DINOSAUR
Encyclopedia

From Dinosaurs to the Dawn of Man

DINOSAUR
Encyclopedia

From Dinosaurs to the Dawn of Man

In association with the
AMERICAN MUSEUM OF NATURAL HISTORY

A Dorling Kindersley Book

LONDON, NEW YORK, MUNICH, PARIS,
MELBOURNE, and DELHI

Senior Editors
Kitty Blount, Maggie Crowley

Senior Art Editor
Martin Wilson

Editors
Kathleen Bada, Susan Malyan,
Giles Sparrow, Rosalyn Thiro,
Marek Walisiewicz

Art Editors
Stephen Bere, Tim Brown, Diane Clouting,
Sarah Crouch, Darren Holt, Robin Hunter,
Rebecca Johns, Clair Watson

Editorial Assistant
Kate Bradshaw

Managing Art Editor
Jacquie Gulliver

US Editors
Cheryl Ehrlich, Margaret Parrish, Gary Werner

Illustrators
Peter Bull Art Studio, Malcolm McGregor,
Peter Visscher, Wildlife Art Ltd

Category Publisher
Jayne Parsons

Paleontological Artist
Luis Rey

Editorial Consultants
Mark Norell, Jin Meng
(American Museum of Natural History, New York)

Digital Models
Bedrock Studios Limited

Authors
David Lambert, Darren Naish, Elizabeth Wyse

DTP Designers
Matthew Ibbotson, Nomazwe Madonko

Production
Kate Oliver

Picture Research
Sean Hunter, Nicole Kaczynski, Bridget Tilly

First American Edition, 2001

01 02 03 04 05 10 9 8 7 6 5 4 3 2 1

Published in the United States by
DK Publishing, Inc.
95 Madison Avenue
New York, New York 10016

Library of Congress Cataloging-in-Publication Data

Lambert, David, 1932-
    Dinosaur encyclopedia/[David Lambert, Darren Naish, Liz Wyse]. – 1st American ed.
        p. cm.
    Includes index.
    ISBN 0-7894-7935-4
    1. Dinosaurs–Encyclopedias, Juvenile. [1. Dinosaurs–Miscellanea. 2. Prehistoric
    animals–Miscellanea.] I. Naish, Darren. II Wyse, Liz. III. Title.

    QE861.3 .L33 2001
    567.9'03–dc21

                                                            2001028433

Color reproduction by Colourscan, Singapore
Printed and bound by Mondadori Printing S.p.A., Verona, Italy

See our complete catalog at
www.dk.com

CONTENTS

FISH AND INVERTEBRATES 20–53

AMPHIBIANS AND REPTILES 54–99

DINOSAURS AND BIRDS 100–191

MAMMALS AND THEIR ANCESTORS 192–275

REFERENCE SECTION 276–376

HOW TO USE THIS BOOK

THE ENCYCLOPEDIA OF DINOSAURS and other prehistoric life begins with an introductory section that provides an overview to understanding fossils, evolution, and prehistoric life. This is followed by the four main sections of the book, which cover the major groups of prehistoric animals – Fish and Invertebrates, Amphibians and Reptiles, Dinosaurs and Birds, and Mammals and their Ancestors. Each entry in these four sections covers a particular prehistoric animal or a group of such animals. An extensive reference section at the back of the book contains a fossil timeline, details of how paleontologists find and study fossils, and biographies of noted researchers.

MAMMALS AND THEIR ANCESTORS

EARLY SYNAPSIDS

SYNAPSIDS ("WITH ARCH") INCLUDE the mammal-like "reptiles" and their descendants, the mammals. They are named for the large hole low in the skull behind each eye. Muscles that worked the jaws passed through this hole, and gave synapsids a wide gape and powerful bite. Synapsids formed a separate group from true reptiles, who gave rise to lizards, dinosaurs, and their relatives. Like living reptiles, however, early kinds were scaly and cold-blooded. Synapsids appeared during the Carboniferous period. Early synapsids are known as pelycosaurs, and were quadrupeds with sprawling limbs. Most pelycosaurs lived in what is now North America and Europe. By early Permian times, pelycosaurs counted for seven out of ten backboned land animals. The early synapsids died out toward the end of the Permian period.

Sunshine could have warmed Dimetrodon's body by heating the blood that flowed through its sail.

SAIL-BACKED KILLER
Dimetrodon was one of the first big land animals to be capable of attacking and killing creatures its own size. This pelycosaur had a large, long, narrow head, with powerful jaws and daggerlike teeth. *Dimetrodon* could grow up to 11 ft 6 in (3.5 m) in length. It survived by attacking and eating large, plant-eating pelycosaurs. *Dimetrodon* lived during the Early Permian in what is now North America and Europe. Its remains have been found in Texas and Oklahoma, and in Europe.

Dimetrodon skull

Canine teeth with serrated blades

TYPES OF TEETH
Most reptiles have teeth of similar shapes. *Dimetrodon's* teeth had different shapes, like a mammal's. The name *Dimetrodon* means "two types of teeth." The differently shaped teeth had various functions. The pointed upper canine teeth were designed for piercing flesh. The sharp front teeth served for biting and gripping. The small back teeth aided in chewing up chunks of flesh.

Dimetrodon

| Cambrian 540–500 | Ordovician 500–435 | Silurian 435–410 | Devonian 410–355 | Carboniferous 355–295 | P |

PALEOZOIC 540–250 MYA

196

Photographs and colorful artworks accompany text.

A specially commissioned model provides a lifelike restoration of a prehistoric animal.

FEATURE PAGES
Realistic restorations of a prehistoric animal set in its natural habitat are found in feature pages throughout the four main sections. Detailed text describes the main animal and other related creatures. These pages (above) describe sea scorpions, and feature the sea scorpion *Pterygotus*.

ANIMAL PAGES
The main sections consist mostly of animal pages, which focus on groups of prehistoric animals. The pages shown above describe early synapsids. A typical animal – here *Dimetrodon* – is displayed prominently. The entry begins with an introduction that describes features of the animal group. It then gives details of the main animal's anatomy and lifestyle, as well as facts on other animals in the group.

Abbreviations used in this book	
MYA	millions of years ago
c.	about
Imperial	
ft	feet
in	inches
°F	degrees Fahrenheit
oz	ounces
lb	pounds
cu in	cubic inches
Metric	
m	meters
cm	centimeters
°C	degrees Celsius
g	grams
kg	kilograms
km	kilometers
cc	cubic centimeters

CLADOGRAM PAGES
The book contains nine cladogram diagrams within the main sections. Each cladogram shows the chain of evolution for a particular group of animals. Color-coded branches make each cladogram easy to follow. Significant features are described in the text. These pages (right) represent the cladogram for ornithischian dinosaurs.

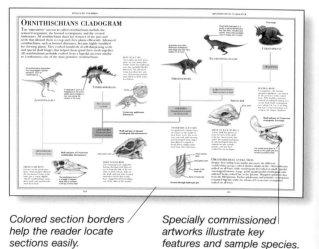

ORNITHISCHIANS CLADOGRAM

Colored section borders help the reader locate sections easily.

Specially commissioned artworks illustrate key features and sample species.

Annotation text in italics explains interesting details in photographs and artworks.

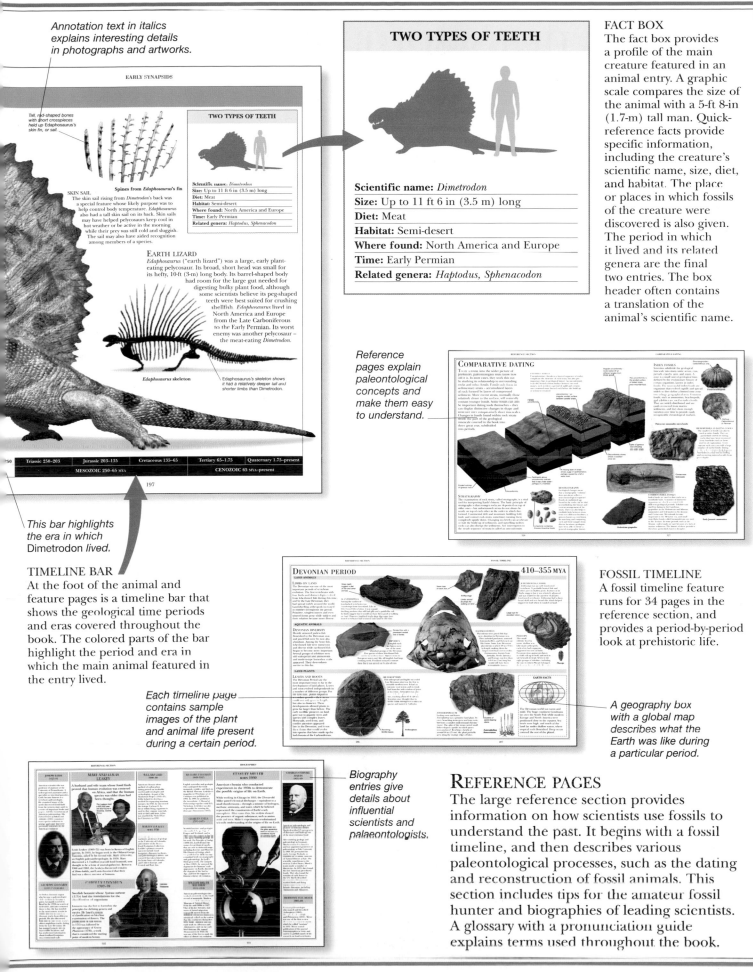

EARLY SYNAPSIDS

Tail, rod-shaped bones with short crosspieces held up Edaphosaurus's skin fin, or sail.

Spines from *Edaphosaurus's* fin

SKIN SAIL
The skin sail rising from *Dimetrodon's* back was a special feature whose likely purpose was to help control body temperature. *Edaphosaurus* also had a tall skin sail on its back. Skin sails may have helped pelycosaurs keep cool in hot weather or be active in the morning while their prey was still cold and sluggish. The sail may also have aided recognition among members of a species.

EARTH LIZARD
Edaphosaurus ("earth lizard") was a large, early plant-eating pelycosaur. Its broad, short head was small for its hefty, 10-ft (3-m) long body. Its barrel-shaped body had room for the large gut needed for digesting bulky plant food, although some scientists believe its peg-shaped teeth were best suited for crushing shellfish. *Edaphosaurus* lived in North America and Europe from the Late Carboniferous to the Early Permian. Its worst enemy was another pelycosaur – the meat-eating *Dimetrodon.*

Edaphosaurus skeleton

Edaphosaurus's skeleton shows it had a relatively deeper tail and shorter limbs than Dimetrodon.

TWO TYPES OF TEETH

Scientific name: *Dimetrodon*
Size: Up to 11 ft 6 in (3.5 m) long
Diet: Meat
Habitat: Semi-desert
Where found: North America and Europe
Time: Early Permian
Related genera: *Haptodus, Sphenacodon*

Triassic 250–203	Jurassic 203–135	Cretaceous 135–65	Tertiary 65–1.75	Quaternary 1.75–present
MESOZOIC 250–65 MYA			CENOZOIC 65 MYA–present	

197

This bar highlights the era in which Dimetrodon lived.

TIMELINE BAR
At the foot of the animal and feature pages is a timeline bar that shows the geological time periods and eras covered throughout the book. The colored parts of the bar highlight the period and era in which the main animal featured in the entry lived.

Each timeline page contains sample images of the plant and animal life present during a certain period.

TWO TYPES OF TEETH

Scientific name: *Dimetrodon*
Size: Up to 11 ft 6 in (3.5 m) long
Diet: Meat
Habitat: Semi-desert
Where found: North America and Europe
Time: Early Permian
Related genera: *Haptodus, Sphenacodon*

FACT BOX
The fact box provides a profile of the main creature featured in an animal entry. A graphic scale compares the size of the animal with a 5-ft 8-in (1.7-m) tall man. Quick-reference facts provide specific information, including the creature's scientific name, size, diet, and habitat. The place or places in which fossils of the creature were discovered is also given. The period in which it lived and its related genera are the final two entries. The box header often contains a translation of the animal's scientific name.

Reference pages explain paleontological concepts and make them easy to understand.

COMPARATIVE DATING

Reference section comparative dating pages

DEVONIAN PERIOD   410–355 MYA

Reference section Devonian period pages

FOSSIL TIMELINE
A fossil timeline feature runs for 34 pages in the reference section, and provides a period-by-period look at prehistoric life.

A geography box with a global map describes what the Earth was like during a particular period.

Biography entries give details about influential scientists and palaeontologists.

Reference section biographies pages

REFERENCE PAGES
The large reference section provides information on how scientists use fossils to understand the past. It begins with a fossil timeline, and then describes various paleontological processes, such as the dating and reconstruction of fossil animals. This section includes tips for the amateur fossil hunter and biographies of leading scientists. A glossary with a pronunciation guide explains terms used throughout the book.

FINDING OUT ABOUT THE PAST

LIFE ON EARTH is almost infinite in its variety – plants, animals, and other forms of life surround us in a multitude of forms. Ever since people first realized that fossils are the remains of once-living things, they have strived to interpret them. Paleontology, the study of ancient life, involves reconstructing the former appearance, lifestyle, behavior, evolution, and relationships of once-living organisms. Paleontological work includes the collection of specimens in the field as well as investigation in the laboratory. Here the structure of the fossil, the way it is fossilized, and how it compares with other forms are studied. Paleontology provides us with a broad view of life on Earth. It shows how modern organisms arose, and how they relate to one another.

Discovery of *Mosasaurus*

EARLY FINDS AND THEORIES
People have always collected fossils. In some cultures, elaborate myths were invented to explain these objects. For example, ammonites, extinct relatives of squids, were thought to be coiled snakes turned to stone. Paleontology as we recognize it today arose in the late 18th century. The discovery of fossil mastodons (American relatives of elephants) and of *Mosasaurus*, a huge Cretaceous marine reptile, led to the acceptance of extinction, an idea previously rejected as contrary to the Bible. With the concept of extinction and life before man established, scientists began to describe remarkable forms of life known only from their fossilized remains.

Paleontologists at work in Mongolia

THE STUDY OF DEATH
Taphonomy is the branch of paleontology concerned with the study of how organisms died and what happened to their bodies between death and discovery. It reveals much about ancient environments and the processes that contribute to fossilization. A fossil's surface can show how much time went by before the dead animal was buried. This may explain its state of preservation and why parts of it are missing. Fossils also preserve evidence of their movements after death – they may be transported by water or moved around by animals.

DIGGING UP FOSSILS
To discover fossils, paleontologists do not generally go out and dig holes. Most fossils are found when they erode onto the surface, so places where there is continual erosion of rock by the wind and water are frequently good sites. Expeditions to suitable locations may involve expensive journeys to regions where travel is difficult. Excavators once dug out fossils with little regard for the context in which they were found. Today we realize that such information is important. The sedimentary layer in which a fossil is found, and its relationship with other fossils, can reveal much about its history prior to preservation.

RECONSTRUCTING THE PAST

How do paleontologists produce reconstructions of prehistoric environments, like the Carboniferous swamp forest shown here? Studies on modern environments show that distinct kinds of sediment are laid down in different environments. Many living things inhabit certain habitats, and the physical features of a fossil may also show what environment it favored when alive. Using these clues, paleontologists can work out what kind of environment a fossil deposit represents. Fossils themselves may reveal features that show how they lived. Interactions between fossils, such as preserved stomach contents and bite marks, are sometimes preserved. Using all of these pieces of evidence, paleontologists can piece together environments and ecosystems that existed in the past.

Preserved Lepidodendron *trunks reveal that this giant clubmoss grew up to 160 ft (50 m) tall, dominating the vegetation in and around large swamps. Trees such as* Lepidodendron *formed the huge coal deposits that give the Carboniferous its name.*

Trunk of *Lepidodendron*

Fossil *Meganeura*

Meganeura's wings recall those of dragonflies, suggesting that it was a fast-flying predator. It probably hunted other insects over the Carboniferous pools and lakes. Fossils of Meganeura and relatives of Eryops are all found fossilized within Carboniferous coal deposits.

Weak limbs, sensory skull grooves, and the position of its eyes and nostrils suggest that the temnospondyl Eryops and its relatives were water-dwelling predators.

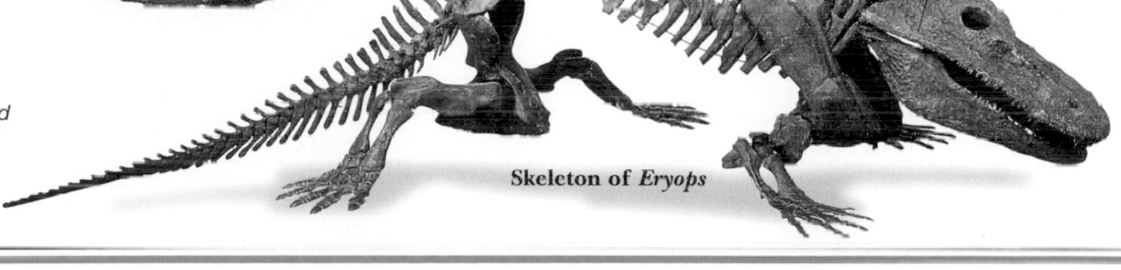

Skeleton of *Eryops*

FOSSILS

NATURALLY PRESERVED REMAINS of once-living organisms, or the traces they made, are called fossils. These objects usually become fossils when they are entombed in sediment and later mineralized. Fossils are abundant throughout the Phanerozoic Eon – the age of "obvious life" from 570 million years ago to the present, so called because of its plentiful fossil remains. Thousands of fossil species, from microscopic organisms to plants, invertebrates, and vertebrate animals, are known from this time. Earlier fossils are revealed by distinctive chemical traces left in rocks as well as fossilized organisms themselves. These extend back in time some 3.8 billion years, to when our planet was young. Because most dead organisms or their remains are usually broken down by bacteria and other organisms, fossilization is relatively rare. Even so, billions of fossils exist.

Animal dies and decomposes in a riverbed.

Riverbed deposits sediment on skeleton

A skeleton buried by sediment is protected from scavengers on the surface.

Rocks are condensed layers of sediments such as sand or mud.

This armor plate comes from a sauropod dinosaur.

Fossilized *Saltasaurus* osteoderm (skin)

Plates may have helped protect the dinosaur from predators.

TYPES OF FOSSIL

The remains of plants and animals (such as shells, teeth, bones, or leaves) are the best known fossils. These are called body fossils. Traces left behind by organisms – such as footprints, nests, droppings, or feeding marks – may also be preserved as fossils, and are called trace fossils. These are often the most abundant kinds of fossil but, unless they are preserved alongside the organism that made them, they are often hard to identify precisely.

When these tracks were formed, this rock surface was soft mud.

These three-toed tracks were probably made by predatory dinosaurs.

Theropod trackway

HOW FOSSILS FORM

The most common form of fossilization involves the burial of an organism, or an object produced by an organism, in sediment. The original material from which the organism or object is made is then gradually replaced by minerals. Some fossils have not formed in this way. Instead, the original object has been destroyed by acidic groundwater, and minerals have later formed a natural replica of the object. Both processes take a long time, but experiments have shown that fossils can be formed much more quickly. In these cases, mineral crystals form in the tissues shortly after death, meaning that they start to fossilize within a few weeks – before decomposition has set in. This type of fossil can preserve blood vessels, muscle fibers, and even feathers in exceptional conditions.

Fossilized hedgehog *Pholidocercus*

EXCEPTIONAL FOSSILS

The soft parts of organisms are usually lost before fossilization begins, as they are broken down quickly by bacteria and other scavengers. For this reason soft-bodied animals (such as jellyfish or molluscs) are poorly represented in the fossil record. However, rapid burial in soft sediment, combined with the presense of certain special bacteria, can mean that soft parts are retained and fossilized. The complete remains of soft-bodied organisms can be preserved under such conditions, as can skin and internal organs.

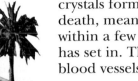

Bacteria and other scavengers under ground may still destroy the skeleton.

More sediments deposited above the fossil bury it deeper in the rock, and may compress or distort it.

Erosion at the surface of the Earth means that new fossils are constantly being revealed.

RESULTS OF FOSSILIZATION

Fossils that are composed of new, replacement minerals are harder, heavier versions of the original. They also usually differ in color from the object that formed them. This ammonite fossil is gold because it is composed of iron pyrite, the mineral often called "fool's gold." Due to pressure inside the rock, fossils may also be altered in shape. Some fossils can be so distorted that experts have difficulty imagining their original shapes.

Minerals in the groundwater may change the fossil's composition.

Moving continental plates may carry sediments far from their original location.

Many exposed fossils are destroyed by the action of wind and water.

Once exposed, a fossil may be discovered by people.

EVOLVING LIFE

THE FOSSIL RECORD PRESERVES the history of life from the earliest single-celled organisms to the complex multicellular creatures – including plants, fungi, and animals – of more recent times. It shows that simple single-celled forms of life called prokaryotes appeared very early on in the history of our planet – traces of microscopic life have been dated to around 3,800 million years ago. More complex, though still single-celled, organisms appear in the fossil record about 2,000 million years ago. In these cells, called eukaryotes, genetic information is stored in a structure called the nucleus. Eukaryotic organisms include algae, plants, fungi, and many other groups. In the Late Precambrian (around 600 million years ago), the first multicellular eukaryotes, or metazoans, arose. By the Cambrian (540–500 million years ago), these metazoans had diversified into a multitude of animals.

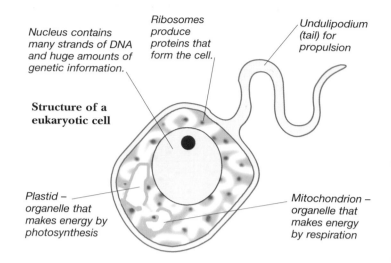

Structure of a eukaryotic cell

Nucleus contains many strands of DNA and huge amounts of genetic information.

Ribosomes produce proteins that form the cell.

Undulipodium (tail) for propulsion

Plastid – organelle that makes energy by photosynthesis

Mitochondrion – organelle that makes energy by respiration

ORIGIN OF EUKARYOTES
Complex eukaryote cells seem to have developed from different kinds of more simple organisms that took to living together and then functioning cooperatively. This cooperation is called symbiosis. Eukaryotes have a central nucleus containing their nucleic acids, such as DNA, and many structures called organelles scattered throughout their fluids. Different organelles have different functions – most are involved in creating energy to fuel the organism itself. Multicellular organisms, probably evolving from single-celled eukaryotes, arose in the Late Precambrian. A great growth of complex lifeforms then took place.

Fossil stromatolite

Flagellum (tail) for propulsion

Ribosomes produce proteins that form the cell.

DNA

Cell wall

FIRST LIFE
The earliest forms of life were prokaryotes. These small, single-celled lifeforms carried DNA, a chemical that codes genetic information, loosely within their cell walls. Prokaryotes developed a wide range of different metabolisms (chemical reactions to generate energy) that may well have helped to produce a planet more suited to advanced lifeforms. Today prokaryotes survive as Archaeobacteria ("ancient bacteria"). They thrive in environments that more advanced lifeforms would find inhospitable or poisonous, such as hot springs and muds devoid of oxygen. Huge fossilized mats of prokaryotic cells are called stromatolites – they show how widespread and dominant these organisms were early on in Earth's history.

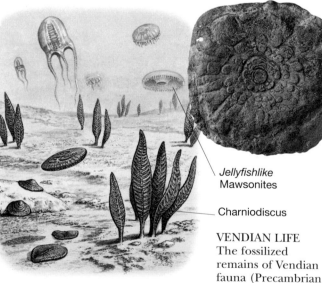

Fossil *Mawsonites*

Jellyfishlike Mawsonites

Charniodiscus

Artist's restoration of Vendian life

VENDIAN LIFE
The fossilized remains of Vendian fauna (Precambrian organisms) were first found at Ediacara Hill in South Australia. This formation, composed of unusual disk- and leaf-shaped fossils such as the *Mawsonites* pictured, provided the first glimpse of the earliest multi-cellular life forms. Vendian fauna vaguely resembled later creatures, for example *Spriggina* looks like a worm while *Charniodiscus* resembles a sea pen. Some paleontologists believe that the Vendian fauna includes the earliest members of several animal groups, but the fossils are generally too incomplete to prove this beyond doubt. Another theory is that Vendian organisms were an independent development in eukaryotic life, unrelated to later organisms.

THE BURGESS SHALE

The Burgess Shale of British Columbia, Canada, is a famous rock unit composed of layers of fine-grained siltstone deposited on the floor of a shallow Cambrian sea. Discovered in 1909 by American paleontologist Charles Walcott, it contains thousands of well-preserved animal fossils, including early members of most modern metazoan groups, as well as other animals that became extinct shortly afterward. The Burgess Shale gives a unique insight into the "Cambrian Explosion" of life. Arthropods, worms, early chordates (relatives of vertebrates), and members of several other groups, many preserved with soft parts intact, are all found here.

Sponges grew on the floor of the Burgess Shale sea, but the reefs of the time were mostly formed by algae.

Marrella was a tiny swimming arthropod. It was probably preyed on by many of the Burgess Shale predators.

Pikaia was an early chordate. It was a wormlike swimmer with tail fins.

Anomalocaris was a large predatory arthropod with a circular mouth, grasping appendages, and swimming fins along its sides.

Anomalocaris was a giant among Burgess Shale animals, growing to 24 in (60 cm) long.

Hallucigenia was originally reconstructed upside-down – the defensive spikes were thought to be legs. The fleshy legs were thought to be feeding tentacles.

Spiky lobopods like Hallucigenia were distant relatives of arthropods.

Hallucigenia was probably a bottom-dweller that fed on organic particles.

Priapulids are burrow-dwelling worms. Today they are rare, but in Burgess Shale times they were abundant.

METAZOAN DIVERSITY

The Burgess Shale shows how well metazoans diversified to fill the available ecological niches. The rest of the Phanerozoic Eon (the age of "obvious life") saw increasing diversification of these groups, the invasion of the land, and a boom in the numbers and variety of arthropods and vertebrates. Animals invaded the air, spread though freshwater environments, and colonized all environments on land. Mollusks and vertebrates have grown to be thousands of times larger than the earliest metazoans. Single-celled organisms, however, have not waned in importance or diversity. Bacteria are present worldwide in all environments, and far outnumber metazoans, so today could still be regarded as part of "the age of bacteria."

Dinosaur   *Bird*   *Mammal*   *Arthropod*

HOW EVOLUTION HAPPENS

ALL LIVING THINGS CHANGE, OR EVOLVE, over generations. This fact can be seen in living populations of animals, plants, and other living things, as well as in fossils. As organisms change over time to adapt to new environments or ways of life, they give rise to new species. The inheritance of features by a creature's descendants is the main component of evolutionary change. An understanding of how evolution happens proved to be one of the key scientific revelations in our understanding of life, and understanding evolution is the key to interpreting the fossil record. By studying evolutionary changes, biologists and paleontologists reveal patterns that have occurred during the history of life.

THE THEORY OF EVOLUTION

The theory that living things change to better suit their environments was first presented by British naturalist Charles Darwin (1809-1882). Darwin argued for the idea of slow changes to species over time, brought about by selection acting on natural variation. Natural variation is present in all living things - all individuals differ from one another in genetic makeup, and therefore in their anatomy and behavior. Natural selection is the mechanism that chooses one variation over another. All individuals compete among themselves and with other organisms for food and territory, and struggle to avoid predators and survive extremes of climate. Those best at passing on their genes – in other words surviving, finding a mate, and raising offspring – will have their features inherited by future generations.

Fishing aboard the *Beagle*

VOYAGE OF THE BEAGLE
Charles Darwin developed his theory of evolution by natural selection following his travels as ship's naturalist on HMS *Beagle* during the 1830s. Darwin studied fossil South American animals as well as living animals on the Galapagos Islands. The similarities and differences that Darwin saw made him realize that species must have changed over time. Darwin was not the only person to propose the idea of evolution, but his ideas were the most influential. His 1859 book, *On the Origin of Species by Means of Natural Selection*, is one of the most famous scientific books ever written.

Tortoises on wet islands only need to reach down to the ground to find food.

Low front of shell originally shared by all Galapagos tortoises

EVOLUTION IN ACTION

Some living animals provide particularly clear examples of evolution in action. On the Galapagos Islands, different kinds of giant tortoises have become suited for different conditions. Tortoises on wet islands where plant growth is thick on the ground have shells with a low front opening. For tortoises on dry islands there is no vegetation on the ground - instead they have to reach up to chew on branches that grow well above ground level. Over time, those tortoises with slightly taller front openings in their shells were better able to reach the higher vegetation. This allowed them to better survive and pass on their genes, so now all the tortoises on dry islands have a tall front opening to their shells.

Tortoises on dry islands have to reach up to find food.

Higher front of shell selected in dry island tortoises.

Horned dinosaurs like Triceratops demonstrate gradual evolution. They were constantly evolving – a genus typically lasted 4–6 million years.

DEVELOPING THE THEORY

When Darwin put forward his theory, he was unable to propose an actual mechanism by which characteristics could pass from one generation to the next. It was several decades before the new science of genetics – the study of inheritance – provided the missing piece of the puzzle and confirmed Darwin's ideas. More recent advances in genetics and paleontology have shown just how complex the relationships between living and fossil species are. Evolution is not as simple as was once thought – for example, organisms do not generally evolve in simple ladder- or chainlike progressions (once a popular image in books). Instead, as new species evolve from old ones, they tend to branch out and diversify, forming complex bush-like patterns. In fact, the main theme of evolution seems to be diversification. Evolution was also traditionally regarded as the development of increasing complexity, but this is not always true. Some living things have become less complex over time, or have lost complicated structures present in their ancestors.

EVOLUTION BY JUMPS

The old view that evolution is a slow and continuous process has been challenged by evidence from the fossil record. Many species seem to stay the same for long periods of time, and then are suddenly replaced by their apparent descendants. This type of evolution is called quantum evolution. The opposite idea, that evolution occurs as slow and gradual change, is the traditional view. It now seems that both kinds of evolution occur, depending on the circumstances. When conditions stay the same, species may not need to change but, if conditions change rapidly, species may need to change rapidly as well.

Fossil humans appear in the Pliocene. Chimpanzees must also have evolved at this time.

Chimpanzees and humans share an enlarged canal in the palate not seen in orangutans.

All great apes (hominids) have an enlarged thumb and other derived characters.

Gar fish demonstrate quantum evolution – the last time they changed was more than 60 million years ago.

HUMAN

CHIMPANZEE

ORANGUTAN

Enlarged palate canal

Large opposable thumb

Canal passing through palate in upper jaw.

Long opposable thumb gives apes and humans an evolutionary advantage.

DERIVED CHARACTERS

Scientists reveal evolutionary relationships by looking for shared features, called "derived characters." The presence of unique derived characters seen in one group of species but not in others shows that all the species within that group share a common ancestor. Such groups are called clades. In the cladogram shown here, humans and chimpanzees share derived characters not seen in orangutans. Humans and chimpanzees therefore share a common ancestor that evolved after the common ancestor of orangutans, chimpanzees and humans. Orangutans, chimpanzees, and humans all share derived characters not seen in other primates and also form a clade. The field of molecular biology has shown that closely related species have similar protein and DNA sequences. Such similarities can also be used as derived characters.

CLASSIFYING LIFE

Jaguar

PEOPLE HAVE ALWAYS CLASSIFIED LIVING THINGS as a way of understanding the world. Organisms could be grouped together based on how they looked, how they moved, or what they tasted like. With the advent of science after the Middle Ages, biologists realized that living things should be grouped together according to common features of their anatomy or habits. However, the concept of evolution was missing from these systems of classification – groups were thought to correspond to strict plans created by God. In the 1960s, biologist Willi Hennig argued that species should only be grouped together when they shared newly evolved features called derived characters. Groups of species united by derived characters, and therefore sharing the same single ancestor, are called clades. This new classification method, called cladistics, has revolutionized biology and palaeontology.

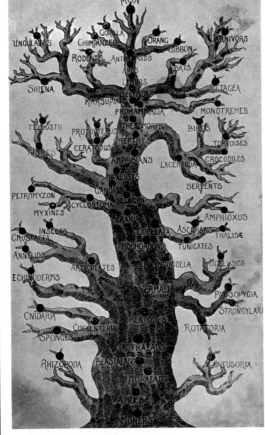

THE TREE OF LIFE
Nineteenth-century scientists thought all living things were part of a ladder-like scheme with humans as the most "advanced" creatures at the top. They classified organisms in a way that reflected this, but this inaccurate view does not reflect the real branching of evolution. Also, evolution does not necessarily result in overall "improvement" but, instead, enables organisms to better cope with their immediate conditions.

Leopard

WHAT IS A SPECIES?
The species is the fundamental biological unit – a population of living things that all look alike, can all interbreed with each other, and cannot interbreed with other species. There are many exceptions to this definition – some species contain individuals that differ radically in appearance, and some can successfully interbreed with others. However, the definition holds true for the majority. Closely related species are grouped into genera (singular: genus). Leopards and jaguars, shown here, are closely related species that both belong within the same genus.

LINNAEAN CLASSIFICATION

The Swedish botanist Carl von Linné (better known by the latinised version of his name, Carolus Linnaeus) was the most influential person to classify organisms in the traditional way. In 1758, he organised all living things into a grand scheme of classification called the *Systema Naturae*. Linnaeus recognized that the basic unit in biology was the species, and he developed an intricate system for grouping species together in increasingly broader groups. Related species were grouped into genera, genera were collected in families, families within orders, orders in classes, classes in phyla, and phyla within kingdoms.

THE CLADISTIC REVOLUTION

By determining the sequence in which their derived characters arose, scientists can arrange species in the order that they probably evolved. However this does not allow them to recognize direct links between ancestors and descendants. When scientists group species into clades, they have to identify and describe the derived features shared by the group. This allows other scientists to examine and test theories about the evolution of a clade – before the introduction of cladistics, this was often not the case. In collecting information on characters, and determining whether they are derived or primitive, scientists amass vast quantities of data that are analysed with computers. Cladistic studies have shown that some traditionally recognised groups really are clades, while others are not.

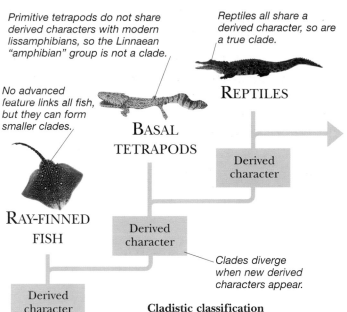

Primitive tetrapods do not share derived characters with modern lissamphibians, so the Linnaean "amphibian" group is not a clade.

Reptiles all share a derived character, so are a true clade.

No advanced feature links all fish, but they can form smaller clades.

REPTILES

BASAL TETRAPODS

RAY-FINNED FISH

Derived character

Derived character

Derived character

Clades diverge when new derived characters appear.

Cladistic classification

Amphibians are an artificial Linnaean group

Acanthostega

AMPHIBIANS

Alligator

REPTILES

Ray

FISH

More advanced groups diverge from the tree at later times. Reptiles, for example, diverged later than amphibians.

Linnaean tree

NATURAL AND UNNATURAL GROUPS

During the twentieth century, it became clear that many of the groups used in the Linnaean system did not correspond to true evolutionary groups because they sometimes excluded many of their own descendants. The Linnaean group Reptilia, for example, was supposed to include the ancestors of birds, but not the birds themselves. So Linnaean groups were not true natural groups, but artificial groupings created by people. Intermediate forms were also a problem for the Linnaean system – should a bird-like reptile be included in the reptile class or the bird class? Cladistics gets round these problems by only recognising natural groups whose members all share the same ancestor. Such groups are called clades. In the cladistic system, birds are a clade, but are themselves part of the reptile clade.

CLADOGRAMS

Cladograms are diagrams that represent the relationships between different organisms. The more derived characters two species share, the closer they will be on the cladogram. Cladograms do not show direct ancestor-descendant sequences but instead portray the branching sequences that occurred within groups. Branching events in the cladogram are marked by nodes – points where a new derived character appears, uniting a narrower, more recently evolved clade. In the section of a bird cladogram shown here, all three groups are united as a clade by a prong on their quadrate bone, a feature that distinguishes them from all other birds. Modern birds and ichthyornithiforms are also united by a rounded head to their humerus bone, not shared with hesperornithiforms – so they also belong in a narrower clade.

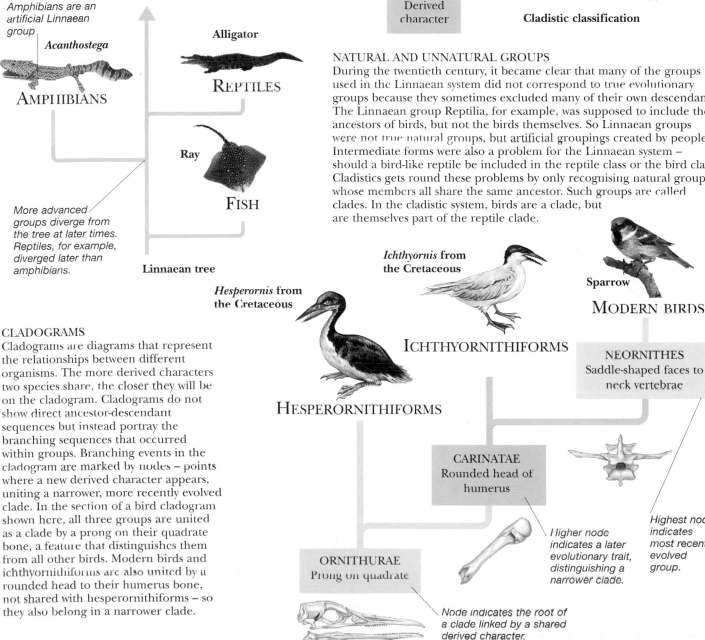

Ichthyornis from the Cretaceous

Sparrow

MODERN BIRDS

Hesperornis from the Cretaceous

ICHTHYORNITHIFORMS

NEORNITHES
Saddle-shaped faces to neck vertebrae

HESPERORNITHIFORMS

CARINATAE
Rounded head of humerus

Higher node indicates a later evolutionary trait, distinguishing a narrower clade.

Highest node indicates most recently evolved group.

ORNITHURAE
Prong on quadrate

Node indicates the root of a clade linked by a shared derived character.

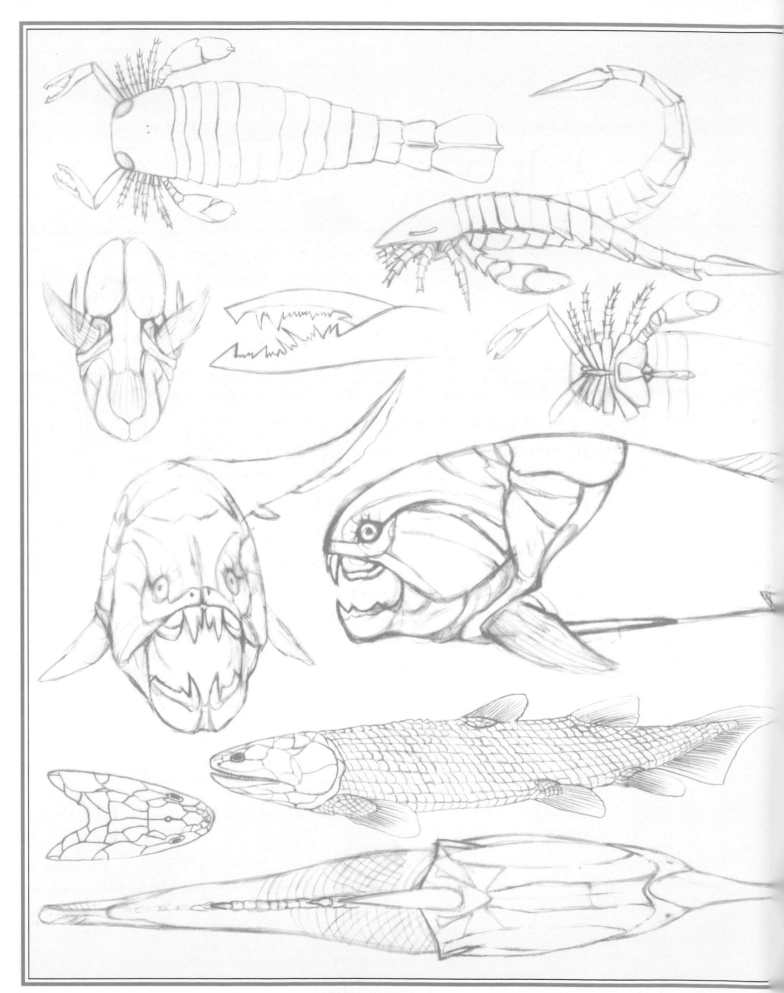

Fish and Invertebrates

Water "woodlice," some as large as serving dishes, dragonflies with the wingspan of hawks, and sea scorpions as big as people are all featured among the prehistoric invertebrates (animals without backbones) in this section. Also displayed are a fantastic variety of fish, the first animals to have backbones. Little jawless creatures with ever-open mouths, armored fish with rocker jaws, spiky-finned spiny acanthodians, and those superbly streamlined swimmers, the sharks and bony fish, are all exhibited here. Finally, lobe-finned fish, an ancient group that is ancestral to humans, are featured. Throughout the section, color photographs depict fossil specimens, and computer models reveal how long-dead organisms actually looked.

INVERTEBRATES CLADOGRAM

THE SIMPLEST ANIMALS ARE INVERTEBRATES whose bodies lack distinct left and right sides. Cnidarians and other primitive groups do not have definite front ends, but their cells are organized into regions that have specialized functions. Members of some higher groups possess hard parts – a feature that evolved in the Early Cambrian. Advanced invertebrates have bodies with distinct left and right sides. Early in the evolution of some of these bilaterally symmetrical animals, the ability to move forward became an advantage, so these animals evolved distinctive head regions to house their primary sensory organs.

CHORDATES

Jurassic starfish
Pentasteria

ECHINODERMS

Rhizopoterion

Jellyfish

SPONGES (PORIFERANS)

CNIDARIANS

Planarian flatworm

DEUTEROSTOMES
Anus develops from blastopore

CTENOPHORES

FLATWORMS
(PLATYHELMINTHS)

Circulation system

Three layers of tissue

THREE TISSUE LAYERS
Flatworms and higher invertebrates are united by the presence of three layers of tissue. These three layers allowed the evolution of a more complex body, and a distinct gut and organs.

Ectoderm

Mesoderm | *Endoderm*

Hollow-ball embryo

HOLLOW-BALL EMBRYO
The development of the embryo from a hollow ball of cells is a feature not seen in sponges. Animals whose embryos go through the hollow ball stage are able to develop more complex bodies than sponges.

CIRCULATION SYSTEM
The presence of a system that circulates blood unites deuterostomes, ecdysozoans, and lophotrochozoans.

Circulation system of a crayfish

ANIMALS
Two cell layers

Ectoderm

Embryo

Blastopore

TWO CELL LAYERS
All animals have two layers of cells in their body walls, which is the simplest type of body organization. The layers form a bag that encloses an internal cavity.

Endoderm | **Hollow, fluid-filled embryo**

ANUS DEVELOPMENT
In deuterostomes, the blastopore – the first hole that forms in the embryo – becomes the anus.

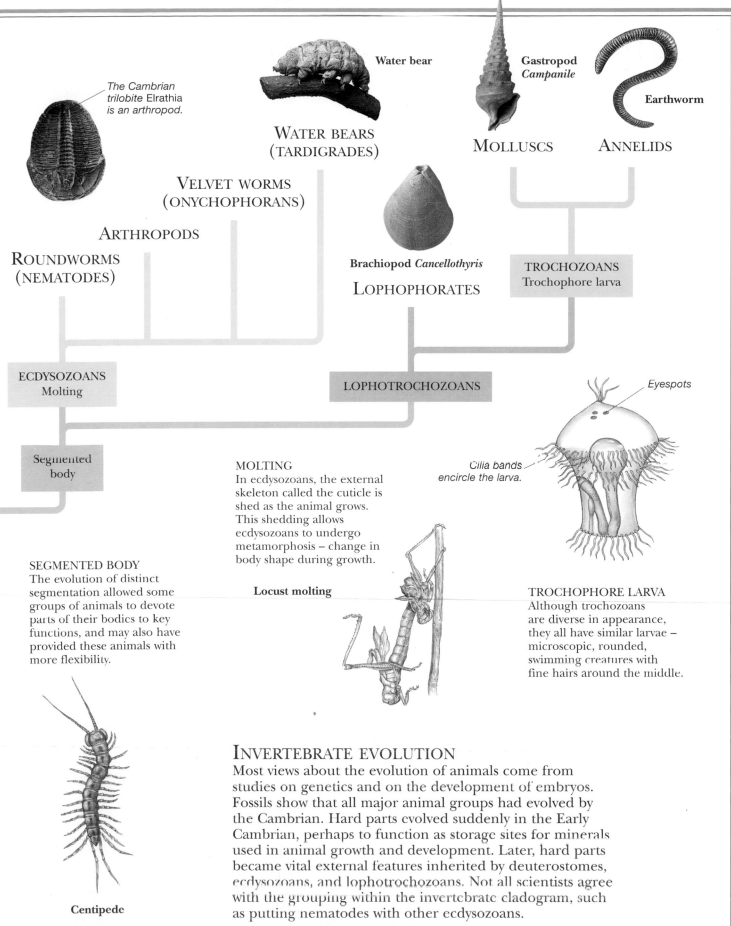

The Cambrian trilobite Elrathia is an arthropod.

Water bear

WATER BEARS (TARDIGRADES)

Gastropod Campanile

Earthworm

MOLLUSCS   **ANNELIDS**

VELVET WORMS (ONYCHOPHORANS)

ARTHROPODS

ROUNDWORMS (NEMATODES)

Brachiopod Cancellothyris

LOPHOPHORATES

TROCHOZOANS
Trochophore larva

ECDYSOZOANS
Molting

LOPHOTROCHOZOANS

Eyespots

Cilia bands encircle the larva.

Segmented body

MOLTING
In ecdysozoans, the external skeleton called the cuticle is shed as the animal grows. This shedding allows ecdysozoans to undergo metamorphosis – change in body shape during growth.

Locust molting

SEGMENTED BODY
The evolution of distinct segmentation allowed some groups of animals to devote parts of their bodies to key functions, and may also have provided these animals with more flexibility.

TROCHOPHORE LARVA
Although trochozoans are diverse in appearance, they all have similar larvae – microscopic, rounded, swimming creatures with fine hairs around the middle.

Centipede

INVERTEBRATE EVOLUTION
Most views about the evolution of animals come from studies on genetics and on the development of embryos. Fossils show that all major animal groups had evolved by the Cambrian. Hard parts evolved suddenly in the Early Cambrian, perhaps to function as storage sites for minerals used in animal growth and development. Later, hard parts became vital external features inherited by deuterostomes, ecdysozoans, and lophotrochozoans. Not all scientists agree with the grouping within the invertebrate cladogram, such as putting nematodes with other ecdysozoans.

TRILOBITES

BEFORE FISH BECAME DOMINANT, ancient seas teemed with trilobites – the relatives of living woodlice, crabs, and insects. Trilobites were among the earliest arthropods. The name trilobite, which means "three-lobed," describes the trilobite body's division lengthwise into three parts separated by two grooves. Most trilobites crawled across the ocean floor, although some species swam. They ranged in size from the microscopically tiny to species that were larger than a platter. With more than 15,000 species, trilobites outnumber any other known type of extinct creature. The trilobites' heyday occured during the Cambrian and Ordovician periods, and the last species vanished during the mass extinction at the end of the Permian period.

TRILOBITE BODY PLAN

Viewed lengthwise, a trilobite's body, such as this *Phacops* (right), has a raised middle lobe, or axis, sandwiched between two flatter lobes called the pleural lobes. Trilobites were also divided crosswise. The three main body parts consisted of the cephalon (head), the thorax, and the pygidium (tail). There were cheeks and eyes on either side of the head. The long thorax was made of many segments, each of which held paired limbs. A tough outer casing protected all parts of the body. After a trilobite died, the casing often broke apart into the three main lobes.

Middle lobe

Pleural lobe

Phacops **rolled up in defense**

A knobbly shield guarded Phacops's head, and its eyes had hard calcite lenses.

DEFENSE

Phacops ("lens eye") curled up in a tight ball or burrowed if attacked. The 12 armored plates of its thorax overlapped like a Venetian blind to protect the legs and underside. Fish were probably *Phacops*'s worst enemies, but trilobites that lived earlier than *Phacops* feared *Anomalocaris*, eurypterids, and nautiloids.

Pygidium (tail)

| Cambrian 540–500 | Ordovician 500–435 | Silurian 435–410 | Devonian 410–355 | Carboniferous 355–295 | Permian |

PALEOZOIC 540–250 MYA

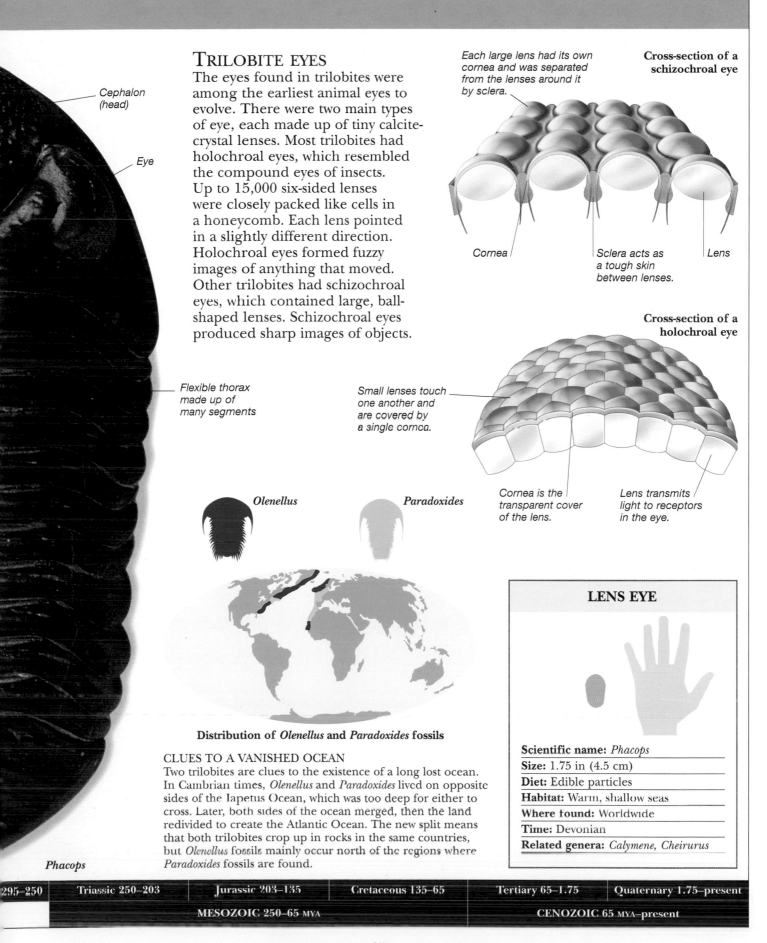

TRILOBITE EYES

The eyes found in trilobites were among the earliest animal eyes to evolve. There were two main types of eye, each made up of tiny calcite-crystal lenses. Most trilobites had holochroal eyes, which resembled the compound eyes of insects. Up to 15,000 six-sided lenses were closely packed like cells in a honeycomb. Each lens pointed in a slightly different direction. Holochroal eyes formed fuzzy images of anything that moved. Other trilobites had schizochroal eyes, which contained large, ball-shaped lenses. Schizochroal eyes produced sharp images of objects.

Cephalon (head)

Eye

Flexible thorax made up of many segments

Phacops

Each large lens had its own cornea and was separated from the lenses around it by sclera.

Cross-section of a schizochroal eye

Cornea

Sclera acts as a tough skin between lenses.

Lens

Cross-section of a holochroal eye

Small lenses touch one another and are covered by a single cornea.

Cornea is the transparent cover of the lens.

Lens transmits light to receptors in the eye.

Olenellus

Paradoxides

Distribution of *Olenellus* and *Paradoxides* fossils

CLUES TO A VANISHED OCEAN

Two trilobites are clues to the existence of a long lost ocean. In Cambrian times, *Olenellus* and *Paradoxides* lived on opposite sides of the Iapetus Ocean, which was too deep for either to cross. Later, both sides of the ocean merged, then the land redivided to create the Atlantic Ocean. The new split means that both trilobites crop up in rocks in the same countries, but *Olenellus* fossils mainly occur north of the regions where *Paradoxides* fossils are found.

LENS EYE

Scientific name:	*Phacops*
Size:	1.75 in (4.5 cm)
Diet:	Edible particles
Habitat:	Warm, shallow seas
Where found:	Worldwide
Time:	Devonian
Related genera:	*Calymene*, *Cheirurus*

295–250	Triassic 250–203	Jurassic 203–135	Cretaceous 135–65	Tertiary 65–1.75	Quaternary 1.75–present
		MESOZOIC 250–65 MYA		CENOZOIC 65 MYA–present	

25

SEA SCORPIONS

EURYPTERIDS

(SEA SCORPIONS) were the largest-ever arthropods. They belong to the chelicerates ("biting claws"), a group that includes scorpions and spiders. Sea scorpions appeared in Ordovician times and persisted into the Permian. Among the largest was *Pterygotus*, which lived more than 400 million years ago and could grow longer than a man. Before predatory fish evolved, sea scorpions were among the most dominant hunters of shallow seas. Some species even crawled ashore, where they breathed air by means of special "lungs," like those of certain land crabs.

BODY PLAN

Like all sea scorpions, *Pterygotus* had a two-part body. Its prosoma (front) bore the mouth, one pair of large eyes, one pair of small eyes, and six pairs of appendages. The long opisthosoma (rear) had 12 plated tail segments called tergites. The first six tergites contained pairs of gills and included the creature's sex organs. *Pterygotus*'s telson, or tail, formed a wide, short paddle. In some sea scorpions, the telson took the shape of pincers or a spike.

Pterygotus swam by beating its broad paddles up and down.

Walking leg

HUNTERS AND SCAVENGERS

Many species of sea scorpion were much smaller and less well-armed than *Pterygotus*. *Eurypterus* was only 4 in (10 cm) long and had two short fangs. It would not have been able to tackle the large prey that *Pterygotus* lived on. These creatures used their legs to pull tiny animals toward their fangs, which tore them up and fed them to the mouth.

| Cambrian 540–500 | Ordovician 500–435 | Silurian 435–410 | Devonian 410–355 | Carboniferous 355–295 | Permian |

PALEOZOIC 540–250 MYA

METHOD OF ATTACK

Pterygotus had big, sharp eyes that could detect the movement of small, armored fish on the muddy sea floor some way ahead. The hunter could have crawled or swum slowly toward its victim, then produced an attacking burst of speed by lashing its telson up and down. Before the fish could escape, it would be gripped between the pincers of a great claw with spiky inner edges. This fang would crush the struggling fish and feed it to *Pterygotus*'s mouth, which lay beneath its prosoma and between its walking legs.

PTERYGOTUS

Scientific name: *Pterygotus*
Size: Up to 7 ft 4 in (2.3 m) long
Diet: Fish
Habitat: Shallow seas
Where found: Europe and North America
Time: Late Silurian
Related genera: *Jaekelopterus, Slimonia*

Small eye

Large eye

Huge fangs (chelicerae) similar to a lobster's claws

295–250	Triassic 250–203	Jurassic 203–135	Cretaceous 135–65	Tertiary 65–1.75	Quaternary 1.75–present
	MESOZOIC 250–65 MYA			CENOZOIC 65 MYA–present	

EVOLVING INSECTS

THE FIRST KNOWN INSECTS were tiny, wingless arthropods that lived in the Devonian. Many scientists think that insects share an ancestor with the crustaceans. By 320 million years ago, some insects had developed wings. Flying insects eventually evolved different types of wings. Flight helped insects find mates, escape enemies, and access new food supplies. The flowering plants that arose in Cretaceous times provided food for nectar-lapping butterflies and pollen-eating bees. By 220 million years ago, antlike termites were forming "cities" in which different individuals performed specialized tasks to help the colony thrive and to raise their young. Later, ants, bees, and wasps also formed colonies. Insects have proven so successful that the world now teems with millions of insect species. No other land-based arthropods are so plentiful or varied.

Antenna

Meganeura fossil

Hard, shiny elytra preserved in a fossil beetle

Fine veins stiffened and strengthened the wings.

Hydrophilus

Six jointed legs, as found in other insects.

WINGS AS SHIELDS

Water beetles almost identical to this Pleistocene *Hydrophilus* fossil still swim in ponds and streams. As in other beetles, their forewings are hard, tough cases called elytra. These cover and protect the flimsy hindwings – the wings that they use to fly. To become airborne, they spread their hinged elytra and flap their hindwings. Beetles designed along these lines date back more than 250 million years to the Permian period.

HAWKLIKE HUNTERS

Meganeura was a gigantic, primitive dragonfly with a 27-in (70-cm) wingspan. It flew to hunt flying insects above tropical forests in Late Carboniferous times. Its features included swiveling, multifaceted eyes like headlights, which were quick to spot movement and sharp enough to allow *Meganeura* to pounce on flying prey. *Meganeura* flew by beating two pairs of wings stiffened by "veins." It dashed to and fro through forests, changing speed and direction almost instantly, grabbing insects with its legs, and bringing them up to its mouth to feed as it flew. Such giant protodragonflies had stronger legs than living dragonflies, and could have tackled flying animals as large as cockroaches.

Cambrian 540–500	Ordovician 500–435	Silurian 435–410	Devonian 410–355	Carboniferous 355–295	Permian

PALEOZOIC 540–250 MYA

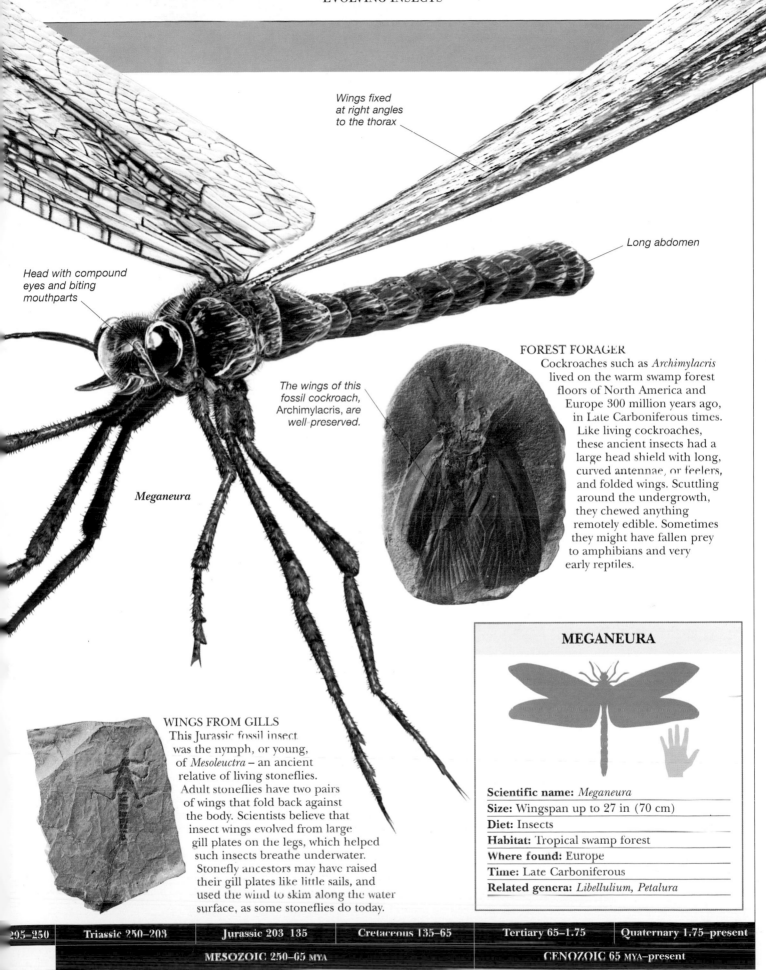

Wings fixed
at right angles
to the thorax

Long abdomen

Head with compound
eyes and biting
mouthparts

The wings of this
fossil cockroach,
Archimylacris, are
well-preserved.

Meganeura

FOREST FORAGER

Cockroaches such as *Archimylacris* lived on the warm swamp forest floors of North America and Europe 300 million years ago, in Late Carboniferous times. Like living cockroaches, these ancient insects had a large head shield with long, curved antennae, or feelers, and folded wings. Scuttling around the undergrowth, they chewed anything remotely edible. Sometimes they might have fallen prey to amphibians and very early reptiles.

WINGS FROM GILLS

This Jurassic fossil insect was the nymph, or young, of *Mesoleuctra* – an ancient relative of living stoneflies. Adult stoneflies have two pairs of wings that fold back against the body. Scientists believe that insect wings evolved from large gill plates on the legs, which helped such insects breathe underwater. Stonefly ancestors may have raised their gill plates like little sails, and used the wind to skim along the water surface, as some stoneflies do today.

MEGANEURA

Scientific name: *Meganeura*

Size: Wingspan up to 27 in (70 cm)

Diet: Insects

Habitat: Tropical swamp forest

Where found: Europe

Time: Late Carboniferous

Related genera: *Libellulium, Petalura*

295–250	Triassic 250–203	Jurassic 203–135	Cretaceous 135–65	Tertiary 65–1.75	Quaternary 1.75–present
		MESOZOIC 250–65 MYA		CENOZOIC 65 MYA–present	

AMMONITES AND BELEMNITES

THE FLAT-SIDED, COILED SHELLS CALLED AMMONITES were named after Ammon, an Egyptian god with coiled horns. Rocks that are rich in ammonite fossils also contain those of belemnites – long, tapering fossils that were named from the Greek word for darts. Both groups were cephalopods – molluscs with soft bodies, such as nautilus, octopus, and squid. Like squid, ammonites and belemnites had tentacles that surrounded beaklike jaws. Both groups lived in the sea and moved by jet propulsion – they squirted water one way to dart in the opposite direction. Ammonites are among the most plentiful fossils from the Mesozoic era, but neither they nor belemnites lasted beyond the Age of Dinosaurs.

ECHIOCERAS

The ammonite *Echioceras* lived and swam in shallow seas around the world in Jurassic times. Its narrow, loosely coiled shell was reinforced by the short, straight ribs that ran across it. In life, *Echioceras*'s tentacled head poked out of the shell's open end as it foraged for food. Paleontologists believe that this ammonite was a slow-swimming scavenger, rather than an active hunter. Like many ammonites, *Echioceras* probably wafted over the seabed and grabbed anything edible it could stuff in its beak.

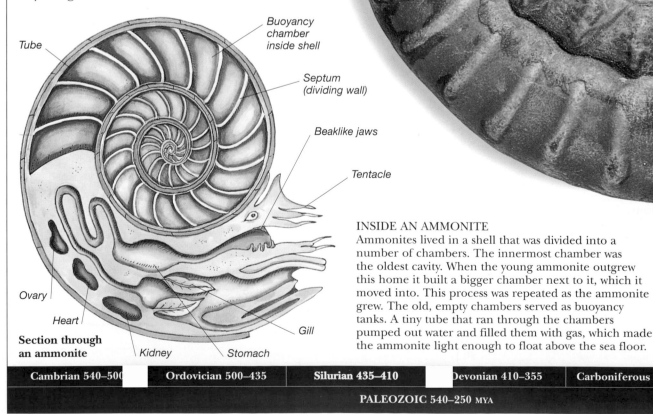

Tube

Buoyancy chamber inside shell

Septum (dividing wall)

Beaklike jaws

Tentacle

Ovary

Heart

Gill

Section through an ammonite

Kidney

Stomach

Ribs spaced well apart strengthened the shell.

INSIDE AN AMMONITE

Ammonites lived in a shell that was divided into a number of chambers. The innermost chamber was the oldest cavity. When the young ammonite outgrew this home it built a bigger chamber next to it, which it moved into. This process was repeated as the ammonite grew. The old, empty chambers served as buoyancy tanks. A tiny tube that ran through the chambers pumped out water and filled them with gas, which made the ammonite light enough to float above the sea floor.

Cambrian 540–500	Ordovician 500–435	Silurian 435–410	Devonian 410–355	Carboniferous 355–295	Permian

PALEOZOIC 540–250 MYA

Loosely coiled shell with many turns, known as whorls

BELEMNOTEUTHIS

Belemnites, such as *Belemnoteuthis*, resembled squid. They were long-bodied creatures with fairly large brains and big eyes. From the head end sprang 10 tentacles armed with suckers and hooks. The muscular mantle – the front of the body – had a winglike fin on either side. The tapering rear end covered the back of the internal shell. *Belemnoteuthis* used its hooked arms to grapple small, slow-moving sea creatures to its beak. To steer or swim slowly, *Belemnoteuthis* flapped its fins. To dart forward or backward for a fast attack or a high speed getaway, it propelled its body by squirting jets of water. *Belemnoteuthis* lived in a Late Jurassic sea that once existed where Europe stands today.

Mantle

Head region

ECHIOCERAS

Scientific name: *Echioceras*

Size: 2.5 in (6 cm) across

Diet: Tiny organisms

Habitat: Shallow seas

Where found: Worldwide

Time: Early Jurassic

Related genus: *Asteroceras*

Hooked tentacle

Chambered phragmocone in the body's broad front end

INSIDE A BELEMNITE

This *Cylindroteuthis* fossil shows the main parts of a belemnite's internal shell. The chambered phragmocone provided buoyancy for the middle of the body and helped to keep it level in the sea. The phragmocone's tapering rear end slotted into the front of the long, narrow guard – a hard part that often fossilized. One of the largest of all belemnites, *Cylindroteuthis* lived in deep offshore waters in Jurassic times.

Long, pointed guard or pen

295–250	Triassic 250–203	Jurassic 203–135	Cretaceous 135–65	Tertiary 65–1.75	Quaternary 1.75–present
		MESOZOIC 250–65 MYA		CENOZOIC 65 MYA–present	

TOWARD THE FIRST FISH

MAJOR STEPS IN EVOLUTION before and early in the Cambrian gave rise to early fish. First, millions of tiny cells clumped together to produce sponges. Then, different types of cells that carried out specialized tasks formed tissues in more advanced animals, the eumetazoans. The first eumetazoans had two layers of tissue. Later eumetazoans had three tissue layers. Further changes created bilaterians – animals with left and right sides, bodies made of many segments, and a front and rear with a mouth and anus. By 535 million years ago, small, long-bodied bilaterians called chordates had evolved a stiffening rod called a notochord that foreshadowed an internal skeleton. Chordates that gained a brain, gills, muscle blocks, and fins became the world's first fish.

Calcite plates protecting the body

Inlet for food and water

Cothurnocystis

Calcite plates framing the head

Slits for expelling water waste

CALCICHORDATES

Cothurnocystis was a strange, boot-shaped animal. One scientist grouped it with the calcichordates ("calcium chordates"), making it a chordate – an organism that has a notochord at some point in its life. Its tail might have contained a notochord, and the small slits in its body might have filtered food, just like the throat slits found in living lancelets. However, most scientists believe it was simply a weird echinoderm. *Cothurnocystis* had an outer "skin" of hard plates like a sea urchin – a living echinoderm.

COTHURNOCYSTIS FOSSIL
Resembling a strange, stalked flower turned to stone, a *Cothurnocystis* fossil lies embedded in an ancient piece of Scottish rock. *Cothurnocystis* belonged to the carpoids – small, oddly flattened creatures that lived on Early Palaeozoic seabeds. More than 400 million years ago, this carpoid – small enough to fit in a human's hand – might have dragged itself across the seabed by its tail. Scientist Richard Jefferies suggested that the tail enclosed a notochord, which might make the carpoids ancestral to fish.

| Cambrian 540–500 | Ordovician 500–435 | Silurian 435–410 | Devonian 410–355 | Carboniferous 355–295 | Permian |

PALEOZOIC 540–250 MYA

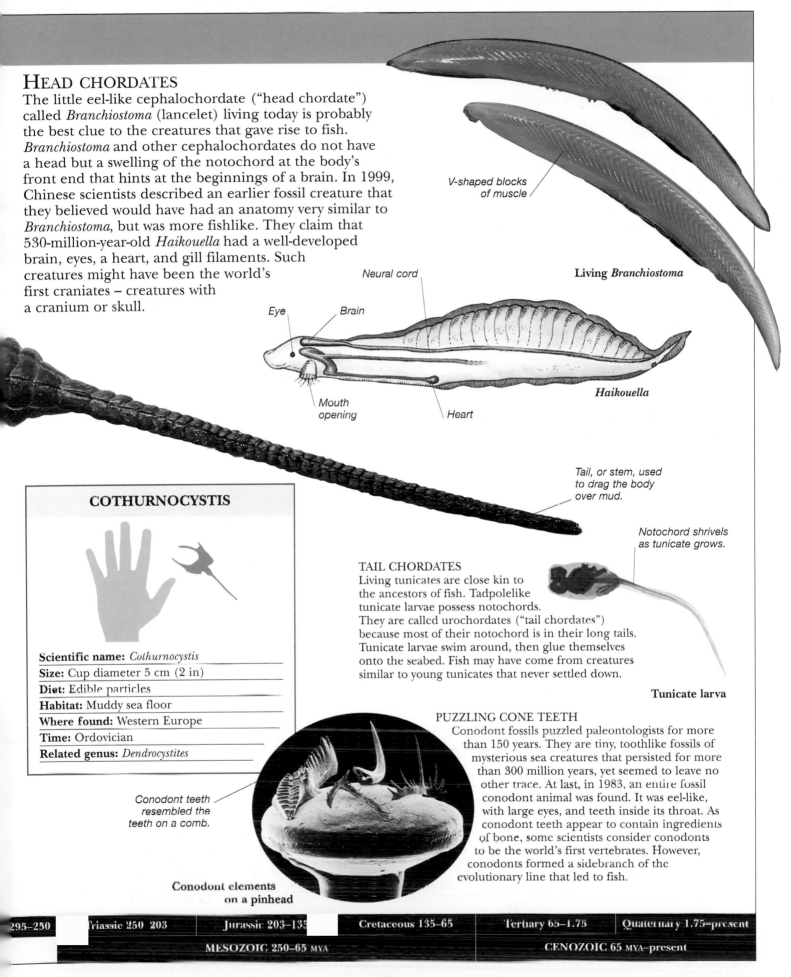

HEAD CHORDATES

The little eel-like cephalochordate ("head chordate") called *Branchiostoma* (lancelet) living today is probably the best clue to the creatures that gave rise to fish. *Branchiostoma* and other cephalochordates do not have a head but a swelling of the notochord at the body's front end that hints at the beginnings of a brain. In 1999, Chinese scientists described an earlier fossil creature that they believed would have had an anatomy very similar to *Branchiostoma*, but was more fishlike. They claim that 530-million-year-old *Haikouella* had a well-developed brain, eyes, a heart, and gill filaments. Such creatures might have been the world's first craniates – creatures with a cranium or skull.

V-shaped blocks of muscle

Living *Branchiostoma*

Neural cord

Eye

Brain

Mouth opening

Heart

Haikouella

Tail, or stem, used to drag the body over mud.

Notochord shrivels as tunicate grows.

COTHURNOCYSTIS

Scientific name: *Cothurnocystis*

Size: Cup diameter 5 cm (2 in)

Diet: Edible particles

Habitat: Muddy sea floor

Where found: Western Europe

Time: Ordovician

Related genus: *Dendrocystites*

Conodont teeth resembled the teeth on a comb.

TAIL CHORDATES

Living tunicates are close kin to the ancestors of fish. Tadpolelike tunicate larvae possess notochords. They are called urochordates ("tail chordates") because most of their notochord is in their long tails. Tunicate larvae swim around, then glue themselves onto the seabed. Fish may have come from creatures similar to young tunicates that never settled down.

Tunicate larva

PUZZLING CONE TEETH

Conodont fossils puzzled paleontologists for more than 150 years. They are tiny, toothlike fossils of mysterious sea creatures that persisted for more than 300 million years, yet seemed to leave no other trace. At last, in 1983, an entire fossil conodont animal was found. It was eel-like, with large eyes, and teeth inside its throat. As conodont teeth appear to contain ingredients of bone, some scientists consider conodonts to be the world's first vertebrates. However, conodonts formed a sidebranch of the evolutionary line that led to fish.

Conodont elements on a pinhead

295–250	Triassic 250–203	Jurassic 203–135	Cretaceous 135–65	Tertiary 65–1.75	Quaternary 1.75–present
	MESOZOIC 250–65 MYA			CENOZOIC 65 MYA–present	

VERTEBRATES CLADOGRAM

ALL VERTEBRATES POSSESS AN INTERNAL SKELETON made of interlocking bones. The evolution of the skeleton allowed vertebrates to support their weight on land better than any other animal group. As a result, vertebrates have grown to sizes and taken to lifestyles that are beyond the scope of most other animals. The most important group of vertebrates are the gnathostomes – the jawed vertebrates. The most successful gnathostomes are the bony fish. Members of this group include the ray-finned fish and the sarcopterygians – the lobe-finned fish and four-footed vertebrates.

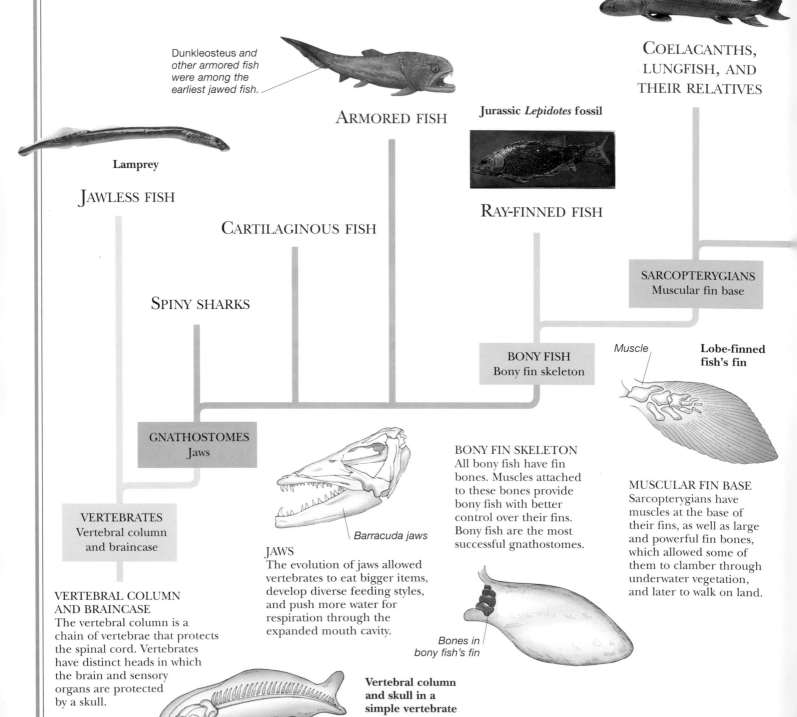

Eusthenopteron **from the Late Devonian**

COELACANTHS, LUNGFISH, AND THEIR RELATIVES

Dunkleosteus *and other armored fish were among the earliest jawed fish.*

ARMORED FISH

Jurassic *Lepidotes* **fossil**

Lamprey

JAWLESS FISH

RAY-FINNED FISH

CARTILAGINOUS FISH

SARCOPTERYGIANS
Muscular fin base

SPINY SHARKS

Muscle

Lobe-finned fish's fin

BONY FISH
Bony fin skeleton

GNATHOSTOMES
Jaws

BONY FIN SKELETON
All bony fish have fin bones. Muscles attached to these bones provide bony fish with better control over their fins. Bony fish are the most successful gnathostomes.

MUSCULAR FIN BASE
Sarcopterygians have muscles at the base of their fins, as well as large and powerful fin bones, which allowed some of them to clamber through underwater vegetation, and later to walk on land.

VERTEBRATES
Vertebral column and braincase

Barracuda jaws

JAWS
The evolution of jaws allowed vertebrates to eat bigger items, develop diverse feeding styles, and push more water for respiration through the expanded mouth cavity.

VERTEBRAL COLUMN AND BRAINCASE
The vertebral column is a chain of vertebrae that protects the spinal cord. Vertebrates have distinct heads in which the brain and sensory organs are protected by a skull.

Bones in bony fish's fin

Vertebral column and skull in a simple vertebrate

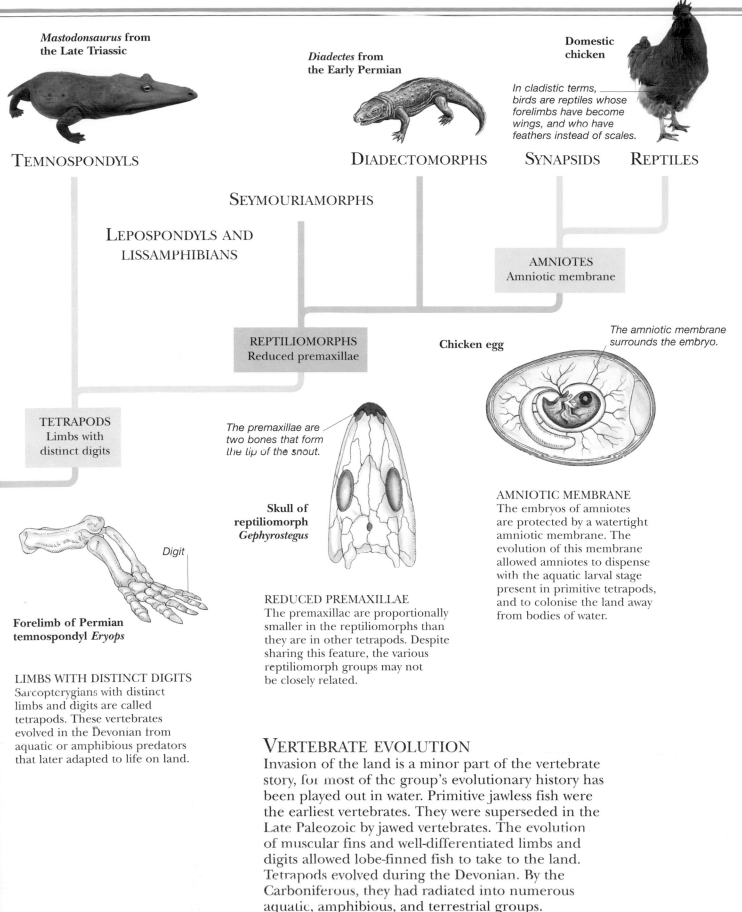

Mastodonsaurus from
the Late Triassic

Diadectes from
the Early Permian

**Domestic
chicken**

*In cladistic terms,
birds are reptiles whose
forelimbs have become
wings, and who have
feathers instead of scales.*

TEMNOSPONDYLS

DIADECTOMORPHS

SYNAPSIDS

REPTILES

SEYMOURIAMORPHS

LEPOSPONDYLS AND
LISSAMPHIBIANS

AMNIOTES
Amniotic membrane

REPTILIOMORPHS
Reduced premaxillae

Chicken egg

*The amniotic membrane
surrounds the embryo.*

TETRAPODS
Limbs with
distinct digits

*The premaxillae are
two bones that form
the lip of the snout.*

**Skull of
reptiliomorph
*Gephyrostegus***

AMNIOTIC MEMBRANE
The embryos of amniotes
are protected by a watertight
amniotic membrane. The
evolution of this membrane
allowed amniotes to dispense
with the aquatic larval stage
present in primitive tetrapods,
and to colonise the land away
from bodies of water.

Digit

**Forelimb of Permian
temnospondyl *Eryops***

REDUCED PREMAXILLAE
The premaxillac are proportionally
smaller in the reptiliomorphs than
they are in other tetrapods. Despite
sharing this feature, the various
reptiliomorph groups may not
be closely related.

LIMBS WITH DISTINCT DIGITS
Sarcoptcrygians with distinct
limbs and digits are called
tetrapods. These vertebrates
evolved in the Devonian from
aquatic or amphibious predators
that later adapted to life on land.

VERTEBRATE EVOLUTION
Invasion of the land is a minor part of the vertebrate
story, for most of the group's evolutionary history has
been played out in water. Primitive jawless fish were
the earliest vertebrates. They were superseded in the
Late Paleozoic by jawed vertebrates. The evolution
of muscular fins and well-differentiated limbs and
digits allowed lobe-finned fish to take to the land.
Tetrapods evolved during the Devonian. By the
Carboniferous, they had radiated into numerous
aquatic, amphibious, and terrestrial groups.

FISH CLADOGRAM

IN CLADISTIC TERMS, THE WORD "FISH" encompasses all vertebrates, as tetrapods – vertebrates that bear limbs with distinct digits – evolved from bony fish. Jawless fish evolved in the Cambrian from chordate animals related to echinoderms. During the Ordovician and Silurian, the gnathostomes, or jawed vertebrates, diversified into four groups – armored fish, cartilaginous fish, spiny sharks, and bony fish. Cartilaginous fish and bony fish have become the dominant forms of vertebrate life, both in water and on land.

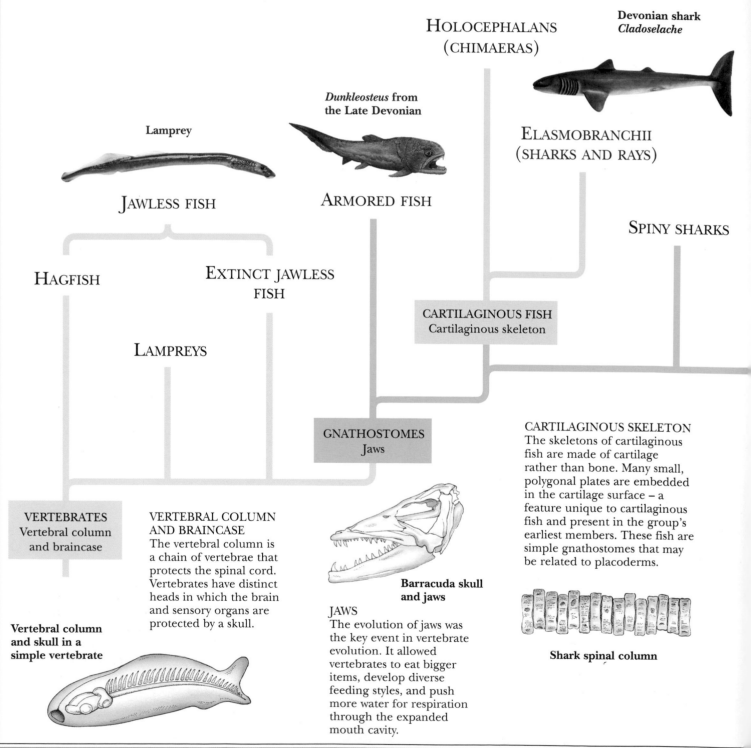

Devonian shark
Cladoselache

HOLOCEPHALANS
(CHIMAERAS)

Dunkleosteus from
the Late Devonian

ELASMOBRANCHII
(SHARKS AND RAYS)

Lamprey

JAWLESS FISH

ARMORED FISH

SPINY SHARKS

HAGFISH

EXTINCT JAWLESS
FISH

CARTILAGINOUS FISH
Cartilaginous skeleton

LAMPREYS

GNATHOSTOMES
Jaws

CARTILAGINOUS SKELETON
The skeletons of cartilaginous fish are made of cartilage rather than bone. Many small, polygonal plates are embedded in the cartilage surface – a feature unique to cartilaginous fish and present in the group's earliest members. These fish are simple gnathostomes that may be related to placoderms.

VERTEBRATES
Vertebral column
and braincase

VERTEBRAL COLUMN
AND BRAINCASE
The vertebral column is a chain of vertebrae that protects the spinal cord. Vertebrates have distinct heads in which the brain and sensory organs are protected by a skull.

**Barracuda skull
and jaws**

JAWS
The evolution of jaws was the key event in vertebrate evolution. It allowed vertebrates to eat bigger items, develop diverse feeding styles, and push more water for respiration through the expanded mouth cavity.

Shark spinal column

**Vertebral column
and skull in a
simple vertebrate**

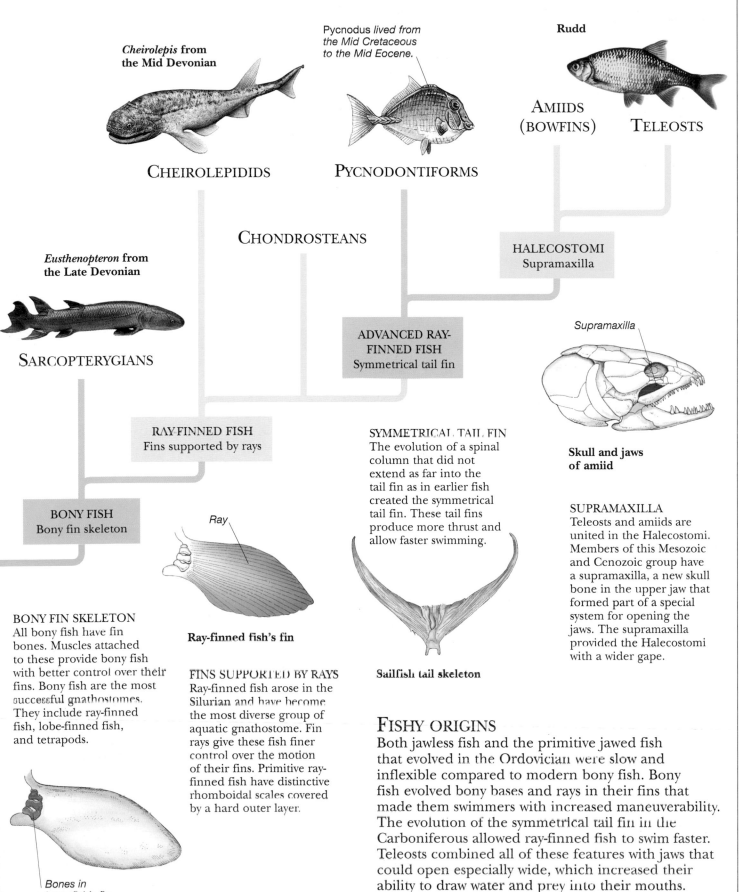

Cheirolepis from
the Mid Devonian

CHEIROLEPIDIDS

*Pycnodus lived from
the Mid Cretaceous
to the Mid Eocene.*

PYCNODONTIFORMS

Rudd

AMIIDS
(BOWFINS)   TELEOSTS

CHONDROSTEANS

HALECOSTOMI
Supramaxilla

Eusthenopteron from
the Late Devonian

SARCOPTERYGIANS

ADVANCED RAY-
FINNED FISH
Symmetrical tail fin

Supramaxilla

**Skull and jaws
of amiid**

RAY-FINNED FISH
Fins supported by rays

SYMMETRICAL TAIL FIN
The evolution of a spinal
column that did not
extend as far into the
tail fin as in earlier fish
created the symmetrical
tail fin. These tail fins
produce more thrust and
allow faster swimming.

SUPRAMAXILLA
Teleosts and amiids are
united in the Halecostomi.
Members of this Mesozoic
and Cenozoic group have
a supramaxilla, a new skull
bone in the upper jaw that
formed part of a special
system for opening the
jaws. The supramaxilla
provided the Halecostomi
with a wider gape.

Ray

BONY FISH
Bony fin skeleton

Ray-finned fish's fin

Sailfish tail skeleton

BONY FIN SKELETON
All bony fish have fin
bones. Muscles attached
to these provide bony fish
with better control over their
fins. Bony fish are the most
successful gnathostomes.
They include ray-finned
fish, lobe-finned fish,
and tetrapods.

FINS SUPPORTED BY RAYS
Ray-finned fish arose in the
Silurian and have become
the most diverse group of
aquatic gnathostome. Fin
rays give these fish finer
control over the motion
of their fins. Primitive ray-
finned fish have distinctive
rhomboidal scales covered
by a hard outer layer.

FISHY ORIGINS

Both jawless fish and the primitive jawed fish
that evolved in the Ordovician were slow and
inflexible compared to modern bony fish. Bony
fish evolved bony bases and rays in their fins that
made them swimmers with increased maneuverability.
The evolution of the symmetrical tail fin in the
Carboniferous allowed ray-finned fish to swim faster.
Teleosts combined all of these features with jaws that
could open especially wide, which increased their
ability to draw water and prey into their mouths.

*Bones in
bony fish's fin*

JAWLESS FISH

AGNATHANS ("WITHOUT JAWS") WERE THE EARLIEST, most primitive fish. Their only living relatives are the hagfishes and lampreys – eel-shaped parasites that fasten onto other fish and feed on their flesh or blood. They were small in size – most less than 6 in (15 cm) long, though some grew to 3 ft 3 in (1 m) – and many were tadpole shaped. They displayed a number of features that are considered to be primitive. Their mouths were fixed open because they lacked jaws, they had no bony internal skeleton, and they lacked paired fins. Because they had fewer fins than more advanced fish, they were not very maneuverable in the water. Early jawless fish lived in the seas, but they later invaded rivers and lakes. They swam by waggling their tails, and sucked in food particles from the mud or water around them. Their bony armor protected them from sea scorpions and other predators.

Backswept horns helped with balance.

The long lower lobe of the tail gave the fish lift as it swam.

Sensory organs, called a lateral line, were present in the sides of the body and in the roof of the skull.

The back of the body was covered with flexible scales.

VERTEBRATE PIONEER

Sacabamsbapis was a tadpole-shaped fish that lived 450 million years ago. It swam by waggling its tail, but had no other fins, which would have made braking and steering almost impossible. Two tiny, headlightlike eyes gazed from the front of its armored head as it sucked in water and food scraps through the ever-open hole of its mouth. *Sacabambaspis* lived in shallow seas, but its fossils have been found in the rocks of Bolivia's high Andes. Old as they are, agnathans 80 million years older are now known from China.

Large bony plates protected the head and chest.

| Cambrian 540–500 | Ordovician 500–435 | Silurian 435–410 | Devonian 410–355 | Carboniferous 355–295 | Permian |

PALEOZOIC 540–250 MYA

A tall, bony spine at the back of the head shield served as a dorsal fin.

Small eyes set in a head shield made of several bony plates

Long, pointed snout

WING SHIELD

Pteraspis ("wing shield") is so named because it had pointed, winglike, armored spines sticking out from its sides. Its heavily armored, pointed head had a long, sharp snout jutting out above and in front of the mouth. Lacking jaws, the mouth was fixed open and the animal might have swum near the surface, guzzling tiny shrimplike creatures. *Pteraspis* and its relatives were very successful during the Late Silurian and Early Devonian in terms of both numbers and diversity.

Bony head shield with eyes on top

BETTER BALANCE

Cephalaspis was a member of the osteostracans, a large group of advanced jawless fish. Its key features included a big, bony head shield with eyes on top, a mouth beneath, and sense organs on the sides and on the top of the head. The upturned tail tended to tilt the head down as it sucked in nourishment from mud on the floors of streams and ponds. Paired scaly flaps, similar to pectoral fins, provided lift and balance, and a dorsal fin helped stop the body rolling.

Body about 8 in (20 cm) long

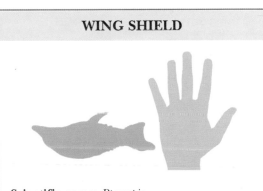

WING SHIELD

Scientific name:	*Pteraspis*
Size:	8 in (20 cm) long
Diet:	Tiny water animals
Habitat:	Shallow seas
Where found:	Europe, Asia, North America
Time:	Early Devonian
Related genera:	*Errivaspis, Protaspis*

295–250	Triassic 250–203	Jurassic 203–135	Cretaceous 135–65	Tertiary 65 1.75	Quaternary 1.75–present
	MESOZOIC 250–65 MYA			CENOZOIC 65 MYA–present	

39

ARMORED FISH

PLACODERMS ("PLATED SKINS") WERE PRIMITIVE jawed fish. They are named for the broad, flat bony plates over the head and front of the body, which protected them from attack by larger placoderms and sea scorpions. They shared many anatomical features with sharks – backbones made of cartilage, for example – hinting that the two groups may have shared a common ancestor. Like sharks, placoderms probably had no swim bladder, and so had to keep swimming to avoid sinking. There were seven main groups of placoderms, including odd forms that were flattened like rays, forms with long, narrow, tapering bodies and tails, and forms with bone-plated "arms." Some lived in the sea, some in fresh water, and they ranged in size from a few inches up to 26 ft (8 m) – the first fish to grow to such a large size. Placoderms were a very successful group. Although they lived almost entirely within a single geological period – the Devonian – they diversified to become the dominant vertebrates of the time.

Each jointed "arm" was a fin inside a bony tube.

FISH WITH "ARMS"

Bothriolepis was among the strangest of placoderms. Up to 3 ft (1 m) in length, it possessed jointed "arms" made of bony tubes that enclosed its long, narrow pectoral fins. *Bothriolepis* might have used these arms to dig for food in the mud of the seabed. Alternatively, the arms could have pulled the fish over dry land as it migrated from one pool to another, breathing air with its "lungs." Fossils of this placoderm are found in marine and freshwater deposits worldwide. Scientists suspect that it lived in shallow Devonian seas, swimming upstream to spawn, just as salmon do today.

Preserved head and trunk shields

Rock slab containing many fossils of *Bothriolepis*

FLAT OUT
The flat-bodied fish *Gemuendina* resembles a modern skate or ray, but in fact it belonged to an ancient group of placoderms called rhenanids. It had broad, winglike pectoral fins. A short, bony shield guarded its foreparts and tiny bony plates ran down its slender tail. Much like living rays, *Gemuendina* swam with rippling movements of its pectoral fins. Patrolling the seabed, it thrust out its jaws and crushed shellfish between its toothlike tubercules. *Gemuendina* lived in Early Devonian times where central Europe now stands, although similar primitive placoderms occurred in North America.

***Gemuendina* fossil in fine-grained rock**

| Cambrian 540–500 | Ordovician 500–435 | Silurian 435–410 | Devonian 410–355 | Carboniferous 355–295 | Permia |

PALEOZOIC 540–250 MYA

Dorsal fin

Head and chest shields connected by a ball-and-socket joint

Unprotected scaleless tail

BONY ONE

One of the largest and most formidable of all placoderms was *Dunkleosteus*, named after American paleontologist D.H. Dunkle. With massive head and jaws, it reached a size of around 16 ft (5 m). Only its head and shoulder areas were covered by a protective shield, leaving the big, fleshy pectoral fins free to help it maneuver. The rest of the body had no armor or scales. Scientists are unsure about the shape and habits of *Dunkleosteus*. It may have been sharklike, swimming and hunting actively, or it may have had an eel-shaped body fringed with long, ribbon-like fins and lived on the sea bed, swimming sinuously.

Bony tooth plates with sharp, cutting cusps

Huge head and chest shield of *Dunkleosteus*

HEAD ARMOR
Dunkleosteus was a member of a group of Late Devonian placoderms called arthrodires or "jointed necks." It rocked back its head to open its jaws, revealing razorlike, self-sharpening bony plates that served as teeth. Its victims probably included small, early sharks.

DUNKLE'S BONY ONE

Scientific name:	*Dunkleosteus*
Size:	16 ft (5 m) or more long
Diet:	Fish
Habitat:	Oceans
Where found:	Europe, Africa, North America
Time:	Late Devonian
Related genera:	*Bruntonichthys, Bullerichthys*

295–250	Triassic 250–203	urassic 203–135	Cretaceous 135–65	ertiary 65–1.75	Quaternary 1.75–present

MESOZOIC 250–65 MYA	CENOZOIC 65 MYA present

DEVONIAN PREDATOR

Sea levels were high in the Devonian, and warm tropical waters teemed with invertebrate life, including corals, echinoderms, trilobites, and sponges. So many new forms of fish evolved during this period that it is sometimes called "the age of fish." Primitive sharks, lobe-finned fish, and lungfish diversified, as did the ray-finned fish and placoderms ("plated skins"). At more than 16 ft (5 m) in length, *Dunkleosteus* was one of the largest of the predatory placoderms, feeding on sharks and other fish.

Cambrian 540–500	Ordovician 500–435	Silurian 435–410	Devonian 410–355	Carboniferous 355–295	Permia

PALEOZOIC 540–250 MYA

SHARKS AND RAYS

SHARKS ARE SUPERB SWIMMING and killing machines and have been among the top ocean predators for more than 400 million years. Their basic features – a streamlined shape and jaws bristling with razor-sharp fangs – have changed little in this time, although many different kinds of sharklike fish have evolved. These include rat fish with big eyes and ratlike tails, and skates and rays with wide, flattened bodies and broad, low teeth. Sharks and their relatives are known as Chondrichthyes ("cartilage fish") because their skeletons are made of cartilage rather than bone. Other features typical of the group include teeth and scales that are continually shed and replaced, no gill covers, and paired fins. Sharks also lack swim bladders, which means they must keep swimming to avoid sinking.

Short main dorsal fin

Streamlined, torpedo-shaped body

Large pectoral fins

Snout shorter and blunter than modern sharks

Rows of teeth grew forward to replace old ones that fell out.

CLADOSELACHE

Cladoselache is one of the earliest known sharks. Its well-preserved fossils have been found in Late Devonian rocks that date back 400 million years. This formidable carnivore hunted fish, squid, and crustaceans that lived in a sea that existed where Ohio now stands. In some ways *Cladoselache* resembled today's sharks, with a torpedo-shaped body, big eyes, large pectoral fins, and large tail, but in other ways it was very different from modern species. Its snout was shorter and more blunt, its mouth was located at the front of the head rather than underneath, and its upper jaw attached to the braincase at the front and back, not just at the back. This meant that the mouth could not open very wide.

CLADOSELACHE

Scientific name: *Cladoselache*
Size: Up to 6 ft 6 in (2 m) long
Diet: Fish and crustaceans
Habitat: Seas
Where found: North America
Time: Late Devonian
Related genus: *Monocladodus*

Cambrian 540–500	Ordovician 500–435	Silurian 435–410	Devonian 410–355	Carboniferous 355–295	Permian

PALEOZOIC 540–250 MYA

Long upper tail
lobe similar to that
of modern sharks

WIDESPREAD PREDATORS

Hybodus was a blunt-headed shark with prominent fin spines
and distinctively shaped scales. Growing up to 8 ft (2.5 m) in
length, it closely resembled modern sharks although its jaws
were of different design, carrying two different types of teeth.
Pointed teeth at the front were used to seize its prey of fish,
while blunt teeth at the back were used to crush bones and
shells. Males had curious barbed hooks on the sides of their
heads, attached to the braincase. The genus *Hybodus*
flourished for much of the Mesozoic Era, and fossils
of different species have been found as far apart
as North America, Europe, Asia, and Africa.

Barbed spines on the head show
that this was a male Hybodus.

Sharp tooth of the
shark Carcharocles

Flat toothplate of
the ray Myliobatis

Large pectoral fins
helped the shark to
maneuver

SUN RAY

The stingray *Heliobatis* ("Sun ray") was a flat-bodied,
freshwater fish that lived in North America about 50
million years ago. Up to 12 in (30 cm) in length, its flat,
round body had a long whip-like tail armed with barbed
spines. *Heliobatis* lay on the bottom of rivers and lakes,
snapping up crayfish and shrimp. When attacked,
it lashed out with its
tail. The spines at the
tip could perhaps
inject a powerful
poison through the
skin of its enemy.

The fin rays radiated
like the rays of the Sun.

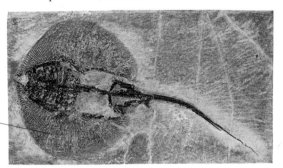

SHARP OR BLUNT

Prehistoric sharks and rays are often identified
from their hard, durable teeth because their gristly
skeletons did not readily fossilize. The sharp, serrated
tooth shown here belongs to the huge Eocene shark
Carcharocles, which killed and ate large sea mammals.
It is very different from the broad flat toothplate of
the ray *Myliobatis*, which was designed to crunch up
the hard shells of armored creatures, such as as
crabs and clams.

Spine-covered "tower"

SPINY CHEST

Among the strangest of all prehistoric creatures was
Stethacanthus ("spiny chest"), a small shark that lived about
360 million years ago. The male carried a bizarre tower on
its back, the broad, flat top of which was covered by a brush
of spines. Another spiny patch grew on top of its head. The
function of the spiny patches is uncertain. Viewed head on,
they may have resembled a pair of huge jaws, thus scaring
off predators, or they may have been important in mating.

95–250	Triassic 250–203	Jurassic 203–135	Cretaceous 135–65	Tertiary 65–1.75	Quaternary 1.75–present

MESOZOIC 250–65 MYA	CENOZOIC 65 MYA present

SPINY SHARKS

ACANTHODIANS OR "SPINY SHARKS" MAY HAVE predated placoderms as the first fish with jaws. They were named for their streamlined, sharklike bodies with upturned tails, and for the thorn-sharp spines that formed the leading edges of their fins. Most spiny sharks had deep, blunt heads, big mouths, and at least two dorsal fins. Although their cartilage backbone reminds us of a shark's, acanthodians had a braincase, gills, and other features more like those of bony fish that dominate the waters of the world today. The oldest known acanthodian fossils come from Early Silurian rocks in China. Evolving in the sea, acanthodians invaded lakes and rivers eventually. Most were small – the largest 6 ft 6 in (2 m) long. The group persisted for maybe 170 million years – as long as the dinosaurs – with a heyday in the Devonian.

Large eyes suggest that Climatius *hunted by sight not scent*

SPINY PROTECTION
Fin spines up to 16 in (40 cm) long are the best known remains of the spiny shark *Gyracanthus*. Fossils of this well-defended animal are found in Carboniferous rocks of North America and Europe. The group to which *Gyracanthus* belongs probably evolved in Antarctica but spread around the world. Some of these acanthodians carried pectoral fin spines that were half their body length as protection against large, fierce predators.

Distinctive ridges on surface of Gyracanthus *fin spine*

INCLINED FISH
Climatius ("inclined fish") was named for its upward tilted tail. This small river fish was a member of the Climatiiformes, the earliest group of acanthodians. It had big eyes and sharp teeth suggesting that it was an active predator. It is likely that *Climatius* zoomed low over the beds of seas or rivers in search of prey – tiny fish and crustaceans. Its defensive features included heavy, bony shoulder armor, spiny fins, and four pairs of extra finlike spines that protected its belly. These helped make *Climatius* difficult for larger predators to tackle.

| Cambrian 540–500 | Ordovician 500–435 | Silurian 435–410 | Devonian 410–355 | Carboniferous 355–295 | Permian |

PALEOZOIC 540–250 MYA

Cheiracanthus fossil in Old Red Sandstone rock

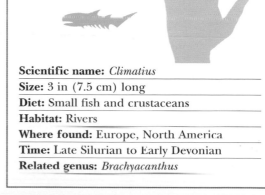

Thick spines on the back and belly made Climatius hard to swallow.

HAND SPINE

Cheiracanthus ("hand spine") was a deep-bodied acanthodian about 12 in (30 cm) in length. It had a blunt head, upturned tail, and fins protected by spines. Unlike many other acanthodians, it had just a solitary dorsal fin. *Cheiracanthus* swam at mid-depth in lakes and rivers, seizing small prey in its gaping jaws. Whole fossils of this fish occur only in Mid-Devonian rocks in Scotland, but its distinctive small, ornamented scales crop up around the world, as far south as Antarctica.

Non-retractable spines added to drag as the fish swam.

Caudal (tail) fin was present only below the upturned tail lobe.

RIGID FINS

The shoulder girdles of spiny sharks such as *Climatius* began as two separate bony plates connected to the spiny pectoral fins on each side of the body. Later they evolved into plates connected by a narrow plate that ran across the chest. Other plates were added later, until they formed a rigid structure that locked the pectoral fins in position. The fixed fins served as hydroplanes, providing lift as *Climatius* swam forward.

Pectoral fins connected to bony plates

Pectoral fins locked in position

INCLINED FISH

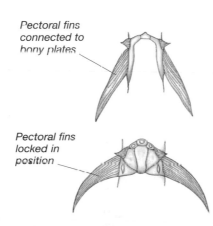

Scientific name: *Climatius*	
Size: 3 in (7.5 cm) long	
Diet: Small fish and crustaceans	
Habitat: Rivers	
Where found: Europe, North America	
Time: Late Silurian to Early Devonian	
Related genus: *Brachyacanthus*	

95–250	Triassic 250–203	Jurassic 203–135	Cretaceous 135–65	Tertiary 65–1.75	Quaternary 1.75–present
	MESOZOIC 250–65 MYA			CENOZOIC 65 MYA–present	

EARLY RAY-FINNED FISH

BONY FISH ARE THE MOST NUMEROUS and diverse of all living vertebrates, and more than 20,000 of them belong to one giant group – the actinopterygians or "ray fins." They are named for the straight bony rays – controlled by muscles in the body wall – that jut out from the body and stiffen the fins. The earliest known ray fins lived 410 million years ago. The first group to evolve were the paleoniscoids ("old, codlike fish"), which were small with thick scales, inflexible stiff fins, long jaws, and long upper tail lobes. By moving air into and out of special "lungs," they could control their level in the water, even though they lacked swim bladders. A few different kinds of paleoniscoids evolved during the Devonian Period but more than 36 family groups appeared later, in the Carboniferous and Permian. After that, new kinds of bony fish called neopterygians ("new fins") began to take their place.

LIVING FOSSILS
About a dozen species of bichirs still live in freshwater habitats in Africa, where they feed on small creatures such as worms and insects. These long-bodied, ray-finned fish can be traced back to ancestors that lived 400 million years ago. Their skeletons are largely made of cartilage, they have big, enamel-covered scales, and their pectoral fins sprout from fleshy lobes.

HAND FIN
Cheirolepis ("hand fin") was one of the earliest ray-finned fish. Only parts of its backbone were actually made of bone – the rest was made of gristle and so was not often preserved in fossils. Unlike modern bony fish, *Cheirolepis* had pectoral fins (the equivalents of arms) that grew from fleshy lobes projecting from its body. It was covered in small overlapping scales thickly coated with a special enamel known as ganoin. This fish was an eager hunter, swimming fast to catch prey in freshwater pools and streams. It could open its jaws very wide to swallow animals two-thirds of its own length. As *Cheirolepis* swam, its tall dorsal fin and the large anal fin below its body helped to stop it rocking in the water.

Relatively large eyes

Long jaws equipped with many tiny teeth

Pectoral fins on fleshy lobes

REDFIELDIUS
About 8 in (20 cm) in length, *Redfieldius* swam in lakes and streams about 210 million years ago. Its group, the redfieldiids, are thought to have evolved in Australia or South Africa and then spread to North Africa and North America in Early Mesozoic times, when all these lands were joined. The skull and fins of *Redfieldius* are more advanced in design than those of the first ray-finned fish.

| Cambrian 540–500 | Ordovician 500–435 | Silurian 435–410 | Devonian 410–355 | Carboniferous 355–295 | Permia |

PALEOZOIC 540–250 MYA

LEPISOSTEUS

This streamlined freshwater predator, about 28 in (70 cm) long, had dorsal and anal fins placed so far back on its body that they almost touched its tail. Despite its "old-fashioned" enameled scales, it is more advanced than the first ray-finned fish. About 50 million years ago, *Lepisosteus* would have lurked in shallow weedy waters of what is now Wyoming. It probably lay in wait for its prey of small fish, seizing them in sudden bursts of speed between its long, narrow, toothy jaws. Living members of its genus include the gars of North America.

Lepisosteus fossil from the Eocene

Tall dorsal fin tended to push the head down when swimming. Paired fins below the body helped to keep the head up.

Characteristic upturned tail

Body flexed powerfully when swimming

HAND FIN

Scientific name: *Cheirolepis*

Size: 10 in (25 cm) long

Diet: Small invertebrates

Habitat: Fresh water

Where found: Europe, North America

Time: Middle to Late Devonian

Related genera: *Moythomasia, Orvikuina*

STURGEON

Best known for producing eggs that people eat as caviar, sturgeons are living "prehistoric" ray-finned fish. The two dozen kinds alive today live in northern seas and swim up rivers to spawn. Several of these species are endangered by over-harvesting, dam construction, and pollution. They feed on small animals and plants, which they suck into their toothless mouths. The largest can grow to lengths of 10 ft (3 m) and weigh up to half a ton (0.5 tonnes). Like bichirs, they have cartilage skeletons, and like *Cheirolepis* they possess uptilted tails and "old-fashioned" scales and fin rays.

295–250	Triassic 250–203	Jurassic 203–135	Cretaceous 135–65	Tertiary 65–1.75	Quaternary 1.75–present
		MESOZOIC 250–65 MYA		CENOZOIC 65 MYA present	

ADVANCED RAY-FINNED FISH

IMPROVED TYPES OF RAY-FINNED FISH called neopterygians ("new fins") began to appear in Mesozoic times – the Age of the Dinosaurs. These new forms had shorter jaws than before, but their mouths could open wider, and tooth plates in their mouths formed bones for grinding up food. Changes in the design of the fins and tail, which became more symmetrical, made neopterygians faster and more agile in the water. However, the biggest changes at this time occurred in the group of neopterygians known as teleosts ("complete bones"). These evolved defensive fin spines, deep but short bodies, and immensely powerful tails to drive them along. Swim bladders – air-filled sacs – helped control their buoyancy, and they could protrude their mouths to seize or suck in food. Spiny teleosts also had lighter, thinner scales than early ray-finned fishes. There are more than 20,000 teleosts living today, demonstrating the success of the design.

Heavily enameled overlapping scales made the body inflexible.

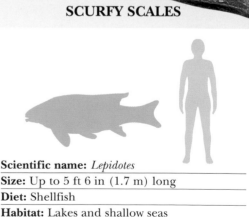

SCURFY SCALES

Lepidotes ("covered in scurfy scales") was a bony fish nearly as long as a human. In many ways it looked very different from the first ray-finned fish. It was far bigger, with a deeper body, a swim bladder for controlling buoyancy, shortened jaws, and a wider gape. Like early ray-finned fish, its body had a coat of thickly enameled scales that resembled rows of shiny tiles. *Lepidotes* cruised above the floors of lakes, lagoons, and shallow coastal waters, crunching shellfish with its strong teeth. Despite its size and protective scales, *Lepidotes* itself was sometimes snatched and gobbled up by big fish-eating dinosaurs: the spinosaurs.

Leptolepides, *a small Late Jurassic teleost from Europe*

PRIMITIVE TELEOST
No longer than a human hand, *Leptolepides* was a primitive bony fish that lived about 150 million years ago. It swam in shoals in tropical lagoons where Germany now stands. Like carp and other modern teleosts, it was able to protrude its mouth to take in its food – plankton in the surface waters. Its bony scales were strong but thin, flexible, and light, making it an agile swimmer, and its tail's supporting rays showed other signs of progressive change.

SCURFY SCALES

Scientific name: *Lepidotes*

Size: Up to 5 ft 6 in (1.7 m) long

Diet: Shellfish

Habitat: Lakes and shallow seas

Where found: Worldwide

Time: Triassic–Cretaceous

Related genera: *Acentrophorus, Corunegenys*

OLD ACARA

Priscacara was a spiny-rayed perchlike teleost that grew to about 6 in (15 cm) in length. It lived in North America about 45 million years ago and was an ancestor of damselfish, small fish found today on coral reefs in warm oceans. Stiff spines protected its dorsal and anal fins, and its short jaws were crammed with tiny teeth allowing it to snap up snails and small crustaceans in lakes and streams.

Short, deep body resembles that of a living cichlid, the acara.

Number of fin rays of anal fin is the same as the number of their support bones – a feature of neopterygians.

Top and bottom tail lobes of equal length

Relatively deep body

SWORD RAY

Xiphactinus was a primitive teleost that swam in Late Cretaceous seas where North America, Europe, and Australia now stand. At up to 14 ft (4.2 m) in length it was as large as today's largest bony fish. Swinging its short "bulldog" jaws open wide to reveal its prominent conical teeth, it could seize and then swallow a fish as long as a human. This is known because the guts of one fossil *Xiphactinus* contain the remains of *Gillicus*, another neopterygian, which was 6 ft (1.8 m) long. It is thought that some *Xiphactinus* died because they tried to swallow prey that was too big.

Large lower jaw

295–250	Triassic 250–203	Jurassic 203–135	Cretaceous 135–65	Tertiary 65–1.75	Quaternary 1.75–present
		MESOZOIC 250–65 MYA		CENOZOIC 65 MYA–present	

51

LOBE-FINNED FISH

THE BONY FISH THAT SWAM IN SEAS and freshwaters 400 million years ago belonged to two large groups – lobe fins and ray fins. Lobe-finned fish, or sarcopterygians, were so called because their fins sprouted from fleshy, muscular lobes reinforced by bone. Many also possessed a type of lung in addition to gills and so could breathe in air and in water. There were two main groups of lobe fins – lungfish and crossopterygians. The latter, also known as "tassel fins," included the coelacanths ("hollow spines") and rhipidistians ("fan sails"), which have an important place in evolutionary history. Certain air-breathing fan sails lost their fins and developed limbs, becoming the ancestors of all land-living vertebrates. By Late Paleozoic times a huge variety of lobe-finned fish thrived in rivers, lakes, and shallow seas worldwide. Today only six species of lungfish and one species of coelacanth survive.

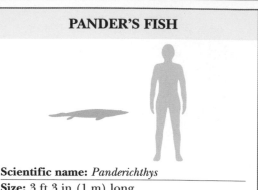

PANDER'S FISH

Scientific name:	*Panderichthys*
Size: 3 ft 3 in (1 m) long	
Diet: Fish and crustaceans	
Habitat: Shallow pools	
Where found: Europe	
Time: Late Devonian	
Related genera: *Elpistostege, Obruchevichthys*	

PANDER'S FISH

In the 1990s, scientists made an important discovery about the Late Devonian fan sail *Panderichthys*. Their studies revealed that this freshwater rhipidistian was one of the closest known ancestors of four-limbed vertebrates – closer even than *Eusthenopteron*. It had a long, narrow body and a long, large, flat head with eyes on top. Its nostrils were low on its snout, and its teeth were covered with enamel folded in the same way as some early four-legged animals. The way its ribs joined its backbone, and the shape of its skull bones also made it more like a tetrapod than a fish.

Ridged upper and lower toothplates of *Ceratodus*

Broad, flat head of Panderichthys, with eyes located on top and undershot mouth, opening below the snout

HORN TEETH

Ceratodus ("horn teeth") was a freshwater lungfish that lived worldwide throughout the Age of Dinosaurs. Tapered at both ends, it grew to a length of 20 in (50 cm). It had two pairs of leaf-shaped, fleshy fins, together with a long, pointed fin formed by the tail fin and two others that had met and joined. The crinkly toothplates anchored to its jaws allowed it to crunch up its food of fish, frogs, and snails. It had gills, but could also breathe through its nostrils at the water surface, using its swim bladder as a kind of lung.

Cambrian 540–500	Ordovician 500–435	Silurian 435–410	Devonian 410–355	Carboniferous 355–295	Permian

PALEOZOIC 540–250 MYA

LIVING COELACANTH

Latimeria, a coelacanth 5 ft (1.5 m) long, shares features with ancestors that lived 350 million years ago. Fleshy lobes support some of its fins and enameled scales protect its body. The tail tip has the characteristic fringe that earned "tassel fins" their name. People thought that coelacanths were extinct until one was caught off South Africa in 1938.

Narrow, fleshy, fin-fringed tail

No dorsal or anal fins

Eusthenopteron **fossil**

Large muscular pectoral fins supported by "arm" bones

GOOD STRONG FIN

Eusthenopteron ("good strong fin") was a long-bodied, predatory freshwater fish with a three-pronged tail. Nostrils opened into its mouth, and details of its skull, teeth, backbone, and the bones of its paired pectoral and pelvic fins were similar to those of the first four-legged animals. It lived in Late Devonian North America and Europe. Scientists once thought that it could haul itself over land from pond to pond on its stubby fins, breathing air through a lunglike swim bladder. However, closer examination of its fins suggests that they may not have worked well as limbs.

Powerful fins, which could push Eusthenopteron through shallow waters

295–250	Triassic 250–203	Jurassic 203–135	Cretaceous 135–65	Tertiary 65–1.75	Quaternary 1.75–present
	MESOZOIC 250–65 MYA			CENOZOIC 65 MYA–present	

LIFE IN A SWAMP FOREST

DURING THE CARBONIFEROUS PERIOD, land-dwelling animals began to diversify and new kinds of terrestrial vertebrates evolved. Lush, forested swamps covered the lowland regions of the northern continents. Ferns and other plants formed the understorey, while giant 100-ft (30-m) trees towered overhead. Dead material from these plants built up over millions of years into thick layers of coal. Humid, tropical conditions and possibly higher amounts of oxygen in the atmosphere favored the evolution of giant arthropods, among them huge, dragonfly-like forms and large, land-dwelling millipedes and scorpions. Among the vertebrates, temnospondyls and anthracosaurs thrived as amphibious and aquatic predators. On land, lepospondyls and the first amniotes hunted invertebrate prey.

GIANT ARTHROPODS

With a wingspan of about 28 in (70 cm), Meganeura was the largest flying insect ever. It was a swift aerial predator, probably living much like a modern dragonfly. It was not a dragonfly however, belonging instead to a more primitive group called the Megasecoptera. Other giant Carboniferous arthropods included scorpions more than 24 in (60 cm) long, and Arthropleura, a flat-bodied millipede 6 ft 6 in (2 m) long.

Skull and body shape suggests that Eryops was an aquatic hunter.

COAL FORMATION

The decaying tissues of Carboniferous plants built up in layers as peat. Later, this became compressed and fossilized to produce lignite and eventually coal – a black sedimentary rock that has been extensively mined for use as a fuel. Plant tissues may not have rotted as quickly in the Carboniferous as they do today – perhaps because fungi and microorganisms responsible for decay were not as efficient or abundant as they are now.

Early reptiles, such as Hylonomus, inhabited the Carboniferous forests. They probably foraged in the leaf litter for insects and other small prey.

| Cambrian 540–500 | Ordovician 500–435 | Silurian 435–410 | Devonian 410–355 | Carboniferous 355–295 | Permia |

PALEOZOIC 540–250 MYA

CARBONIFEROUS PLANTS

A number of plant groups, including clubmosses, horsetails, and ferns, formed the Carboniferous swamp forests. The largest clubmosses, such as the giant *Lepidodendron*, reached 165 ft (50 m) in height while the biggest horsetails grew to 50 ft (15 m). Living members of these groups rarely exceed a few feet in height. Dense groups of plants would have grown in and around the swampy pools, and broken stems, branches, and shed leaves would have lain in the waters.

Eryops may have crawled onto the shore or onto fallen tree trunks to bask or rest.

LONGFACE

Scientific name:	*Eryops*
Size:	6 ft 6 in (2 m) long
Diet:	Fish, amphibious tetrapods
Habitat:	Swamps and lakes
Where found:	North America
Time:	Late Carboniferous to Permian
Related genera:	*Clamorosaurus, Intasuchus*

AQUATIC HUNTERS

Various large predators haunted the dark waters of the Carboniferous forests, including amphibious temnospondyls called eryopids ("longfaces") that survived into the Permian period. Their long, somewhat flattened skulls contained numerous sharp teeth. Eyes and nostrils were located on the top of their heads, suggesting that they kept as much of their bodies under water as possible when stalking prey. They had short weak limbs, and scaly skin scattered with bony nodules.

05–250	Triassic 250–203	Jurassic 203–135	Cretaceous 135–65	Tertiary 65–1.75	Quaternary 1.75–present
		MESOZOIC 250–65 MYA		CENOZOIC 65 MYA–present	

LEPOSPONDYLS AND LISSAMPHIBIANS

LEPOSPONDYLS WERE A GROUP OF CARBONIFEROUS and Permian tetrapods that probably included the ancestors of lissamphibians, the group that includes frogs, salamanders, and caecilians. They lived in a warm, humid world where giant temnospondyls were the dominant predators. Microsaurs were lizard-like lepospondyls from the Carboniferous and Early Permian. Some were well-adapted for life on land, while others were aquatic. Nectrideans were salamanderlike, and more at home in the water – the best-known nectridean is *Diplocaulus*, with its distinctive boomerang-shaped skull. Lissamphibians evolved early in the Mesozoic, perhaps from microsaurs. Frogs are known from the Triassic, while salamanders and caecilians first appear in the Jurassic. Today there are more lissamphibian than mammal species – around 5,000.

Diplocaulus would not have exposed its vulnerable underside for long.

SNAKELIKE AÏSTOPODS

One of the most bizarre groups of Paleozoic tetrapods are the aïstopods, eel-like animals with more than 200 vertebrae and without any limbs or limb girdles. Aïstopods have large eyes, suggesting that they hunted by sight. Some may have been able to open their jaws very wide, like snakes, and so could have eaten large prey. Scientists argue over whether aïstopods were aquatic eel-like predators or land-living burrowers. It may be that different aïstopods followed each of these lifestyles.

Snakelike body with no sign of limbs

Some aïstopods had extra joints in their jaws for engulfing large prey.

Aïstopod *Aornerpeton*

BOOMERANG HEAD

Diplocaulus from the Permian of Texas was one of the most unusual lepospondyls. The "boomerang" shape of the skull was formed by hornlike extensions from the hind-corners of the back of the skull. Baby *Diplocaulus* did not have the boomerang-shaped skulls of adults, but as they became older the hornlike structures became larger. *Diplocaulus'* skull was just one of several bizarre designs found among nectrideans – several later examples grew extremely long snouts. *Diplocaulus'* short body and tail are also unusual for a nectridean, and some experts have speculated that it propelled itself by rippling its body up and down, rather than by using its tail.

LISSAMPHIBIAN DIVERSITY

Since their first appearance, lissamphibians have evolved into a wide variety of forms. Frogs are bizarre lissamphibians with dramatically reduced skeletons. They lack ribs and a tail, have only a few vertebrae, and have a pelvis reduced to a V-shaped structure. *Triadobatrachus* from Triassic Madagascar is the earliest known frog. Salamanders first appear as fossils in the Jurassic, and modern groups, such as giant salamanders, are known from the Eocene (53–33.7 MYA) onward. The earthworm-like, limbless lissamphibians called caecilians also originate in Jurassic times.

Giant salamander *Andrias*

Early frog *Triadobatrachus*

| Cambrian 540–500 | Ordovician 500–435 | Silurian 435–410 | Devonian 410–355 | Carboniferous 355–295 | Permi |

PALEOZOIC 540–250 MYA

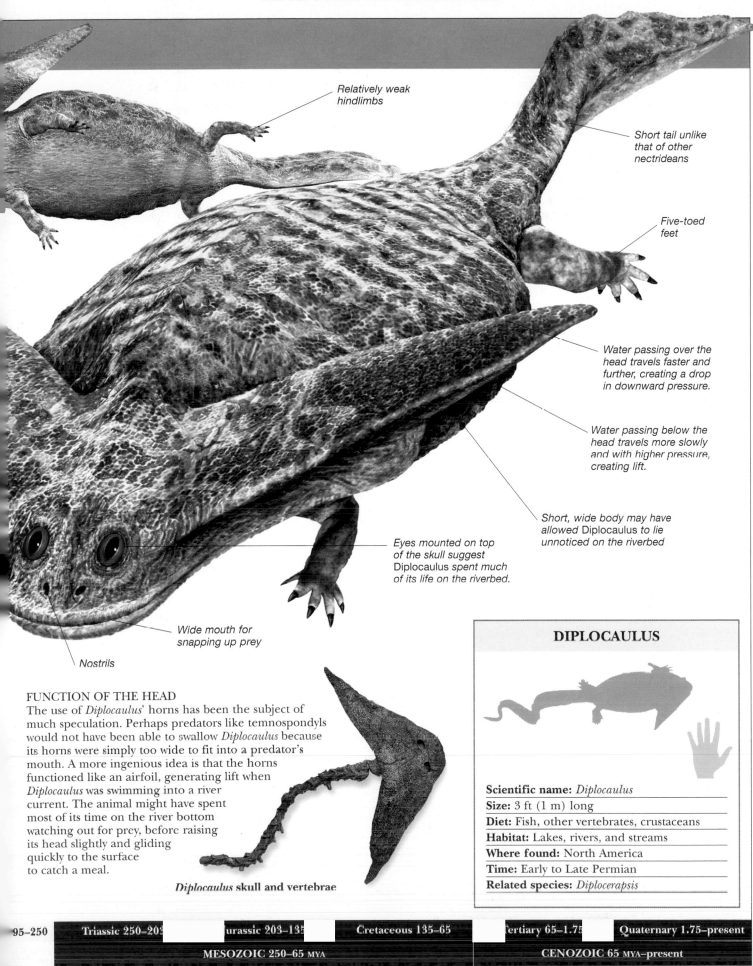

Relatively weak hindlimbs

Short tail unlike that of other nectrideans

Five-toed feet

Water passing over the head travels faster and further, creating a drop in downward pressure.

Water passing below the head travels more slowly and with higher pressure, creating lift.

Short, wide body may have allowed Diplocaulus to lie unnoticed on the riverbed

Eyes mounted on top of the skull suggest Diplocaulus spent much of its life on the riverbed.

Wide mouth for snapping up prey

Nostrils

FUNCTION OF THE HEAD

The use of *Diplocaulus'* horns has been the subject of much speculation. Perhaps predators like temnospondyls would not have been able to swallow *Diplocaulus* because its horns were simply too wide to fit into a predator's mouth. A more ingenious idea is that the horns functioned like an airfoil, generating lift when *Diplocaulus* was swimming into a river current. The animal might have spent most of its time on the river bottom watching out for prey, before raising its head slightly and gliding quickly to the surface to catch a meal.

Diplocaulus skull and vertebrae

DIPLOCAULUS

Scientific name: *Diplocaulus*

Size: 3 ft (1 m) long

Diet: Fish, other vertebrates, crustaceans

Habitat: Lakes, rivers, and streams

Where found: North America

Time: Early to Late Permian

Related species: *Diplocerapsis*

95–250	Triassic 250–203	urassic 203–135	Cretaceous 135–65	Tertiary 65–1.75	Quaternary 1.75–present
	MESOZOIC 250–65 MYA			CENOZOIC 65 MYA–present	

REPTILIOMORPHS

THE REPTILIOMORPHS, OR "REPTILE FORMS," include the ancestors of amniotes, and the amniotes – the group that includes reptiles – themselves. Though some specialized reptiliomorphs, like *Crassigyrinus*, were amphibious or aquatic, generally their skeletons became steadily better suited for carrying weight on land. Some reptiliomorphs are found preserved in environments well away from water, and are not associated with other water-dependent species. It seems that these terrestrial reptiliomorphs were very amniote-like, and they have at times even been classified as amniotes. Whether they actually laid eggs on land, as amniotes do, is still uncertain, but at least some of them are known to have produced aquatic larvae. Most amphibious and terrestrial reptiliomorphs were sprawling predators that ate arthropods and small vertebrates. The terrestrial diadectomorphs were herbivores, while the long-bodied aquatic anthracosaurs, some of which reached nearly 16 ft (5 m) in length, probably preyed on fish and other animals.

The tail is unknown, but it was probably long and used in swimming.

The back part of the skull anchored large chewing muscles.

Diadectes had a stout skull and deep lower jaws.

Strong fingers to dig up plants

Molarlike back teeth for chewing

Front teeth were spoon-shaped and projected forward.

Powerful limbs sprawled sideways from the body.

Short claws with blunt, rounded tips

FIRST HERBIVORES

Diadectomorphs were reptilelike animals that evolved in the Late Carboniferous and survived into the Early Permian. They had massive limb girdles and short, strong limbs. *Diadectes* from North America and Europe is the best known diadectomorph. The shape of their teeth shows that diadectomorphs were herbivores, and thus the very first land vertebrates to evolve a plant-eating lifestyle. Features of their skeletons show that diadectomorphs were very closely related to amniotes, and they may have been very similar in lifestyle and anatomy.

| Cambrian 540–500 | Ordovician 500–435 | Silurian 435–410 | Devonian 410–355 | Carboniferous 355–295 | Permia |

PALEOZOIC 540–250 MYA

BIZARRE AQUATIC PREDATOR

Crassigyrinus from the Early Carboniferous of Scotland is regarded by some experts as a reptiliomorph. It was about 6 ft (2 m) long, with a massive, blunt head and tiny limbs. *Crassigyrinus* was probably an aquatic predator of fish and other vertebrates. Several of its features were very primitive, perhaps because of its specialization to aquatic life. Among these were its pelvis and a prominent notch in the back of its skull. This may have been for a spiracle – a remnant of the gill slits seen in fish and the earliest limbed vertebrates.

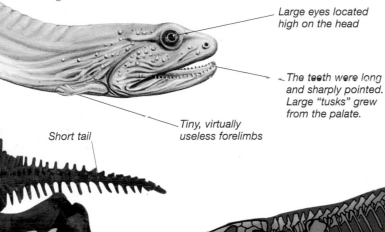

Large eyes located high on the head

The teeth were long and sharply pointed. Large "tusks" grew from the palate.

Short tail

Tiny, virtually useless forelimbs

Limb bones were heavily built and powerfully muscled.

Barrel-shaped body probably housed massive abdomen.

Toes were short and composed of stout bones.

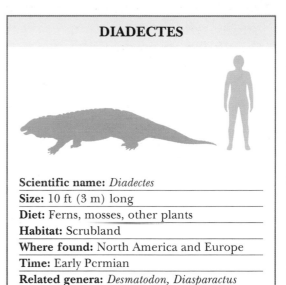

DIADECTES

Scientific name:	*Diadectes*
Size:	10 ft (3 m) long
Diet:	Ferns, mosses, other plants
Habitat:	Scrubland
Where found:	North America and Europe
Time:	Early Permian
Related genera:	*Desmatodon, Diasparactus*

Skeletal structure of *Seymouria*

SEYMOURIAMORPHS

The Permian saw the appearance of the seymouriamorphs, a group of small predatory reptiliomorphs. Many were aquatic, giving birth to young with gills. Like fish, these juveniles had sensory canals on their skull bones. Pits on the skulls of *Discosauriscus* larvae might have housed organs to detect electrical signals from the muscles of their prey. *Seymouria*, from Europe and North America, was a land-based form. It had stocky limbs and lived in dry upland environments. Unlike those of *Discosauriscus*, juveniles of *Seymouria* lacked gills.

Westlothiana probably preyed on insects.

Limbs show that Westlothiana was suited for life on the ground.

Long, flexible body

Lizardlike tail

LIZZIE THE LIZARD

Westlothiana from the Early Carboniferous of Scotland – nicknamed "Lizzie the lizard" – was originally regarded as the first reptile. It was later identified as a reptiliomorph only distantly related to amniotes. However, scientists have recently suggested that *Westlothiana* is not even a close relation of reptiliomorphs. Instead, it may be a far more primitive kind of tetrapod (four-footed vertebrate). The same has also been argued for seymouriamorphs.

INTRODUCING AMNIOTES

IN THE LATE CARBONIFEROUS, a group of animals appeared that would come to dominate life on land – the amniotes. Descended from reptiliomorphs, these were the first creatures to protect their embryos within a sealed structure called the amniotic egg. The evolution of amniotic eggs was probably the key development that allowed tetrapods to conquer the land – they could now move into environments that were far away from water. Amniotes consist of two major groups: synapsids (mammals and their fossil relatives) and reptiles. Many later dispensed with the eggshell and retained their embryos internally, thus affording them even better protection.

The rotten tree stumps that trapped Hylonomus mostly belonged to Sigillaria, a 100 ft (30 m) tall clubmoss.

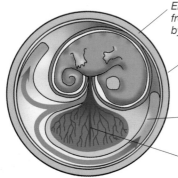

Embryo is protected from the outside world by the shell.

Microscopic shell pores let gases in and out.

Waste material collects in the allantois.

Yolk feeds the embryo during development.

AMNIOTE EGGS

Amniotic eggs have a semipermeable shell that protects the embryo from drying out on land. An internal membrane called the amnion surrounds the embryo as well as the yolk, the embryo's food source. A sac called the allantois stores waste material. Development of the embryo in a protective sealed structure meant that the free-swimming larval stage seen in earlier tetrapods could be dispensed with.

EARLY FOSSIL AMNIOTES

Paleontologists can identify skeletal features that are unique to synapsids and reptiles, such as their teeth. These features allow them to recognize early fossil amniotes without direct proof that they laid amniotic eggs. The earliest fossil reptiles are Carboniferous animals such as *Hylonomus* and *Paleothyris*. The earliest fossil synapsid is *Archaeothyris* from the same Carboniferous Canadian locality as *Hylonomus* and *Paleothyris*. All these early amniotes were very similar in appearance.

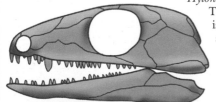

Skull of *Paleothyris*

Hylonomus *wasn't the only vertebrate that perished in these traps. Several species of microsaurs have also been recovered from the tree stumps, as have anthracosaurs and temnospondyls.*

Trapped at the bottom of a hollow tree stump, specimens of Hylonomus eventually died of starvation.

| Cambrian 540–500 | Ordovician 500–435 | Silurian 435–410 | Devonian 410–355 | Carboniferous 355–295 | Permia |

PALEOZOIC 540–250 MYA

Hylonomus and other early reptiles had more powerful jaw muscles than earlier tetrapods.

Stout skull and sharp pointed teeth were suitable for biting and crushing small arthropods.

More than thirty fossil tree stumps have now been discovered at Joggins.

Repeated floods allowed sediments to build up around the rotting stump, until the ground was level with the top. As flooding continued, the stump began to fill with sediments from within.

SETTING THE TRAP

Carboniferous trees were sometimes killed as flood waters covered their bases with sediment, smothering their roots. Alternatively, the water may have killed the trees because it was salty. Eventually these dead trees rotted and fell over, leaving only a broken stump. The center of the stump then rotted away, and as repeated floods gradually raised the level of the forest floor around it, the hollow stump eventually formed a pitlike trap. The larger animals of Joggins are thought to have fallen into these traps while fleeing from forest fires. Some of these creatures could have survived for awhile by feeding on snails and arthropods caught in the trap, but eventually they would have starved.

LIFE AND DEATH OF HYLONOMUS

The early reptile Hylonomus ("forest mouse") comes from a famous fossil site called Joggins in Nova Scotia, Canada. Many specimens are preserved remarkably well as complete skeletons in which the smallest bones, and sometimes even body scales, are preserved intact. The superb preservation arises because the skeletons were preserved inside forest-floor traps formed from rotten tree stumps.

Floods brought sand into the forest, surrounding and killing the tree. Under pressure, this layer transformed into sandstone.

Millipedes and insects fell into the hollow tree stumps. These may have attracted Hylonomus and other small vertebrates looking for an easy meal.

Mud deposits around base of tree allowed it to grow to maturity, and were later compressed into shale.

FOREST MOUSE

Scientific name:	*Hylonomus*
Size:	8 in (20 cm) long
Diet:	Millipedes and other arthropods
Habitat:	Tropical forest floors
Where found:	Nova Scotia, Canada
Time:	Late Carboniferous
Related genera:	*Paleothyris, Cephalerpeton*

95–250	Triassic 250–203	Jurassic 203–135	Cretaceous 135–65	Tertiary 65–1.75	Quaternary 1.75–present

MESOZOIC 250–65 MYA	CENOZOIC 65 MYA–present

69

REPTILES CLADOGRAM

DURING THE PALAEOZOIC AND THE MESOZOIC, the clade of amniotes called the reptiles dominated life on Earth. In the form of birds, snakes, and lizards, reptiles are the most successful group of living amniotes. The earliest reptiles, such as *Hylonomus,* were tiny insectivores. However, early parareptiles – a radiation of armoured herbivorous and insectivorous forms – included the largest land animals of the Permian. Turtles are surviving members of this early parareptile radiation. The diapsids – a major reptile group – evolved late in the Carboniferous. The Late Permian saw the rise of the archosaurs – the group that includes dinosaurs, birds, pterosaurs, and crocodiles. Living alongside the archosaurs were the squamates, the diapsid group that includes lizards, snakes, and their relatives.

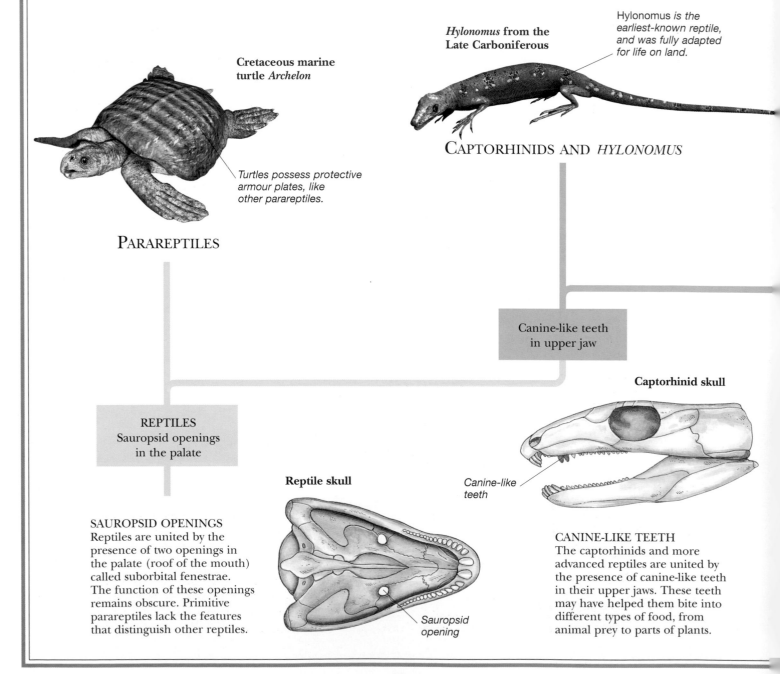

Cretaceous marine turtle *Archelon*

Hylonomus **from the Late Carboniferous**

Hylonomus *is the earliest-known reptile, and was fully adapted for life on land.*

Turtles possess protective armour plates, like other parareptiles.

CAPTORHINIDS AND *HYLONOMUS*

PARAREPTILES

Canine-like teeth in upper jaw

Captorhinid skull

REPTILES
Sauropsid openings in the palate

Reptile skull

Canine-like teeth

SAUROPSID OPENINGS
Reptiles are united by the presence of two openings in the palate (roof of the mouth) called suborbital fenestrae. The function of these openings remains obscure. Primitive parareptiles lack the features that distinguish other reptiles.

Sauropsid opening

CANINE-LIKE TEETH
The captorhinids and more advanced reptiles are united by the presence of canine-like teeth in their upper jaws. These teeth may have helped them bite into different types of food, from animal prey to parts of plants.

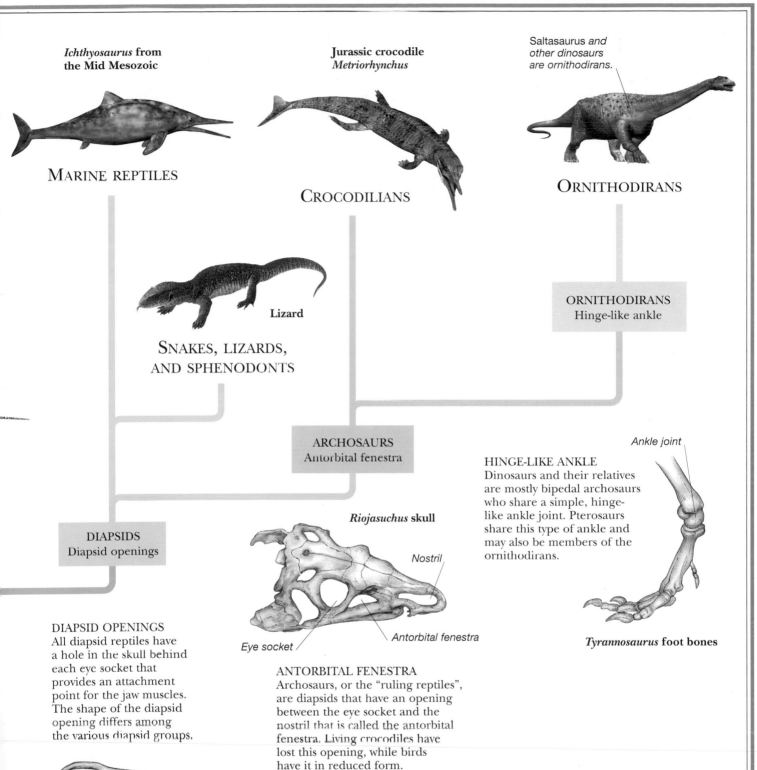

Ichthyosaurus **from the Mid Mesozoic**

MARINE REPTILES

Jurassic crocodile
Metriorhynchus

CROCODILIANS

Saltasaurus and other dinosaurs are ornithodirans.

ORNITHODIRANS

Lizard

SNAKES, LIZARDS, AND SPHENODONTS

ORNITHODIRANS
Hinge-like ankle

ARCHOSAURS
Antorbital fenestra

Riojasuchus **skull**

Ankle joint

HINGE-LIKE ANKLE
Dinosaurs and their relatives are mostly bipedal archosaurs who share a simple, hinge-like ankle joint. Pterosaurs share this type of ankle and may also be members of the ornithodirans.

Nostril

DIAPSIDS
Diapsid openings

Eye socket

Antorbital fenestra

Tyrannosaurus **foot bones**

DIAPSID OPENINGS
All diapsid reptiles have a hole in the skull behind each eye socket that provides an attachment point for the jaw muscles. The shape of the diapsid opening differs among the various diapsid groups.

ANTORBITAL FENESTRA
Archosaurs, or the "ruling reptiles", are diapsids that have an opening between the eye socket and the nostril that is called the antorbital fenestra. Living crocodiles have lost this opening, while birds have it in reduced form.

Diapsid reptile skull

The diapsid openings may help reduce the stress placed on the back of the skull during biting.

REPTILE EVOLUTION

Many reptile key features signify improvements in catching and biting food. The canine-like teeth that evolved in the Carboniferous perhaps helped early reptiles grab food, while the evolution of diapsid openings may have lightened and strengthened the skull. The antorbital fenestra of archosaurs may have further lightened the skull, allowing faster head strikes. Parts of the reptile cladogram remain controversial. Experts argue over whether marine reptiles are closest to lizards and their relatives or to archosaurs.

PARAREPTILES

PARAREPTILES ARE A GROUP OF UNUSUAL REPTILES that include small lizardlike forms as well as larger animals, some of them bristling with spikes and armor plates. Unlike most other reptiles, many parareptiles lack holes, called fenestrae, at the back of their skulls. These fenestrae helped to lighten the skulls in more advanced reptiles such as dinosaurs. Many parareptiles appear to have been herbivorous, with blunt, peglike teeth, while others probably ate insects and other arthropods. Probably the most primitive group of parareptiles were the lizardlike milleretids from Late Permian South Africa. Traditionally, turtles – which also lack fenestrae at the back of their skulls – have been included among the parareptiles.

Conical defensive spikes covering back

Extra vertebrae attached to hips helped Scutosaurus support its body weight.

Short tail did not reach the ground.

Massive, columnlike hindlimbs for supporting weight

Large eyes suggest acute vision.

Blunt-tipped, short snout

Short, stumpy toes suited for slow walking

PROCOLOPHONIDS

The procolophonids were parareptiles that lived worldwide from the Late Permian to the Late Triassic. They were shaped like chunky lizards, with broad-cheeked skulls. Their cheeks sported a stout backward-pointing spike, though *Hypsognathus*, from Late Triassic North America, had several cheek spikes. *Procolophon*, the best-known procolophonid, is unusual in that some species possessed skull fenestrae. More primitive parareptiles did not have these, so *Procolophon* must have evolved them independently from other reptiles. Procolophonids had blunt, peglike teeth at the back of their mouths, and may have eaten tough plants or insects.

Strong, robust limbs perhaps used for digging

Fragmented *Procolophon* fossil

Robust, rounded body probably housed large digestive system.

Short legs and toes suggest Procolophon was not a fast runner.

Large, thin horn

Cheek spikes may have been used in shoving matches.

Skull surface covered in lumps and bumps

ARMORED SKULL

Elginia was a pareiasaur – a member of a group of Late Permian parareptiles which grew up to 10 ft (3 m) long. *Elginia* was a dwarf form, about 2 ft (60 cm) long, found in Scotland. Its head was covered in spikes and there were two particularly long ones growing out of the back of its skull. These were probably used for display rather than combat. Some dwarf pareiasaurs had extensive body armor and were strikingly turtle-like.

| Cambrian 540–500 | Ordovician 500–435 | Silurian 435–410 | Devonian 410–355 | Carboniferous 355–295 | Permia |

PALEOZOIC 540–250 MYA

Large, projecting cheek
flanges (platelike projections),
perhaps for self-defense

Nasal horn
developed in
adults

Blunt, broad snout
with broad mouth

Teeth were
serrated, and
leaf-shaped in
profile.

Large spikes growing
from lower jaw
developed with age.

Powerfully muscled,
sprawling forelimbs

PAREIASAURS

Giant pareiasaurs like *Scutosaurus* ("shield lizard") were
heavily built parareptiles with massive, rounded bodies.
Their teeth were suited for biting and chewing tough
foliage, and their huge bodies probably housed enormous
abdomens to digest low-quality plant material. *Scutosaurus*
and its relatives were covered with bony spikes, bosses,
and horns. Some of these structures, such as the cheek
projections and nose and jaw spikes, only developed with
age and could have been used in mating displays or in
fights with rivals. The structures could also have been
defensive, as pareiasaurs would probably have been
preyed upon by large therapsids and early archosaurs.

MESOSAURS

A sister group to the parareptiles,
and all other reptiles, were the
mesosaurs, small aquatic reptiles
from Permian times. They had
elongated jaws and needlelike
teeth that would have helped
them strain small fishes and
arthropods out of the water.
Paddlelike tails, webbed fingers and
toes, and thickened ribs would have
helped them stay below the water
surface and maneuver when hunting.

Fossil mesosaurs

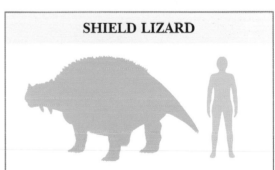

SHIELD LIZARD

Scientific name: *Scutosaurus*

Size: 8 ft (2.5 m) long

Diet: Ferns, horsetails, and other plants

Habitat: Marshes and floodplains

Where found: Eastern Europe

Time: Late Permian

Related genera: *Sanchuanasaurus, Elginia*

295–250	Triassic 250–203	Jurassic 203–135	Cretaceous 135–65	Tertiary 65–1.75	Quaternary 1.75–present
	MESOZOIC 250–65 MYA			CENOZOIC 65 MYA–present	

TURTLES

TURTLES OR CHELONIANS ARE UNIQUE REPTILES that first appeared in the Triassic as small amphibious omnivores. During the Mesozoic, they diverged into land-dwelling herbivores, freshwater omnivores and predators, and giant, fully marine creatures with a diet of sponges and jellyfish. Today they flourish as more than 250 species. Although some early turtles still had teeth on their palate, all turtles have a distinctive toothless beak. This beak is highly adaptable, and has been used by various turtle species to cut plant material, strip flesh from carcasses, catch fish, and bite poisonous or abrasive food items like jellyfish and sponges. The origins of turtles are still controversial. Some experts say that turtles are parareptiles and that they evolved from dwarf armored pareiasaurs. Others think that they are highly modified diapsid reptiles.

Interior of *Araripemys* shell

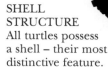

SHELL STRUCTURE

All turtles possess a shell – their most distinctive feature. Remarkably, the shell is a modified ribcage covered by armor plates. Unlike any other vertebrate, turtles have modified their skeleton so that their shoulder and hip girdles are inside their ribcage. Advanced turtles can pull their limbs, neck, and tail inside their shell and some forms even have hinges in their shells allowing them to shut their entire body away from the outside world. The earliest turtles, like *Proganochelys* from Late Triassic Germany, could not draw their neck or limbs inside their shell.

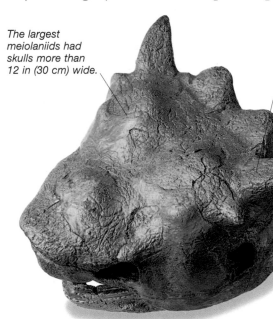

The largest meiolaniids had skulls more than 12 in (30 cm) wide.

Large side horns, perhaps used in fighting.

HORNED LAND TURTLES

The meiolaniids were an unusual group of giant terrestrial turtles that lived in South America and Australasia from the Cretaceous to the recent past, and grew up to 8 ft (2.5 m) long. Large horns on their skulls pointing sideways or backward and upward meant that meiolaniids could not withdraw their heads into their shells. They also wielded a defensive bony club on the end of their tail tip, similar to that of the ankylosaurid dinosaurs. One meiolaniid from Quaternary Australia is named *Ninjemys* ("ninja turtle").The very last meiolaniids were still living on Lord Howe Island in the Pacific Ocean 120,000 years ago.

Nostrils high up on the snout.

MARINE GIANT

Seagoing turtles first evolved in the Early Cretaceous and are just one of many groups that developed into giant forms. *Archelon*, among the biggest of all, reached nearly 13 ft (4 m) long – twice the length of a large modern marine turtle. Turtles never grew much larger than this because they still needed to come ashore and lay eggs, and this meant they had to be able to support their weight on land. In contrast to land turtles, such as tortoises, some marine turtles reduced the weight of their shell and gained buoyancy by losing armor plates and developing a thick leathery covering. However, some species then evolved defensive spikes along the middle ridge of their shells, perhaps to discourage attacks from large predators such as mosasaurs and plesiosaurs.

Cambrian 540–500	Ordovician 500–435	Silurian 435–410	Devonian 410–355	Carboniferous 355–295	Permia
		PALEOZOIC 540–250 MYA			

TWO KINDS OF TURTLES
Early in their evolution, turtles split into two groups, depending on how they pulled their necks into their shells. Pleurodires such as *Stupendemys* and the modern snake-necked turtles are all freshwater animals, and pull their necks in sideways. *Stupendemys*, from South America 4 million years ago, was the largest freshwater turtle ever, growing up to 6 ft 6 in (2 m) long. Cryptodires, which pull their necks in vertically, include tortoises, marine turtles, and terrapins.

Hind flippers shorter and broader than the front ones

Spaces between the ribs were probably visible in the live animal.

Living relatives of Stupendemys eat water plants, fruit, and fish.

Male turtles have shorter tails than female ones.

Stupendemys probably spent most of its time in water.

Female sea turtles use their hind paddles to dig nests.

Archelon may have been prey for giant mosasaurs like Tylosaurus.

Archelon's similarities to modern leatherback turtles suggest its shell may have been covered in thick skin, rather than armor plates.

Large winglike paddles used for underwater flight.

Of five fingers in the paddle, the third and fourth were the longest.

ARCHELON

Scientific name: *Archelon*

Size: 13 ft (4 m)

Diet: Probably jellyfish

Habitat: Warm, shallow seas

Where found: North America

Time: Late Cretaceous

Related genera: *Protostega, Calcarichelys*

95–250	Triassic 250–203	Jurassic 203–135	Cretaceous 135–65	Tertiary 65–1.75	Quaternary 1.75–present
	MESOZOIC 250–65 MYA			CENOZOIC 65 MYA–present	

DIVERSIFYING DIAPSIDS

LATE IN THE PERMIAN, THE DIAPSIDS – the reptilian group that includes the lizards, archosaurs, and marine ichthyosaurs and plesiosaurs – underwent an extraordinary burst of evolution. Evolving from small insect-eating ancestors from the Carboniferous, the diapsids soon produced gliders, swimmers, and diggers. Many of these new diapsids shared special features of the skull and skeleton, and are grouped together as the neodiapsids ("new diapsids"). Most early neodiapsids were small and inhabited environments where large synapsids, such as dinocephalians and dicynodonts, were the dominant herbivores and carnivores. By the beginning of the Triassic, many neodiapsids were extinct, but choristoderes survived throughout the Mesozoic and into the Cenozoic. Other neodiapsid groups were ancestors of the two great reptile groups of the Mesozoic – the squamates (lizards, snakes, and relatives) and the archosaurs (dinosaurs, birds, crocodiles, and relatives).

Each wing was supported by 22 curving, rodlike bones.

Back of skull raised up into a serrated crest

The back of the skull was very broad but the snout was pointed.

Claws were curved, sharp, and good at grasping.

Sharp, conical teeth were suited for catching insects.

The back of the skull resembles that of lizards. This once led experts to think that lizards descended from younginiforms.

Youngina had a particularly long, narrow snout.

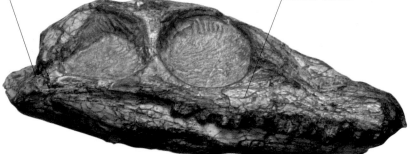

YOUNGINA AND RELATIVES

The younginiforms were among the most primitive neodiapsids. They were agile Permian reptiles with short necks and large openings at the back of the skull. Though some younginiforms were aquatic, most were land dwellers. *Youngina* itself was a burrowing reptile – young specimens have been found preserved together in a fossil burrow, perhaps clustered together to regulate body heat when the weather was too hot or too cold. *Thadeosaurus*, a younginiform from Madagascar, had a strikingly long tail and very long toes. It may have been a fast runner like modern long-tailed lizards.

COELUROSAURAVUS

Scientific name: *Coelurosauravus*

Size: 2 ft (60 cm) long

Diet: Insects

Habitat: Open forest

Where found: Madagascar and Europe

Time: Late Permian

Related genera: *Weigeltisaurus, Wapitisaurus*

Cambrian 540–500	Ordovician 500–435	Silurian 435–410	Devonian 410–355	Carboniferous 355–295	Permia

PALEOZOIC 540–250 MYA

EARLY GLIDERS

The weigeltisaurids were unusual tree-dwelling diapsids. They glided using skin membranes stretched over long rods that grew from the sides of the body. These "wings" could be folded away when not in use. The gliding rods of *Coelurosauravus*, the best known weigeltisaurid, were at first mistaken for a fish's fin spines. When they were identified as part of *Coelurosauravus*, they were thought to be extendable ribs like those seen on *Draco*, the modern gliding lizard of southeast Asia. Recent studies have shown that the wing struts of weigeltisaurids are completely unconnected to the ribs – they are unique features not seen in any other animal, living or extinct. Weigeltisaurids are rather primitive and appear to be separate from the neodiapsids.

The body was long and flattened from top to bottom.

Skin membranes stretched across the bony rods.

LIFE IN THE WATER

Several Permian neodiapsids were among the earliest reptiles to take to life in the water, hunting fish and other prey. The younginiform *Hovasaurus* from Late Permian Madagascar had a deepened, paddlelike tail for swimming. Its fossil stomach contents show that it swallowed stones, perhaps for use as ballast. Other swimming neodiapsids, like *Claudiosaurus*, also evolved in the Late Permian. *Claudiosaurus* may be a close relative of later marine reptiles such as the plesiosaurs and ichthyosaurs.

Restoration of *Hovasaurus*

Arms and legs show that Hovasaurus could also walk on land.

CHORISTODERES

The choristoderes were a group of aquatic and land-dwelling neodiapsids whose fossil record extends from the Triassic to the mid-Tertiary. They evolved from younginiform-like ancestors in the Permian. None were bigger than 10 ft (3 m) in length. Some, like *Champsosaurus* shown here, looked superficially like river-dwelling crocodiles, and probably hunted fish. *Shokawa* from Cretaceous Japan was long-necked, and resembled a miniature plesiosaur. Short-snouted *Lazarussuchus* was also small, but built for life on land.

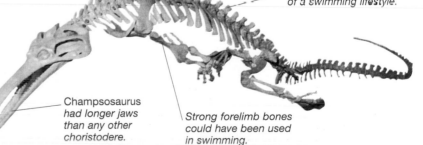

Vertebrae show evidence of a swimming lifestyle.

Champsosaurus had longer jaws than any other choristodere.

Strong forelimb bones could have been used in swimming.

295–250	Triassic 250–203	Jurassic 203–135	Cretaceous 195–65	Tertiary 65 1.75	Quaternary 1.75–present
	MESOZOIC 250–65 MYA			CENOZOIC 65 MYA–present	

77

MOSASAURS

LARGE SEA LIZARDS CALLED MOSASAURS dominated the shallow continental seas of the Cretaceous. Related to land lizards, such as monitors and gila monsters, the earliest mosasaurs were amphibious predators about 3 ft (1 m) in length. Later mosasaurs grew to more than 49 ft (15 m) long and were among the most awesome marine predators of all time. With large, conical teeth and strong jaws, they preyed on large fish, turtles, and plesiosaurs. Some mosasaurs evolved blunt, crushing teeth and probably ate shelled molluscs, such as ammonites. Because of their size and specialization for life in water, it seems unlikely that later mosasaurs could move on land, so females probably gave birth to live young at sea.

Spines suggest tail would have been deep but narrow – like that of a living sea snake.

TYLOSAURUS

This giant, long-skulled mosasaur was part of a group of mosasaurs called the russellosaurines. One of the most distinctive features of *Tylosaurus* was a hard, bony tip to its snout. *Tylosaurus* may have used this snout as a ramming weapon for stunning prey. Some specimens have been found with damaged snouts, which suggests that such behavior was likely. However, the snout tip was not made of solid bone, so it was probably more fragile than it looked.

Like modern sea creatures, tylosaurs probably had a dark upper surface and a light underside.

Some mosasaurs had small, smooth scales. Others had scales with ridges across the middle.

Bony tip to snout

Mosasaurs did not just have teeth lining their jaws, they also had teeth on the bones of their palate.

The tip of the lower jaw was blunt and rectangular.

Monitor lizard

MOSASAUR SENSES
Like their lizard relatives on land, mosasaurs probably had long forked tongues. Their skulls show that they had the Jacobson's organ, a structure used by snakes and lizards to detect scent particles in air or water. This indicates that mosasaurs probably used smell to hunt their prey and to detect other members of their species. All mosasaurs had large eyes and, probably, acute eyesight.

Cambrian period 540–500	Ordovician 500–435	Silurian 435–410	Devonian 410–355	Carboniferous 355–295	Permia
		PALEOZOIC 540–250 MYA			

Skeleton of *Tylosaurus*

FLIPPERS AND FINS

Mosasaurs had evolved streamlined flippers from the arms and legs of their land-living ancestors. Extra finger and toe bones made the flippers longer. Mosasaurs probably moved their long, flexible tails from side to side when swimming, a method called sculling, and steered with their flippers. Long, bony spines on the tail vertebrae show that the tail was deep, but narrow in width.

Mosasaurs had mobile skull bones that would have allowed them to swallow large prey.

Internal spaces in the bones were probably filled by fat. Modern whales also have fatty spaces in their bones.

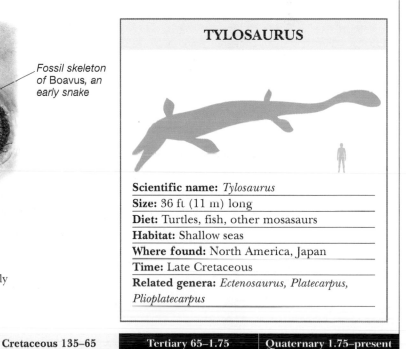

Its powerful tail propelled Tylosaurus through the water.

Tylosaurus had long, winglike flippers. Some mosasaurs had broad, paddlelike flippers.

Fossil skeleton of Boavus, an early snake

A LINK WITH SNAKES?

The most controversial area in the study of mosasaurs is whether or not they were close relatives of snakes. Like snakes, mosasaurs had long, flexible bodies, reduced limbs, and very mobile skull bones. So some experts argue that snakes and early mosasaurs both descended from the same swimming ancestor. However, other experts argue that snakes are not related to mosasaurs and that the similarities are only superficial.

TYLOSAURUS

Scientific name: *Tylosaurus*

Size: 36 ft (11 m) long

Diet: Turtles, fish, other mosasaurs

Habitat: Shallow seas

Where found: North America, Japan

Time: Late Cretaceous

Related genera: *Ectenosaurus, Platecarpus, Plioplatecarpus*

95–250	Triassic 250–203	Jurassic 203–135	Cretaceous 135–65	Tertiary 65–1.75	Quaternary 1.75–present
	MESOZOIC 250–65 MYA			CENOZOIC 65 MYA–present	

PLACODONTS AND NOTHOSAURS

THESE TWO GROUPS OF CREATURES were marine reptiles. They were related to plesiosaurs and formed part of a larger group called the Sauropterygia. Placodonts and nothosaurs were largely restricted to the warm, shallow seas of Triassic Europe, northern Africa, and Asia and none of them were particularly large – most were around 3 ft (1 m) long. Nothosaurs were amphibious, long-necked predators with numerous sharp teeth. Their fossils have been found in sea rocks. This suggests that they were sea-going creatures, but they probably rested and bred on land, much like modern seals. Placodonts were armored sauropterygians with teeth suited for crushing shellfish.

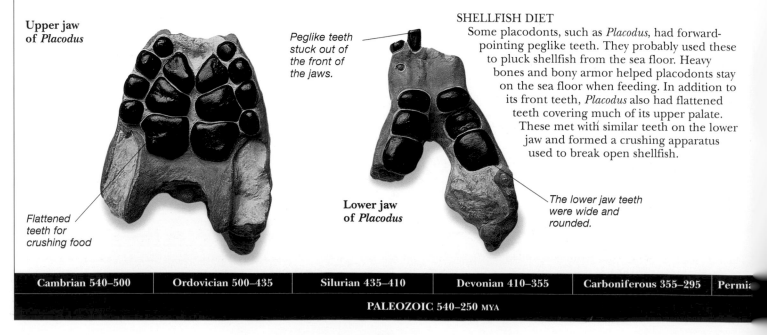

Nothosaurus *had tall vertebral spines in the shoulder region.*

Long, pointed front teeth

Smaller teeth at the back of the jaw

A nothosaur's shoulder and chest bones formed large, flattened plates.

NOTHOSAURUS

The best known nothosaur is *Nothosaurus*. It had a long, narrow snout and fanglike teeth. Small teeth lined its jaws all the way to the back of the cheek region. Eight species of *Nothosaurus* have been found in Europe and the Near East. In the Early Triassic, a rise in sea levels allowed *Nothosaurus* to invade a shallow sea in what is now Israel. New species of *Nothosaurus* evolved there, including a specialized dwarf species.

Upper jaw of *Placodus*

Peglike teeth stuck out of the front of the jaws.

Flattened teeth for crushing food

Lower jaw of *Placodus*

The lower jaw teeth were wide and rounded.

SHELLFISH DIET

Some placodonts, such as *Placodus*, had forward-pointing peglike teeth. They probably used these to pluck shellfish from the sea floor. Heavy bones and bony armor helped placodonts stay on the sea floor when feeding. In addition to its front teeth, *Placodus* also had flattened teeth covering much of its upper palate. These met with similar teeth on the lower jaw and formed a crushing apparatus used to break open shellfish.

Cambrian 540–500	Ordovician 500–435	Silurian 435–410	Devonian 410–355	Carboniferous 355–295	Permia

PALEOZOIC 540–250 MYA

REPTILIAN RAYS

Placochelyids, such as this *Psephoderma*, were turtlelike placodonts with long, whiplike tails, paddle-shaped limbs, and sharply pointed snouts. Their body shape was similar to that of rays, a group of fish that first appeared in the Jurassic. Like rays, placochelyids might have hidden underneath sand or gravel on the sea floor. They probably foraged for shellfish.

Nothosaurus probably moved its tail from side to side when swimming.

Nothosaurus's hips were strongly connected to its backbone. This was not true of all nothosaurs.

Like more primitive reptiles, nothosaurs had long, flexible tails.

Its fingers and toes may have been webbed.

Powerful limb muscles were attached to the underside of the body.

Unlike plesiosaurs, nothosaurs had flexible knee and ankle joints.

HENODUS

In some placodonts, the body armor became very extensive and formed a shell resembling that of a turtle. *Henodus* was a particularly turtlelike placodont. It lived in a lagoonlike sea where the water would have been slightly salty. Living in this kind of water is difficult because any changes in the salt levels are stressful to animals. Shelled animals, such as turtles and *Henodus*, are better equipped to cope with this stress.

Henodus had no teeth. It may have filtered its food out of the water.

NOTHOSAURUS

Scientific name: *Nothosaurus*

Size: Different species ranged from 3–10 ft (1–3 m) in length.

Diet: Fish

Habitat: Shallow tropical seas

Where found: Europe, Near East

Time: Triassic

Related genera: *Germanosaurus, Lariosaurus*

95–250	Triassic 250–203	Jurassic 203–135	Cretaceous 135–65	Tertiary 65–1.75	Quaternary 1.75–present
	MESOZOIC 250–65 MYA			CENOZOIC 65 MYA–present	

SHORT-NECKED PLESIOSAURS

PLESIOSAURS WERE MARINE REPTILES. They belonged to the same group as nothosaurs and placodonts, the Sauropterygia. All plesiosaurs had four winglike flippers and many pointed teeth. They probably used their flippers to "fly" underwater in a similar way to marine turtles or penguins. While many plesiosaurs had long necks and small skulls, others, the pliosaurs, were short-necked and had enormous skulls. The biggest pliosaurs, such as *Liopleurodon* and *Kronosaurus*, had skulls 10 ft (3 m) long with huge pointed teeth. It seems likely that pliosaurs were predators that fed on other marine reptiles. This is confirmed by long-necked plesiosaur skeletons that bear pliosaur tooth marks.

Maybe pliosaurs like this Simolestes were not close relatives of forms like Kronosaurus.

SOUTHERN HEMISPHERE GIANT

Kronosaurus was a giant pliosaur from Australia and South America. It is best known from the reconstructed skeleton displayed at the Harvard Museum of Comparative Zoology in Massachusetts. This measures 43 ft (13 m) from nose to tail, with a very long body. Its immense skull supports a massive bony crest. Recent work has shown that this reconstruction is inaccurate: there should not be a huge skull crest and the body should be shorter, meaning that *Kronosaurus* was probably only about 30 ft (9 m) long. Pliosaurs like *Kronosaurus* lived worldwide throughout the Jurassic and Cretaceous periods.

WERE PLIOSAURS A NATURAL GROUP?
Several different pliosaur groups are known. These include rhomaleosaurs, pliosaurids, brachaucheniids (which may include *Kronosaurus*), and polycotylids. All of these groups might share the same single ancestor, and therefore form a clade. Alternatively, different pliosaurs might descend from different long-necked plesiosaur ancestors. Plesiosaur experts still argue over these opposing views.

The flippers were formed of long fingers and toes with numerous small bones.

The large eyes faced slightly forward, suggesting an overlapping field of vision.

Water leaves skull through the external nostrils.

Water enters mouth and flows into the internal nostrils.

Large eye socket

Skull of *Plesiosaurus*

External nostrils

The biggest teeth were 10 in (25 cm) long but much of this length was embedded in the bones of the jaw.

UNDERWATER SNIFFING
Plesiosaurs' internal nostrils – two holes on the palate – are located farther forward than the nostrils on the outside of the snout. This suggests that water flowed through the snout and into the internal nostrils, where scent particles could have been detected, then out through the external nostrils. Plesiosaurs could therefore have "sniffed" the water they swam through, as modern sharks do, to detect prey.

Cambrian 540–500	Ordovician 500–435	Silurian 435–410	Devonian 410–355	Carboniferous 355–295	Permia

PALEOZOIC 540–250 MYA

Pliosaurs had short tails that were probably not used for moving around. Some fossils suggest that there may have been a diamond-shaped fin at the tip of the tail.

Massive muscles gave the flippers a very powerful downstroke. Perhaps while one pair of flippers was in the downstroke, the other pair was in the upstroke.

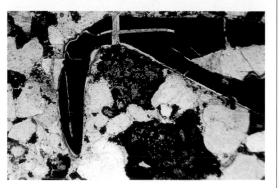

PLIOSAUR STOMACH CONTENTS

This photograph shows quartz grains and a hooklet from a squid found in a pliosaur's stomach. We know from their stomach contents that pliosaurs preyed on all kinds of marine animal, from small fish and squid to other plesiosaurs. One pliosaur specimen even appears to have swallowed armor plates from a thyreophoran dinosaur. Pliosaurs may have eaten floating dinosaur carcasses, or perhaps they grabbed swimming dinosaurs or those that got too close to the water's edge.

In pliosaurs the hind pair of flippers were larger than the front pair.

All plesiosaurs had belly ribs, or gastralia, that were tightly interlocked and helped to keep the body stiff.

Unlike terrestrial reptiles, in plesiosaurs the bones of the shoulder and hip girdles were located on the underside of the body.

Kronosaurus

KRONOSAURUS

Scientific name: *Kronosaurus*

Size: 30 ft (9 m) long

Diet: Marine reptiles, fish, and mollusks

Habitat: Open ocean

Where found: Australia and South America

Time: Early Cretaceous

Related genus: *Brachauchenius*

LONG-NECKED PLESIOSAURS

WHILE SOME PLESIOSAURS were big-headed predators, others had small skulls and very long necks. One group of plesiosaurs, the elasmosaurs, had necks up to 16 ft (5 m) long. Most long-necked plesiosaurs fed on fish and mollusks, though some may have eaten seafloor invertebrates and others perhaps preyed on other marine reptiles. Both short- and long-necked plesiosaurs became extinct at the very end of the Cretaceous.

FILTER FEEDING PLESIOSAURS

One group of long-necked plesiosaurs, the cryptoclidids, had numerous interlocking needlelike teeth. These were probably used as a filtering device to capture small fish and swimming shrimps. The cryptoclidid would have closed its mouth around a group of prey and then pushed the water out of its mouth with its tongue. Any small animals in its mouth would have been trapped there by the interlocking teeth.

LONG NECKS

Elasmosaurus had 72 vertebrae in its neck, more than any other plesiosaur, or indeed any other animal. Studies of plesiosaur vertebrae suggest that their necks were fairly flexible, but experts are still unsure how they used them. *Elasmosaurus* may have approached a shoal of fish from behind and used its neck to plunge its head into them, or it may have "flown" slowly above the sea floor, using its neck to reach down and graze on bottom-dwelling invertebrates.

PLESIOSAUR SKULLS

Compared to the sizes of their bodies, long-necked plesiosaurs had small skulls. The shape of the bony ring that supported the eyeball suggests that plesiosaurs had flattened eyeballs, so their eyes would have been better suited to seeing underwater than in air. Some plesiosaurs have been found with earbones. These are fused to the surrounding skull bones, which suggests that their ears were not suited to detecting sound waves carried through the air.

Cambrian 540–500	Ordovician 500–435	Silurian 435–410	Devonian 410–355	Carboniferous 355–295	Permia

PALEOZOIC 540–250 MYA

"PLATE LIZARD"

Elasmosaurus was a Late Cretaceous representative of the elasmosaurs, a group of long-necked plesiosaurs that originated in the Jurassic. Like all advanced elasmosaurs, *Elasmosaurus* had a tremendously long neck, a light skull lined with vicious interlocking teeth, and winglike flippers with slim pointed tips. The name *Elasmosaurus* means "plate lizard" and comes from the large, platelike shoulder bones that covered its chest and formed its arm sockets. The huge muscles that powered its flippers were anchored to these bones.

PLATE LIZARD

Scientific name:	*Elasmosaurus*
Size:	46 ft (14 m) long
Diet:	Fish and swimming mollusks
Habitat:	Shallow seas
Where found:	North America
Time:	Late Cretaceous
Related genera:	*Callawayasaurus, Libonectes*

05–250	Triassic 250–20	urassic 203–135	Cretaceous 135–65	ertiary 65–1.75	Quaternary 1.75–present
		MESOZOIC 250–65 MYA		CENOZOIC 65 MYA–present	

ICHTHYOSAURS

THESE MESOZOIC MARINE REPTILES are famous for resembling sharks or dolphins. Many ichthyosaur fossils have been found, some of which have impressions of the skin preserved. These show that advanced ichthyosaurs, such as *Ichthyosaurus*, had a triangular dorsal fin, two pairs of paddlelike fins, and a forked, vertical tail like that of a shark. Long, snapping jaws and conical teeth suggest that ichthyosaurs ate fish and squid. This has been confirmed by their stomach contents. While the smaller ichthyosaurs were only about 3 ft (1 m) long, giant ichthyosaurs from the Triassic and early Jurassic grew to more than 65 ft (20 m) in length, making them the largest marine reptiles of them all. Ichthyosaurs were already rare in the Cretaceous and did not survive to the end of the Mesozoic.

Ichthyosaur earbones are not separated from the other skull bones, as they are in dolphins, so there is no reason to think that they used sonar.

SHARK–SHAPED REPTILE

Ichthyosaurus is one of the best known of all ichthyosaurs and many specimens have been found in Jurassic rocks in England and Germany. Like other members of the advanced group of ichthyosaurs called thunnosaurs, *Ichthyosaurus* had a shark-shaped body. It was a medium-sized ichthyosaur, with a slim, pointed snout and fore flippers twice as large as its hind flippers. *Ichthyosaurus* had very broad front fins with six or more digits. Some later ichthyosaurs had even more digits than this. *Platypterygius* from the Cretaceous, for example, had eight or more.

Ichthyosaurus

In all chthyosaurs the nostril was positioned close to the eye.

Small, pointed teeth for grabbing fish

Long, slim jaws for snapping up fish and swimming mollusks

This ichthyosaur fossil is preserved with the babies still inside the mother.

Skeleton of *Stenopterygius*

BIRTH AND BABIES
Some ichthyosaurs have been found with the bones of babies preserved in their abdominal region. At first, experts thought that these babies were stomach contents and therefore evidence of cannibalism. But it is now clear that these were babies that died before or during birth. Most pregnant ichthyosaurs preserve only one or two babies, though some have as many as 11. The babies were born tail-first and fully able to swim.

| Cambrian 540–500 | Ordovician 500–435 | Silurian 435–410 | Devonian 410–355 | Carboniferous 355–295 | Permia |

PALEOZOIC 540–250 MYA

HOW DID ICHTHYOSAURS SWIM?

Experts argue over how exactly ichthyosaurs swam. They probably used their forked tails to propel them through the water. Stiffening fibers helped the tail base to act as a hinge, so that the tail could be flapped rapidly from side to side. Their powerful shoulders and wing-shaped flippers suggest to some experts that ichthyosaurs flapped their flippers and "flew" underwater.

Impressions of ichthyosaur dorsal fins show that they were triangular in shape.

Fossil of *Stenopterygius*

Preserved ichthyosaur skin is smooth and apparontly without scales.

Skin impressions show that ichthyosaurs had an upper lobe to their tails.

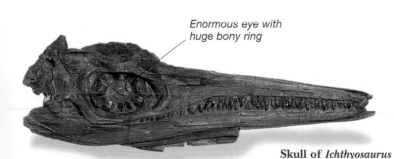

Baby ichthyosaurs had proportionally larger heads and shorter bodies than adults.

The bones at the end of the tail grew downward to support the tail's bottom lobe.

The small hind fins may have acted as stabilizers, helping the animal to stay upright.

Enormous eye with huge bony ring

Skull of *Ichthyosaurus*

BIG EYES AND DEEP DIVING

Ichthyosaurs had huge eye sockets, filled by a ring of bones called the sclerotic ring. This helped support the massive eyeball. Their large eyes suggest that ichthyosaurs used eyesight to hunt. They may have been able to hunt prey at night, in murky waters, or in perpetually dark, deep waters. *Temnodontosaurus*, a Jurassic ichthyosaur from Europe, had the largest eyes of any vertebrate animal. Each of its eyes was 10 in (26 cm) wide.

ICHTHYOSAURUS

Scientific name:	*Ichthyosaurus*
Size:	10 ft (3 m) long
Diet:	Fish and squid
Habitat:	Open ocean
Where found:	Europe
Time:	Early Jurassic
Related genus:	*Stenopterygius*

5–250	Triassic 250–203	Jurassic 203–135		Tertiary 65–1.75	Quaternary 1.75–present
	MESOZOIC 250–65 MYA			CENOZOIC 65 MYA–present	

87

EARLY RULING REPTILE GROUPS

ARCHOSAURS – THE GROUP OF ANIMALS that includes crocodiles, dinosaurs, and birds – belong to a larger group called the archosauromorphs, or "ruling reptile forms." During the Permian and Triassic, several archosauromorph groups evolved. Some, such as the prolacertiforms, were four-legged meat eaters that resembled long-necked lizards. Others, such as the trilophosaurs and rhynchosaurs, were plant eaters whose skulls and teeth were suited to slicing tough plants. All early archosauromorphs were extinct by the end of the Triassic.

Tanystropheus had long, slender limbs. Its hands were proportionally small.

GIRAFFE-NECKED FISHER

The prolacertiform *Tanystropheus* was among the most peculiar of all Triassic reptiles. Many prolacertiforms had long necks, but in *Tanystropheus* this was taken to an extreme, and its neck was twice as long as its body. *Tanystropheus* had only about 10 very long vertebrae in its neck, which suggests that its neck was not very flexible. Most specimens of *Tanystropheus* are preserved in marine rocks, so it probably either fished from the water's edge or swam.

Lizardlike body shape

Fracture lines in the tail bones suggest that Tanystropheus's tail could break off when bitten by a predator.

Tanystropheus had long feet and its toes may have been webbed. It probably used its feet for swimming.

Stout skull with toothless snout tip

Lizardlike body shape

TRILOPHOSAURS

Experts know from their skeletons that trilophosaurs were archosauromorphs, but they are unusual because, unlike other members of the group, they had grown new bone over the lower of the two diapsid skull openings. Trilophosaurs had robust skulls and toothless, beaklike snout tips. They had broad teeth for slicing and chewing tough plants.

Long limbs suited to running and digging

All trilophosaurs were less than 3 ft 3 in (1m) in length.

Skeleton of *Trilophosaurus*

Cambrian 540–500	Ordovician 500–435	Silurian 435–410	Devonian 410–355	Carboniferous 355–295	Permi

PALEOZOIC 540–250 MYA

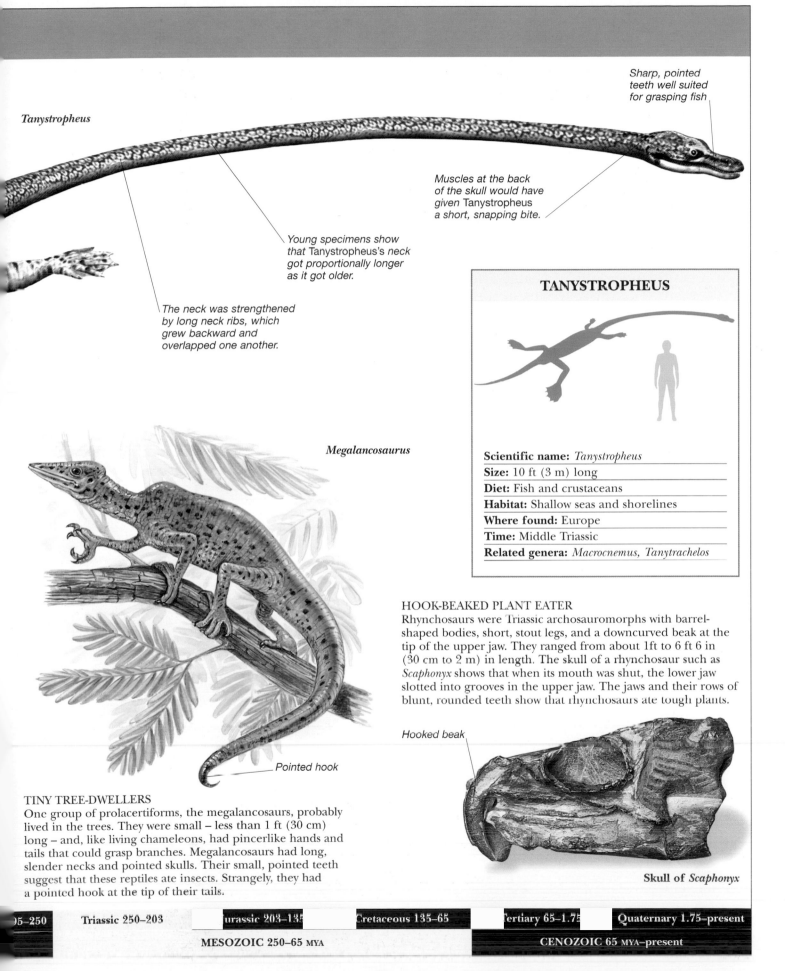

Tanystropheus

Sharp, pointed teeth well suited for grasping fish

Muscles at the back of the skull would have given Tanystropheus a short, snapping bite.

Young specimens show that Tanystropheus's *neck* got proportionally longer as it got older.

The neck was strengthened by long neck ribs, which grew backward and overlapped one another.

Megalancosaurus

TANYSTROPHEUS

Scientific name: *Tanystropheus*

Size: 10 ft (3 m) long

Diet: Fish and crustaceans

Habitat: Shallow seas and shorelines

Where found: Europe

Time: Middle Triassic

Related genera: *Macrocnemus, Tanytrachelos*

HOOK-BEAKED PLANT EATER

Rhynchosaurs were Triassic archosauromorphs with barrel-shaped bodies, short, stout legs, and a downcurved beak at the tip of the upper jaw. They ranged from about 1ft to 6 ft 6 in (30 cm to 2 m) in length. The skull of a rhynchosaur such as *Scaphonyx* shows that when its mouth was shut, the lower jaw slotted into grooves in the upper jaw. The jaws and their rows of blunt, rounded teeth show that rhynchosaurs ate tough plants.

Hooked beak

Pointed hook

TINY TREE-DWELLERS

One group of prolacertiforms, the megalancosaurs, probably lived in the trees. They were small – less than 1 ft (30 cm) long – and, like living chameleons, had pincerlike hands and tails that could grasp branches. Megalancosaurs had long, slender necks and pointed skulls. Their small, pointed teeth suggest that these reptiles ate insects. Strangely, they had a pointed hook at the tip of their tails.

Skull of *Scaphonyx*

05–250	Triassic 250–203	urassic 203–135	Cretaceous 135–65	Tertiary 65–1.75	Quaternary 1.75–present
		MESOZOIC 250–65 MYA		CENOZOIC 65 MYA–present	

EARLY CROCODILE-GROUP REPTILES

ARCHOSAURS – CROCODILES, PTEROSAURS, dinosaurs, and their relatives –
evolved in the Late Permian and diversified into many different groups
during the Triassic. Early on, archosaurs split into two clades, both of
which have living representatives. Ornithodirans included pterosaurs,
dinosaurs, and birds. Crocodylotarsians, the crocodile-group reptiles,
included numerous extinct groups and crocodiles. Unlike dinosaurs
and their relatives, crocodile-group reptiles had ankle joints that allowed
them to twist their feet to the side when walking. These joints gave
crocodylotarsians their name, which means "crocodile ankle." In the
Triassic, amphibious, long-jawed crocodylotarsians called phytosaurs
dominated waterways, while, on land, predatory rauisuchians and
plant-eating aetosaurs were important. Yet, despite their
success, all crocodylotarsians except crocodiles
became extinct at the end of the Triassic.

Two rows of armor plates ran along the top of the spine.

Large muscles connected the tail to the thigh bone.

DEEP-SKULLED GIANTS

Many crocodile-group reptiles
were large, land-living predators,
called rauisuchians. They had long limbs
and deep skulls with long, serrated teeth. Some
were huge, reaching lengths of up to 33 ft (10 m).
Prestosuchus, shown here, was a rauisuchian from
Triassic Brazil. Similar rauisuchians lived in Europe,
Argentina, and elsewhere. *Prestosuchus* reached
about 16 ft (5 m) in length and had a distinctive
downward bend at the tip of its snout.

The short fifth toe was turned backwards

HOW RAUISUCHIANS WALKED

Rauisuchians' limbs were positioned directly
underneath their bodies, perhaps enabling
them to run faster. This evolved in a different
way from dinosaurs and their relatives. In
dinosaurs, the top of the thigh bone was turned
inward to meet the hip socket, allowing an
erect posture. But rauisuchian thigh bones did
not have an inturned head, so they supported
the hips from directly underneath.

Side view of rauisuchian hip joint

Ilium

Ischium

Pubic bone

Thigh bones

Front view of hip joint

Ilium

Thigh bone directly under hip

Pubic bone

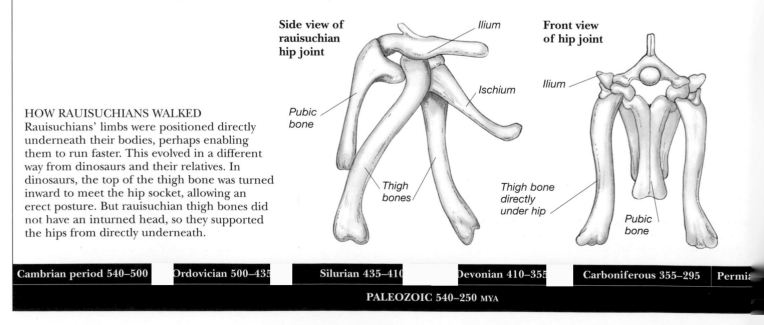

Cambrian period 540–500	Ordovician 500–435	Silurian 435–410	Devonian 410–355	Carboniferous 355–295	Permia

PALEOZOIC 540–250 MYA

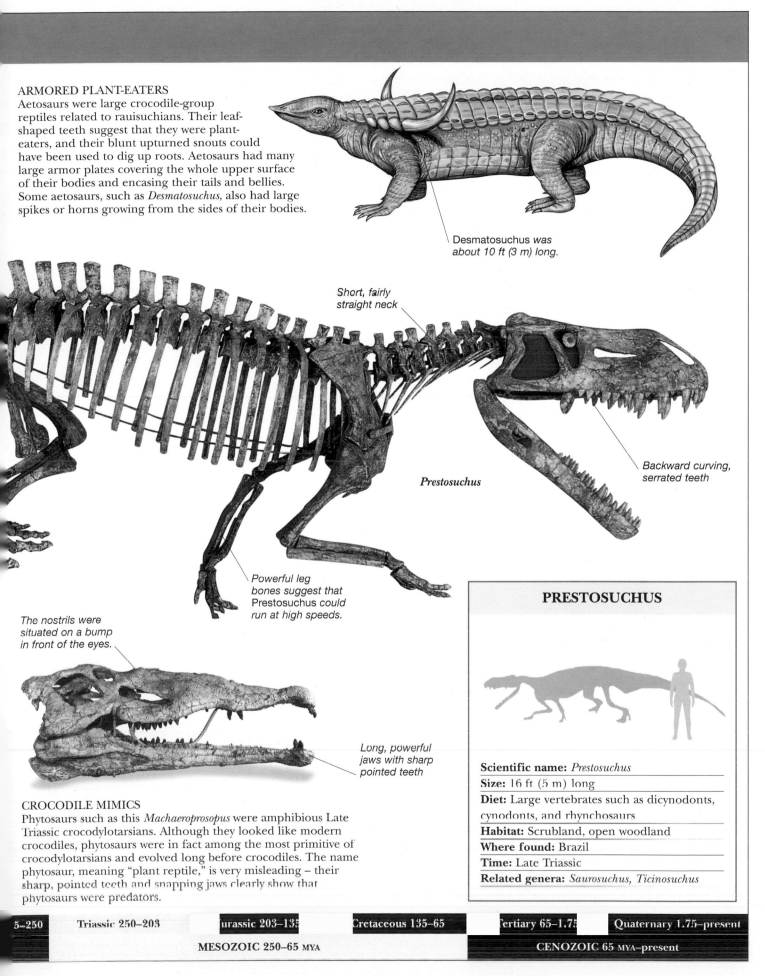

ARMORED PLANT-EATERS

Aetosaurs were large crocodile-group reptiles related to rauisuchians. Their leaf-shaped teeth suggest that they were plant-eaters, and their blunt upturned snouts could have been used to dig up roots. Aetosaurs had many large armor plates covering the whole upper surface of their bodies and encasing their tails and bellies. Some aetosaurs, such as *Desmatosuchus*, also had large spikes or horns growing from the sides of their bodies.

Desmatosuchus was about 10 ft (3 m) long.

Short, fairly straight neck

Backward curving, serrated teeth

Prestosuchus

Powerful leg bones suggest that Prestosuchus could run at high speeds.

The nostrils were situated on a bump in front of the eyes.

Long, powerful jaws with sharp pointed teeth

CROCODILE MIMICS

Phytosaurs such as this *Machaeroprosopus* were amphibious Late Triassic crocodylotarsians. Although they looked like modern crocodiles, phytosaurs were in fact among the most primitive of crocodylotarsians and evolved long before crocodiles. The name phytosaur, meaning "plant reptile," is very misleading – their sharp, pointed teeth and snapping jaws clearly show that phytosaurs were predators.

PRESTOSUCHUS

Scientific name: *Prestosuchus*

Size: 16 ft (5 m) long

Diet: Large vertebrates such as dicynodonts, cynodonts, and rhynchosaurs

Habitat: Scrubland, open woodland

Where found: Brazil

Time: Late Triassic

Related genera: *Saurosuchus*, *Ticinosuchus*

5–250	Triassic 250–203	Jurassic 203–135	Cretaceous 135–65	Tertiary 65–1.75	Quaternary 1.75–present
	MESOZOIC 250–65 MYA			CENOZOIC 65 MYA–present	

CROCODILIANS

APART FROM BIRDS, CROCODILIANS are the last survivors of the archosaurs or "ruling reptiles" – the group to which the dinosaurs belonged. They evolved at about the same time as the dinosaurs and for most of their 200-million-year history crocodilians have been large, long-bodied, aquatic carnivores. Armor-plating in the form of bony scutes set in their hides, deep tails, short, strong limbs, and powerful, sharp-toothed jaws made them formidable predators. Lying loglike in a lake or river, they seized passing fishes or ambushed large creatures coming for a drink. In the Age of Dinosaurs, when climates everywhere were warm, these cold-blooded creatures spread throughout the world. Some became suited for life on land, others for life at sea. Some were fast runners, no bigger than a dog, but one monster, *Deinosuchus*, was as heavy as an elephant and as long as a tennis court is wide.

Limbs designed to steer and brake

Forelimbs shaped like hydrofoils

Skull broader behind the eyes than in front

Slender jaws

Small but sharp teeth

SEA BEAST

Metriorhynchus was a seagoing crocodilian from the Mesozoic. Its webbed toes and fingers formed paddles for efficient swimming, and its jaws bristled with razor-sharp teeth for seizing slippery fishes and prehistoric relatives of squid. Lacking the heavy armor typical of other crocodilans *Metriorhynchus* was quite light and flexible. It probably lay with its nostrils above water, ready to launch an attack, and hunted by making sudden rushes after slowly swimming up on unsuspecting prey or waiting in ambush. From time to time, it would have hauled itself ashore to lay eggs on sandbanks and perhaps to bask in the warm sun.

Male has a knob at the tip of his slender snout

SLENDER-JAWED FISH EATER
Gharials, also known as gavials, are large, living crocodilians. Their long, slender jaws armed with small but sharp teeth are ideal for catching fish. With relatively weak legs they are poor walkers and seldom venture far from water. Gharials now live only in the north of the Indian subcontinent, but their genus, *Gavialis*, goes back 50 million years and was once spread throughout Africa, Asia, and North and South America.

| Cambrian 540–500 | Ordovician 500–435 | Silurian 435–410 | Devonian 410–355 | Carboniferous 355–295 | Permia |

PALEOZOIC 540–250 MYA

Deinosuchus *lived to an age of about 50 years old, growing throughout its life.*

Broad, powerful snout

TERROR OF THE DINOSAURS

Deinosuchus ("terrible crocodile") may have been the largest crocodilian that ever lived. Up to five times larger than today's species, this Late Cretaceous giant from North America grew to 33 ft (10 m) in length and weighed 5 tons (5 tonnes). Lying near the water's edge, *Deinosuchus* probably lunged to seize large prey, such as duck-billed dinosaurs, before spinning them over and over in the water to tear off great lumps of flesh. Like modern crocodiles, *Deinosuchus* is thought to have swallowed stones which served as ballast in the water.

Downturned tail

Tail lashed from side to side to swim forward

Hind limbs much longer than front limbs

Relatively broad, short head

Tail protected by two rows of armored plates

LIGHTWEIGHT LANDLUBBER

Protosuchus ("first crocodile") from Early Jurassic Arizona was one of the earliest land-based crocodilians. About 3 ft (1 m) in length, this agile hunter could run semi-upright on its long hind legs and was able to catch speedy lizards and mammals. Its agility on land is still shown by modern crocodiles, which can lift their bodies off the ground to walk briskly. *Protosuchus* had short jaws that broadened out at the base of the skull to maximize the surface to which muscles could attach. This gave it a powerful bite. When its jaws clamped shut, the pointed canine teeth on its lower jaw slotted into sockets in the upper jaw to lock the bite.

METRIORHYNCHUS

Scientific name:	*Metriorhynchus*
Size:	10 ft (3 m) long
Diet:	Fish
Habitat:	Seas
Where found:	Europe and South America
Time:	Mid-Jurassic to Cretaceous
Related genera:	*Geosaurus, Pelagosaurus*

05–250	Triassic 250–203	Jurassic 203–135	Cretaceous 135–65	Tertiary 65–1.75	Quaternary 1.75–present
		MESOZOIC 250–65 MYA		CENOZOIC 65 MYA–present	

EARLY PTEROSAURS

PTEROSAURS WERE FLYING ARCHOSAURS that may have been closely related to dinosaurs. A pterosaur's wings were made of a large skin membrane that stretched from the end of its incredibly long fourth finger to its body and back legs. This wing membrane was reinforced with stiffening fibers and muscles. Exceptional fossils show that some pterosaurs had furry bodies and may have been warm-blooded, like modern day birds and mammals. Early toothed pterosaurs from the Triassic and Jurassic differ from later pterosaurs in having long tails, unfused bones in their backs, and relatively short bones in their wrists. Most early pterosaurs were small compared to later types, and none had a wingspan of more than 10 ft (3 m).

Fossil skeleton of Dimorphodon

Like birds, all pterosaurs probably had beaks.

Dimorphodon

PRIMITIVE PTEROSAURS

The earliest pterosaurs are from the Triassic. Though they are primitive compared to later forms, having shorter wing bones for example, they are still true pterosaurs. One possible "proto-pterosaur" has been found – a Russian fossil called *Sharovipteryx*. While clearly not a pterosaur, it shares many features in common with them. *Dimorphodon*, shown here, was an Early Jurassic pterosaur, notable for its enormous skull and differently sized teeth. The teeth at the front of its skull were much larger and more pointed than the others, while the teeth at the back of its lower jaw were tiny.

ANUROGNATHIDS

One early pterosaur group, the anurognathids, had short tails like advanced pterosaurs, but still had the short wrist bones and other features of early pterosaurs. Anurognathids had short, tall skulls, sharply pointed teeth and long, slim wings. These features suggest that they were fast-flying predators that fed on insects.

Anurognathus *snapped up insects in its huge beak.*

| Cambrian 540–500 | Ordovician 500–435 | Silurian 435–410 | Devonian 410–355 | Carboniferous 355–295 | Permia |

PALEOZOIC 540–250 MYA

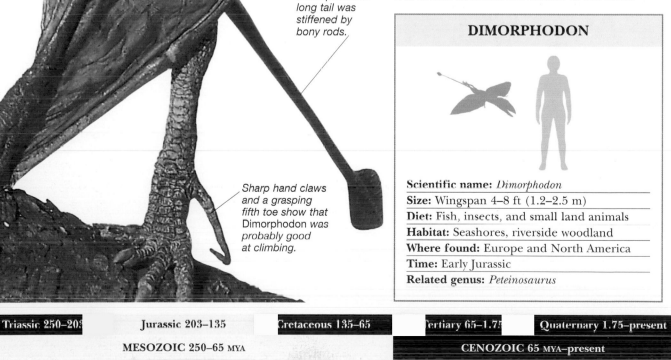

BIRDLIKE SKULL

Sophisticated flight requires good vision and a well-developed sense of balance. All pterosaur skulls have huge eye sockets, showing that their eyes were large and their eyesight was probably excellent. Some pterosaur skulls have internal casts of their brains preserved. These show that the parts of the brain responsible for sight and control of movement were well-developed and similar to the same parts of the brain in modern birds.

The bones in Dimorphodon's flexible neck were lightened by air-filled sacs.

Experts disagree about whether pterosaur wing membranes were connected to the whole leg or just to the thigh region.

The wing finger was made of four long, rodlike bones.

Dimorphodon's long tail was stiffened by bony rods.

Sharp hand claws and a grasping fifth toe show that Dimorphodon was probably good at climbing.

FISH GRABBERS

This fossilized skeleton of the Jurassic pterosaur *Rhamphorhynchus* was found in Germany with skin impressions and the wing membranes preserved. These show that it had a throat pouch and a diamond-shaped structure on the end of its tail. *Rhamphorhynchus* had a beak with several prominent, forward-pointing teeth at the tips of both upper and lower jaws. This would have allowed it to snatch fish from the surface of the water.

DIMORPHODON

Scientific name: *Dimorphodon*

Size: Wingspan 4–8 ft (1.2–2.5 m)

Diet: Fish, insects, and small land animals

Habitat: Seashores, riverside woodland

Where found: Europe and North America

Time: Early Jurassic

Related genus: *Peteinosaurus*

DIMORPHODON

Remains of *Dimorphodon* and related pterosaurs have been found in both seafloor and riverside environments, so they may have lived in a variety of different habitats. *Dimorphodon* and its relations were probably opportunistic predators who preyed on a wide variety of small animals. They may have eaten insects, caught lizards and other small reptiles, and captured fish and crustaceans from rivers or the sea. Experts do not know whether pterosaurs like *Dimorphodon* caught their prey while aloft, or while standing on all fours.

| Cambrian 540–500 | Ordovician 500–435 | Silurian 435–410 | Devonian 410–355 | Carboniferous 355–295 | Permi |

PALEOZOIC 540–250 MYA

05–250	Triassic 250–203	Jurassic 203–135	Cretaceous 135–65	Tertiary 65–1.75	Quaternary 1.75–present
		MESOZOIC 250–65 MYA		CENOZOIC 65 MYA–present	

97

ADVANCED PTEROSAURS

PTERODACTYLOIDS WERE ADVANCED PTEROSAURS that first evolved in the Late Jurassic. As earlier kinds of pterosaurs became extinct, they came to dominate the Cretaceous skies. Some pterodactyloids were toothless, while some had hundreds of bristlelike teeth. Other pterodactyloids had huge interlocking teeth for grabbing fish, while a group called dsungaripterids had blunt teeth, perhaps used for crushing shellfish. Only one or two species of pterodactyloid were left by the end of the Cretaceous. These were the last of the pterosaurs. Pterosaurs may have declined because newly evolving waterbirds took over their habitats.

WINGS AND NO TEETH

Pteranodon, meaning "wings and no teeth," is one of the most famous pterosaurs. Until *Quetzalcoatlus* was described in 1975, *Pteranodon* was the largest pterosaur known. It had a large headcrest, and the shape of its lower jaw suggests that *Pteranodon* had a pouch under its bill, something like that of a pelican. Several species of *Pteranodon* have been identified, all of them found in North America.

Wing bones of Rhamphorhynchus

WINGS AND WRISTS

The main part of the pterosaur wing skeleton was an elongated fourth finger, composed of four bones. A bone called the pteroid, unique to pterosaurs, pointed forward and inward from the front of the wrist joint. It supported an extra wing membrane called the propatagium. This stretched from the wrist to the shoulder and would have been used to help control the flow of air over the wing.

Pteranodon ingens *had a long, backward-pointing, triangular crest.*

One Pteranodon *fossil had fish bones preserved where its throat pouch would have been.*

Female

MALES AND FEMALES

Different specimens of *Pteranodon* have differently shaped head crests. Some have a large, very prominent crest – others a small crest. These two kinds have been found together, so it seems that they are males and females of the same species. The males are probably the ones with the bigger crests. They probably used their crests to impress females and intimidate other males.

Pteranodon sternbergi

Male

Pterodaustro *probably waded on all fours when feeding.*

PTERODAUSTRO

Some pterodactyloids had long jaws and hundreds of slim teeth. The best example is *Pterodaustro* from Early Cretaceous South America. Its jaws curved upward and its lower jaws were filled with about 1,000 straight, bristlelike teeth. It probably strained beakfuls of water through these teeth, leaving plankton trapped in its mouth.

Bristlelike teeth

| Cambrian 540–500 | Ordovician 500–435 | Silurian 435–410 | Devonian 410–355 | Carboniferous 355–295 | Permia |

PALEOZOIC 540–250 MYA

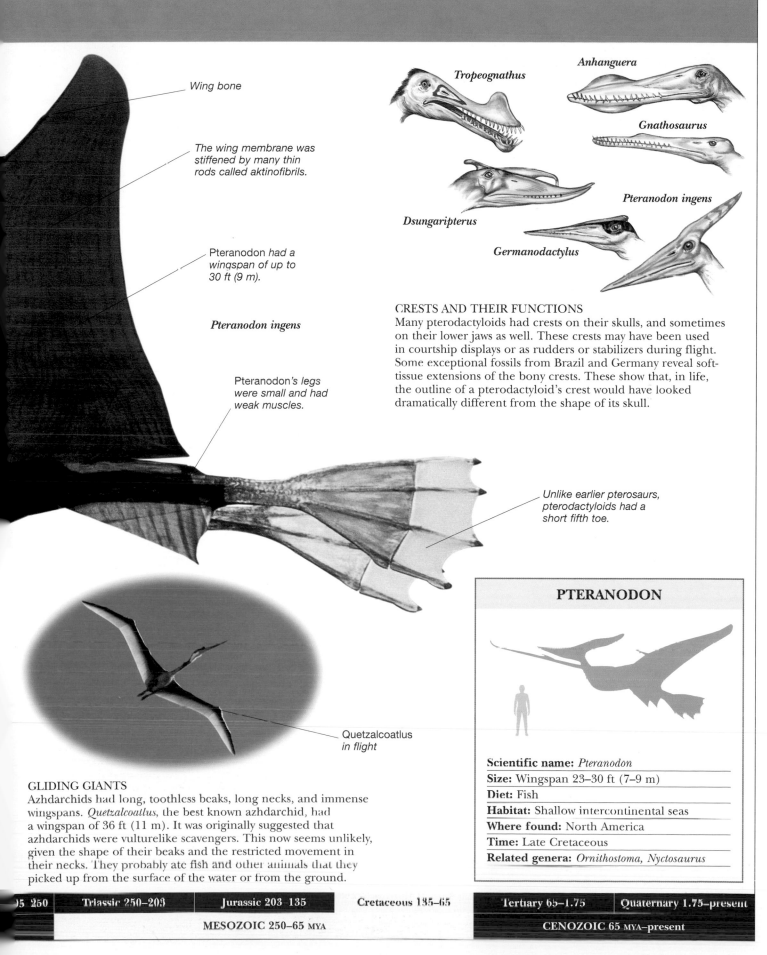

Wing bone

The wing membrane was stiffened by many thin rods called aktinofibrils.

Pteranodon had a wingspan of up to 30 ft (9 m).

Pteranodon ingens

Pteranodon's legs were small and had weak muscles.

Tropeognathus

Anhanguera

Gnathosaurus

Dsungaripterus

Pteranodon ingens

Germanodactylus

CRESTS AND THEIR FUNCTIONS
Many pterodactyloids had crests on their skulls, and sometimes on their lower jaws as well. These crests may have been used in courtship displays or as rudders or stabilizers during flight. Some exceptional fossils from Brazil and Germany reveal soft-tissue extensions of the bony crests. These show that, in life, the outline of a pterodactyloid's crest would have looked dramatically different from the shape of its skull.

Unlike earlier pterosaurs, pterodactyloids had a short fifth toe.

Quetzalcoatlus in flight

GLIDING GIANTS
Azhdarchids had long, toothless beaks, long necks, and immense wingspans. *Quetzalcoatlus*, the best known azhdarchid, had a wingspan of 36 ft (11 m). It was originally suggested that azhdarchids were vulturelike scavengers. This now seems unlikely, given the shape of their beaks and the restricted movement in their necks. They probably ate fish and other animals that they picked up from the surface of the water or from the ground.

PTERANODON

Scientific name: *Pteranodon*

Size: Wingspan 23–30 ft (7–9 m)

Diet: Fish

Habitat: Shallow intercontinental seas

Where found: North America

Time: Late Cretaceous

Related genera: *Ornithostoma, Nyctosaurus*

05 250	Triassic 250–203	Jurassic 203–135	Cretaceous 135–65	Tertiary 65–1.75	Quaternary 1.75–present
		MESOZOIC 250–65 MYA		CENOZOIC 65 MYA–present	

Dinosaurs and Birds

A bee-sized hummingbird seems worlds apart from a dinosaur as heavy as a whale. Yet birds almost certainly evolved from feathered dinosaurs. This section brings to life those ancient reptiles that between them dominated life on land for an astonishing 160 million years. Realistic models, many shown in prehistoric settings, reveal dinosaurs' likely shapes, colors, and weaponry. The fantastic range includes armor-plated herbivores and theropods with jaws big enough to swallow people whole, had people existed. Read on to discover how small theropods gave rise to birds with teeth and claws, and how these clumsy flyers evolved into today's aerial acrobats.

DINOSAURS DEFINED

THE MESOZOIC AGE IS OFTEN CALLED the "Age of the Dinosaurs," because for more than 150 million years, a single, extremely diverse group of reptiles dominated life on land. The first dinosaurs were probably two-legged hunters no bigger than a dog, but they soon evolved into a huge variety of shapes and sizes, and spread around the world. In time, they came to range from giants as heavy as a great whale to little birdlike beasts no bigger than a hen. No individual dinosaur species lasted longer than a few million years, but new species always arose to take their place – some scientists list 900 genera of dinosaur that lived at some time between 230 million and 65 million years ago.

DINOSAUR STANCE

One of the keys to dinosaur success was their upright posture. Most reptiles sprawl with their legs at the side of their bodies, but dinosaurs carried their limbs directly below their bodies, just like modern mammals, so their weight was carried straight down. Since they did not have to use large amounts of energy just to keep their bodies off the ground, dinosaurs were free to develop more active lifestyles.

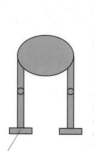

Erect stance of mammals and dinosaurs

Sprawling posture of most reptiles

Dinosaur skulls lack a postfrontal bone.

Allosaurus, a lizard-hipped dinosaur

All dinosaurs have three or more sacral vertebrae (vertebrae linked to hip girdle).

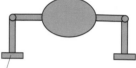

Long crest on humerus (upper arm bone)

Ridge above acetabulum (hole in hipbones) rests on head of femur.

Fourth finger (where present) had three or fewer bones.

Fully open acetabulum to receive femur

Femur (thighbone) has a ball-shaped head turned inward to slot into hipbones.

Cnemial crest (ridge) on tibia

WHAT MAKES A DINOSAUR?

Paleontologists can tell a dinosaur apart from other kinds of fossil animal by details in the bones of its skull, shoulders, vertebrae, hands, hips, and hindlimbs. These show that dinosaurs walked with limbs erect and on their toes, not flat-footed like bears. Without living specimens to study, we cannot know for sure just how their bodies worked, but such active animals were almost certainly warm-blooded. Small kinds probably generated internal heat as birds and mammals do. Large ones were simply too big to cool down at night. Neither kind grew sluggish in the cold like ordinary reptiles, so dinosaurs were always ready to hunt for food or find a mate.

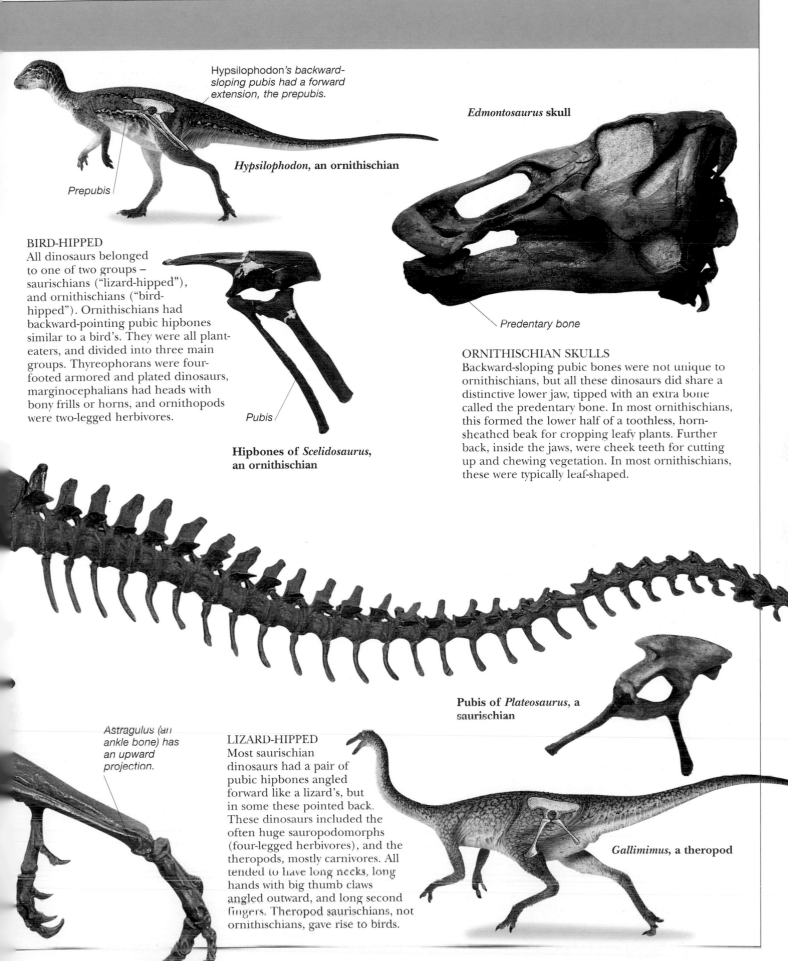

Hypsilophodon's *backward-sloping pubis had a forward extension, the prepubis.*

Edmontosaurus **skull**

***Hypsilophodon*, an ornithischian**

Prepubis

BIRD-HIPPED

All dinosaurs belonged to one of two groups – saurischians ("lizard-hipped"), and ornithischians ("bird-hipped"). Ornithischians had backward-pointing pubic hipbones similar to a bird's. They were all plant-eaters, and divided into three main groups. Thyreophorans were four-footed armored and plated dinosaurs, marginocephalians had heads with bony frills or horns, and ornithopods were two-legged herbivores.

Pubis

Hipbones of *Scelidosaurus*, an ornithischian

Predentary bone

ORNITHISCHIAN SKULLS

Backward-sloping pubic bones were not unique to ornithischians, but all these dinosaurs did share a distinctive lower jaw, tipped with an extra bone called the predentary bone. In most ornithischians, this formed the lower half of a toothless, horn-sheathed beak for cropping leafy plants. Further back, inside the jaws, were cheek teeth for cutting up and chewing vegetation. In most ornithischians, these were typically leaf-shaped.

Pubis of *Plateosaurus*, a saurischian

Astragulus (an ankle bone) has an upward projection.

LIZARD-HIPPED

Most saurischian dinosaurs had a pair of pubic hipbones angled forward like a lizard's, but in some these pointed back. These dinosaurs included the often huge sauropodomorphs (four-legged herbivores), and the theropods, mostly carnivores. All tended to have long necks, long hands with big thumb claws angled outward, and long second fingers. Theropod saurischians, not ornithischians, gave rise to birds.

***Gallimimus*, a theropod**

SAURISCHIANS CLADOGRAM

THE "LIZARD-HIPPED" DINOSAURS CALLED saurischians were one of the two great groups of dinosaurs. Key saurischian features include an elongated neck, a long second finger, and cavities in the bones that housed air-filled sacs connected to the lungs. Primitive saurischians had a pubic bone that pointed forward, as in other amniotes. This was a primitive feature inherited from the early dinosaur ancestors of saurischians. The saurischians included groups specialized for both herbivorous and carnivorous lifestyles. Saurischians survived the extinction event at the end of the Cretaceous in the form of birds.

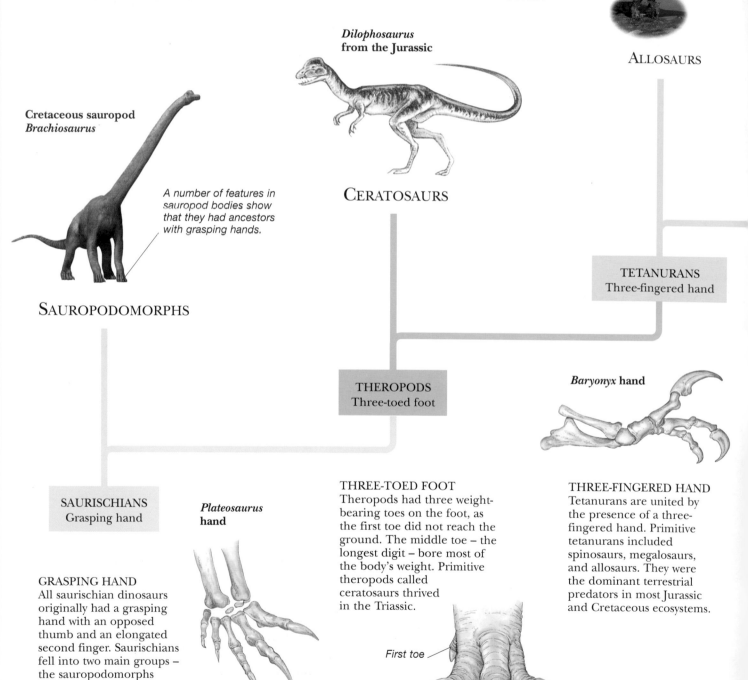

Allosaurus from the Jurassic

ALLOSAURS

Dilophosaurus from the Jurassic

CERATOSAURS

Cretaceous sauropod
Brachiosaurus

A number of features in sauropod bodies show that they had ancestors with grasping hands.

SAUROPODOMORPHS

TETANURANS
Three-fingered hand

THEROPODS
Three-toed foot

Baryonyx hand

SAURISCHIANS
Grasping hand

Plateosaurus hand

GRASPING HAND
All saurischian dinosaurs originally had a grasping hand with an opposed thumb and an elongated second finger. Saurischians fell into two main groups – the sauropodomorphs and the theropods.

THREE-TOED FOOT
Theropods had three weight-bearing toes on the foot, as the first toe did not reach the ground. The middle toe – the longest digit – bore most of the body's weight. Primitive theropods called ceratosaurs thrived in the Triassic.

First toe

Allosaurus foot

THREE-FINGERED HAND
Tetanurans are united by the presence of a three-fingered hand. Primitive tetanurans included spinosaurs, megalosaurs, and allosaurs. They were the dominant terrestrial predators in most Jurassic and Cretaceous ecosystems.

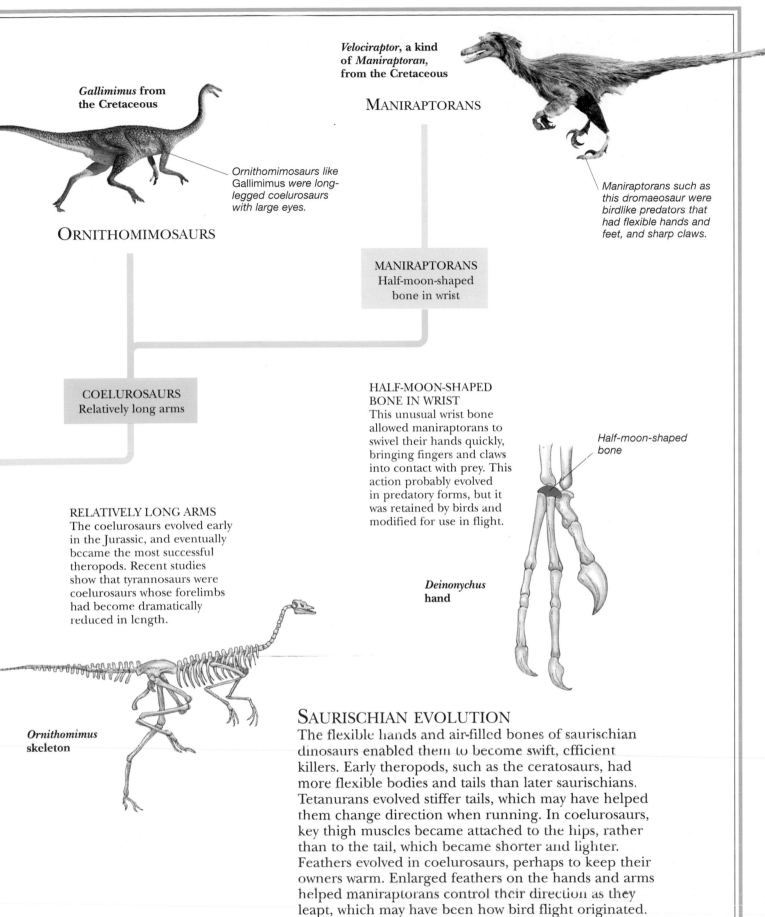

Velociraptor, a kind
of *Maniraptoran*,
from the Cretaceous

MANIRAPTORANS

**Gallimimus from
the Cretaceous**

Ornithomimosaurs like
Gallimimus *were long-
legged coelurosaurs
with large eyes.*

ORNITHOMIMOSAURS

Maniraptorans such as
this dromaeosaur were
birdlike predators that
had flexible hands and
feet, and sharp claws.

MANIRAPTORANS
Half-moon-shaped
bone in wrist

COELUROSAURS
Relatively long arms

**HALF-MOON-SHAPED
BONE IN WRIST**
This unusual wrist bone
allowed maniraptorans to
swivel their hands quickly,
bringing fingers and claws
into contact with prey. This
action probably evolved
in predatory forms, but it
was retained by birds and
modified for use in flight.

Half-moon-shaped
bone

RELATIVELY LONG ARMS
The coelurosaurs evolved early
in the Jurassic, and eventually
became the most successful
theropods. Recent studies
show that tyrannosaurs were
coelurosaurs whose forelimbs
had become dramatically
reduced in length.

Deinonychus
hand

Ornithomimus
skeleton

SAURISCHIAN EVOLUTION

The flexible hands and air-filled bones of saurischian
dinosaurs enabled them to become swift, efficient
killers. Early theropods, such as the ceratosaurs, had
more flexible bodies and tails than later saurischians.
Tetanurans evolved stiffer tails, which may have helped
them change direction when running. In coelurosaurs,
key thigh muscles became attached to the hips, rather
than to the tail, which became shorter and lighter.
Feathers evolved in coelurosaurs, perhaps to keep their
owners warm. Enlarged feathers on the hands and arms
helped maniraptorans control their direction as they
leapt, which may have been how bird flight originated.

EARLY THEROPODS

FOSSILS FROM ARGENTINA AND BRAZIL show that some of the earliest dinosaurs were two-legged, sharp-toothed, sharp-clawed saurischian ("lizard-hipped") hunters. Three such dinosaurs lived in South America about 228 million years ago. Their bones show a mixture of old-fashioned and advanced designs, but all three share features with theropods, the group all other known meat-eating dinosaurs belong to. When these creatures lived, dinosaurs seem to have been small and fairly uncommon creatures. Recent finds in Brazil and Madagascar hinted at even earlier saurischians, though – small plant-eating prosauropods. Another very early herbivore was *Pisanosaurus*, an ornithischian ("bird-hipped") dinosaur from Argentina.

Double-hinged jaws gripped struggling prey.

Shoulder joint

FIRST SAURISCHIAN

Eoraptor lived about 228 million years ago in Argentina. The near-complete skeleton was discovered in 1991, revealing that *Eoraptor* was only 3 ft 3 in (1 m) long, and weighed just 24 lb (11 kg). A small but fierce long-legged hunter, it had a lower snout and shorter grasping hands than its neighbor *Herrerasaurus*. *Eoraptor* would have looked somewhat like a miniature, lightly built version of later theropods, yet it had many more primitive features. For instance, it had more fingers, weaker claws, and fewer vertebrae supporting the hips. It probably hunted lizards and small mammal-like creatures.

HERRERA'S LIZARD

Herrerasaurus was a large-jawed theropod that could grow longer than a family car and as heavy as a pony. It lived about 228 million years ago in what are now the foothills of the Andes. *Herrerasaurus* was one of the largest hunters of its day, only smaller than land-based relatives of crocodilians, such as *Saurosuchus*. Its likely prey included the rhynchosaur *Scaphonyx* and the small plant-eating ornithischian dinosaur *Pisanosaurus*. Running on its long hind legs, it could easily have overtaken slower-moving, four-legged prey.

Leaflike teeth, similar to those in prosauropods

Sharp curved cutting teeth

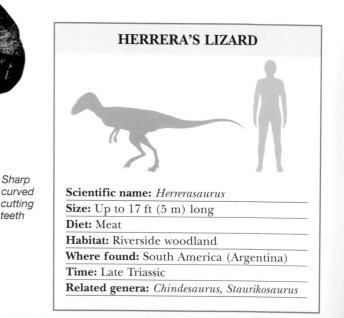

HERRERA'S LIZARD

Scientific name: *Herrerasaurus*

Size: Up to 17 ft (5 m) long

Diet: Meat

Habitat: Riverside woodland

Where found: South America (Argentina)

Time: Late Triassic

Related genera: *Chindesaurus, Staurikosaurus*

Cambrian 540–500	Ordovician 500–435	Silurian 435–410	Devonian 410–355	Carboniferous 355–295	Permia

PALEOZOIC 540–250 MYA

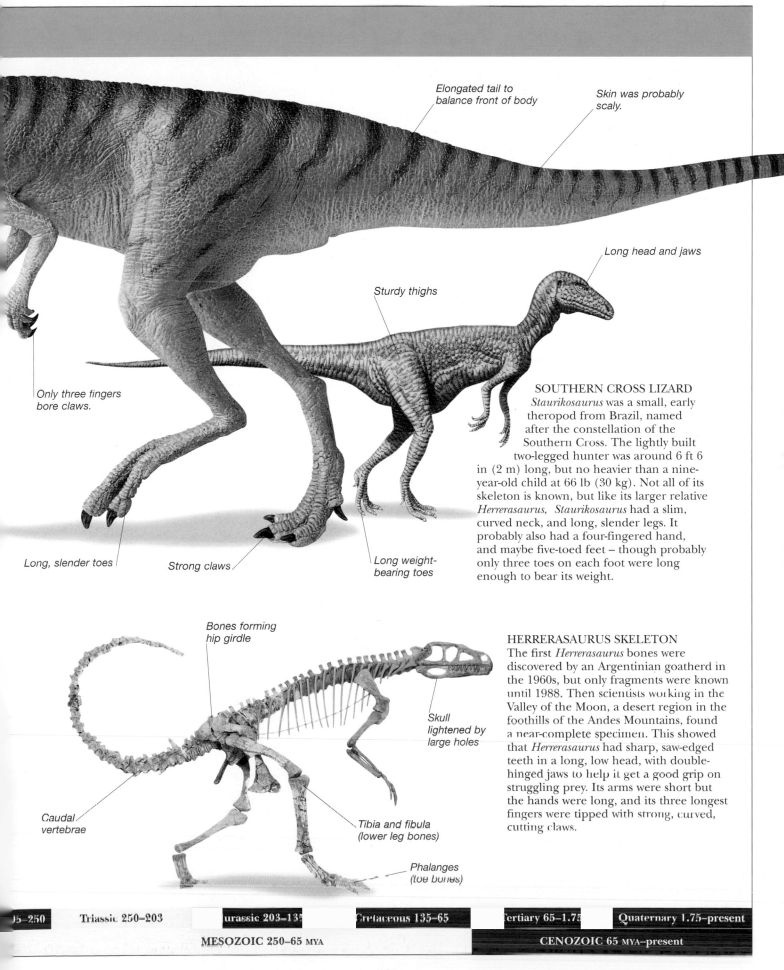

Elongated tail to balance front of body

Skin was probably scaly.

Long head and jaws

Sturdy thighs

Only three fingers bore claws.

Long, slender toes

Strong claws

Long weight-bearing toes

SOUTHERN CROSS LIZARD
Staurikosaurus was a small, early theropod from Brazil, named after the constellation of the Southern Cross. The lightly built two-legged hunter was around 6 ft 6 in (2 m) long, but no heavier than a nine-year-old child at 66 lb (30 kg). Not all of its skeleton is known, but like its larger relative *Herrerasaurus*, *Staurikosaurus* had a slim, curved neck, and long, slender legs. It probably also had a four-fingered hand, and maybe five-toed feet – though probably only three toes on each foot were long enough to bear its weight.

Bones forming hip girdle

Skull lightened by large holes

Caudal vertebrae

Tibia and fibula (lower leg bones)

Phalanges (toe bones)

HERRERASAURUS SKELETON
The first *Herrerasaurus* bones were discovered by an Argentinian goatherd in the 1960s, but only fragments were known until 1988. Then scientists working in the Valley of the Moon, a desert region in the foothills of the Andes Mountains, found a near-complete specimen. This showed that *Herrerasaurus* had sharp, saw-edged teeth in a long, low head, with double-hinged jaws to help it get a good grip on struggling prey. Its arms were short but the hands were long, and its three longest fingers were tipped with strong, curved, cutting claws.

J5–250	Triassic 250–203	Jurassic 203–135	Cretaceous 135–65	Tertiary 65–1.75	Quaternary 1.75–present
		MESOZOIC 250–65 MYA		CENOZOIC 65 MYA–present	

HORNED LIZARDS

HORNS OR BUMPS ON THEIR HEADS earned some meat-eating dinosaurs the name ceratosaurs ("horned lizards"). At least 20 species are known – the largest grew 23 ft (7 m) long and weighed more than a ton, while the smallest was no bigger than a dog. Horns were not unique to ceratosaurs, and not all ceratosaurs were actually horned, but all shared certain skeletal features. They also kept primitive features that other theropods lost – for instance, each hand had four digits (not three). Ceratosaurs spread worldwide and lasted nearly right through the Age of Dinosaurs. Early on, they were the main predatory dinosaurs, but later they seem to have petered out in northern continents as deadlier tetanuran ("stiff-tailed") killers took their place.

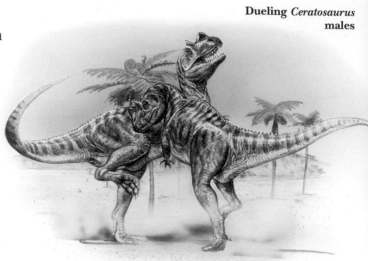
Dueling *Ceratosaurus* males

CERATOSAURUS
Ceratosaurus was one of the biggest ceratosaurs, found in Late Jurassic North America and Tanzania. It had a large, deep head with a blade-like horn over its nose, two hornlets on its brows, and great curved fangs. The arms were short but strong, with sharply hooked claws. *Ceratosaurus* probably hunted ornithopods such as *Camptosaurus*, and the sick and young of large four-legged plant-eaters such as *Stegosaurus* and *Diplodocus*. The horns might have been used for intimidation by rival males.

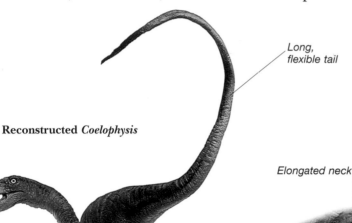

Reconstructed *Coelophysis*

Long, flexible tail

Primitive four-fingered hand

Elongated neck

Long, narrow jaws with sharp, curved teeth

Remains of a swallowed baby Coelophysis – this dinosaur was a cannibal.

HOLLOW FORM
Coelophysis ("hollow form") was a slim theropod as long as a small car but as light as an eight-year-old child. With a head like a stork's, a long, curved neck, and slender legs it resembled a long-legged bird – but unlike living birds Coelophysis had teeth, clawed hands, and a long, bony tail. One of the earliest-known ceratosaurs, it roamed Arizona and New Mexico in the Late Triassic, about 225 million years ago. Coelophysis probably snapped up lizards and small mammals, and may have hunted in packs to bring down larger prey.

Coelophysis **skeleton**

Cambrian 540–500	Ordovician 500–435	Silurian 435–410	Devonian 410–355	Carboniferous 355–295	Permia

PALEOZOIC 540–250 MYA

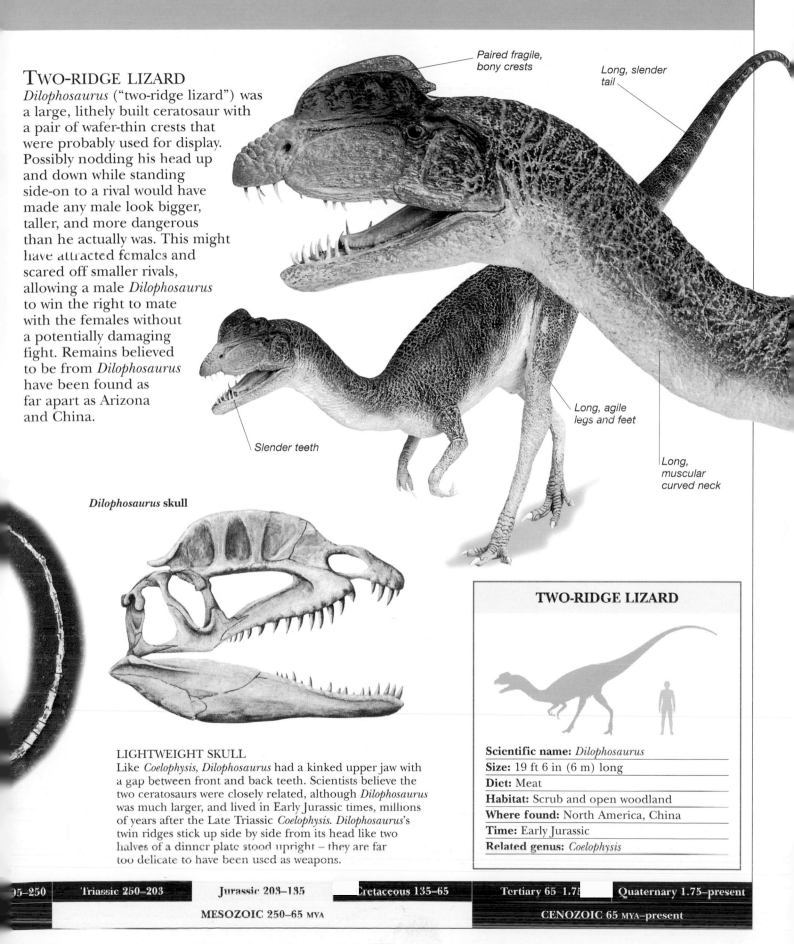

TWO-RIDGE LIZARD

Dilophosaurus ("two-ridge lizard") was a large, lithely built ceratosaur with a pair of wafer-thin crests that were probably used for display. Possibly nodding his head up and down while standing side-on to a rival would have made any male look bigger, taller, and more dangerous than he actually was. This might have attracted females and scared off smaller rivals, allowing a male *Dilophosaurus* to win the right to mate with the females without a potentially damaging fight. Remains believed to be from *Dilophosaurus* have been found as far apart as Arizona and China.

Paired fragile, bony crests

Long, slender tail

Slender teeth

Long, agile legs and feet

Long, muscular curved neck

Dilophosaurus **skull**

LIGHTWEIGHT SKULL

Like *Coelophysis*, *Dilophosaurus* had a kinked upper jaw with a gap between front and back teeth. Scientists believe the two ceratosaurs were closely related, although *Dilophosaurus* was much larger, and lived in Early Jurassic times, millions of years after the Late Triassic *Coelophysis*. *Dilophosaurus*'s twin ridges stick up side by side from its head like two halves of a dinner plate stood upright – they are far too delicate to have been used as weapons.

TWO-RIDGE LIZARD

Scientific name:	*Dilophosaurus*
Size:	19 ft 6 in (6 m) long
Diet:	Meat
Habitat:	Scrub and open woodland
Where found:	North America, China
Time:	Early Jurassic
Related genus:	*Coelophysis*

95–250	Triassic 250–203	Jurassic 203–135	Cretaceous 135–65	Tertiary 65–1.75	Quaternary 1.75–present
		MESOZOIC 250–65 MYA		CENOZOIC 65 MYA–present	

ABEL'S LIZARDS

IN 1985 ARGENTINIAN PALEONTOLOGISTS José Bonaparte and Fernando Novas named a large carnivorous dinosaur with a skull unlike any discovered before. They called it *Abelisaurus* ("Abel's lizard") after Roberto Abel, the museum director who discovered it. Similarities with *Ceratosaurus* made the scientists believe it belonged to a previously unknown group of ceratosaurs ("horned lizards"), which they called the abelisaurids. Abelisaurids' unusual features included a short, steep snout with thickened bone or horns above the eyes. Soon, more members of the group came to light, including *Xenotarsosaurus* from South America, *Majungatholus* from Madagascar, *Indosaurus* and *Indosuchus* from India, and perhaps others from Europe. Most were large meat-eaters – they must have terrorized the plant-eating dinosaurs of southern continents in Cretaceous times.

Lower jaw slender compared to deep head

Very short, stubby arms and hands

Short, thick stubby horns

Eyes see sideways and forward

Nostrils on short, deep snout

HORNED HEAD

A victim's view of *Carnotaurus* shows how its small eyes faced partly forward, perhaps helping to focus on its prey. Above the eyes, two short, pointed horns stuck out sideways and upward. Scientists are unsure what the horns were for – they are too short to kill, but perhaps they were used by males to display to females or threaten rival males. Perhaps a big male would bob its head up and down to scare smaller rivals away, or maybe rival males stood side by side with lowered heads, butting each other in the head or neck.

Slender lower jaw

Teeth rather long and delicate

MEAT-EATING BULL

By far the weirdest looking abelisaurid was *Carnotaurus* ("meat-eating bull") from Late Cretaceous Argentina. *Carnotaurus* grew up to 25 ft (7.6 m) long, and had a very short, deep head with horns like a bull's. Other key features included tiny, useless-looking arms and long, slim legs. Perhaps *Carnotaurus* hunted by attacking young sauropods or medium-sized ornithopods headfirst, or scavenging from those it found already dead. *Carnotaurus* left behind detailed fossil skin impressions showing that it had large, bluntly pointed scales running in rows along its back and sides. The body's skin was also covered by a mass of disc-shaped scales – perhaps all big theropods had scaly skins like this.

| Cambrian 540–500 | Ordovician 500–435 | Silurian 435–410 | Devonian 410–355 | Carboniferous 355–295 | Permia |

PALEOZOIC 540–250 MYA

Rows of large, blunt scales

Body balanced
above the hips

Carnotaurus jawbones

PUZZLING JAWLINE

The lower jaw of *Carnotaurus* is another mystery of this unusual theropod. In contrast to the massive head, it is slender and delicate, and its teeth seem too lightly built to cope with big, struggling prey. This is more evidence that *Carnotaurus* might have scavenged or had a unique hunting strategy.

Skull of *Majungatholus*

MAJUNGA DOME

Another large abelisaurid was *Majungatholus*, found in Madagascar. *Majungatholus* was another fierce predator with a bony bump on its deep head, and it grew to over 30 ft (9 m) long. In 1998, a near-complete skull was discovered on the island where it lived.

Very powerful
thighs

Strong shins

High ankle
joint

Tiny hallux
(big toe)

Large, weight-
bearing toes

Upper foot with
elongated bones

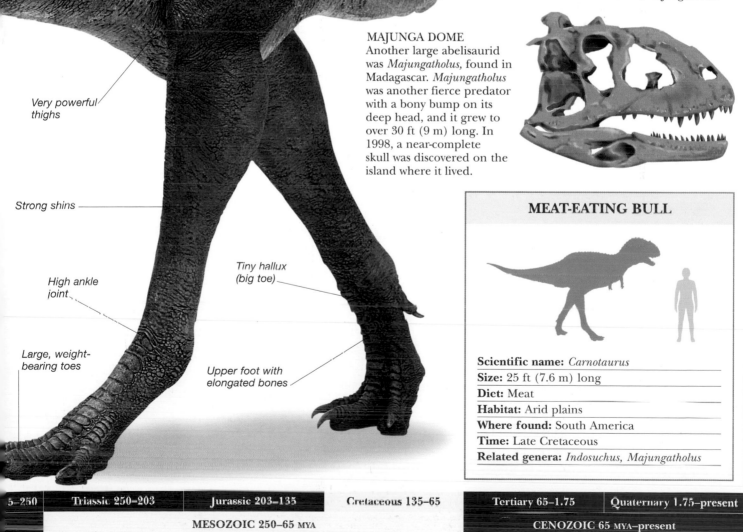

MEAT-EATING BULL

Scientific name:	*Carnotaurus*
Size:	25 ft (7.6 m) long
Diet:	Meat
Habitat:	Arid plains
Where found:	South America
Time:	Late Cretaceous
Related genera:	*Indosuchus, Majungatholus*

STIFF TAILS

MOST OF THE LATER THEROPODS are known as tetanurans ("stiff tails"). The name tetanuran comes from a change that probably affected their legs and tails. In early theropods, muscles linked the thigh bones to the middle of the tail, which waggled from side to side as they walked. Tetanurans evolved shortened tail-thigh muscles, and this meant that their tails' rear ends became less mobile. In time some tetanurans lost their tails altogether. Tetanuran skulls were less solid than ceratosaurs'; the jaws only had teeth forward of their eyes, and each hand bore no more than three fingers. The first known tetanurans included *Eustreptospondylus, Megalosaurus,* and other so-called megalosaurs ("big lizards"). These medium to large theropods are mostly known from scrappy fossils dating from Early Jurassic to Early Cretaceous times. New finds of big theropods from Asia, Africa, and Europe show the wide variety of early tetanuran theropods.

WELL-CURVED VERTEBRAE
Eustreptospondylus was an early tetanuran living in England more than 170 million years ago. It grew up to 23 ft (7 m) long. Despite its size, long tail, and long, thick legs, it was lightly built, with weight-saving holes in its skull, and short, three-fingered hands. This sharp-toothed theropod could have hunted the four-legged, plant-eating dinosaurs that shared its habitat – the plated *Lexovisaurus,* armored *Sarcolestes,* and perhaps even the huge sauropod *Cetiosaurus.*

Tail-thigh muscle became shortened in tetanurans.

Tetanurans had distinctive lower leg and ankle bones.

Bladelike teeth 2 in (5 cm) long

AFRICAN HUNTER
At 30ft (9 m) long, *Afrovenator* ("African hunter") was lightly built, fast-moving, and armed with 2-in (5-cm) bladelike teeth and sharp, hooked claws. It roamed a lush, hot countryside with shallow lakes and rivers. Fossil bite marks found in the ribs of a young sauropod called *Jobaria* suggest that sauropods were its major food supply. *Afrovenator*'s discovery in the Sahara desert in 1994 showed that primitive tetanurans still thrived in Early Cretaceous Africa 135 million years ago, 35 million years after *Eustreptospondylus* flourished in Europe.

Three large, weight-bearing toes

| Cambrian 540–500 | Ordovician 500–435 | Silurian 435–410 | Devonian 410–355 | Carboniferous 355–295 | Permia |

PALEOZOIC 540–250 MYA

Air-filled bones lightened tetanuran skulls.

Tetanurans had teeth only at the front of their jaws.

Muscular arms

MIGHTY JAWBONE

The first *Megalosaurus* jaw to be discovered was armed with great curved teeth, and must have formed part of a long, deep head. It even shows where new teeth had begun to grow, replacing the old ones when they fell out, as sometimes happened when *Megalosaurus* bit into its victims.

Tetanurans had three-fingered hands.

Replacement tooth

Tooth

Interdental plate

Large, muscular legs

BIG LIZARD

Megalosaurus was the first dinosaur to get a scientific name still used today. In 1824, British scientist William Buckland described it from a tantalizing broken piece of lower jaw. *Megalosaurus* probably grew longer and stronger than *Eustreptospondylus*, with a large head, thick neck, short strong arms, and long powerful legs. The three main digits on each hand and foot bore murderously long sharp claws. Yet no whole skeleton has ever been found, and many details are guesswork. *Megalosaurus*, like *Eustreptospondylus*, lived in the Mid Jurassic. Fossils have been found in England, France, and Portugal.

BIG LIZARD

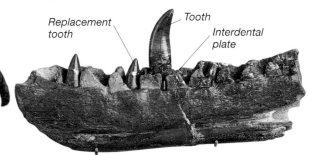

Scientific name: *Megalosaurus*

Size: 30 ft (9 m) long

Diet: Meat

Habitat: Coastal woodland

Where found: Western Europe

Time: Middle Jurassic

Related genus: *Eustreptospondylus*

05-95–250	Triassic 250–203	Jurassic 203–135	Cretaceous 135–65	Tertiary 65–1.75	Quaternary 1.75–present

MESOZOIC 250–65 MYA   CENOZOIC 65 MYA–present

GIANT KILLERS

GREAT MEAT-EATING DINOSAURS were roaming the world long before *Tyrannosaurus* terrorized North America. Several may even have exceeded that monster in size. These great hunters were tetanuran theropods – a name once used for all large carnivorous dinosaurs, but now used only for the allosaurs and close relatives. Allosaurid heads had deep skulls with distinctive bones and large weight-saving openings. Sometimes they had ridges or crests on the snout or over the eyes. Their jaws were immense, with narrow, curved fangs, though weaker than *Tyrannosaurus*'s. Their arms were stronger, with three-fingered hands armed with sharp claws, and their great muscular legs with three-toed feet resembled those of a gigantic bird. Allosaurids flourished from Late Jurassic to Late Cretaceous times, in places as far apart as North and South America, Europe, and Africa.

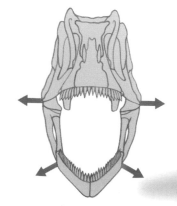

Tail strengthened by sturdy vertebrae

Tail probably wagged widely from side to side.

Thigh joined to hip girdle by a femur more massive than *Tyrannosaurus*'s.

DIFFERENT LIZARD
Allosaurus roamed western North America, East Africa, and southwest Europe in Late Jurassic times. Small adults weighed as much as a heavy horse, while large ones grew as heavy as an elephant. Individuals of various sizes perhaps belonged to several species. Some scientists once thought the biggest fossils came from another genus altogether. *Allosaurus* preyed upon plant-eating dinosaurs such as two-legged *Camptosaurus* and four-legged *Stegosaurus* and *Apatosaurus*. It probably hunted by ambush, hiding in trees until a slow-moving herbivore came by.

EXPANDING JAWS
Two views of *Allosaurus*'s jaws show how they first gaped open (left) then moved apart (right), to bite a huge mouthful from its victim. Skull bones with movable joints allowed this to happen. *Allosaurus* could also slide its skull back over its lower jaw, to let its knifelike teeth slice through muscle and gristle. Some scientists now think the slim lower jaw was too fragile for fighting, and was used only for feeding after *Allosaurus* had weakened its prey with axelike blows from the upper jaw, and ripped out chunks of flesh by pulling back with its powerful neck muscles.

Claws up to 10 in (25 cm) long seized prey.

Strongly curved narrow claw

Forward extensions of pubic bones made these look like boots.

Cambrian 540–500	Ordovician 500–435	Silurian 435–410	Devonian 410–355	Carboniferous 355–295	Permi

PALEOZOIC 540–250 MYA

Head twice as large as that of *Allosaurus*

Bladelike, saw-edged teeth 8 in (20 cm) long

Grasping, three-fingered hand with sharp claws

Relatively small shoulder

Very strong, three-toed foot

Each foot supported up to 3.9 tons (4 tonnes) of body weight.

GIANT SOUTHERN LIZARD

Giganotosaurus from Late Cretaceous Argentina was an immense carnivore, perhaps even longer and more massive than *Tyrannosaurus*. It is thought to have been as heavy as 125 people and up to 45 feet (13.7 m) long, with a bony skull crest, deep head, short arms, and immensely powerful legs. This big-game hunter could have attacked one of the largest-ever sauropods, *Argentinosaurus*, or scavenged meat from its corpse. *Giganotosaurus* flourished about 90 MYA, but, like all allosaurids, seemingly died out before the end of the Cretaceous Period. In various parts of the world they were replaced by abelisaurids or tyrannosaurids. Perhaps these proved more efficient hunters than allosaurids.

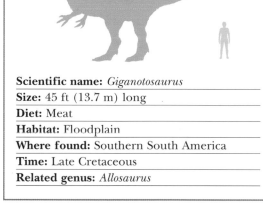

GIANT SOUTHERN LIZARD

Scientific name: *Giganotosaurus*

Size: 45 ft (13.7 m) long

Diet: Meat

Habitat: Floodplain

Where found: Southern South America

Time: Late Cretaceous

Related genus: *Allosaurus*

SHARK-TOOTHED LIZARD

Carcharodontosaurus was another huge Cretaceous "hangover": an allosaurid theropod from mid Cretaceous North Africa. This dinosaur lent its name to the carcharodontosaurines, a subgroup that also includes *Giganotosaurus* and another massive South American theropod, perhaps the largest of all. At nearly 46 ft (14 m) long and weighing at least 6.9 tons (7 tonnes), *Carcharodontosaurus* could have been as large and heavy as *Giganotosaurus*, although its head was shorter, and its brain was smaller than *Tyrannosaurus*'s.

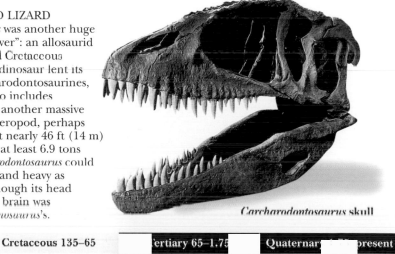

Carcharodontosaurus skull

)5 250	Triassic 250–203	Jurassic 203–135	Cretaceous 135–65	Tertiary 65–1.75	Quaternary 1.75–present
	MESOZOIC 250–65 MYA			CENOZOIC 65 MYA–present	

PREDATOR TRAP

ABOUT 145 MILLION YEARS AGO IN UTAH, one predator after another homed in on a feast that proved too good to be true. The scent of plant-eating dinosaurs and the sounds of their cries led the great hunters one by one to a pool of water where they found their prey stuck deep in mud. To an *Allosaurus* the sight of the giant herbivores was like an invitation to lunch. But instead of wading out into clear water, it soon found itself sucked into something more like thick porridge. Floundering about, it might have managed to scramble onto the back of its prey, but soon both sank and drowned. More theropods would arrive and die the same way. Before they sank, though, many had time to bite chunks from the herbivores and trample on them and each other.

THE VICTIMS
The predator trap claimed the lives of at least 40 *Allosaurus*, from adults 40 ft (12 m) long and weighing 2.2 tons (2 tonnes), to youngsters one-quarter their size. *Allosaurus* was not the only predatory dinosaur there. Others included *Ceratosaurus* and two small hunters; *Marshosaurus* and *Stokesosaurus*. Among their prey was the medium-sized ornithopod *Camptosaurus*, the plated dinosaur *Stegosaurus*, and the sauropods *Barosaurus* and *Camarasaurus*.

LAYING THE TRAP
Scientists suspect that a volcano in the young Rocky Mountains was responsible for forming this deadly mud trap. When the volcano erupted, it hurled out masses of ash, some of which accumulated in a local waterhole, creating a deep mass of wet mud with a patch of clear water in the middle. Seeing the water, thirsty plant-eating dinosaurs ventured in to drink and were trapped. Perhaps the mud near the edges was solid enough for them not to sink in, for most seem to have died in the middle.

The bleached skull of a long-drowned Allosaurus shows how the two living dinosaurs will meet their ends.

Cambrian 540–500	Ordovician 500–435	Silurian 435–410	Devonian 410–355	Carboniferous 355–295	Permia

PALEOZOIC 540–250 MYA

EVIDENCE FOR THE TRAP

The pool where the dinosaurs died is now the Cleveland-Lloyd Dinosaur Quarry in Utah. Since 1927, when scientists began digging fossils out of the quarry, they have found more than 10,000 bones. In any given area, big plant-eaters should normally outnumber big predators, yet here far more bones belonged to *Allosaurus* than to any of its victims. This is why scientists believe the pool was a predator trap – a deadly place where over weeks, months, and even years, a few trapped victims would lure large numbers of the creatures that preyed on them.

Pterosaurs passing overhead ignore the struggling animals below.

An *Allosaurus homes in on a* Stegosaurus *sucked down by wet mud. Moments later, the predator too will begin to sink.*

DIFFERENT LIZARD

Scientific name: *Allosaurus*

Size: 40 ft (12 m) long

Diet: Meat

Habitat: Open countryside

Where found: North America

Time: Late Jurassic

Related genus: *Giganotosaurus*

J5–250	Triassic 250–203	Jurassic 203–135	Cretaceous 135–65	Tertiary 65–1.75	Quaternary 1.75–present
		MESOZOIC 250–65 MYA		CENOZOIC 65 MYA–present	

HOLLOW-TAIL LIZARDS

THE JURASSIC LANDSCAPE PROBABLY TEEMED with small predators – the dinosaur equivalent of mammals such as foxes and jackals – but because their bones were so thin and fragile very few left fossil remains. Among the best known of these are *Compsognathus* from Germany and France, and *Ornitholestes* from the United States. Both were probably fast runners, chasing and eating lizards, small mammals, and other creatures smaller than themselves. They were early members of a new tetanuran theropod group – the coelurosaurs or "hollow-tail lizards." This great group of predatory dinosaurs eventually gave rise to huge tyrannosaurs, birdlike ornithopods, and the likely ancestors of birds.

COMPSOGNATHUS LIFESTYLE

Compsognathus lived on warm desert islands in what are now southern Germany and France, and was was probably the largest predator there (small islands rarely have enough food to support large meateaters). The little dinosaur's slender build, with a long neck, balancing tail, and birdlike legs, would have made it a fast mover. It caught and ate lizards such as *Bavarisaurus* among the scrubby vegetation, and perhaps also hunted the primitive bird *Archaeopteryx*. *Compsognathus* may also have scavenged dead king crabs and other creatures washed up on the shore.

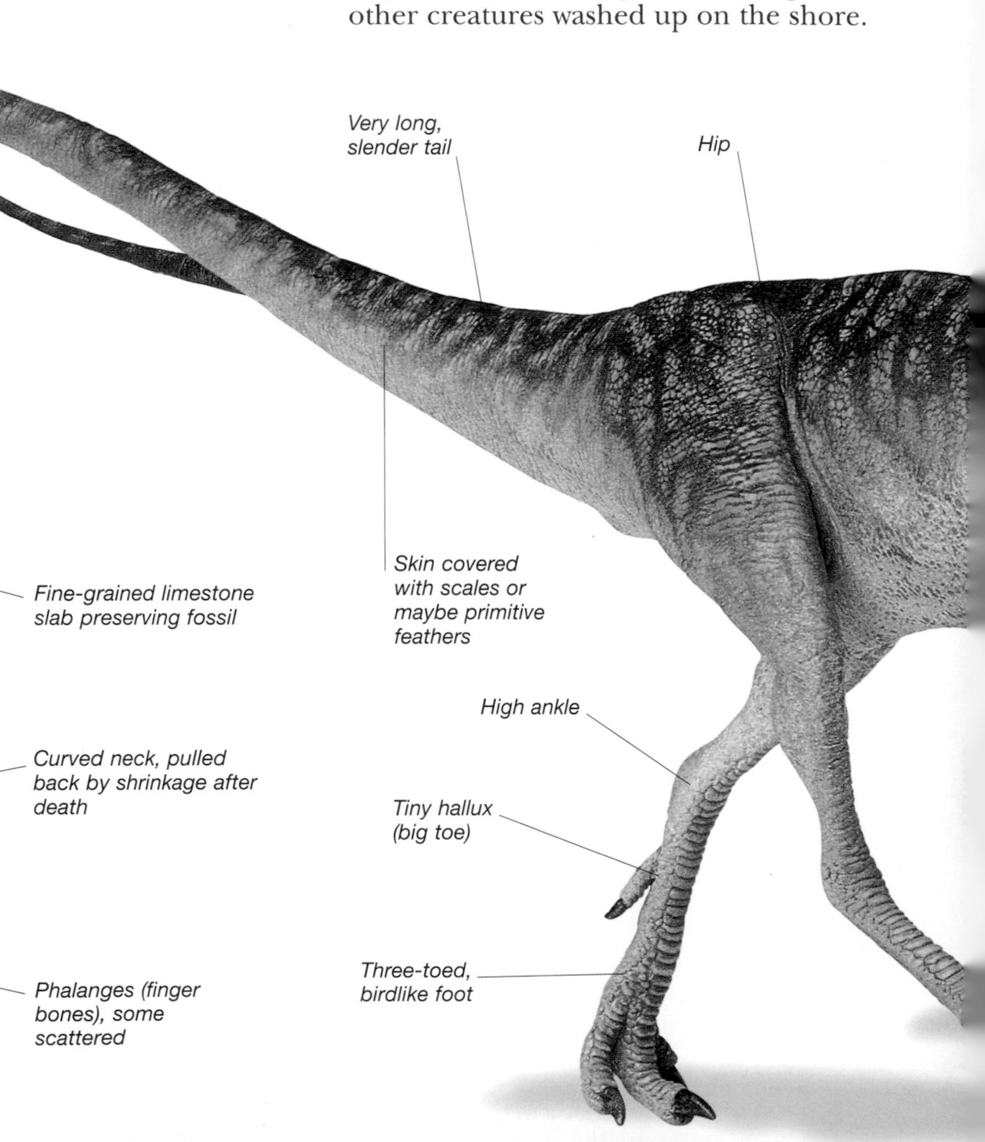

Very long, slender tail

Hip

THE LIZARD EATER

The fossil *Compsognathus* shown below is one of only two so far discovered. This well-preserved German specimen had swallowed a small lizard called *Bavarisaurus*. Half-grown, the theropod was no bigger than a chicken, but a French specimen was the size of a turkey. *Compsognathus* might have had only two fingers on each hand. Other coelurosaurs had three, including a large thumb claw.

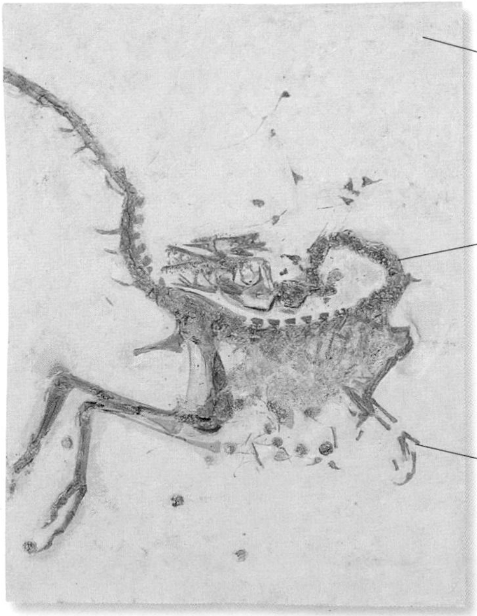

Fine-grained limestone slab preserving fossil

Skin covered with scales or maybe primitive feathers

High ankle

Curved neck, pulled back by shrinkage after death

Tiny hallux (big toe)

Phalanges (finger bones), some scattered

Three-toed, birdlike foot

| Cambrian 540–500 | Ordovician 500–435 | Silurian 435–410 | Devonian 410–355 | Carboniferous 355–295 | Perm |

PALEOZOIC 540–250 MYA

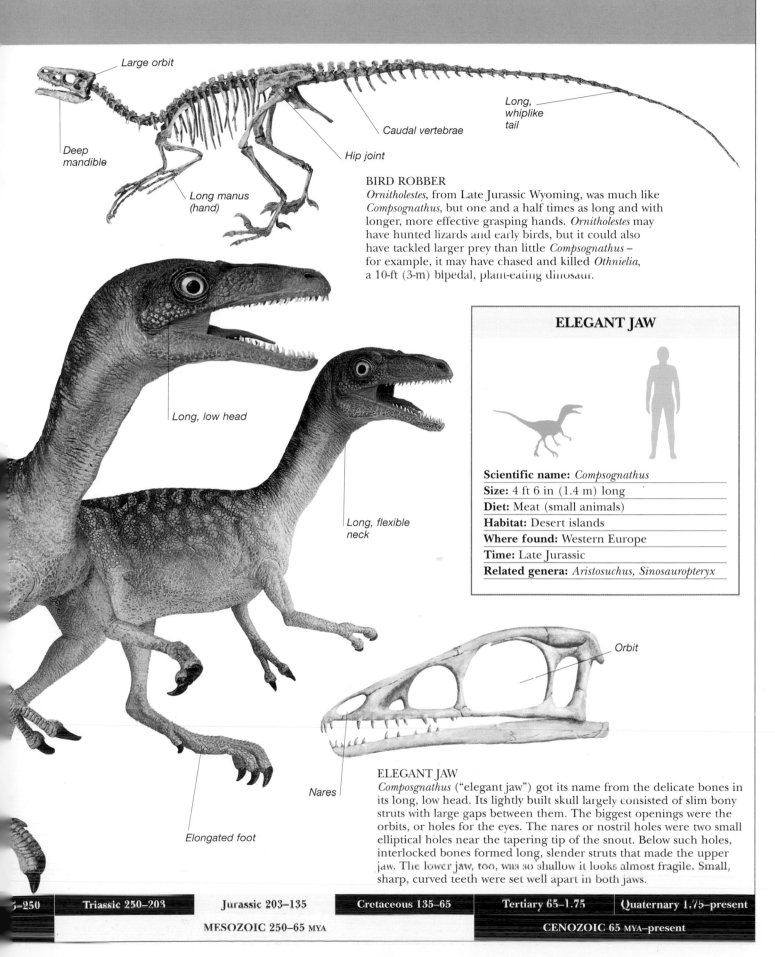

Large orbit

Long,
whiplike
tail

Caudal vertebrae

Deep
mandible

Hip joint

Long manus
(hand)

BIRD ROBBER

Ornitholestes, from Late Jurassic Wyoming, was much like
Compsognathus, but one and a half times as long and with
longer, more effective grasping hands. *Ornitholestes* may
have hunted lizards and early birds, but it could also
have tackled larger prey than little *Compsognathus* –
for example, it may have chased and killed *Othnielia*,
a 10-ft (3-m) bipedal, plant-eating dinosaur.

Long, low head

ELEGANT JAW

Scientific name: *Compsognathus*

Size: 4 ft 6 in (1.4 m) long

Diet: Meat (small animals)

Habitat: Desert islands

Where found: Western Europe

Time: Late Jurassic

Related genera: *Aristosuchus, Sinosauropteryx*

Long, flexible
neck

Orbit

Nares

Elongated foot

ELEGANT JAW

Composgnathus ("elegant jaw") got its name from the delicate bones in
its long, low head. Its lightly built skull largely consisted of slim bony
struts with large gaps between them. The biggest openings were the
orbits, or holes for the eyes. The nares or nostril holes were two small
elliptical holes near the tapering tip of the snout. Below such holes,
interlocked bones formed long, slender struts that made the upper
jaw. The lower jaw, too, was so shallow it looks almost fragile. Small,
sharp, curved teeth were set well apart in both jaws.

| 5–250 | Triassic 250–203 | Jurassic 203–135 | Cretaceous 135–65 | Tertiary 65–1.75 | Quaternary 1.75–present |

MESOZOIC 250–65 MYA · CENOZOIC 65 MYA–present

OSTRICH DINOSAURS

ORNITHOMIMID OR "BIRD MIMIC" DINOSAURS were built like flightless, long-legged birds such as ostriches. Unlike most nonbird theropods, ornithomimids evolved a birdlike beak. However, unlike modern birds, they had a long, bony tail core and arms with clawed fingers, rather than wings. Ornithomimids lived mainly in Late Cretaceous times in parts of North America, East Asia, and Europe, and probably in Africa and Australia too. Ornithomimids may have roamed open countryside, pecking at plants and maybe sometimes snapping up small animals. Large eyes helped them spot prey and watch for danger. If a tyrannosaur caught an ornithomimid by surprise, it could deliver a terrible kick with its sharp toe claws, but it was more likely to sprint away from danger.

SPECIALIZED LEGS
Scientists think ostrich dinosaurs such as *Struthiomimus* ("ostrich mimic") and *Dromiceiomimus* ("emu mimic") ran as quickly as an ostrich. All three had evolved sprinters' legs with longer shins than thighs, and long foot and toe bones. Ostriches are one of the fastest living land animals, sprinting at up to 50 mph (80 kmh). Some ornithomimids could have matched that. For short bursts perhaps one or two could run even faster.

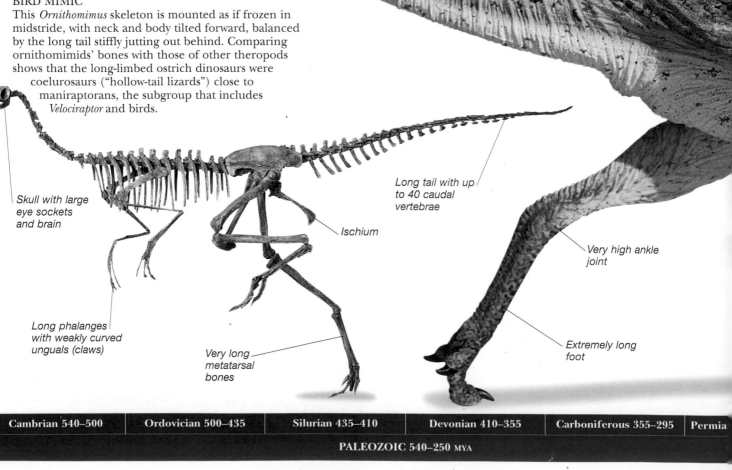

BIRD MIMIC
This *Ornithomimus* skeleton is mounted as if frozen in midstride, with neck and body tilted forward, balanced by the long tail stiffly jutting out behind. Comparing ornithomimids' bones with those of other theropods shows that the long-limbed ostrich dinosaurs were coelurosaurs ("hollow-tail lizards") close to maniraptorans, the subgroup that includes *Velociraptor* and birds.

Skull with large eye sockets and brain

Long phalanges with weakly curved unguals (claws)

Very long metatarsal bones

Ischium

Long tail with up to 40 caudal vertebrae

Very high ankle joint

Extremely long foot

Cambrian 540–500	Ordovician 500–435	Silurian 435–410	Devonian 410–355	Carboniferous 355–295	Permia

PALEOZOIC 540–250 MYA

More than 70 tiny teeth in upper jaw

About 150 tiny teeth in lower jaw

Skin throat pouch, perhaps to store food

Eyes at sides of head, giving a wide view

Toothless beak covered with a horny sheath

PELICAN MIMIC

Pelecanimimus ("pelican mimic") was an early ornithomimid from Europe. It had more, but tinier, teeth than any other known theropod (more than 200).The sharp, close-packed teeth formed long cutting edges – in later ostrich dinosaurs teeth must have become smaller still, until in time they all disappeared. Another apparent oddity was a skin throat pouch like a pelican's. *Pelecanimimus* was found near an ancient lake, so perhaps it had waded out in shallow water to catch fish. These could have been stored in its pouch before it swallowed them or took them back to a nestful of young.

Hand could have served as a hook.

CHICKEN MIMIC

Gallimimus ("chicken mimic"), the largest known ostrich dinosaur, was three times as long as a tall man. It had a small, birdlike head on a long, flexible neck, a long, narrow beak, and big eyes on the sides of its head to spot danger from almost any direction. Slender arms ended in gangly, three-fingered hands held with palms facing into the body. Their long, curved claws might have hooked leafy twigs or seized small mammals and lizards. The hindlimbs had long shin and upper foot bones, ending in three long toes tipped with sharp claws. A long, tapered tail stuck out stiffly to balance the head and neck. *Gallimimus* roamed a dry region of semi-desert, where plants were most plentiful along moist river banks.

Flexible shoulder joint

Shin longer than thigh, designed for sprinting

Toes short compared to rest of foot

Hand shorter than in most ornithomimids

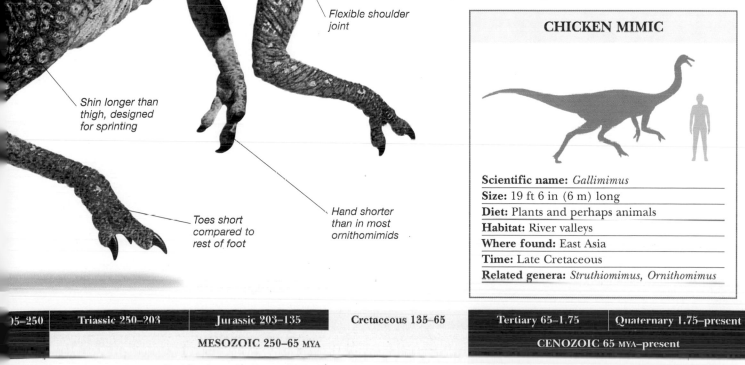

CHICKEN MIMIC

Scientific name: *Gallimimus*

Size: 19 ft 6 in (6 m) long

Diet: Plants and perhaps animals

Habitat: River valleys

Where found: East Asia

Time: Late Cretaceous

Related genera: *Struthiomimus, Ornithomimus*

05–250	Triassic 250–203	Jurassic 203–135	Cretaceous 135–65	Tertiary 65–1.75	Quaternary 1.75–present
		MESOZOIC 250–65 MYA		CENOZOIC 65 MYA–present	

TYRANNOSAURIDS

THE TYRANNOSAURIDS OR "TYRANT LIZARDS" were the fiercest predators in western North America and Asia 65 million years ago. Among the largest and most terrifying of all meat-eating dinosaurs, they first appeared about 80 million years ago, and were among the last dinosaurs to become extinct. Surprisingly, their closest relatives seem to have been the lightly built dinosaurs that gave rise to birds. Despite this, tyrannosaurids evolved to immense size – an adult *Tyrannosaurus* could grow longer than the width of a tennis court, as heavy as an elephant, and tall enough to look into a first-story window. Massive legs bore its weight on three large, birdlike clawed toes. Tyrannosaurid arms were absurdly short, but were also strong, ending in fearsome two-clawed hands. However, their chief weapons were awesome jaws, armed with huge fangs able to deliver a bite as powerful as an alligator's.

Immensely powerful thigh muscles

Elongated upper part of foot

Each foot supported a load half as heavy as an elephant.

BONY SCAFFOLDING

Compared to most other theropods, tyrannosaurids had larger skulls, more powerful jaws, stouter teeth, a thicker neck, a shorter body, and very tiny arms. The skull was nearly half as long as the backbone between hips and head – the thick neck must have had extremely strong muscles to support and move its weight. Arms were typically no longer than a man's, but very muscular. All this suggests tyrannosaurids were predators designed around their bone-crunching, flesh-shredding mouths. Recently discovered skeletons have included the largest *Tyrannosaurus* specimens ever discovered. These have sparked controversy about whether tyrannosaurids showed sexual differences – perhaps with females larger than males.

**Skeleton of
Tyrannosaurus rex**

Ungual (bone sheathed with a horny claw)

Paired rockerlike pubic bones

Birdlike leg bones might imply the ability to run.

Middle metatarsal narrows to a splint.

Stable ankle for walking on rough ground

THE TYRANT'S SKULL

A short, deep snout helped give *Tyrannosaurus*'s great skull a boxlike shape when seen from the side. Big holes between the bones helped to reduce its weight. The immensely powerful jaws – big enough to swallow a human whole – were curved, so that as they closed, their great fangs all met at once. The teeth themselves had sawlike edges at the back and front, leaving distinctive puncture marks in the bones of prey such as the horned dinosaur *Triceratops*. Eye holes and the tell-tale shape of its brain-case reveal that *Tyrannosaurus* had big eyes and a well-developed sense of smell.

Thick teeth, almost as wide as long

| Cambrian 540–500 | Ordovician 500–435 | Silurian 435–410 | Devonian 410–355 | Carboniferous 355–295 | Permia |

PALEOZOIC 540–250 MYA

Massive head with
rigidly joined bones
for a strong bite

The lower jaw's
bones showed
some flexibility.

Thick, muscular neck
supported by short,
wide vertebrae

ON THE HUNT

Tyrannosaurus rex ("king of the tyrant lizards") walked
heavily on its great hind limbs, with head jutting forward,
and a level back and tail. It probably trailed after herds of
horned and duck-billed dinosaurs browsing through woods
and flowery, ferny glades. *Tyrannosaurus rex* would have
eaten large meaty dinosaurs it found already dead, but also
attacked any individual too sick, old, or young to keep up with
the rest. Some scientists believe it sprinted after prey, while
others think it could only manage a fast walk. *Tyrannosaurus rex*
would have moved in for the kill with gaping jaws. Seizing
small dinosaurs in its mouth it could have shaken them to
death. Biting a mighty mouthful of flesh from a larger victim,
it could have hooked its finger claws into the creature's hide to
hold the body still. When its prey collapsed from loss of blood,
Tyrannosaurus rex would use one great clawed foot to hold the
creature down, grip its neck or flank between its teeth, then
jerk its head back, tearing out colossal chunks of meat.

Two-fingered
hand on a small
but sturdy arm

Ankle joint
with bones
forming a
simple hinge.

Only the toes
touched the
ground.

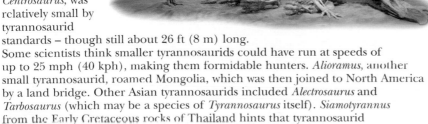

ALBERTA LIZARD
Albertosaurus, shown
here above a felled
Centrosaurus, was
relatively small by
tyrannosaurid
standards – though still about 26 ft (8 m) long.
Some scientists think smaller tyrannosaurids could have run at speeds of
up to 25 mph (40 kph), making them formidable hunters. *Alioramus*, another
small tyrannosaurid, roamed Mongolia, which was then joined to North America
by a land bridge. Other Asian tyrannosaurids included *Alectrosaurus* and
Tarbosaurus (which may be a species of *Tyrannosaurus* itself). *Siamotyrannus*
from the Early Cretaceous rocks of Thailand hints that tyrannosaurid
ancestors probably first arose in Asia, about 120 million years ago.

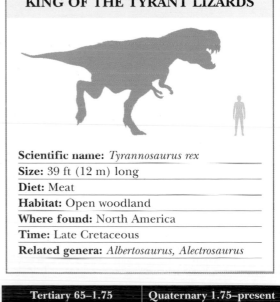

KING OF THE TYRANT LIZARDS

Scientific name:	*Tyrannosaurus rex*
Size:	39 ft (12 m) long
Diet:	Meat
Habitat:	Open woodland
Where found:	North America
Time:	Late Cretaceous
Related genera:	*Albertosaurus*, *Alectrosaurus*

95–250	Triassic 250–203	Jurassic 203–135	Cretaceous 135–65	Tertiary 65–1.75	Quaternary 1.75–present
		MESOZOIC 250–65 MYA		CENOZOIC 65 MYA–present	

SCYTHE LIZARDS

THERIZINOSAURS ("SCYTHE LIZARDS") were the oddest of all known dinosaurs. For many years, scientists had to guess what they looked like from scraps of fossils that included four-toed feet like a prosauropod's and scythe-shaped claws. Paleontologists named the mysterious owner of the giant claws *Therizinosaurus*. In 1988, more complete skeletons of an earlier relative, *Alxasaurus*, turned up in China. Comparison of this therizinosaur's bones with previous finds enabled scientists to picture "scythe lizards" as large, slow-moving, bipedal creatures. The biggest resembled bizarre, extinct, hoofed mammals called chalicotheres. Therizinosaurs' wrist and toe bones show they were "stiff-tailed" theropods related to *Oviraptor*. Therizinosaurs lived in East Asia and North America. Most kinds lived in Cretaceous times, but a therizinosaur has been reported from the Early Jurassic.

Small head supported by a long neck

Socket where the claw joined its finger bone

Therizinosaur claw fossil

HOW SCYTHE LIZARDS LIVED

Therizinosaurus seems to have been built for the kind of life led by gorillas or by large, extinct mammals such as giant ground sloths and chalicotheres. It ambled around on its long hind limbs, sometimes propping up the forepart of its body on its finger claws. Sitting on its haunches, supported by its tail, *Therizinosaurus* could have craned its long, straight neck to crop trees with its toothless beak and stretched its hands to claw more leafy twigs toward its mouth.

UNUSUAL CLAWS
The first digit claw on *Therizinosaurus*'s hand grew longer than a man's arm, but the other two claws were shorter. All three claws resembled scythe blades, being gently curved, flat-sided, and tapering to a narrow point. The claws were so long that *Therizinosaurus* might have walked upon its knuckles when on all fours. Its huge claws still puzzle scientists. Compared to a dromaeosaurid's talons, *Therizinosaurus*'s claws appear unsuited to aggression. If not used in courtship or for raking plants, they might have been used to rip open termites' nests.

The first digit's claw tended to be the longest.

Cambrian 540–500	Ordovician 500–435	Silurian 435–410	Devonian 410–355	Carboniferous 355–295	Permia

PALEOZOIC 540–250 MYA

SCYTHE LIZARD

Therizinosaurus was one of the last and most awkwardly built of all therizinosaurs. Paleontologists Dale and Donald Russell reinvented *Therizinosaurus*'s appearance by matching its incomplete bones with the known bones of other therizinosaurs. They borrowed its small head from *Erlikosaurus*, based its lower jaw's length on *Segnosaurus*, and made its jaws toothless. Its long neck, back, and broad hips were based on *Nanshiungosaurus*.

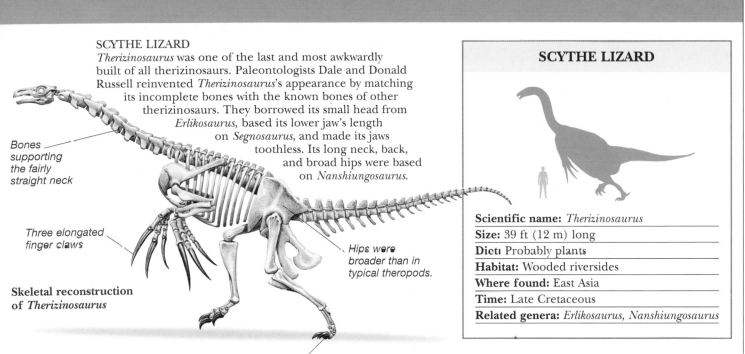

Bones supporting the fairly straight neck

Three elongated finger claws

Skeletal reconstruction of *Therizinosaurus*

Hips were broader than in typical theropods.

Short, broad, four-toed foot

Broad body containing a large digestive system

Three stampeding Beipiaosaurus *alarm small birds and feathered dinosaurs.*

SCYTHE LIZARD

Scientific name:	*Therizinosaurus*
Size:	39 ft (12 m) long
Diet:	Probably plants
Habitat:	Wooded riversides
Where found:	East Asia
Time:	Late Cretaceous
Related genera:	*Erlikosaurus, Nanshiungosaurus*

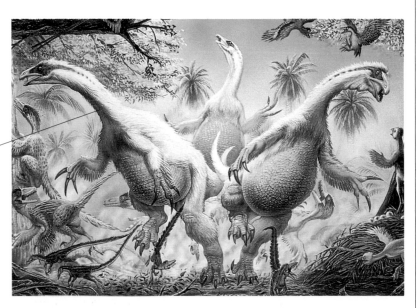

BEIPIAO LIZARD

Beipiaosaurus was named after Beipiao, the Chinese city near to where its fossils were discovered in 1996. As long as a tall man, but more heavily built, *Beipiaosaurus* lived more than 120 million years ago, making it older than other "scythe lizards." It was also less highly evolved. Its body had a sizable head with lower tooth crowns, hands longer than thighs, three-toed feet, and long shins. The most exciting discovery was that fine feathery filaments had covered its arms, legs, and maybe the rest of its body. This find strengthened the evidence that many theropods were not scaly, but covered in long down that resembled an emu's hairlike feathers.

5–250	Triassic 250–203	Jurassic 203–135	Cretaceous 135–65	Tertiary 65–1.75	Quaternary 1.75–present

MESOZOIC 250–65 MYA   CENOZOIC 65 MYA–present

CRETACEOUS CONFLICT

Rearing in intimidating poses, a group of therizinosaurs confronts a hungry *Tarbosaurus* in the riverside forests of Cretaceous Asia. *Therizinosaurus*'s claws were unsuitable for tearing flesh, despite their great length, so it may have used its large size to frighten attackers. Although it was the smaller dinosaur, *Tarbosaurus* could mount a vicious attack. The tyrannosaur preyed upon other dinosaurs, as well as therizinosaurs.

Cambrian 540–500	Ordovician 500–435	Silurian 435–410	Devonian 410–355	Carboniferous 355–295	Permia

PALEOZOIC 540–250 MYA

EGG THIEVES

OVIRAPTOR ("EGG THIEF") was a long-legged theropod with large eyes, a toothless beak, and a bony tail. *Oviraptor* and its close relatives seem to have been the dinosaurs most closely related to birds. The scientist who described *Oviraptor* in 1924 believed he had found one that was killed while stealing the eggs of the horned plant-eater *Protoceratops*. He named his find *Oviraptor philoceratops* ("egg thief, fond of horned dinosaurs"). In the 1990s, however, more *Oviraptor* dinosaurs were found with similar eggs. In one of these eggs lay the tiny bones of an *Oviraptor* embryo. Far from stealing other dinosaurs' eggs, the adults had died protecting their own, in the way ground-nesting birds do today. *Oviraptor* lived about 80 million years ago in what is now the Gobi Desert of Mongolia and China.

DESERT DISASTER
Fossil bones and eggs show where an oviraptorid died guarding a nest of 22 long eggs, laid in a circle. This nest lay on sandy ground, probably at the edge of a desert oasis. To protect the eggs from a rare desert downpour, the parent had seemingly spread its clawed arms over the nest as a bird might spread its wings. Suddenly, a rain-drenched dune slid down over the nest, and buried the dinosaur and its eggs beneath a sandy avalanche.

Fossils of an oviraptorid nesting with eggs

DEVOTED MOTHERS

This lifelike model shows an *Oviraptor* mother settling down to brood her clutch of eggs. The nest is a sandy mound with a hollow scooped out in the middle. Inside, she has laid in a circle more than 18 long eggs. Crouching low, the big, birdlike creature uses her own body heat to keep her eggs warm at night. By day, the soft, downy feathers that cover her body and arms shield her eggs from the Sun's fierce heat, and from sand blown about by strong winds. If another dinosaur tries to steal her eggs, she might scratch it with her sharp finger claws or, like an ostrich, deliver a terrible kick.

Hard-shelled eggs, like a bird's

Oviraptorid embryo in egg

EMBRYO
Tiny bones still cradled by fragments of eggshell reveal the remains of an oviraptorid embryo in an egg laid 80 million years ago. The unhatched dinosaur lay curled up in an egg no more than 3 in (7 cm) across. Had it hatched, the baby would have grown to be 6 ft 6 in (2 m) long. Finds of dinosaur embryos are rare because their bones were often too fragile to be preserved.

Cambrian 540–500	Ordovician 500–435	Silurian 435–410	Devonian 410–355	Carboniferous 355–295	Permia

PALEOZOIC 540–250 MYA

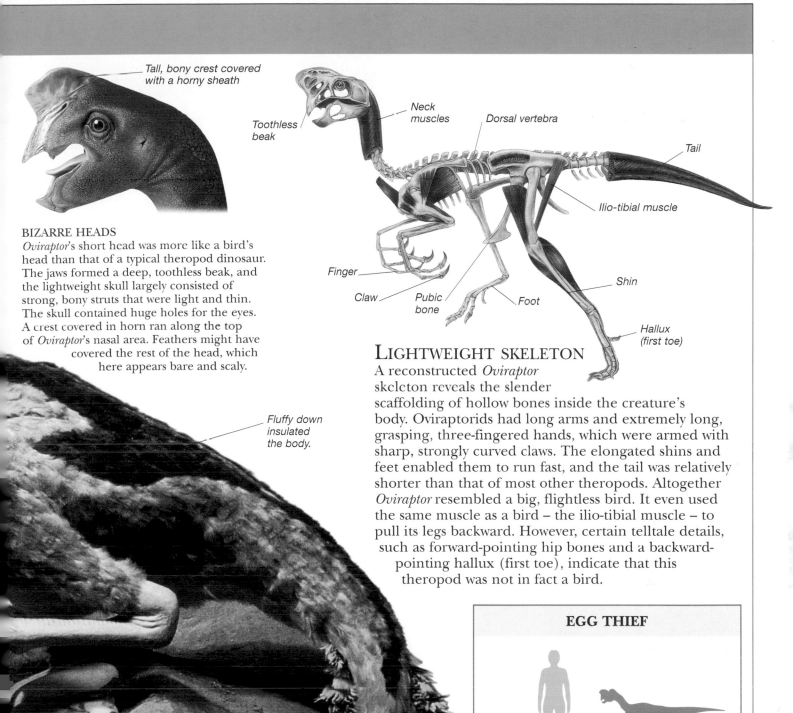

Tall, bony crest covered with a horny sheath

Toothless beak

Neck muscles

Dorsal vertebra

Tail

Ilio-tibial muscle

Finger

Claw

Pubic bone

Foot

Shin

Hallux (first toe)

Fluffy down insulated the body.

BIZARRE HEADS

Oviraptor's short head was more like a bird's head than that of a typical theropod dinosaur. The jaws formed a deep, toothless beak, and the lightweight skull largely consisted of strong, bony struts that were light and thin. The skull contained huge holes for the eyes. A crest covered in horn ran along the top of *Oviraptor*'s nasal area. Feathers might have covered the rest of the head, which here appears bare and scaly.

LIGHTWEIGHT SKELETON

A reconstructed *Oviraptor* skeleton reveals the slender scaffolding of hollow bones inside the creature's body. Oviraptorids had long arms and extremely long, grasping, three-fingered hands, which were armed with sharp, strongly curved claws. The elongated shins and feet enabled them to run fast, and the tail was relatively shorter than that of most other theropods. Altogether *Oviraptor* resembled a big, flightless bird. It even used the same muscle as a bird – the ilio-tibial muscle – to pull its legs backward. However, certain telltale details, such as forward-pointing hip bones and a backward-pointing hallux (first toe), indicate that this theropod was not in fact a bird.

EGG THIEF

Scientific name: *Oviraptor*

Size: 6 ft 6 in (2 m) long

Diet: Uncertain

Habitat: Semi-desert

Where found: Central Asia

Time: Late Cretaceous

Related genera: *Conchoraptor, Ingenia*

95–250	Triassic 250–203	Jurassic 203–135	Cretaceous 135–65	Tertiary 65–1.75	Quaternary 1.75–present

MESOZOIC 250–65 MYA

CENOZOIC 65 MYA–present

TAIL FEATHER

OF ALL CHINA'S AMAZING NON-BIRD dinosaurs and birds, none has proven more astonishing than *Caudipteryx* ("tail feather"). This long-legged, turkey-sized creature seems a mixture of both kinds of animal, with a birdlike beak, feathers, and short tail, but teeth and bones that proclaim it a non-bird theropod dinosaur. *Caudipteryx* lived in Early Cretaceous times, not long after the first known bird. Scientists have suggested it might have been either a strange theropod dinosaur, a theropod dinosaur with ancestors that flew, or a bird that evolved from birds that had lost the power to fly. It is most probable that *Caudipteryx* was a dinosaur, and the maniraptoran ("grasping hand") and oviraptorid dinosaurs were its nearest relatives.

UNUSUAL BODY

Caudipteryx had a short head and a beak with sharp, buck teeth in the front upper jaw. From its lightly built body sprouted shorter arms than those of most advanced theropods, although there were long, three-fingered hands that ended in short claws. Long legs and birdlike toes indicate that this dinosaur was a fast runner. *Caudipteryx*'s bony tail was among the shortest of all known dinosaur's, and most of the animal was covered in some type of feathering.

Caudipteryx *had wing feathers that were symmetrical in shape, like this wild turkey feather.*

Down feather

Wing feather

FEATHER FUNCTION
Feathers of different kinds covered most of *Caudipteryx*. Short down provided insulation, and implied that *Caudipteryx* was warm-blooded. Feathers with 8-in (20-cm) long quill shafts sprouted from its arms, fingers, and tail, but *Caudipteryx* could not fly. Its wing feathers were symmetrical, whereas the wing feathers found in birds that can fly are asymmetrical. *Caudipteryx*'s feathers might have been brightly colored and used for mating display.

Cambrian 540–500	Ordovician 500–435	Silurian 435–410	Devonian 410–355	Carboniferous 355–295	Permia

PALEOZOIC 540–250 MYA

PUZZLING RELATIONSHIPS

Scientists stressing *Caudipteryx*'s birdlike nature have claimed it had a reversed "big" toe, and used muscles like a bird's to pull back its legs as it walked. Other scientists believe both suppositions are unproved, and stress details indicating that this was a non-bird dinosaur. For instance, the pubic hip bones pointed forward, while the beak, tail bones, and other hip bones hint that *Caudipteryx* was closely related to the dinosaur *Oviraptor*.

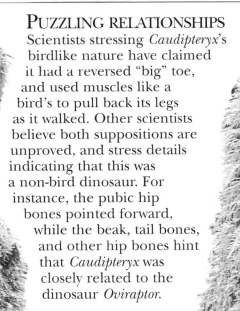

TAIL FEATHER

Scientific name: *Caudipteryx*
Size: 2 ft 4 in (70 cm) tall
Diet: Plants and possibly animals
Habitat: Woodland
Where found: East Asia
Time: Early Cretaceous
Related genus: Possibly *Oviraptor*

05 250	Triassic 250–203	Jurassic 203–135	Cretaceous 135–65	Tertiary 65–1.75	Quaternary 1.75–present

MESOZOIC 250–65 MYA — **CENOZOIC 65 MYA–present**

TERRIBLE CLAWS

DEINONYCHUS ("TERRIBLE CLAW") and other dromaeosaurids ("running lizards") were small, aggressive, hunting dinosaurs. Few theropods matched their intelligence, and none brandished such a terrifying combination of weapons. The jaws of dromaeosaurids bristled with big, curved, bladelike fangs, their three-fingered hands bore hooked claws, and curved claws sprouted from their long, birdlike toes. The huge switchblade claws on their second toes were twice as long as any of their other claws. Dromaeosaurids ranged from about 6 ft 6 in (2 m) to 20 ft (6 m) in length. They probably evolved during the Jurassic period, although their known fossils date from Cretaceous times. Dromaeosaurids spread through northern continents after these separated from the southern supercontinent Gondwana.

Skull deeper and more strongly built than that of Velociraptor.

One of a number of skeletons of Deinonychus found in Montana and Wyoming.

Large claw swung down to deliver slashing attacks.

CAMOUFLAGE
No one knows what colors dromaeosaurids might have been. Most likely their scaly or feathered skins were tinted or patterned in ways that made their bodies blend in with their surroundings. If *Deinonychus* lived in woodland, stripes or spots on its skin would have helped to conceal it in the dappled light beneath the trees. Its camouflage would have made it less visible to its prey.

Skin is striped like that of a living tiger.

Striped *Deinonychus*

TERRIBLE CLAW
Mounted as if leaping in for the kill, this *Deinonychus* skeleton shows some of the key anatomical features that made dromaeosaurids so feared. Its jaws gape to bare wicked-looking rows of fangs. The gangly arms unfold like a bird's wings and stretch out to hook their curved claws into a victim's scaly hide. The switchblade toe claws could rise, ready to flick forward and disembowel prey. Bony rods sprouted forward from the tail bones to overlap the bones in front and form a bundle that stiffened the tail. The leaping dinosaur would swing its tail around to help it keep its balance. The tail acted as a flexible rod, darting in all directions as the dinosaur moved.

Cambrian 540–500	Ordovician 500–435	Silurian 435–410	Devonian 410–355	Carboniferous 355–295	Permia

PALEOZOIC 540–250 MYA

FEATHERED VELOCIRAPTOR

Velociraptor ("quick robber"), a dromaeosaurid the length of a tall man, appears below as a model covered with feathers, not scales. Fine, hair-like strands protect its body from heat and cold, and long, showy feathers sprout from its head and arms. Since 1996, fossil feathers like these have turned up in China with superbly preserved small theropods including the dromaeosaurids *Sinornithosaurus* ("Chinese bird lizard") and *Microraptor* ("tiny robber"). Working with Chinese scientists in 2001, Mark Norell of the American Museum of Natural History revealed yet more evidence that all such theropods closely related to birds had feathers not scales. No feathers have been found with *Deinonychus* or *Velociraptor*, but as fossilized feathers survive only in fine-grained rocks they could well have had feathers too.

This *Velociraptor's* sharp claws and agility failed to save its life.

DUEL TO THE DEATH

Two tangled fossils found in the Mongolian desert were a *Velociraptor* and a *Protoceratops* that died while fighting. This scene shows that even an aggressive theropod ran risks when it fought a well-defended plant-eater. The lithe hunter *Velociraptor* had grasped the plant-eater's snout while delivering kicks to its throat. The *Protoceratops* had gripped its attacker's arm in its strong beak. Suddenly, sand loosened from a dune by wind or rain smothered both of them.

Hairlike feathery filaments probably insulated the body.

Each hand had three, long, narrow fingers with sharp claws.

TERRIBLE CLAW

Scientific name: *Deinonychus*

Size: 10 ft (3 m)

Diet: Meat

Habitat: Open woodland

Where found: North America

Time: Early Cretaceous

Related genera: *Dromaeosaurus, Velociraptor*

Tail stiffened by bony struts except at its base, just behind the hips.

Velociraptor had to keep its great second-toe claw raised when it walked.

)5–250	Triassic 250–203	Jurassic 203–135	Cretaceous 135–65	Tertiary 65–1.75	Quaternary 1.75–present
		MESOZOIC 250–65 MYA		CENOZOIC 65 MYA–present	

ROAD RUNNERS

CRETACEOUS LANDS TEEMED WITH small, hunting dinosaurs designed, like prehistoric roadrunners (swift, ground-dwelling birds), for dashing around and seizing small, backboned animals. Many of these small-game hunters belonged to the maniraptoran ("seizing hands") dinosaurs – the theropod group to which birds belong. Their long, clawed hands stretched out to seize prey, then pulled in and back, much as a bird's wings flap. Like birds, some maniraptorans had feathers. Traces of feathering survive in the well-preserved fossils of *Caudipteryx* ("tail feather") and *Sinornithosaurus* ("Chinese bird lizard") from China. Feathers or down very likely also covered the North American theropods *Bambiraptor* and *Troodon*.

Troodon *might have had vertical pupils that helped it hunt at night.*

Head of *Troodon*

SMART DINOSAUR
With a large brain for the size of its body, *Troodon* was one of the most intelligent dinosaurs. *Troodon*'s eyes could focus on objects directly in front of it, which helped *Troodon* to judge when a victim came within range. *Troodon* may well have hunted at dusk, as its big eyes very likely saw clearly in dim light.

WOUNDING TOOTH
Named for its curved, saw-edged teeth, *Troodon* was a big-brained, long-legged hunter that was the length of a tall human. It flourished in western North America about 70 million years ago. Like *Velociraptor*, *Troodon* was built on slim, birdlike lines, and had a switchbladelike second toe claw that it held clear of the ground as it walked. Unlike *Velociraptor*, however, *Troodon*'s big toe claw was too small to allow it to tackle large game. *Troodon* might have killed baby dinosaurs, but its main prey were birds, lizards, snakes, and small mammals.

Troodontids' hip bone shapes are partly guesswork, but the pubic bones jutted forward, not back, as in more birdlike theropods.

Flattened chevrons, stiffening the tail

Ischium

Long, slim tibia

Long, slender arms bearing three-fingered hands with sharply curved claws

Gastralia (belly ribs)

Close-fitting metatarsal bones

Small, raised "switchblade" second toe claw

| Cambrian 540–500 | Ordovician 500–435 | Silurian 435–410 | Devonian 410–355 | Carboniferous 355–295 | Perm |

PALEOZOIC 540–250 MYA

A rather deep snout and large teeth were among Bambiraptor's least birdlike features.

A wrist joint like a bird's allowed it to fold its hands as a bird folds its wings.

BAMBI RAIDER

Discovered in 1994 in Montana, the 75-million-year-old skeleton of *Bambiraptor* is one of the most complete and birdlike of any non-avian North American dinosaur. The 3-ft 3-in (1-m) long individual was not yet fully grown. An agile runner, with shins long like a bird's, *Bambiraptor* had large eye sockets, and a bigger brain for the size of its body than any other known dinosaur. Some of its bones contained air sacs linked to the lungs, as in a bird. They supplied extra oxygen for a creature that was likely very active. *Bambiraptor* was probably warm-blooded, with downy feathering that helped to conserve body heat.

Bambiraptor skeleton

WOUNDING TOOTH

Scientific name:	*Troodon*
Size:	6 ft 6 in (2 m) long
Diet:	Meat
Habitat:	Open woodland
Where found:	North America
Time:	Late Cretaceous
Related genera:	*Byronosaurus, Saurornithoides*

Forward-facing eyes

Its wishbone and shoulders helped it to swing its long arms out to grab.

BAMBIRAPTOR IN ACTION

Bambiraptor was an agile hunter of small game. Stepping watchfully through the undergrowth, it was ready to leap into action if a frog jumped or a mammal moved. The theropod strode rapidly after its intended victim. If its prey suddenly darted away, *Bambiraptor* followed swiftly, keeping its balance by shifting its stiffened tail from side to side. The hunter probably ended most chases by grabbing its prey in its hands and delivering a fatal bite.

Half-moon-shaped wrist bones made possible a grabbing action, like the flight stroke of a bird.

TROODON SKELETON

Arms outstretched, as if running to attack a victim, this mounted skeleton gives a good idea of *Troodon* as an active, agile hunter. The maniraptoran's long, low skull housed a brain as big as an emu's, and its jaws bore about 120 of the small, sharp, cutting teeth that earned this troodontid dinosaur its name. This theropod's basket of gastralia, or "belly ribs," perhaps acted in a similar way to a diaphragm, which helps the lungs to work.

Slashing kicks from the long claw on each foot could disembowel larger prey.

250	Triassic 250–203	Jurassic 203–135	Cretaceous 135–65	Tertiary 65–1.75	Quaternary 1.75–present
		MESOZOIC 250–65 MYA		CENOZOIC 65 MYA–present	

BIRDS CLADOGRAM

SEVERAL FEATURES ALLOW BIRDS TO BE distinguished from their closest relatives, the dromaeosaurid dinosaurs, and allow *Archaeopteryx* – the earliest known bird – to be included in the birds cladogram. Skeletal details such as a reduced tail and distinctive feet set birds apart from other animals. Although all birds possess feathers, these are not a unique feature of birds, as feathers are also present in non-avian theropod dinosaurs, such as *Caudipteryx*. Birds more advanced than *Archaeopteryx* originated around the Jurassic-Cretaceous boundary. Their tail, hand, and chest bones were much like those of modern birds.

Iberomesornis, *from Early Cretaceous Spain, was the earliest member of the Ornithothoraces.*

Confuciusornis was *a jay-sized bird from Early Cretaceous China.*

CONFUCIUSORNITHIDS

ENANTIORNITHINES

ARCHAEOPTERYX

ORNITHOTHORACES
Alula

Pygostyle

Pygostyle

AVES
Shortened tail

Skeleton of Early Cretaceous bird

ALULA
Ornithothoracines are united by the alula – a feather that helps direct air over the upper surface of the main wing. Enantiornithines were a Cretaceous radiation of the Ornithothoraces.

Alula

SHORTENED TAIL
A tail with less than 25 vertebrae sets birds apart from other maniraptorans. This feature reflects a need to lighten the skeleton. The long tail of *Archaeopteryx* would have made it quite a clumsy flier.

Tail

PYGOSTYLE
Birds more advanced than *Archaeopteryx* have their last five tail vertebrae further reduced and fused into a plate of bone called the pygostyle. These birds include confuciusornithids and the Ornithothoraces.

Heron wing

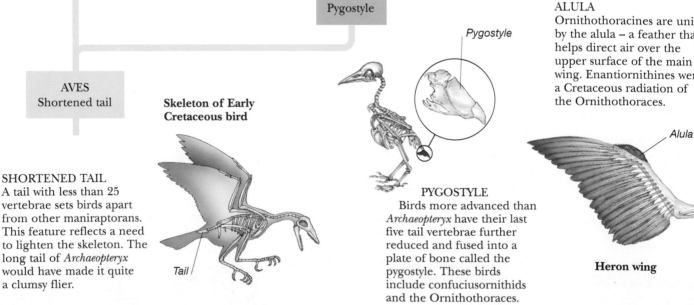

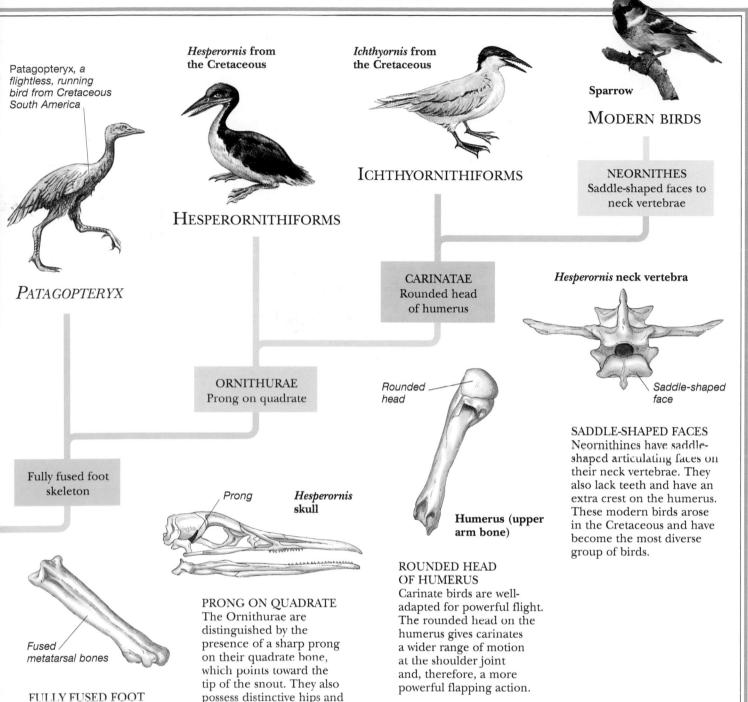

Patagopteryx, a flightless, running bird from Cretaceous South America

Hesperornis from the Cretaceous

Ichthyornis from the Cretaceous

Sparrow

MODERN BIRDS

ICHTHYORNITHIFORMS

NEORNITHES
Saddle-shaped faces to neck vertebrae

HESPERORNITHIFORMS

PATAGOPTERYX

Hesperornis neck vertebra

CARINATAE
Rounded head of humerus

ORNITHURAE
Prong on quadrate

Rounded head

Saddle-shaped face

Fully fused foot skeleton

Prong   *Hesperornis* **skull**

Humerus (upper arm bone)

SADDLE-SHAPED FACES
Neornithines have saddle-shaped articulating faces on their neck vertebrae. They also lack teeth and have an extra crest on the humerus. These modern birds arose in the Cretaceous and have become the most diverse group of birds.

Fused metatarsal bones

ROUNDED HEAD OF HUMERUS
Carinate birds are well-adapted for powerful flight. The rounded head on the humerus gives carinates a wider range of motion at the shoulder joint and, therefore, a more powerful flapping action.

FULLY FUSED FOOT
In the ornithurines and *Patagopteryx*, the elongate foot bones called the metatarsals are completely fused to form a structure called the tarsometatarsus. These bones were not completely fused together in earlier birds.

PRONG ON QUADRATE
The Ornithurae are distinguished by the presence of a sharp prong on their quadrate bone, which points toward the tip of the snout. They also possess distinctive hips and a shortened back that has less than 11 vertebrae.

BIRD EVOLUTION
Whether flight in birds originated from running or climbing dinosaurs remains the subject of argument. Primitive birds possess features associated with flight, but some may have lived on the ground. Trends such as the loss of serrations on the teeth and the shortening of the tail reflect a move toward a lighter skeleton and more agile flying abilities. The evolution of the alula allowed birds to become even better fliers. Later birds evolved stronger wing and chest bones, and more flexible necks. Teeth were retained in birds until the Neornithes.

ARCHAEOPTERYX

THE OLDEST KNOWN BIRD is *Archaeopteryx* ("ancient wing"). About 150 million years ago, this crow-sized creature walked and fluttered on tropical desert islands, now part of southwest Germany. Feathers sprouted from its arms and hands, its tail was long and feathered, and its big toes pointed backward, much like a perching bird's. Yet the creature's sharp teeth, clawed hands, bony tail core, and many other features resemble a small carnivorous dinosaur's. Indeed two of the seven fossil skeletons found between 1855 and 1992 were at first misidentified as a small theropod that shared the same islands. The number of similarities between small theropods and *Archaeopteryx* convince most paleontologists that birds are simply a kind of dinosaur that learned to fly.

Slender snout had small, sharp teeth curving back.

Horn-tipped claws on front of wings

Each long flight feather had an asymmetrical shaft.

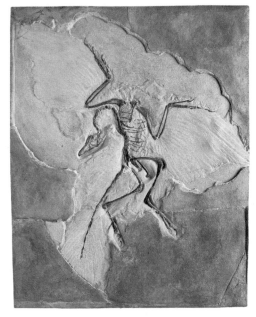

FEATHER PRESERVATION
Fine-grained Bavarian limestone preserves the delicate feather impressions of this *Archaeopteryx*. Feathers probably evolved in theropods from fuzzy down that helped keep the body warm, and the first long feathers may have been for show. But *Archaeopteryx*'s primary feathers were made for flight – each had a shaft closer to one edge than the other, as in flying birds today. Only such asymmetrical feathers are capable of flight. Long legs would have helped the bird to leap off the ground, and arms and wrists were adapted for flapping.

ARCHAEOPTERYX RECONSTRUCTED
Archaeopteryx's skeleton hints at key features inherited from increasingly advanced types of theropods. Between them these gave the first bird a mobile head, sharp curved teeth, a long, slim neck, shortened body, and a stiffened tail. Other similarities included hollow bones, long, folding arms, three weight-bearing toes per foot, and long, grasping three-fingered hands with swiveling wrists. Even the wishbone and feathers were inherited from nonbird theropod ancestors. In dinosaur terms, *Archaeopteryx* appears to be a maniraptoran related to dromaeosaurids, a group of theropods that included *Velociraptor*.

Abdominal ribs as in reptiles but not in modern birds

Half-moon-shaped wrist bone fanning the hand for flight stroke

Cambrian 540–500	Ordovician 500–435	Silurian 435–410	Devonian 410–355	Carboniferous 355–295	Perm

PALEOZOIC 540–250 MYA

TREES DOWN OR GROUND UP?

Perched on a branch, this reconstruction of *Archaeopteryx* shows one way in which early birds might have taken to the air. Some scientists suppose it used its claws to climb up trees, then fluttered weakly back to the ground. Yet the desert islands where *Archaeopteryx* lived had no tall trees. Instead, perhaps it ran after flying insects, leaped to catch them in mid air, then stayed aloft by flapping its wings. The downstroke movement probably evolved from the way its ancestors stretched out their hands to grab at prey, but took on a new role when coupled with feathers. Fluttering down or leaping in the air, *Archaeopteryx* could not have flown far or fast – its breastbone was too small to anchor strong flight muscles.

Feathers sprouted
from a bony tail
core like that of
most dinosaurs.

Horny claws
helped to grasp
branches.

Tail feathers
helped the bird
keep its balance
during flight.

Tail core of 23 bones
– fewer than in almost
all nonflying dinosaurs –
reduced the bird's weight.

Fully reversed
hallux (big toe),
as in all birds

STRANGE CLAWS

The young of a strange South American bird, called the hoatzin, are born with claws on the leading edge of each wing, much like those of *Archaeopteryx*. If a snake scares them out of their nest, they leap out and fall to the ground, then claw their way back up the tree using their fingers, toes, and beak. Some scientists believe *Archaeopteryx* used the horny tips of its fingers in a similar way, slowly hauling itself up trees until it gained enough height to launch itself. Hoatzins may be among the most primitive modern birds, with no close living relatives, but they are still far more advanced than *Archaeopteryx*.

ANCIENT WING

Scientific name:	*Archaeopteryx*
Size:	2 ft (60 cm) long
Diet:	Small animals
Habitat:	Tropical desert islands
Where found:	Western Europe
Time:	Late Jurassic
Related genus:	Perhaps *Rahonavis*

5–250	Triassic 250–20?	Jurassic 203–135	Cretaceous 135–65	ertiary 65–1.7?	Quaternary 1.75–present
		MESOZOIC 250–65 MYA		CENOZOIC 65 MYA–present	

EARLY BIRDS

FOR MORE THAN A CENTURY after the discovery of *Archaeopteryx*, no one knew how such bony tailed, toothy, claw-fingered, weak-winged "bird dinosaurs" evolved into today's beaked, toothless, effortless flyers. Since 1990, though, new finds of early fossil birds from Spain, China, and elsewhere have helped solve this puzzle. The first of these birds lived in Early Cretaceous times, millions of years after Late Jurassic *Archaeopteryx*. Cretaceous birds show step-by-step changes that transformed the first clumsy flappers into masters of the air. Yet among these new fossil finds are strange birds that branched off, forming once-successful lines that petered out, leaving no descendants, including the extremely varied enantiornithines ("opposite birds"). Both of these groups died out in the Late Cretaceous, about 5 million years before the Age of Dinosaurs ended.

CRETACEOUS BIRD RELATIVES

Late Cretaceous alvarezsaurids, such as *Shuvuuia*, were long-legged, feathered, flightless, and had tiny teeth in their beaks. Their ridged breastbones seem designed to anchor flight muscles, and their wrist and hand bones are fused together, as if to form a strong support for flight feathers. These features at first led to them being identified as a group of primitive flightless birds, but they have now been reclassified as close relatives of real birds. Their forelimbs were absurdly short and each ended in a single massive finger with a powerful claw. Some scientists suggest that they used their claws to open termite nests and feast upon the grubs inside.

Legs set far back made walking difficult.

Elongated body with long, narrow hip bones

Cervical vertebrae supporting very long neck

Splintlike bones bore tiny wings incapable of flight.

Long, sharp, narrow beak, with little teeth

Two long, showy tail feathers present on males.

EARLY SEABIRDS

Hesperornis was an enormous, long-necked seabird up to 6 ft (1.8 m) long, which hunted fish in the shallow seas covering Late Cretaceous Kansas. It had a big head and long beak armed with small, pointed teeth. Unlike many other seabirds of the time, *Hesperornis* had lost the ability to fly, and its forelimbs had shrunk until only a pointed humerus bone remained. Seabirds like this evolved from earlier fliers to become powerful swimmers and deadly fish-hunters. Their large back feet were probably webbed for propulsion, and the stubs of their wings could have been used for steering.

CONFUCIUS BIRD

Scientific name:	*Confuciusornis*
Size:	Up to 24 in (60 cm) long
Diet:	Probably plants
Habitat:	Lakeside forest
Where found:	East Asia
Time:	Early Cretaceous
Related genus:	*Changchengornis*

Cambrian 540–500	Ordovician 500–435	Silurian 435–410	Devonian 410–355	Carboniferous 355–295	Pe

PALEOZOIC 540–250 MYA

CONFUCIUS BIRD

Confuciusornis was a magpie-sized bird that lived in Early Cretaceous China, more than 120 million years ago. It perched in trees, ate plants, and bred in colonies of hundreds. Some of the birds (probably the males) had long tail feathers, possibly for display, while others (probably females) were smaller with much stubbier tails. *Confuciusornis* flew more strongly than *Archaeopteryx*, but showed a strange mixture of advanced and old-fashioned features. Its clawed fingers, flattish breastbone, wrists, hips, and legs remind scientists of *Archaeopteryx*. Newer features included its deeper chest, strut-shaped coracoid (a shoulder bone), horny, toothless beak, and a pygostyle – a shortened tail core of fused bones. So me scientists put *Confuciusornis* in a group of birds called the Pygostylia.

Confuciusornis females had a short tail

Three fingers with curved claws projecting from each wing

Toothless beak covered by a horny sheath

Flight feathers well designed for powered flight

Tail feathers grew from fused tail bones.

Hallux (big toe) reversed as in living birds

Deepened breast bone anchoring strong flight muscles

Thumb supporting feathers used in slow flight

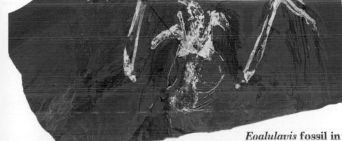

Eoalulavis fossil in ultraviolet light

DAWN LITTLE-WING BIRD

Described in 1996, sparrow-sized *Eoalulavis* from Early Cretaceous Spain is the earliest known bird to have a tuft of feathers sprouting from its thumb. Projecting from its main wing's leading edge, this tiny wing or "alula" kept *Eoalulavis* airborne at low speeds, helping it to land and perch on trees. The alula was an important innovation, found in birds today. *Eoalulavis* belonged to the Ornithothoraces ("bird chests"), stronger and more maneuverable flyers than *Confuciusornis* and its kin. Yet *Eoalulavis* was on a side branch from the line of evolution that led to modern birds, and might not even have been warm-blooded.

Triassic 250–203	Jurassic 203–135	Cretaceous 135–65	Tertiary 65–1.75	Quaternary 1.75–present
	MESOZOIC 250–65 MYA		CENOZOIC 65 MYA–present	

50

NEW BIRDS

ALTHOUGH THE REPTILES that we think of
as dinosaurs died out 65 million years ago,
their probable descendants – birds – survived.
Throughout the Cenozoic they evolved,
diversifying into different species suited for
life in almost all parts of the world. Today,
birds flourish – their 9,000 or so living species
outnumber mammal species nearly two to
one. But countless Cenozoic bird species did
not survive to the present day. Most are still
unknown, but all the Cenozoic fossil birds so
far discovered belong to the same great group
as present day birds – the Neornithes or "new
birds." Their hallmarks are a toothless, horny
beak, fused limb bones, and an efficient, four-
chambered heart to aid rapid muscle movement
in flying. Extinct neornithines, however,
included flightless giants, strange waterbirds,
and also land birds unlike any still around.

Argentavis – *wingspan*
25 ft (7.6 m)

Andean condor –
wingspan 11 ft
(3.2 m)

FLYING GIANT
Discovered in 1979, *Argentavis magnificens*
("magnificent Argentine bird") was probably the largest
bird that ever flew. It had an enormous 25 ft (7.6 m) wingspan,
greater than was once thought possible for a flying bird, and
may have weighed as much as a jaguar. This vast bird was a
teratorn – a gigantic relative of the turkey vultures seen in
the Americas today. Like these, it possibly had a bare head
and neck for burrowing deep into a corpse without messing
up its feathers. Although huge, the feet of these birds were
extremely weak, so they would not have been capable of lifting
prey from the ground. Instead, they probably soared above
grassy pampas, swooping down on grazing flightless birds
and mammals to kill them on the ground, or feeding
from corpses of those that had already died.

Bone   Skin

Preserved Moa foot

**Early illustration
of a moa and kiwis**

Claw

FLIGHTLESS GIANTS
Subfossil bones like this moa foot have yielded
molecules revealing relationships between giant flightless
birds extinct for up to 1500 years. In 2001 scientists proved
that New Zealand's moas, birds up to 11 ft (3.5 m) tall, and
Madagascar's mighty elephant birds shared ancestors with
the still-living South American rhea, African ostrich, and
Australian emu. Such so-called ratites must have spread
through the southern continents before they were separated
by sea about 70 million years ago. Ratites represent
the Paleognathae ("old jaws") – a less advanced type
of neornithine than the Neognathae ("new jaws"),
to which almost all other living birds belong.

| Cambrian 540–500 | Ordovician 500–435 | Silurian 435–410 | Devonian 410–355 | Carboniferous 355–295 | Permi |

PALEOZOIC 540–250 MYA

Titanis *may* have had an ornamental crest

Beak with strong, sharp, hooked upper mandible

Lower mandible much smaller than upper

Head supported on a long neck

Broad, flat beak like a duck's

Presbyornis skeleton

Long, curved, slender neck

PUZZLING PRESBYORNIS

Presbyornis was a weird waterbird with a ducklike head and beak, certain skull features like a flamingo, and some limb bones like a shorebird. Despite this confusing mixture of ingredients, most scientists group it with the ducks, geese, and swans. It probably waded in shallow, salty lakes and fed much like a flamingo, by filtering algae from the water. *Presbyornis* fossils are found worldwide, and this long-lived genus may have first appeared in the age of the dinosaurs. However, it is best known from North American fossils of around 50 million years ago, some in large nesting colonies.

Long legs like a shorebird's

Clawed fingers capable of seizing prey

Long toes to prevent sinking in soft mud

TERROR CRANE

The huge carnivorous *Titanis* ("giant") was a phorusrhacid or "terror crane" – one of a group of flightless birds that rivaled mammals as top predators in South America for millions of years. Standing 8 ft (2.5 m) tall, with a big head, powerful hooked beak, and long legs with powerful talons, *Titanis* was among the last phorusrhacids, and crossed the Panama Isthmus into North America when the continents joined around 3 million years ago. It probably hunted on open plains, seizing prey with wings that had re-evolved digits tipped with huge claws, before holding it down with its feet and tearing out chunks of flesh with its beak. *Titanis*'s arms are unique – earlier phorusrhacids had stubby, useless wings.

Three-toed foot capable of giving a knockout kick

Sharp toe claws could inflict severe wounds.

GIANT

Scientific name: *Titanis*

Size: 8 ft (2.5 m)

Diet: Meat

Habitat: Grassland

Where found: North America

Time: Tertiary and Quaternary

Related species: *Ameginornis, Phorusrhacus*

05–250	Triassic 250–203	Jurassic 203–135	Cretaceous 135–65	Tertiary 65–1.75	Quaternary 1.75 present
		MESOZOIC 250–65 MYA		CENOZOIC 65 MYA–present	

TITANIS

Four million years ago on a Central American plain, the primitive horse *Hipparion* flees from the sudden appearance of the area's most formidable predator out of nearby pampas grass. As *Hipparion* bolts, the 8-ft (2.5-m) *Titanis* turns in pursuit, arms outstretched with two vicious claws ready to seize the hapless little horse. Despite weighing more than 330 lb (150 kg), *Titanis* is surprisingly agile, with powerful legs capable of bringing down even the fastest prey. When North and South America link up, and North American wildlife floods south, *Titanis* will be the only major predator to make the journey in the opposite direction, surviving until perhaps 400,000 years ago.

Cambrian 540–500	Ordovician 500–435	Silurian 435–410	Devonian 410–355	Carboniferous 355–295	Permi

PALEOZOIC 540–250 MYA

INTRODUCING SAUROPODOMORPHS

THE LIZARD-HIPPED OR SAURISCHIAN DINOSAURS were divided into two great groups – theropods, which gave rise to birds, and sauropodomorphs ("lizard-foot forms"). Sauropodomorphs had small heads, teeth shaped for cropping plants, long necks, and roomy bodies for digesting large amounts of low-quality leafy foods. Most possessed large thumb claws, evolved from small bipedal ancestors. By Late Triassic times there were already two types of sauropodomorph: prosauropods ("before the lizard feet") and sauropods ("lizard feet"). Prosauropods ranged from small two-legged forms to great four-legged beasts. Sauropods were immense herbivores propped up by pillarlike limbs, with stubby feet and hands much like those of an elephant. They included the largest, heaviest animals that ever lived on land. Both groups spread around the world – prosauropods perhaps evolved first, but died out in Early Jurassic times. Sauropods persisted almost right through the Age of Dinosaurs.

All sauropods had at least 44 caudal vertebrae

This famous reconstruction shows Apatosaurus's tail dragging on the ground. In fact, it was probably carried horizontally.

Thick bones, supporting pillarlike limbs

PROSAUROPODS
Scientists have disagreed about exactly which anatomical "ingredients" set prosauropods apart from sauropods. A list of key prosauropod features drawn up in 1990 included small, "saw-edged," leaf-shaped teeth, a skull half as long as the thigh bone, and jaws hinged below the level of the upper teeth. They also had broad pubic hip bones forming a kind of apron, large, pointed thumb claws, and traces of tiny fifth toes on the feet. Some scientists believe prosauropods could also have had a horny beak and fleshy cheeks.

Small, saw-edged, leaf-shaped front teeth

Tail has about 50 caudal vertebrae.

Broad foot with four long toes

Paired pubic bones project like an apron.

Sternal plates form a heart-shaped shield.

Large strong, curved thumb claw

Lufengosaurus skeleton

Narrow track made by a sauropod's erect limbs

Fossilized sauropod footprint left in soft ground

HOW SAUROPODS WALKED
Scientists used to think that the heaviest sauropods must have lived in lakes and swamps, buoyed up by water. Finds of fossil footprints have disproved this old idea. They also show quite narrow tracks, proving that sauropods walked with limbs erect beneath their bodies, like cows or elephants, not sprawling to either side like the limbs of lizards and turtles.

Cambrian 540–500	Ordovician 500–435	Silurian 435–410	Devonian 410–355	Carboniferous 355–295	Permia

PALEOZOIC 540–250 MYA

Eleven or fewer
dorsal vertebrae

At least 12 cervical
vertebrae reinforcing
the long neck

Nostril openings far
back on the skull

Broad, short,
stubby foot bones

Large thumb
and toe claws

KEY SAUROPOD FEATURES

Apatosaurus ("deceptive lizard") was a diplodocid, or double-beam, sauropod, also known as *Brontosaurus* ("thunder lizard"). The diplodocids are named after the dual extensions on the chevrons of their tail vertebrae, but they also display distinctive features seen in other sauropods. Many of these affect the dinosaur's overall shape. Sauropods "borrowed" back vertebrae to extend their necks, resulting in at least 12 neck bones, but just 11 or fewer back vertebrae. These bones' neural spines were typically V-shaped, to cradle a strong ligament that helped to raise the weight of the neck and head. The columnlike limbs were also adapted to bear huge weight – ankles were cushioned by springy cartilage; and they had a full set of five fingers on each hand, but the number of bones in each digit was reduced. Sauropods walked on their toes with palms raised, and a fleshy pad supporting most of the weight. Their thumbs and three toes bore large claws. Sauropod teeth also show tell-tale wear marks made by biting off leaves, and their skulls have large nostril openings far back on the head.

DID SAUROPODS REAR?
Prosauropods could certainly reach to nip at high leaves, but could the immense sauropods also stand on hind legs? In this model for a museum display, a *Barosaurus* rears to protect her young one from a marauding *Allosaurus*, preparing to stamp down on the predator or lash at it with her tail. However, some scientists still doubt whether sauropods could have pumped the blood so high to their brains, or whether mothers took care of their young like this.

An *Allosaurus*
threatens a young
Barosaurus.

Adult Barosaurus *might
have raised its head
up to 50 ft (15 m).*

Young Barosaurus
shelters behind
its mother.

DECEPTIVE LIZARD

Scientific name: *Apatosaurus*

Size: 69 ft (21 m) long

Diet: Plants

Habitat: Floodplain

Where found: North America

Time: Late Jurassic

Related species: *Barosaurus, Diplodocus*

95–250	Triassic 250–203	Jurassic 203–135	Cretaceous 135–65	Tertiary 65–1.75	Quaternary 1.75–present
	MESOZOIC 250–65 MYA			CENOZOIC 65 MYA–present	

PROSAUROPODS

THE PROSAUROPODS ("BEFORE SAUROPODS") thrived between about 230 and 178 million years ago. They were among the first plant-eating dinosaurs, and the first land animals tall enough to browse on trees. Various groups evolved, with species ranging from creatures lighter than a man and walking on their hindlimbs to ponderous four-legged giants – the first dinosaurs to grow as heavy as an elephant. However, they all shared certain key features, including a small head, long neck, heavy body, long tail, and huge, curved thumb claws. Their size and adaptations for feeding on available vegetation made the prosauropods hugely successful – they probably lived all over the world, and came to outnumber all other large land animals. Eventually, though, they were replaced by their possible descendants, the even more huge and specialized sauropods.

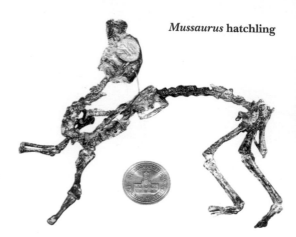

Mussaurus hatchling

MOUSE LIZARD
Prosauropod nests have been found, proving that some young hatched from surprisingly tiny eggs, often no larger than a small songbird's. However, even such sparrow-sized hatchlings could eventually grow into adults weighing about 260 lb (120 kg). This discovery was made in Argentina, where paleontologists unearthed the nest, eggshells, and five little hatchlings of a prosauropod they called *Mussaurus* ("mouse lizard"), which may in fact be babies of a previously described species.

Jaws contained many small, flat-sided teeth.

Teeth snipped off leafy twigs with a powerful bite.

Plateosaurus hand

Long, sharp, bony core of the thumb claw

Second digit's long, curved claw

LONG THUMB CLAW
Plateosaurus's forelimbs had five digits of varying lengths – two short outer fingers, two much longer middle fingers, and a huge curving thumb. This claw was so long that it would have got in the way while walking on all fours, and probably had to be held off the ground. It would have made a formidable defensive weapon for jabbing at attacking theropods. With the rest of the hand, this claw could also have grasped tree trunks for support or pull down branches as *Plateosaurus* reared to nibble the leaves.

Horny sheath covering thumb claw

Thumb claw held clear of the ground when walking

Cambrian 540–500	Ordovician 500–435	Silurian 435–410	Devonian 410–355	Carboniferous 355–295	Permia

PALEOZOIC 540–250 MYA

Hollows in spinal
bones cut down
their weight.

Large gut probably
filled with bulky
plant food

Limb bones were solid
and heavy.

BUS-LENGTH BEAST

Riojasaurus was one of the largest prosauropods, and one of the first truly large dinosaurs. A heavy quadruped that could grow up to 36 ft (11 m) long, one calculation puts its weight as great as 5 tons (4.5 tonnes). As prosauropods grew larger, the great weight of intestines in front of their forward-sloping hip bones helped to make them front-heavy, eventually forcing them to spend their whole life on all fours.

FLAT LIZARD

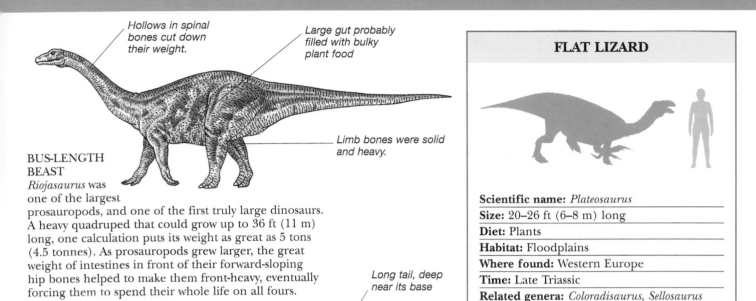

Scientific name:	*Plateosaurus*
Size:	20–26 ft (6–8 m) long
Diet:	Plants
Habitat:	Floodplains
Where found:	Western Europe
Time:	Late Triassic
Related genera:	*Coloradisaurus, Sellosaurus*

Long tail, deep
near its base

The tail tapered
toward the end.

Sturdy toes bore
most of the weight.

Toe claws were
short but strong.

FLAT LIZARD

Plateosaurus, ("flat lizard"), one of the best-known prosauropods, was found widely in Western Europe. It grew up to 26 ft (8 m) long, with strong arms and hands, able to support a share of its weight. Most of the time *Plateosaurus* would have ambled along on all fours, but its long, strong rear legs would have allowed it to rear and perhaps even trot along on two legs to escape danger, its tail balancing the weight of its body. By rising and craning its elongated neck, it could crop tree leaves beyond the reach of other animals. *Plateosaurus*'s small skull was equipped with saw-edged, leaf-shaped teeth for chopping up these leafy foods and a low jaw joint designed to give a powerful bite. The teeth were set in slightly from the jaw rim. The flexible neck led to a long ribcage containing a long gut to process bulky plant food, with the help of swallowed stones to grind it to a pulp.

95–250	Triassic 250–203	Jurassic 203–135	Cretaceous 135–65	Tertiary 65–1.75	Quaternary 1.75–present
	MESOZOIC 250–65 MYA			CENOZOIC 65 MYA–present	

151

EARLY SAUROPODS

SAUROPODS ("LIZARD FEET"), THE LARGEST DINOSAURS of all, probably evolved from ancestors no bigger than a dog; yet the earliest known sauropod was already sizeable. *Isanosaurus* ("Isan lizard") from the Late Triassic of northeast Thailand, around 220 million years old, had thigh bones nearly twice as long as human thighs. The next earliest sauropod, *Vulcanodon* ("volcano tooth") from Early Jurassic Zimbabwe, measured 20 ft (6.5 m), as long as a large crocodile. Other early sauropods included India's *Barapasaurus* ("big leg lizard"), Europe's *Cetiosaurus* ("whale lizard"), and China's *Shunosaurus* ("Shuo lizard"). At up to 60 ft (18 m) from snout to tail, the biggest of these Early to Mid Jurassic dinosaurs matched the length of a large sperm whale. Between them, finds of fossil bones and footprints indicate that sauropods had spread worldwide by the beginning of the Jurassic Period.

Some tail bone chevrons are shaped like those of the later Diplodocus.

Relatively short and deep tail, shown here trailing on the ground, but probably carried off the ground in life

This model skull is guesswork – no Cetiosaurus skull is known with certainty.

The neck bones' design made them rather inflexible.

WHALE LIZARD

Cetiosaurus was a Mid Jurassic sauropod first discovered in England in the early 1800s. In 1 841 it became the first sauropod to get a scientific name. Paleontologist Richard Owen, who named it, knew this was a giant reptile, but its fossil vertebrae were huge and spongy, somewhat like a whale's. Owen thought the creature might have swum in the sea. Later finds revealed that *Cetiosaurus* had been a land animal up to 60 ft (18 m) long, and as heavy as several elephants. This rather primitive sauropod's weight was largely in its heavy limbs and vertebrae.

Pubic bones probably helped to support the large, heavy gut.

Only pale bones in this reconstruction are real – others were invented.

STIFF-NECKED CETIOSAURUS

Most reconstructions have pictured *Cetiosaurus* as a swan-necked treetop browser. In fact the dinosaur's stiff neck stuck straight out, counterbalanced by a raised tail, and *Cetiosaurus* could not raise its head much higher than its shoulders. However, it could lower its head to drink, or swing it in an arc 10 ft (3 m) across to crop fern fronds or small, leafy trees. This sauropod roamed low-lying shores of an ancient sea that covered much of England.

Cambrian 540–500	Ordovician 500–435	Silurian 435–410	Devonian 410–355	Carboniferous 355–295	Permia

PALEOZOIC 540–250 MYA

Shoulder blade –
two fused bones,
the scapula and
coracoid

Skull, one of the few
kinds of sauropod
skulls to survive

Neck relatively
short for a
sauropod

SHUO LIZARD

Shunosaurus from Middle Jurassic China grew about 33 ft (10 m) long. Early sauropods like this already show the basic characteristics of small head, long neck and tail, deep body, and pillarlike legs, but these were not yet fully developed. Their necks and tails were relatively short, fewer vertebrae had fused to their hip bones to help support the body, and their spinal bones were not yet deeply scooped out to reduce weight. Shunosaurus had only 12 neck bones, 13 back vertebrae, 4 vertebrae fused with its hip bones, and 44 bones in its tail. Later, larger sauropods had many more vertebrae – for instance, *Apatosaurus* had nearly twice as many tail bones. Finds of many *Shunosaurus* fossils, some almost complete, make this among the best-known of the sauropods. Some skeletons show that the last tail bones were fused together and swollen to form a club. Like an ankylosaurid dinosaur, *Shunosaurus* could have swung its tail as a formidable defensive weapon.

Large foot
with long,
deep claws

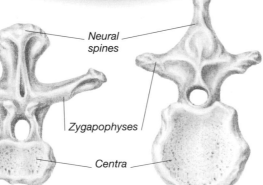

Neural
spines

Zygapophyses

Centra

CHANGING VERTEBRAE
A rather solid, heavy *Cetiosaurus* spinal bone (above right) contrasts with a *Brachiosaurus* dorsal vertebra (above left). *Brachiosaurus* was a later, more advanced, type of sauropod. In *Brachiosaurus*, any bone not needed in the centrum has been lost, but the neural spine and zygapophyses are long and strong. In more advanced sauropods, bone growth was concentrated along the lines of greatest stress, like the steel tubes of scaffolding.

SHUO LIZARD

Scientific name:	*Shunosaurus*
Size:	33 ft (10 m) long
Diet:	Plants
Habitat:	Floodplain
Where found:	East Asia
Time:	Middle Jurassic
Related genera:	*Datousaurus*

95–250	Triassic 250–203	Jurassic 203–135	Cretaceous 135–65	Tertiary 65–1.75	Quaternary 1.75–present

MESOZOIC 250–65 MYA   CENOZOIC 65 MYA–present

153

DOUBLE BEAMS

THE DIPLODOCIDS ("DOUBLE BEAMS") were immense four-legged sauropods. They had small heads shaped much like a horse's, and peg-shaped teeth only at the front of the jaws. Their front limbs seem ridiculously short, but all four legs were built like an elephant's in order to support the heavy body. An incredibly long neck was balanced by an even longer tail that tapered to a slender "whiplash." Diplodocids get their name from twin extensions called chevrons in the bones of their middle tail. These "double beams" may have protected the blood vessels in their tails if they pressed down on the ground for the animals to rear. Similar chevrons are found in some other sauropods, perhaps close relatives. Almost all diplodocids lived in the Late Jurassic. The best known, such as *Apatosaurus*, *Diplodocus*, and *Seismosaurus*, are from the western United States.

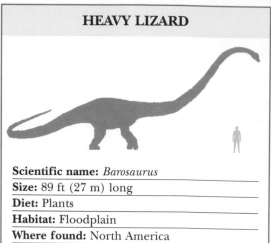

HEAVY LIZARD

Scientific name:	*Barosaurus*
Size:	89 ft (27 m) long
Diet:	Plants
Habitat:	Floodplain
Where found:	North America
Time:	Late Jurassic
Related genera:	*Apatosaurus*, *Diplodocus*

DOUBLE BEAM
Diplodocus grew longer than a tennis court, yet weighed no more than two large elephants. Most of its length came from its slender neck and tail, and deep hollows in the spinal bones reduced their weight. New calculations suggest that this huge creature could not lift its long, stiff neck much higher than its shoulders. Instead of browsing on high leafy twigs, as most people imagine, it would have grazed low-growing ferns. Standing in a fern meadow, *Diplodocus* could have swung its neck from side to side, stripping the fronds with its peg-shaped teeth, and using swallowed stones to help to mash them up inside its stomach.

Ten tall dorsal vertebrae formed the spinal bones on the back.

Chevrons

At least 80 caudal vertebrae made up the tail's core.

The straight, slim femur was shaped like a stove pipe.

Thirty rodlike bones formed the tail's "whiplash" end.

Barosaurus's center of gravity was near its hips.

Front limbs were short compared to the hindlimbs.

Bones just like Diplodocus's supported the limbs.

Cambrian 540–500	Ordovician 500–435	Silurian 435–410	Devonian 410–355	Carboniferous 355–295	Permia

PALEOZOIC 540–250 MYA

DECEPTIVE LIZARD

Apatosaurus grew nearly as long as *Diplodocus*, but became far heavier – as heavy as four or five elephants. Much of its weight lay in its thick heavy bones, and it is equally well known as *Brontosaurus* ("thunder lizard") for its supposed stomping walk. In fact, fossil bones named *Brontosaurus* turned out to match those from the already named *Apatosaurus*. Another error involved the creature's head, which was not discovered for many years. People mistakenly believed *Apatosaurus* had had a box-shaped skull like *Camarasaurus*'s, but when a real *Apatosaurus* skull was finally unearthed, it was long and low, with peg-shaped teeth, like *Diplodocus*'s.

Very long bones in the neck

EARTH-SHAKING LIZARD

Seismosaurus ("earth-shaking lizard"), from New Mexico, has been called the longest dinosaur of all, probably measuring around 110 ft (34 m) and weighing up to 33 tons (30 tonnes). The Late Jurassic rocks that this monster came from have yielded other North American diplodocid giants. *Amphicoelias* and *Supersaurus* may have been even longer and heavier than *Seismosaurus*. The skeletons of all three genera are very incomplete, though, and two or more kinds of diplodocid may eventually prove to be just one. Recent discoveries suggest that even larger sauropods may have evolved in Cretaceous South America.

Tail contained diplodocid-type vertebrae.

"Stretched" bones supported the neck.

Comparatively tiny head

The flexible tail may have cracked like a whip.

HEAVY LIZARD

At up to 89 ft (27 m) long, *Barosaurus* had a strong resemblance to *Diplodocus*, but with one important difference. One third of this creature's length was made up by its amazingly long neck. *Barosaurus* had the same number of neck vertebrae as *Diplodocus* (fifteen), but each was remarkably stretched to create an astounding reach. Strangely, while diplodocid necks were longer than those of other sauropods, their forelimbs were shorter. If these giants grazed only on all fours, this would have limited their reach, but if they could rear on their hindlegs, then reduced weight in the front of the body would have been an advantage. *Barosaurus* is therefore one of the best arguments for this kind of behavior – at full stretch, a rearing *Barosaurus* could hold its head 49 ft (15 m) above the ground.

95–250	Triassic 250–203	Jurassic 203–135	Cretaceous 135–65	Tertiary 65–1.75	Quaternary 1.75–present
		MESOZOIC 250–65 MYA		CENOZOIC 65 MYA–present	

CHAMBERED LIZARDS

CAMARASAURUS ("CHAMBERED LIZARD") gets its name from the roomy hollows in its backbone that helped to limit the weight of this sturdy creature. *Camarasaurus* lived in Late Jurassic western North America. Fossil hunters in Colorado, Wyoming, and Utah have found the remains of individuals ranging from babies to adults. The tiniest fossil belonged to an embryo 3 ft 3 in (1 m) long that was almost ready to hatch from an egg smaller than some birds' eggs. This was the first sauropod embryo ever discovered. Outside North America, close relatives of *Camarasaurus* lived at about the same time in what are now Portugal and Spain. Less closely related sauropods that share similar features with *Camarasaurus* lived as far away as Mongolia, China, and Thailand.

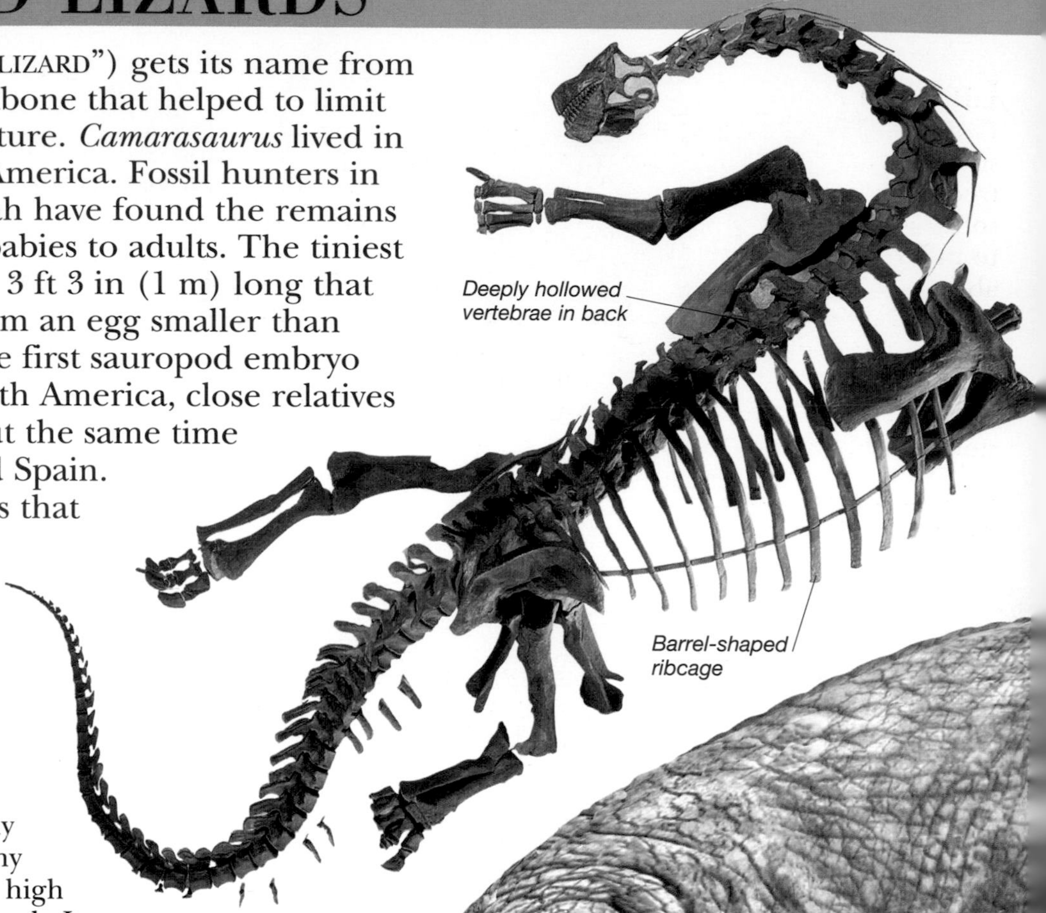

Deeply hollowed vertebrae in back

Barrel-shaped ribcage

BONY SCAFFOLDING

Scientists know more about this dinosaur's skeleton than almost any other sauropod's, thanks to its many fossil remains. *Camarasaurus* had a high skull that was short from front to back. Its vertebrae included 12 short neck bones with long, straight ribs that overlapped those behind to stiffen the neck. There were also 12 back bones, five sacral vertebrae fused to the hip bones, and 53 tail bones. The weight-bearing bones of each limb ended in stubby digits.

Moderately short, but sturdy tail

Massive hindlimbs, with clawed toes supported by a fleshy pad.

| Cambrian 540–500 | Ordovician 500–435 | Silurian 435–410 | Devonian 410–355 | Carboniferous 355–295 | Permia |

PALEOZOIC 540–250 MYA

LIFESTYLE

Camarasaurus adults probably fed below shoulder height, swinging their strong necks stiffly sideways and down to strip tough leaves from shrubby trees with their teeth. Young camarasaurids seem to have eaten plants with softer leaves. Signs of wear on the teeth of adult camarasaurids hold clues to this sauropod's diet. They hint that an adult *Camarasaurus* ate more abrasive plants than sauropods such as *Diplodocus*. This would have meant that both types of sauropod could have lived in the same place at the same time without competing for food. Perhaps camarasaurid young shared the diplodocids' diet because they could not yet digest tough leaves.

Short, blunt, deep head, with eyes and nostrils far back

Shoulders perhaps higher than most sauropods'

Antorbital fenestra ("window in front of the orbit") – an air-filled hole in the skull found in most dinosaurs and other archosaurs

BOXY SKULL

Camarasaurus's short, deep skull had a muzzle that was blunt like a bulldog's. Its orbits, or eye sockets, lay far back in the head, where the tiny braincase was also located. The nares – two holes for the nostrils – were set high up in front of the eyes. Only slim, bony struts separated these sockets and holes, but the jaw bones provided solid supports for the deeply rooted, spoon-shaped teeth that ran around *Camarasaurus*'s mouth. Below each orbit, muscles that worked the jaws bulged from a skull hole called an infratemporal fenestra, or "window below the temporal bone."

Forelimbs ending in short, stubby toes with sharp thumb claws

CHAMBERED LIZARD

Scientific name: *Camarasaurus*

Size: 59 ft (18 m) long

Diet: Plants

Habitat: Floodplain

Where found: North America, western Europe

Time: Late Jurassic

Related genera: *Aragosaurus, Opisthocoelicaudia*

.95–250	Triassic 250–203	Jurassic 203–135	Cretaceous 135–65	Tertiary 65–1.75	Quaternary 1.75–present
		MESOZOIC 250–65 MYA		CENOZOIC 65 MYA–present	

ARM LIZARDS

LONG, PILLARLIKE FORELIMBS earned *Brachiosaurus* ("arm lizard") its name and gave it a back that sloped steeply down to its hindquarters. This high-shouldered sauropod was built like a mighty giraffe. With a long neck much like the boom of a crane, *Brachiosaurus* could lift or lower its head to browse on tree leaves or fern fronds. This giant plant-eater's fossils crop up in the Late Jurassic rocks of western North America, southern Europe, and east Africa. Similar sauropods have been said to include *Bothriospondylus*, *Lapparentosaurus*, *Pelorosaurus*, and *Pleurocoelus*. However, some of these supposed brachiosaurids ("arm lizards") seem to have been more closely related to *Brachiosaurus* than others. Many sauropods are known from so few bones that comparing their relationships is often difficult.

Shaft – long middle section – of femur (thigh bone)

A DINOSAURIAN GIRAFFE

Powerful muscles might have raised *Brachiosaurus*'s head 43 ft (13 m) high, making it more than twice as tall as a giraffe and high enough to peer over a four-story building. *Brachiosaurus* was not the longest of dinosaurs, but it was probably among the heaviest. One expert estimated that it weighed 76 tons (78 tonnes) – as much as 13 African bull elephants – although others have put its weight lower, at 31–46 tons (32–47 tonnes). Certainly, the hollows in its vertebrae and the air spaces in its ribs helped to lighten some of its bones. However, its thick-walled limb bones were immensely heavy.

PILLARLIKE LIMBS

As long as a very tall man and massively thick, the *Brachiosaurus* femur (thigh bone) was one of the largest, strongest, and most solid of the bones in its body. *Brachiosaurus*'s upper arm bones were even longer than its thigh bones – unusual for a sauropod. The scientist who described *Brachiosaurus* initially mistook one of its upper arm bones for a femur.

| Cambrian 540–500 | Ordovician 500–435 | Silurian 435–410 | Devonian 410–355 | Carboniferous 355–295 | Permian |

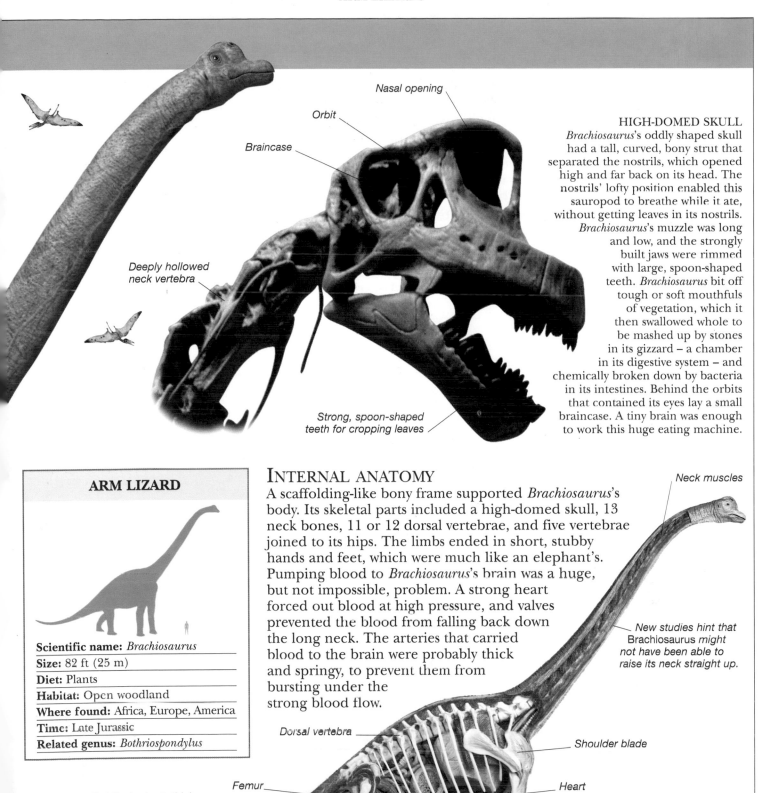

Nasal opening

Orbit

Braincase

Deeply hollowed neck vertebra

Strong, spoon-shaped teeth for cropping leaves

HIGH-DOMED SKULL

Brachiosaurus's oddly shaped skull had a tall, curved, bony strut that separated the nostrils, which opened high and far back on its head. The nostrils' lofty position enabled this sauropod to breathe while it ate, without getting leaves in its nostrils. *Brachiosaurus*'s muzzle was long and low, and the strongly built jaws were rimmed with large, spoon-shaped teeth. *Brachiosaurus* bit off tough or soft mouthfuls of vegetation, which it then swallowed whole to be mashed up by stones in its gizzard – a chamber in its digestive system – and chemically broken down by bacteria in its intestines. Behind the orbits that contained its eyes lay a small braincase. A tiny brain was enough to work this huge eating machine.

ARM LIZARD

Scientific name: *Brachiosaurus*

Size: 82 ft (25 m)

Diet: Plants

Habitat: Open woodland

Where found: Africa, Europe, America

Time: Late Jurassic

Related genus: *Bothriospondylus*

INTERNAL ANATOMY

A scaffolding-like bony frame supported *Brachiosaurus*'s body. Its skeletal parts included a high-domed skull, 13 neck bones, 11 or 12 dorsal vertebrae, and five vertebrae joined to its hips. The limbs ended in short, stubby hands and feet, which were much like an elephant's. Pumping blood to *Brachiosaurus*'s brain was a huge, but not impossible, problem. A strong heart forced out blood at high pressure, and valves prevented the blood from falling back down the long neck. The arteries that carried blood to the brain were probably thick and springy, to prevent them from bursting under the strong blood flow.

Neck muscles

New studies hint that Brachiosaurus might not have been able to raise its neck straight up.

Dorsal vertebra

Shoulder blade

Femur

Heart

Relatively short, thick tail carried far off the ground

Gizzard

Ulna and radius in forearm

Internal anatomy of *Brachiosaurus*

05–250	Triassic 250–203	Jurassic 203–135	Cretaceous 135–65	Tertiary 65–1.75	Quaternary 1.75–present
		MESOZOIC 250–65 MYA		CENOZOIC 65 MYA–present	

JURASSIC BROWSER

Small herds of brachiosaurids roamed riverside forests of conifers, cycads, and ferns that grew in the warm, Late Jurassic climate. *Brachiosaurus* stood at the edge of woods, swinging its long neck to reach the leaves of tall trees. Lowering its neck, the massive creature grazed on fronds of low-growing ferns. A dinosaur as large as this needed a lot of plant food to survive, so *Brachiosaurus* probably spent most of its time eating.

| Cambrian 540–500 | Ordovician 500–435 | Silurian 435–410 | Devonian 410–355 | Carboniferous 355–295 | Permi |

PALEOZOIC 540–250 MYA

05–250	Triassic 250–203	Jurassic 203–135	Cretaceous 135–65	Tertiary 65–1.75	Quaternary 1.75–present
		MESOZOIC 250–65 MYA		CENOZOIC 65 MYA–present	

ORNITHISCHIANS CLADOGRAM

THE "BIRD-HIPPED" DINOSAURS called ornithischians include the armored stegosaurs, the horned ceratopsians, and the crested hadrosaurs. All ornithischians share key features of the jaws and teeth that allowed them to crop and chew plants efficiently. Advanced ornithischians, such as horned dinosaurs, became highly modified for chewing plants. They evolved hundreds of self-sharpening teeth and special skull hinges that helped them grind their teeth together. All ornithischians probably evolved from a bipedal ancestor similar to *Lesothosaurus,* one of the most primitive ornithischians.

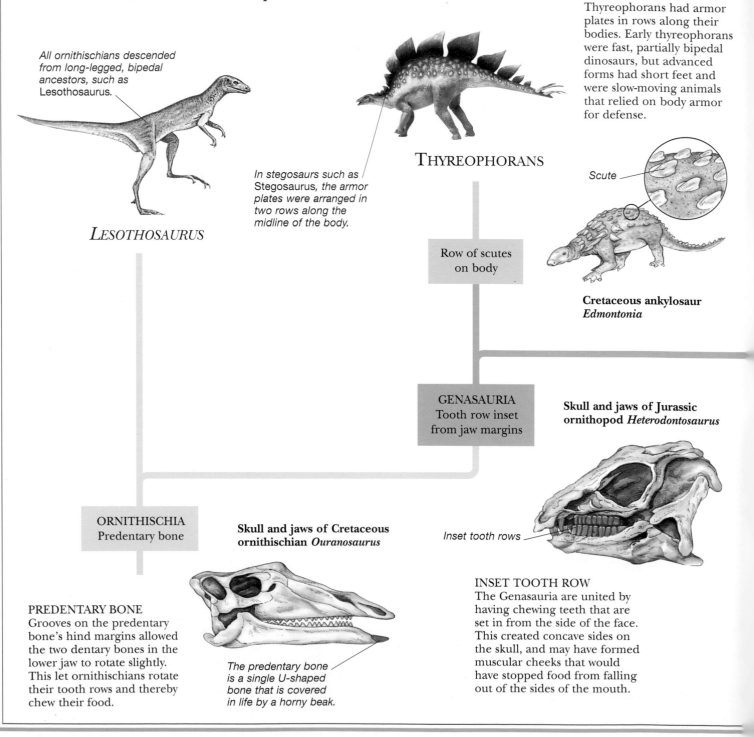

ROW OF SCUTES
Thyreophorans had armor plates in rows along their bodies. Early thyreophorans were fast, partially bipedal dinosaurs, but advanced forms had short feet and were slow-moving animals that relied on body armor for defense.

All ornithischians descended from long-legged, bipedal ancestors, such as Lesothosaurus.

THYREOPHORANS

In stegosaurs such as Stegosaurus, the armor plates were arranged in two rows along the midline of the body.

Scute

LESOTHOSAURUS

Row of scutes on body

Cretaceous ankylosaur
Edmontonia

GENASAURIA
Tooth row inset from jaw margins

Skull and jaws of Jurassic ornithopod *Heterodontosaurus*

ORNITHISCHIA
Predentary bone

Skull and jaws of Cretaceous ornithischian *Ouranosaurus*

Inset tooth rows

PREDENTARY BONE
Grooves on the predentary bone's hind margins allowed the two dentary bones in the lower jaw to rotate slightly. This let ornithischians rotate their tooth rows and thereby chew their food.

The predentary bone is a single U-shaped bone that is covered in life by a horny beak.

INSET TOOTH ROW
The Genasauria are united by having chewing teeth that are set in from the side of the face. This created concave sides on the skull, and may have formed muscular cheeks that would have stopped food from falling out of the sides of the mouth.

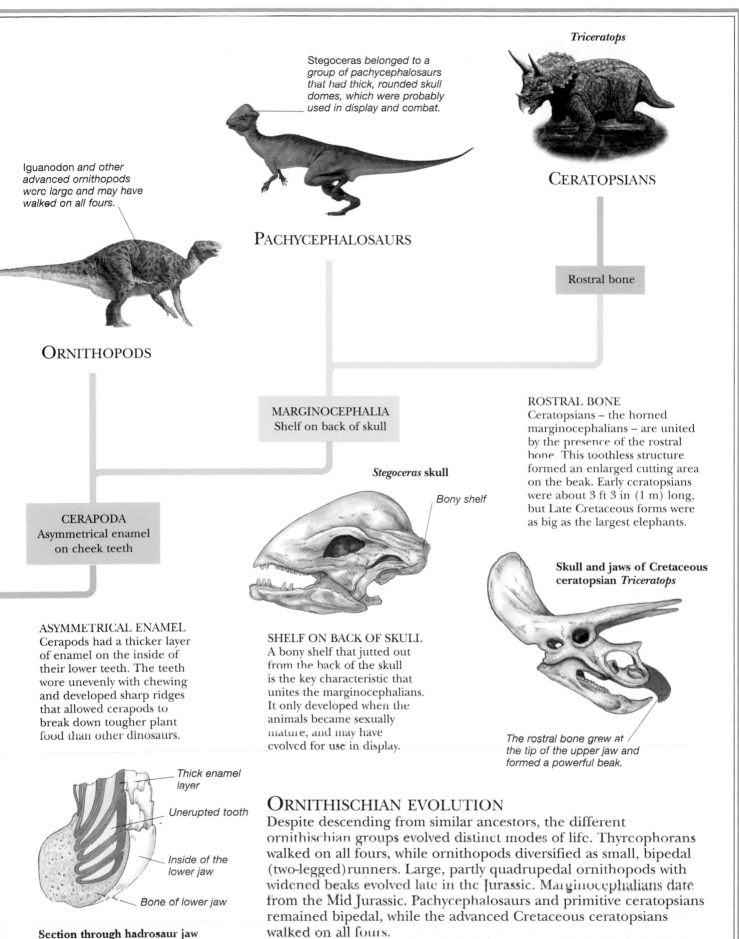

Triceratops

Stegoceras *belonged to a group of pachycephalosaurs that had thick, rounded skull domes, which were probably used in display and combat.*

CERATOPSIANS

Iguanodon and other advanced ornithopods were large and may have walked on all fours.

PACHYCEPHALOSAURS

Rostral bone

ORNITHOPODS

MARGINOCEPHALIA
Shelf on back of skull

ROSTRAL BONE
Ceratopsians – the horned marginocephalians – are united by the presence of the rostral bone. This toothless structure formed an enlarged cutting area on the beak. Early ceratopsians were about 3 ft 3 in (1 m) long, but Late Cretaceous forms were as big as the largest elephants.

Stegoceras **skull**

Bony shelf

CERAPODA
Asymmetrical enamel on cheek teeth

Skull and jaws of Cretaceous ceratopsian *Triceratops*

ASYMMETRICAL ENAMEL
Cerapods had a thicker layer of enamel on the inside of their lower teeth. The teeth wore unevenly with chewing and developed sharp ridges that allowed cerapods to break down tougher plant food than other dinosaurs.

SHELF ON BACK OF SKULL
A bony shelf that jutted out from the back of the skull is the key characteristic that unites the marginocephalians. It only developed when the animals became sexually mature, and may have evolved for use in display.

The rostral bone grew at the tip of the upper jaw and formed a powerful beak.

Thick enamel layer

Unerupted tooth

Inside of the lower jaw

Bone of lower jaw

ORNITHISCHIAN EVOLUTION
Despite descending from similar ancestors, the different ornithischian groups evolved distinct modes of life. Thyreophorans walked on all fours, while ornithopods diversified as small, bipedal (two-legged) runners. Large, partly quadrupedal ornithopods with widened beaks evolved late in the Jurassic. Marginocephalians date from the Mid Jurassic. Pachycephalosaurs and primitive ceratopsians remained bipedal, while the advanced Cretaceous ceratopsians walked on all fours.

Section through hadrosaur jaw

SMALL BIPEDAL PLANT EATERS

DURING THE JURASSIC PERIOD, several types of two-legged ornithischian ("bird-hipped") dinosaurs evolved. Early kinds were no bigger than a dog, but later some grew to lengths of 30 ft (9 m). They walked on hindlimbs much longer than their arms and had horny beaks and ridged teeth for crushing leafy plant food. Scientists are unsure how some of the small early forms are related to one another and so group most kinds together as ornithopods, or "bird-footed" ornithischians. Their hind feet resembled those of a bird, with three large, forward-pointing toes tipped with claws or blunt nails. Without daggerlike teeth or talons to defend themselves, most ornithopods ran away from danger and some were among the fastest of all dinosaurs.

Small head with large eyes and strong jaws

Level back balanced by a long tail

Five-fingered hand with tiny fifth finger

LESOTHO LIZARD

The dog-sized early plant eater *Lesothosaurus*, which lived in southern Africa and Venezuela in Early Jurassic times, is too primitive to be classified with the true ornithopods. Its jaws moved only up and down, not side to side, so it is likely to have fed by slicing rather than grinding leaves. With long sprinter's shins, the animal could race away from its enemies at high speeds. At other times, *Lesothosaurus* would have gone down on all fours to eat low-growing plants, raising its head frequently to watch out for sneaky predators.

HIGH RIDGE BROWSER

Hypsilophodon ("high ridge tooth") was named for its grooved, high-ridged cheek teeth, which made it very efficient at chewing tough Cretaceous vegetation. Its jaws hinged below the level of the teeth, giving it a strong bite, and as its upper jaws moved out, the lower jaws moved in, with the result that upper and lower teeth constantly sharpened one another. This 5 ft (1.5 m) long animal lived in North America and Western Europe.

Feet as long as the shins, designed for sprinting

Short arms with stubby fingers

Long, lightly-built legs

Cambrian 540–500	Ordovician 500–435	Silurian 435–410	Devonian 410–355	Carboniferous 355–295	Permi...

PALEOZOIC 540–250 MYA

LESOTHO LIZARD

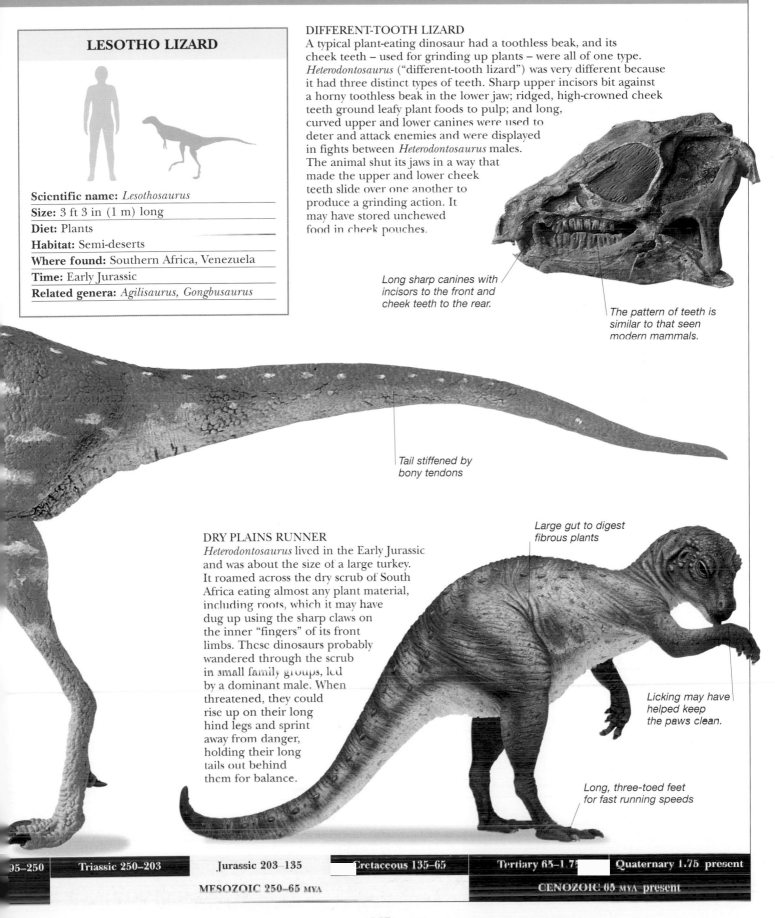

Scientific name: *Lesothosaurus*

Size: 3 ft 3 in (1 m) long

Diet: Plants

Habitat: Semi-deserts

Where found: Southern Africa, Venezuela

Time: Early Jurassic

Related genera: *Agilisaurus, Gongbusaurus*

DIFFERENT-TOOTH LIZARD

A typical plant-eating dinosaur had a toothless beak, and its cheek teeth – used for grinding up plants – were all of one type. *Heterodontosaurus* ("different-tooth lizard") was very different because it had three distinct types of teeth. Sharp upper incisors bit against a horny toothless beak in the lower jaw; ridged, high-crowned cheek teeth ground leafy plant foods to pulp; and long, curved upper and lower canines were used to deter and attack enemies and were displayed in fights between *Heterodontosaurus* males. The animal shut its jaws in a way that made the upper and lower cheek teeth slide over one another to produce a grinding action. It may have stored unchewed food in cheek pouches.

Long sharp canines with incisors to the front and cheek teeth to the rear.

The pattern of teeth is similar to that seen modern mammals.

Tail stiffened by bony tendons

Large gut to digest fibrous plants

DRY PLAINS RUNNER

Heterodontosaurus lived in the Early Jurassic and was about the size of a large turkey. It roamed across the dry scrub of South Africa eating almost any plant material, including roots, which it may have dug up using the sharp claws on the inner "fingers" of its front limbs. These dinosaurs probably wandered through the scrub in small family groups, led by a dominant male. When threatened, they could rise up on their long hind legs and sprint away from danger, holding their long tails out behind them for balance.

Licking may have helped keep the paws clean.

Long, three-toed feet for fast running speeds

| 05–250 | Triassic 250–203 | Jurassic 203–135 | Cretaceous 135–65 | Tertiary 65–1.75 | Quaternary 1.75 present |

MESOZOIC 250–65 MYA

CENOZOIC 65 MYA present

EARLY SHIELD BEARERS

ARMED WITH SHOWY PROTECTIVE bony spikes and plates, stegosaurs and ankylosaurs rightly earned their name of thyreophorans or "shield bearers." Yet these plodding quadrupeds – the dinosaur equivalents of armored cars – evolved from smaller, more agile plant eaters, which merely had rows of small bony plates and studs set in their skin. Two of these early thyreophorans are known from well-preserved Jurassic fossils. *Scutellosaurus*, which was built lightly to run on its long hind limbs lived in North America, while the bigger, bulkier *Scelidosaurus* lived in Europe. Incomplete fossils of other early thyreophorans, including *Emausaurus*, *Echinodon*, and *Tatisaurus*, have also been found.

ARMORED SKIN
Scelidosaurus's hide was covered in tiny, pebbly scales and rows of bony studs. Small, low, bony plates – some ridged, some cone-shaped – added protection to its neck and back, while hornier bony plates formed clusters that protected the head. This knobby armor was sufficient to resist attacks by Jurassic theropods, which had not yet developed powerful muscles and sharp claws and teeth.

Long, narrow, armored tail

BONY PLATES
These three scutes, or horny plates, give some idea of the body armor that protected *Scelidosaurus* from predators. If a theropod bit into the animal's pebbly hide, its teeth would have come to a crunching full stop.

Small, bony studs arranged in rows

UNIVERSITY LIZARD
Emausaurus was an early Jurassic herbivore, about 6 ft 6 in (2 m) in length. Its unusual name, which is short for "Ernst-Moritz-Arndt-Universität lizard," comes from a university town in northern Germany, where its fossil was discovered in 1990. Only parts of the skull, skeleton, and small pieces of its armor were unearthed, so little is known about its habits. Like its relatives *Scelidosaurus* and *Scutellosaurus*, *Emausaurus* was protected from theropod attack by flat and cone-shaped lumps set into its skin.

LOWER HIND LIMB LIZARD

Among the most primitive of the ornithischian ("bird hipped") dinosaurs was *Scelidosaurus* ("lower hind limb lizard") from the Early Jurassic. When walking, it carried its long, heavy body on four sturdy limbs, and was highest at the hips. Its long feet had toes with hooflike claws on their tips. Rows of low, ridged, horn-sheathed bones reinforced its skin. These, together with its curved lower jaw and distinctive skull bones, identify *Scelidosaurus* as a thyreophoran dinosaur. Although its front upper jaw had teeth, these were not used for chewing but bit up and down, slicing and crushing the soft "flowers" of palmlike plants.

Cambrian 540–500	Ordovician 500–435	Silurian 435–410	Devonian 410–355	Carboniferous 355–295	Permia

PALEOZOIC 540–250 MYA

LITTLE SHIELD

Scutellosaurus ("little shield lizard") had a long body, slim limbs, and an elongated tail. More than 300 little, horn-sheathed, bony scutes guarded its back, flanks, and the base of its tail. The largest scutes formed one or two rows down the middle of the back. *Scutellosaurus* could walk on its hind limbs, its long body balanced by its even longer tail. However, its bony armor made its body heavy at the front, so it probably also ambled on all fours. *Scutellosaurus* used its simple cheek teeth to slice and crush soft, fleshy, low-growing vegetation.

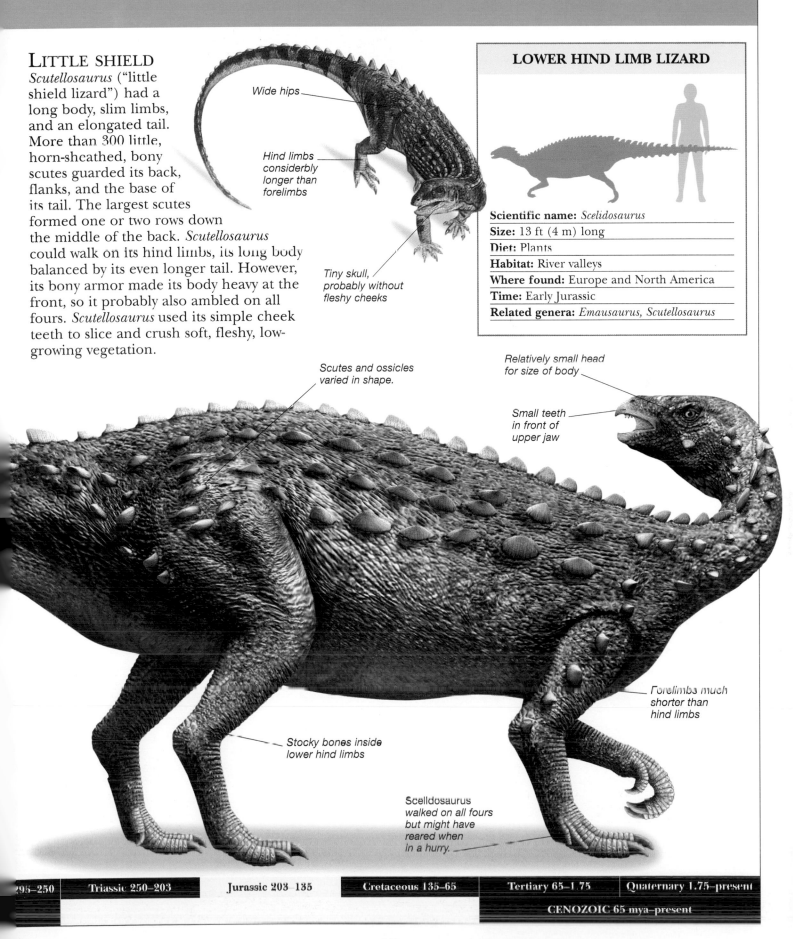

Wide hips

Hind limbs considerbly longer than forelimbs

Tiny skull, probably without fleshy cheeks

LOWER HIND LIMB LIZARD

Scientific name: *Scelidosaurus*
Size: 13 ft (4 m) long
Diet: Plants
Habitat: River valleys
Where found: Europe and North America
Time: Early Jurassic
Related genera: *Emausaurus, Scutellosaurus*

Scutes and ossicles varied in shape.

Relatively small head for size of body

Small teeth in front of upper jaw

Stocky bones inside lower hind limbs

Forelimbs much shorter than hind limbs

Scelldosaurus walked on all fours but might have reared when in a hurry.

PLATED DINOSAURS

STEGOSAURS ("ROOF LIZARDS") WERE A GROUP OF four-legged, plant-eating dinosaurs that reached lengths of up to 30 ft (9 m). Named for the two rows of tall bony plates jutting up from the neck, back, and tail, most also had a pair of spikes jutting out from their shoulders. Their bulky, ponderous bodies carried characteristically tiny, low-slung heads. Stegosaurs first appeared in East Asia in Early Jurassic times, and by the Late Jurassic the group included *Tuojiangosaurus* from China, *Kentrosaurus* from East Africa, *Lexovisaurus* from Europe, and *Stegosaurus* from North America. Late Jurassic times were their heyday, and the group seems to have petered out in Early Cretaceous times. Perhaps their spiky defenses proved no match for new formidable kinds of theropod dinosaur.

TUO RIVER LIZARD

Scientific name: *Tuojiangosaurus*
Size: 23 ft (7 m) long
Diet: Plants
Habitat: Open woodland
Where found: East Asia (China)
Time: Late Jurassic
Related genera: *Lexovisaurus, Paranthodon*

TUOJIANGOSAURUS

The Chinese dinosaur *Tuojiangosaurus* ("Tuo River lizard") was longer but lighter than a rhinoceros. Its skeleton clearly shows a low skull, high, humped back, long, heavy tail, and solid limb bones. Up to 15 pairs of pointed bony plates rose from this stegosaur's neck, back, and tail. Two pairs of long, slim spikes stuck up and out from the end of the tail, and a long spine jutted from each shoulder. Horny sheaths would have covered the tail and shoulder spikes, making these even longer than their bony cores suggest.

SKULLS AND TEETH

Most stegosaur skulls were long, low, and narrow, ending in a slim, toothless beak. The jaws were hinged low down at the back and had small, ridged cheek teeth set in from the sides. Fleshy cheeks may have stopped food from falling out of the mouth when eating. Stegosaurs must have consumed huge amounts of plant matter to sustain their great bulk.

Stegosaurus skull and ridged cheek tooth

Tuojiangosaurus skeleton

Bones of the forelimbs much shorter than those of the hind limbs

The forelimbs may have been erect or splayed out at the elbows.

Cambrian 540–500	Ordovician 500–435	Silurian 435–410	Devonian 410–355	Carboniferous 355–295	Permiar

PALEOZOIC 540–250 MYA

SPIKY BACK

Kentrosaurus ("sharp point lizard") takes its name from the long spines that stuck up from its back, tail, and flanks. Up to 17 ft (5 m) in length, this stegosaur had a long but narrow skull, which was held low off the ground when walking. Its jaws were equipped with small cheek teeth to browse ferns and other low-growing plants that grew along river banks. The back legs were twice as long as the front legs, suggesting that *Kentrosaurus* could rear up to reach higher vegetation.

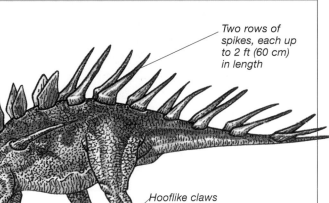

Two rows of spikes, each up to 2 ft (60 cm) in length

Hooflike claws on toes

ONE BRAIN OR TWO

For such a large dinosaur, *Kentrosaurus* had a small brain – no bigger than a walnut. However, the olfactory bulb was well developed, giving the animal a good sense of smell. It was once believed that the tiny brain was too small to control the animal's body and that another larger brain was located near the hips, as in other dinosaurs. Scientists now know that the larger "brain" merely held nerves that controlled the hind limbs and tail, and stored glycogen – food energy for powering its muscles.

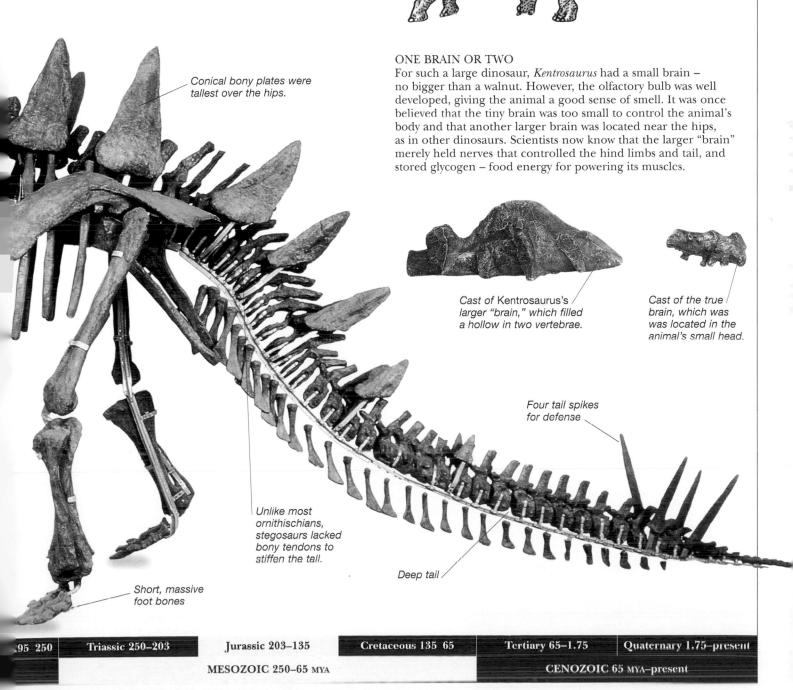

Conical bony plates were tallest over the hips.

Cast of Kentrosaurus's larger "brain," which filled a hollow in two vertebrae.

Cast of the true brain, which was was located in the animal's small head.

Four tail spikes for defense

Unlike most ornithischians, stegosaurs lacked bony tendons to stiffen the tail.

Deep tail

Short, massive foot bones

95 250	Triassic 250–203	Jurassic 203–135	Cretaceous 135 65	Tertiary 65–1.75	Quaternary 1.75–present
		MESOZOIC 250–65 MYA		CENOZOIC 65 MYA–present	

SPIKY BACKS

THE MOST STRIKING FEATURE of any stegosaur is the array of plates sticking up from its neck, back, and tail. The largest member of this group was *Stegosaurus* ("roof lizard") – a North American dinosaur that could grow to the size of a bus. Its back was crowned by huge plates shaped like upended sidewalk slabs. The first *Stegosaurus* fossil was discovered in the western United States in the 1870s, and dozens have been unearthed since. Despite being one of the most intensely studied of all dinosaurs, experts have long disagreed about how the plates were arranged on the giant's back and about their function. Were they for defense or for show, or did they help regulate temperature?

STING IN THE TAIL
Stegosaurus was well protected by a tough, studded hide, and it was also able to deter predators with its mace-like tail. Sticking out and back from the end of the tail were at least two pairs of long, sharp bony spikes, covered in horn. Standing alongside an attacking *Allosaurus* or other predator, *Stegosaurus* could have lashed its tail, inflicting frightful stabbing blows.

Downcurved neck held the head low off the ground.

Broad hind foot with three short, blunt toes.

Four-toed forefoot with toes tipped by hooflike nails

Cambrian 540–500	Ordovician 500–435	Silurian 435–410	Devonian 410–355	Carboniferous 355–295	Permia

PALEOZOIC 540–250 MYA

172

PLATE DEBATE

Scientists once thought that the paired bony plates on *Stegosaurus's* back protected it from attack. This now seems unlikely, because the plates were made of thin bone and were probably covered with skin, not horn. Instead, they perhaps served as radiators, helping *Stegosaurus* to warm up when it turned perpendicular to the Sun's rays, and to cool down when it turned away. Another theory is that the plates were for show, helping males and females of the same species to recognize each other.

The plates may have alternated rather than forming two paired rows.

Although small, the brain effectively coordinated the bulky body.

The narrow beak was suited to cropping low-growing soft, fleshy plants.

CHAINMAIL
Stegosaurus's vulnerable throat was protected from the claws and teeth of theropods by bony studs set in the skin. These studs – also present on the hips, thighs, and tail – were the equivalent of the chainmail worn by medieval knights. They prevented puncture while leaving the skin itself quite flexible.

ROOF LIZARD

Scientific name:	*Stegosaurus*
Size:	Up to 30 ft (9 m) long
Diet:	Plants
Habitat:	Open woodland
Where found:	North America
Time:	Late Jurassic
Related genera:	*Tuojiangosaurus, Wuerhosaurus*

05 250	Triassic 250–20?	Jurassic 203–135	Cretaceous 135–65	Tertiary 65–1.75	Quaternary 1.75–present
		MESOZOIC 250–65 MYA		CENOZOIC 65 MYA–present	

NODE LIZARDS

THE ARMORED DINOSAURS CALLED ANKYLOSAURS ("fused lizards") were heavily plated, four-legged plant-eaters. They had characteristic low-slung heads, fairly short necks, broad, barrel-shaped bodies, and long, rather thick tails. These tanklike beasts were too slow to sprint away from danger, and their stubby claws and small, ridged teeth were no match for a large theropod's talons and fangs. Instead, they relied for protection on bony plates or spikes sheathed with horn and set into their thick, tough hides like cobblestones in a road. Ankylosaurs' armor may have proved more effective than the defenses of stegosaurs, relatives that they replaced. First emerging in the Jurassic, ankylosaurs spread through northern continents during Cretaceous times, and appeared as far south as Australia and Antarctica. Their three main groups were nodosaurids ("node lizards"), polacanthids, and ankylosaurids.

Ridged, bony, horn-covered scute ("shield")

Second collar of bony plates

First collar of bony plates

Spike protecting against a flank attack

Long bony spike guarding the shoulder

Short, broad, sturdy foot

Mouth ending in narrow beak

Ankylosaurs probably had roomy cheeks to hold food being chewed

ARMORED GIANT

As long as a soccer goal is wide and twice the weight of a large rhino, *Edmontonia* was one of the largest and latest of the nodosaurids. These ankylosaurs tended to have a fairly narrow, pear-shaped skull, covered with big scales, protecting the braincase. Many had spiky shoulder spines, but none had a tail club. *Edmontonia* shielded the back of its neck with two collars of flat bony plates. A third collar lay between the shoulders, and rows of smaller, ridged bony plates covered the rest of the back and tail. Long, bony spikes projecting from the shoulders were its main weapons, and could have crippled an attacking tyrannosaur's leg.

Cambrian 540–500	Ordovician 500–435	Silurian 435–410	Devonian 410–355	Carboniferous 355–295	Permi

PALEOZOIC 540–250 MYA

Broad-based "thorny" plates guarding tail

Sharp, low plates shielding hips

Raised bony shields on the hindlimb

Tall, ridged scutes over shoulders

Rows of ridged plates running down muscular tail

AN ARMORED DINOSAUR DOWN UNDER

Found near Minmi Crossing in Queensland, *Minmi* was the first armored dinosaur discovered south of the Equator. At only 10 ft (3 m) long, this Early Cretaceous ankylosaur was smaller than most others. Small bony plates guarded its belly, and beside each dorsal vertebra was a bony plate joined to a bony rod that might have helped to reinforce its backbone. Such unusual features make scientists suspect that *Minmi* was neither a nodosaurid nor an ankylosaurid, but belonged to another, so-far nameless group of armored dinosaurs.

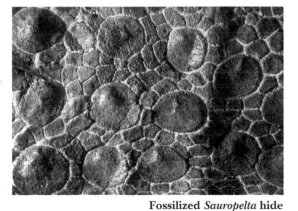

Fossilized *Sauropelta* hide

ARMORED HIDE

Sauropelta ("shielded lizard") from the Early Cretaceous of North America was smaller and less heavily armored than *Edmontonia*. Seen from above, *Sauropelta*'s armor resembles a knight's chain mail. Rows of bony cones set among small studs protected its back but left its body quite flexible. Bony spikes jutted from the sides of its neck. If attacked, *Sauropelta* might have crouched to guard its unarmored belly.

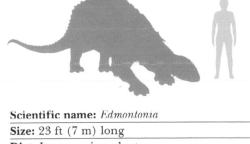

EDMONTONIA

Scientific name:	*Edmontonia*
Size:	23 ft (7 m) long
Diet:	Low-growing plants
Habitat:	Open woodland
Where found:	North America
Time:	Late Cretaceous
Related genera:	*Panoplosaurus, Sauropelta*

Largest bony plate over braincase

Edmontonia **skull**

Impressions of large scales

SHEEPLIKE HEAD

Edmontonia's skull looked much like a sheep's head when seen from one side. Its narrow, toothless beak was probably suited to cropping soft, juicy, low-growing plants, which were then sliced up by its small, ridged cheek teeth. A top view shows bony plates tightly fitting together like bits of a jigsaw puzzle to thicken the skull. A theropod's teeth might have simply skidded off *Edmontonia*'s skull like human teeth trying to crunch up a coconut shell.

5–250	Triassic 250–203	Jurassic 203–135	Cretaceous 135–65	Tertiary 65 1.75	Quaternary 1.75–present
	MESOZOIC 250–65 MYA			CENOZOIC 65 MYA–present	

FUSED LIZARDS

THE ANKYLOSAURIDS ("FUSED LIZARDS") were armored dinosaurs 10–33 ft (3–10 m) long. Like their relatives the nodosaurids, their main defenses were the thick, solid bones of the skull, and bands of bony plates, studs, and spikes shielding the neck and back. Unlike nodosaurids, most ankylosaurids had a skull as broad as it was long, with small "horns" projecting from the back, and a convoluted airway inside. Their common feature was the massive bony club on the end of the tail, and some early "ankylosaurids" without a club arguably formed a third family, called the polacanthids. The ankylosaurids appeared by the Late Jurassic and thrived throughout the Cretaceous in Asia, North America, and Europe. Some Late Cretaceous ankylosaurids were the largest armored dinosaurs of all.

Pattern where scales were stuck to the skull

AN ANKYLOSAURID SKULL

This reconstruction reveals *Euoplocephalus*'s bizarrely armored skull. Thick skull bones with a "crazy paving" pattern closed holes that lightened the skull in other dinosaurs. Its bony eyelid could flick up or down, like a window shutter, to protect the eye. Broad, short, thornlike spikes projected at the rear, protecting the back of the skull. Behind the heavy, toothless beak, the cheek teeth seem tiny and inadequate. They merely sliced up soft plant foods that were mainly mashed up in the gut.

Spine-fringed tail could lash from side to side.

Thickened bone gave the tail a club shape.

Muscular tail could swing club from side to side.

Broad, flat spikes to ward off attack from the side

THORNY BEAST
Named after fossil hunter Robert Gaston, *Gastonia* resembled a walking thorn bush the length of a large car. *Gastonia* roamed Utah in Early Cretaceous times. Big spines stuck out sideways from its shoulders and tail, and two rows of long spines stuck up from its back. Many smaller bony spines and a bony shield across its hips completed this dinosaur's jaw-breaking defense. *Gastonia*'s broad skull resembles an ankylosaurid's, but it was in fact a polacanthid. Despite the lack of a club, spines could have made its tail a formidable weapon.

WELL-ARMORED HEAD

Scientific name: *Euoplocephalus*
Size: 23 ft (7 m) long
Diet: Low–growing plants
Habitat: Open woodland
Where found: North America
Time: Late Cretaceous
Related genera: *Ankylosaurus, Pinacosaurus*

Cambrian 540–500	Ordovician 500–435	Silurian 435–410	Devonian 410–355	Carboniferous 355–295	Permi

PALEOZOIC 540–250 MYA

WELL-ARMORED HEAD

Resembling a cross between an armadillo and a huge rhinoceros, *Euoplocephalus* ("well-armored head") was one of the most common ankylosaurids of Late Cretaceous North America. With its broad beak, *Euoplocephalus* would not have been a choosy feeder – its main foods were very likely ferns, and the weedy, soft-stemmed flowering plants now spreading north. As it ambled slowly across woodland glades, four sturdy limbs bore the weight of its barrel-shaped body and the heavy load of plant food in its gut. If it had to, *Euoplocephalus* could break into a trot, but speed was not its best defense.

Flexible armored bands on back

Lateral division between bands

Pointed scutes ran in rows down back.

Bony "thorns" tallest over the shoulders

Broad toothless beak for cropping low vegetation

One of two large bony tail plates

Broad thighs partly supported by wide, shelf-shaped hipbones

Short digits with blunt nails

Short and broad three-toed feet

BONY TAIL CLUB

This fossil shows the construction of what was probably an ankylosaurid's main counterattacking weapon. At the tip of the tail, four swollen bony lumps – two large and two small – had fused to one another and the tail-tip vertebrae. Outside these bones, long, ropelike tendons stiffened and reinforced the tail's tip. The tail's muscular base was flexible, though – free to swing the club from side to side, delivering a heavy, powerful blow. Any attacking tyrannosaurid might have risked a fractured shin or ankle.

Bony tendons reinforced end of the tail.

One of two small bony tail plates

)5–250	Triassic 250–203	Jurassic 203–135	Cretaceous 135–65	Tertiary 65 1.75	Quaternary 1.75–present
		MESOZOIC 250–65 MYA		CENOZOIC 65 MYA=present	

CAMPTOSAURS AND DRYOSAURS

IGUANODONTIANS evolved during the Jurassic. They were the most successful ornithopod (bird-footed) dinosaurs and include the famous *Iguanodon (see pp180–81).* The most primitive iguanodontians, such as *Dryosaurus,* were relatively small and lightly built and would have relied on fast running to escape from predators. They might have used their arms for walking when moving very slowly, but, in contrast to *Iguanodon,* their arms and fingers were short. Unlike earlier ornithopods, iguanodontians did not have teeth at the tip of their upper jaw. With the evolution of *Camptosaurus,* iguanodontians began to become larger, heavier, and less agile.

Holes for nerves and blood vessels show that camptosaurs had beaked lower and upper jaws.

CAMPTOSAURUS

The best-known camptosaur was *Camptosaurus* from the Late Jurassic and Early Cretaceous of North America and England. It had stout hind limbs, a vaguely horselike skull, and a large, deep body. *Camptosaurus* was originally named *Camptonotus* meaning "flexible back." This was because the hip vertebrae of the first specimen seemed not to be fused together. However, *Camptonotus* had already been given to another animal, so *Camptosaurus,* meaning "flexible lizard" was chosen. In fact, *Camptosaurus* does have fused hip vertebrae like other dinosaurs, so the name is inaccurate.

Camptosaurus *had strong arms. Fossil tracks suggest that it may sometimes have walked slowly on all fours.*

The arms were slim and the hands were small. Hatchlings had stronger forelimbs and appear to have walked on all fours.

Palpebral bone

The teeth were leaf-shaped with serrated margins.

CAMPTOSAURUS SKULL
Features of its skull show that *Camptosaurus* was well suited for cropping and chewing plant material. The toothless beaks of the upper and lower jaws were broad and would have had sharp cutting edges. Mobile joints allowed the cheeks to move in and out so that the teeth in the upper jaw could grind against those in the lower jaw. An unusual bone called the palpebral grew across the eye socket, but its function is unknown.

Dryosaur legs and feet were built for fast running. Unlike in Camptosaurus, *the small first toe was not present.*

Cambrian 540–500	Ordovician 500–435	Silurian 435–410	Devonian 410–355	Carboniferous 355–295	Permia

PALEOZOIC 540–250 MYA

The bones of the lower part of the pelvis are directed backward to allow space for larger guts.

Crisscross pattern of tendons

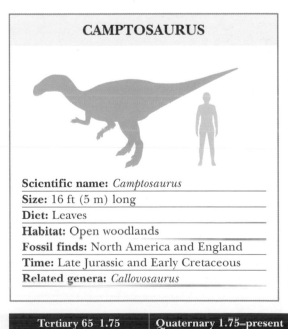

VERTEBRAE OF CAMPTOSAURUS

Like other ornithopods, *Camptosaurus* had a criss-cross pattern of tendons growing on the sides of the spines of its vertebrae. Arranged in three overlapping layers, these helped reinforce the spine and keep the back stiff. Its sacrum – the part of the vertebral column where the vertebrae are connected to the pelvis – consisted of either five or six vertebrae. *Camptosaurus* shared with *Iguanodon* special peg-and-socket joints between each of the sacral vertebrae. These further helped reinforce the backbone.

The last thumb bone was a pointed, spurlike structure. It was different from the specialized thumb spike seen in Iguanodon.

Hooflike fingertip

HAND OF CAMPTOSAURUS

Camptosaurus had five short fingers, the first three of which had hooves. Fossil trackways show that its fingers were not joined together in a large pad as they were in *Iguanodon*. Several of the wrist bones were fused together, perhaps for strength when the hand was used to support weight.

Camptosaurs have massive toe bones. The small first toe is turned backward and would not have reached the ground.

DRYOSAURUS

Dryosaurs have been found in North America, Africa, and Europe. The name means "tree lizard" and is a reference to the idea that this dinosaur lived in a woodland environment. Dryosaurs have short skulls with large eyes. Their peculiar nostrils are not covered over on their upper side by a bony bridge, as they are in virtually all other dinosaurs.

CAMPTOSAURUS

Scientific name:	*Camptosaurus*
Size:	16 ft (5 m) long
Diet:	Leaves
Habitat:	Open woodlands
Fossil finds:	North America and England
Time:	Late Jurassic and Early Cretaceous
Related genera:	*Callovosaurus*

95–250	Triassic 250 203	Jurassic 203–135	Cretaceous 135–65	Tertiary 65 1.75	Quaternary 1.75–present
		MESOZOIC 250–65 MYA		CENOZOIC 65 MYA–present	

179

IGUANODON

FOSSILS OF IGUANODON have been found in Europe, Asia, and North America, and it is one of the best-known and most successful dinosaurs. Officially brought to attention in 1825 by Gideon Mantell, a doctor from Lewes, England, it was the second dinosaur after *Megalosaurus* to be named and described. Mantell thought that *Iguanodon* was an immense lizardlike animal, while other scientists of the time argued that it resembled a rhinoceros more. In 1878, numerous complete skeletons were discovered in a coal mine in Belgium, which showed what *Iguanodon* really looked like. It had stout three-toed bird-limbs, powerful arms with a thumb shaped like a spike, and a vaguely horselike skull with a toothless beak. Fossilized footprints suggest that *Iguanodon* moved around in herds.

Scientists once believed that Iguanodon's tail would have sloped down close to the ground as shown here. More recent research has shown that this was not the case. Like virtually all dinosaurs, the structure of Iguanodon's spine suggests that its tail would have been held horizontally and off the ground.

Iguanodon's powerful arms were long enough to reach the ground. The three middle fingers appear suited for bearing weight. These features suggest that Iguanodon often walked on all fours.

PECULIAR HANDS

Iguanodon has the most specialized hands of any dinosaur. They could have been used as weapons, for walking on, and for grasping vegetation. A large conical spike, originally thought to be located on the tip of the nose, turned out to be *Iguanodon's* highly modified thumb. The second, third, and fourth fingers are strongly built and webbed together, and tipped with blunt hooves. Its fifth finger is slim and flexible.

Cambrian 540–500	Ordovician 500–435	Silurian 435–410	Devonian 410–355	Carboniferous 355–295	Permia

PALEOZOIC 540–250 MYA

IGUANODON

Scientific name: *Iguanodon*
Size: 8-12 m (26-40 ft)
Diet: Leaves, branches, fronds, and ferns
Habitat: Woodlands
Where found: Europe, Asia, and North America
Time: Early Cretaceous
Related genera: *Altirhinus, Ouranosaurus*

The woodland habitat of Iguanodon contained giant tree ferns and conifers. Flowering plants such as magnolias had also evolved by this time.

Iguanodon *was stoutly built and probably walked with its body held horizontally for most of the time.*

VEGETARIAN

Iguanodon was a large browsing herbivore with a deep skull, toothless beak, and many powerful cropping teeth. Special hinges in the skull and mobile lower jaws allowed *Iguanodon* to chew tough plants. Its height may have allowed it to feed from trees.

5–250	Triassic 250–203	Jurassic 203–135	Cretaceous 135–65	Tertiary 65–1.75	Quaternary 1.75–present
		MESOZOIC 250–65 MYA		CENOZOIC 65 MYA–present	

DUCK-BILLED DINOSAURS

IN THE CRETACEOUS an important group called the hadrosaurs ("duck-billed" dinosaurs) descended from *Iguanodon*-like ancestors. As their name suggests, duck-billed dinosaurs are characterized by an expanded toothless beak. They had hundreds of tightly packed teeth that were well equipped to grind up tough vegetation. Some had bizarre crests. Duck-billed dinosaurs are best known from North America and eastern Asia but they are also known from Europe, South America, and Antarctica. They were among the biggest dinosaurs, but they were preyed on by tyrannosaurs and other theropods. An old theory is that the hadrosaurs were amphibious animals, but their stiff tails, short toes, and small hands show that they more likely lived on land. Fossilized tracks, piles of bones, and nesting sites suggest that they were herding animals and formed nesting colonies.

Skull features show that duck-billed dinosaurs had large eyes, acute hearing, and a good sense of smell.

CORYTHOSAURUS

Corythosaurus was a crested duck-billed dinosaur, with a crest that was shaped like a plate. The name *Corythosaurus* means "helmet lizard," referring to the similarity between its crest and the helmets worn by soldiers in ancient Greece. *Corythosaurus* is one of the best-known hadrosaurs thanks to the discovery of a complete skeleton in 1912. The similar-looking *Hypacrosaurus* is probably a descendant of *Corythosaurus*.

Hatchlings were about 20 in (50 cm) long.

MAIASAURA FAMILY
Maiasaura was a flat-headed duck-billed dinosaur. Like other hadrosaurs without crests, it had hollow areas around the nostrils which perhaps housed large, inflatable skin pouches. It has been preserved with nests, broken eggshells, and babies. The babies clearly stayed in the nest for some time after hatching (as shown by the trampled eggshell) and therefore they may have been cared for by their parents.

Duck-billed dinosaurs had lost their thumbs, and their forelimbs were slimmer and less powerful than in Iguanodon.

Cambrian 540–500	Ordovician 500–435	Silurian 435–410	Devonian 410–355	Carboniferous 355–295	Permi

PALEOZOIC 540–250 MYA

Hadrosaur skin was covered in small, rounded tubercles.

LAMBEOSAUR CRESTS

Duck-billed dinsoaurs with crests were called lambeosaurs. These crests were hollow with a complex series of tubes inside, and the shape varied tremendously between species and individuals. The crests are connected to the noses and throats of the animals. Lambeosaurs probably used them as resonating devices, with the various shapes creating different sounds.

Parasaurolophus had a backward pointing tube.

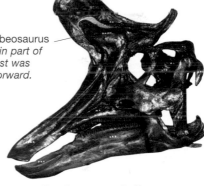

Evolution of the crest resulted in the nostrils being pulled backward.

Parasaurolophus skull

Hypacrosaurus skull

Stiff and narrow tail

In Lambeosaurus the main part of the crest was tilted forward.

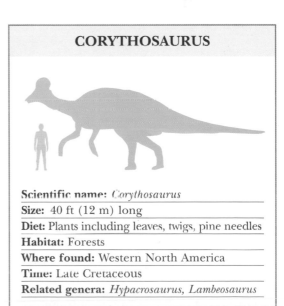

Lambeosaurus skull

Stout and powerful hind limbs

Fossilized tracks show that duck-billed dinosaurs often walked on all fours, though they could walk on two legs as well.

SWAMPLAND

Corythosaurus is shown here wading through a forest swamp. Most hadrosaurs lived in warm plains between the Rocky Mountains and a vast inland sea that divided North America into western and eastern halves. As well as cypress swamps, there were pine forests, fern prairies, and coastal marshes. The first flowering plants – the plants and trees that dominate the world today – were beginning to spread.

CORYTHOSAURUS

Scientific name:	*Corythosaurus*
Size:	40 ft (12 m) long
Diet:	Plants including leaves, twigs, pine needles
Habitat:	Forests
Where found:	Western North America
Time:	Late Cretaceous
Related genera:	*Hypacrosaurus, Lambeosaurus*

5–250	Triassic 250–203	Jurassic 203–135	Cretaceous 135–65	Tertiary 65–1.75	Quaternary 1.75–present
	MESOZOIC 250–65 MYA			CENOZOIC 65 MYA–present	

THICK-HEADED LIZARDS

PACHYCEPHALOSAURS were Cretaceous dinosaurs that are famous for having specially thickened bones on the tops of their skulls. In some, such as the Late Cretaceous North American forms *Pachycephalosaurus* and *Stegoceras*, the top of the skull formed a thickened dome, shaped like a bowling ball. Others, such as *Homalocephale* from Mongolia, had flat skull roofs. All known pachycephalosaurs come from the northern hemisphere and most are smaller than humans. The earliest is the Early Cretaceous *Yaverlandia*, from the Isle of Wight in England. It is known only from the top of its skull and is unique in having two small domes on the skull roof. Many specimens have been found in North America and Asia. A small pachycephalosaur from the Late Cretaceous of China is distinguished by having the longest name of any dinosaur – *Micropachycephalosaurus*.

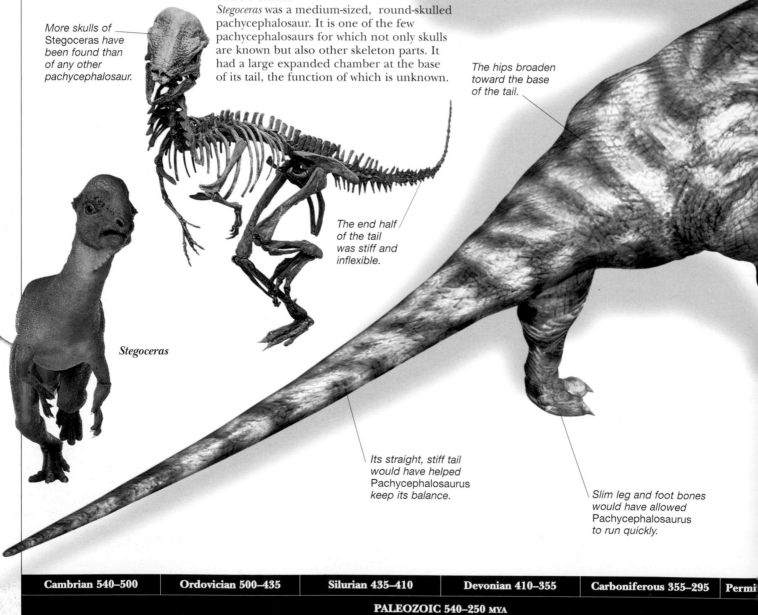

Prominent ridges grow along the side of the skull and over the eyes.

Pachycephalosaurs had curved, fanglike teeth at the front of the mouth. They also had beaks.

STEGOCERAS

Stegoceras was a medium-sized, round-skulled pachycephalosaur. It is one of the few pachycephalosaurs for which not only skulls are known but also other skeleton parts. It had a large expanded chamber at the base of its tail, the function of which is unknown.

More skulls of Stegoceras *have been found than of any other pachycephalosaur.*

The hips broaden toward the base of the tail.

The end half of the tail was stiff and inflexible.

Stegoceras

Its straight, stiff tail would have helped Pachycephalosaurus keep its balance.

Slim leg and foot bones would have allowed Pachycephalosaurus to run quickly.

Cambrian 540–500	Ordovician 500–435	Silurian 435–410	Devonian 410–355	Carboniferous 355–295	Permi

PALEOZOIC 540–250 MYA

The top of the head of Pachycephalosaurus looks like the shape of a bowling ball.

The bony shelf is one of the features common to all pachycephalosaurs.

Skull and mandible of *Stegoceras*

BONY SHELF
All pachycephalosaurs have a bony shelf jutting out from the back of their skulls, as seen on the *Stegoceras* example above. The related genus *Prenocephale* has a less distinct shelf. The bony shelf is also seen in the ceratopsians (horned dinosaurs). Thus, pachycephalosaurs and ceratopsians are united in a group called the Marginocephalia ("margin-headed ones").

The arms and hands of Pachycephalosaurus are small in proportion to the very broad body.

Skull of *Prenocephale*

Prenocephale had a less distinct, rounded shelf.

PACHYCEPHALOSAURUS

The thickened skull roofs of dome-headed pachycepha-losaurs suggest that these dinosaurs used their heads for fighting off rivals during the breeding season, much like goats and sheep do. However, the skull roof in goats and sheep forms a contact area that can be more than 12 in (30 cm) wide. In contrast, the bowling-ball shape of dome-headed pachycephalosaurs would have a small contact area, which would have placed a dangerous sideways strain on the neck. If pachycephalosaurs did not butt heads, they may have butted each other's bodies instead. Features of the vertebrae suggest that their spines may have had some shock-absorbing ability.

PACHYCEPHALOSAURUS

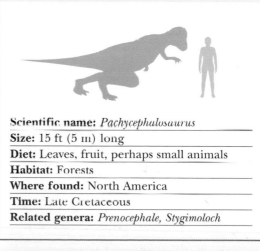

Scientific name: *Pachycephalosaurus*

Size: 15 ft (5 m) long

Diet: Leaves, fruit, perhaps small animals

Habitat: Forests

Where found: North America

Time: Late Cretaceous

Related genera: *Prenocephale, Stygimoloch*

95–250	Triassic 250–203		Jurassic 203–135	Cretaceous 135–65		Tertiary 65–1.75	Quaternary 1.75 present
		MESOZOIC 250–65 MYA				CENOZOIC 65 MYA–present	

PARROT LIZARDS

PSITTACOSAURS (PARROT LIZARDS) were small bipedal (two-footed) ceratopians (bird-hipped dinosaurs) that have proved abundant in the Lower Cretaceous rocks of eastern Asia. Their short, deep skulls are like those of modern parrots. Originally classified as ornithopods related to *Hypsilophodon*, psittacosaurs were later recognized as relatives of the horned dinosaurs of the Late Cretaceous. Both these groups possess a unique bone (the rostral) at the tip of the upper jaw. With the exception of *Chaoyangsaurus*, psittacosaurs are the most primitive known ceratopians. Elongated, slim hindlegs suggest they were fast runners, and this is probably how they escaped from predators. More than 100 specimens are known.

Like most ornithischians, psittacosaurs had bony tendons arranged along the length of their tail.

PSITTACOSAURUS

Eleven different species, all in genus *Psittacosaurus*, are distinguished by proportions, features of the teeth, and shape of the skull. Psittacosaurs have four fingers on the hand, unlike later ceratopians which all have five fingers. This suggests that psittacosaurs were not the actual ancestors of later ceratopians. *Psittacosaurus* was around for about 40 million years, making it one of the longest lived dinosaur genera.

Psittacosaurus would have run around on its hind legs.

LITTLE BABIES

Baby psittacosaurs are among the smallest reported dinosaur fossils. One specimen is estimated to have been 9 in (23 cm) long. Like other baby animals, these psittacosaurs have huge eyes, short snouts, and proportionally larger heads than adults. Some babies are found preserved together, suggesting that they stayed in groups. As with many dinosaurs, experts are unsure as to whether the babies were cared for by their parents, or if they were independent.

Actual size skull of fossilized baby *Psittacosaurus*

FOSSILIZED PSITTACOSAURUS

Skeletons are often found in desert areas with sand dunes. This suggests that *Psittacosaurus* was adapted to life in dry environments. Several psittacosaur specimens are preserved as if lying on their bellies, their legs folded up underneath them. One expert has suggested that this shows their legs had great mobility.

This skeleton, found in the 1920s, was the first psittacosaur to be discovered.

| Cambrian 540–500 | Ordovician 500–435 | Silurian 435–410 | Devonian 410–355 | Carboniferous 355–295 | Permi |

PALEOZOIC 540–250 MYA

Like many other similar dinosaurs, psittacosaurs had bones called palpebrals jutting out above their eyeballs. Experts remain unsure as to what these were for.

The rostral bone, a parrotlike beak

Psittacosaurus skull

Unlike psittacosaurs, parrots can move their upper jaw independently of the rest of the skull.

Modern parrot head

Horns, perhaps used in fighting or displaying, project from the cheek.

PARROTLIKE HEADS

The psittacosaurs' remarkably deep skulls are superficially like those of parrots. Their toothless beaks and blunt teeth suggest that they were herbivores, but they could have been omnivores that also ate carrion and small animals. Unlike later ceratopians, psittacosaurs swallowed stones and used these to help grind up their food.

Long toes and sharp claws suggest that Psittacosaurus could have been a good digger.

PSITTACOSAURUS

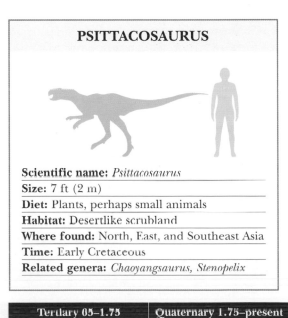

Scientific name: *Psittacosaurus*

Size: 7 ft (2 m)

Diet: Plants, perhaps small animals

Habitat: Desertlike scrubland

Where found: North, East, and Southeast Asia

Time: Early Cretaceous

Related genera: *Chaoyangsaurus, Stenopelix*

EARLY HORNED DINOSAURS

THE GROUP OF HORNED DINOSAURS called the Neo-ceratopsia ("new horned faces") can be divided into early and advanced forms. The early horned dinosaurs did not have the large horns of the advanced forms and they were relatively small, at about 3–12 ft (1–4 m) long. Early neoceratopsians probably ate mainly plants. Unlike their ceratopsomorph descendants, some of these early neoceratopsians had pointed teeth in their upper jaws. These primitive neoceratopsians were mostly from eastern Asia, including the well-known *Protoceratops*. Two others, *Leptoceratops* and *Montanoceratops,* were North American.

The deep tail was originally thought to indicate that Protoceratops *could swim. However, the animal lived in a desert.*

BURIED IN SAND
Several *Protoceratops* specimens from Mongolia are preserved buried in sand. Perhaps these were killed when the sand dunes they were hiding behind collapsed on top of them. Because their bones were then protected from scavengers, these specimens are very well preserved. Some of them are preserved in twisted or standing positions. New finds show *Protoceratops* babies clustered together.

The skeleton is seen here from beneath.

***Protoceratops* preserved in sand**

PROTOCERATOPS
Protoceratops is one of the few dinosaurs known from tens of specimens. In the Gobi Desert in Mongolia its fossils are so abundant that fossil-hunting paleontologists there call it the "sheep of the Gobi." Individuals with larger, taller neck frills and deeper snouts appear to be males. *Protoceratops* has very tall spines on the top of its tail vertebrae, which were perhaps used in display.

Protoceratops *had long, slender limbs suggesting that it was a fast runner.*

STAGES OF DEVELOPMENT
Because of the abundance of *Protoceratops* specimens, experts have been able to make a detailed study of the different stages of development. Specimens range from tiny babies to full-grown adult males and females. These reveal important changes that occurred in proportions during growth, particularly in the frill, as can be seen in the sequence of skulls shown here. Up to the juvenile stage, the frill or snout shape does not differ between males and females. Older females have narrow frills and low snouts, while older males have larger cheeks, snout, and frills.

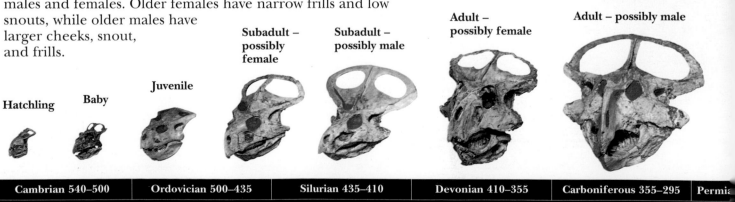

Hatchling **Baby** **Juvenile** **Subadult – possibly female** **Subadult – possibly male** **Adult – possibly female** **Adult – possibly male**

| Cambrian 540–500 | Ordovician 500–435 | Silurian 435–410 | Devonian 410–355 | Carboniferous 355–295 | Permia |

PALEOZOIC 540–250 MYA

Most horned dinosaur frills had thin bony borders and skin-covered gaps in the bone. These suggest that they were not for the attachment of large jaw muscles as once thought.

Protoceratops

Velociraptor

The Velociraptor's arm is gripped by the Protoceratops' beak.

FOSSILIZED PROTOCERATOPS FIGHTING VELOCIRAPTOR

This famous fossil was discovered in the Gobi Desert in 1971. It preserves a *Protoceratops* locked in combat with a *Velociraptor*. Both animals appear to have died while fighting. This might be because they both died of their injuries, or it might be because they were buried by a sand dune as they fought.

Some Protoceratops fossils include the bony rings that supported the eyeballs. These show that the eyes were large.

Protoceratops had a very small nasal horn between the eyes. The nasal horn was present in all advanced horned dinosaurs.

Two pairs of fanglike teeth may have been used in fighting or biting.

PROTOCERATOPS

Scientific name: *Protoceratops*

Size: 7 ft (2.5 m) long

Diet: Mostly desert vegetation

Habitat: Desert and desertlike scrubland

Where found: East Asia

Time: Late Cretaceous

Related genera: *Breviceratops, Udanoceratops, Leptoceratops*

05–250	Triassic 250–203	Jurassic 203–135	Cretaceous 135–65	Tertiary 65–1.75	Quaternary 1.75–present
	MESOZOIC 250–65 MYA			CENOZOIC 65 MYA–present	

ADVANCED HORNED DINOSAURS

IN THE LATE CRETACEOUS a group of horned dinosaurs, called the ceratopsomorphs, developed. These were distinguished from earlier horned dinosaurs by their mostly large body size, hooflike (rather than clawlike) bones on their fingers and toes, and large horns. They were robust, short-tailed, four-legged dinosaurs that superficially resembled horned rhinos today. All have massive hooked beaks and shearing teeth and would have been highly efficient eaters of most kinds of plant material. With the exception of two controversial fragmentary specimens from eastern Asia and South America – all known ceratopsomorphs are North American. About 14 different genera evolved there.

Many advanced horned dinosaurs have bones called epoccipitals arranged around the edges of the frill. The large frill spikes of Styracosaurus are probably enlarged epoccipitals.

Straight nose horn

CENTROSAURUS
Centrosaurus is a common horned dinosaur. Its nose horn is sometimes straight and points upward, as here. In other individuals it curves backward or forward to overhang the tip of the snout.

STYRACOSAURUS
A group of horned dinosaurs called the centrosaurines had relatively small brow horns and enlarged nose horns. Some centrosaurines also grew prominent backward-pointing spikes on the back of the frill. This trend was carried to its extreme in *Styracosaurus*, a genus that has six markedly elongate spikes on the back of the frill. The spikes would have looked imposing if the head was dipped in display.

Like other centrosaurines, Styracosaurus had an enlarged elongate nasal horn.

Centrosaurines have enormous nostril openings and incredibly deep snouts. The function of these nostrils is unknown.

Cambrian 540–500	Ordovician 500–435	Silurian 435–410	Devonian 410–355	Carboniferous 355–295	Permi

PALEOZOIC 540–250 MYA

LIFE AND DEATH IN HERDS

At least some horned dinosaurs appear to have been herding animals. Like living wildebeest, shown here, and other herding mammals, many horned dinosaurs seem to have drowned during the panic of river crossing. Their bones were then trampled and scavenged by theropods and other animals.

Like other horned dinosaurs, the body of Styracosaurus was covered in a thick hide.

The hips are connected to about 10 vertebrae bones – more than in any other dinosaur group, except birds.

The nose horn and two brow horns give Triceratops its name, which means "three-horned face."

TRICERATOPS

The most famous horned dinosaur is *Triceratops*, a member of the chasmosaurine group. Chasmosaurines mostly had elongate frills with large openings, but *Triceratops* is unusual in having a fairly short frill that lacks openings. Growing to 30 ft (10 m) in length and weighing about 10 tons, it was a gigantic animal and one of the last nonbird dinosaurs.

Some experts think that horned dinosaurs could gallop despite the shortness of their limbs.

The robust four-toed feet were built to support weight. The hooves were blunt, unlike the clawlike hooves of more primitive horned dinosaurs.

STYRACOSAURUS

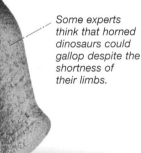

Scientific name:	*Styracosaurus*
Size:	17 ft (5 m) long
Diet:	Ferns, cycads, and other plants
Habitat:	Open woodland
Where found:	North America
Time:	Late Cretaceous
Related species:	*Achelousaurus, Einiosaurus*

95–250	Triassic 250–203	Jurassic 203–135	Cretaceous 135–65	Tertiary 65–1.75	Quaternary 1.75–present

MESOZOIC 250–65 MYA   CENOZOIC 65 MYA–present

191

Mammals and their Ancestors

Sprawling, scaly pelycosaurs with tall fins on their backs, featured below, look nothing like tigers or cows. Yet the pages in this section show that today's hairy, warm-blooded mammals all owe their origins to such reptile-like creatures. Startling images reveal other prehistoric mammals that looked just as strange as pelycosaurs – elephantine sloths, snaky whales, cats with dagger-like canine teeth, and hoofed mammals with bizarrely horned heads. Discover extinct ape-like creatures that walked erect, and their increasingly intelligent descendants – the mammals called humans.

SYNAPSIDS CLADOGRAM

MAMMALS AND THEIR EXTINCT RELATIVES are called synapsids. These amniotes are named after the bony opening behind the eye, known as the synapsid opening. Typical mammalian features, such as fur, a warm-blooded metabolism, and a lower jaw that consists of a single bone, appeared gradually during synapsid evolution. True mammals evolved in the Triassic. The earliest members of the three living groups – the egg-laying monotremes, the pouched marsupials, and the placentals – appeared in the Cretaceous. Placental mammals include the most familiar synapsid groups.

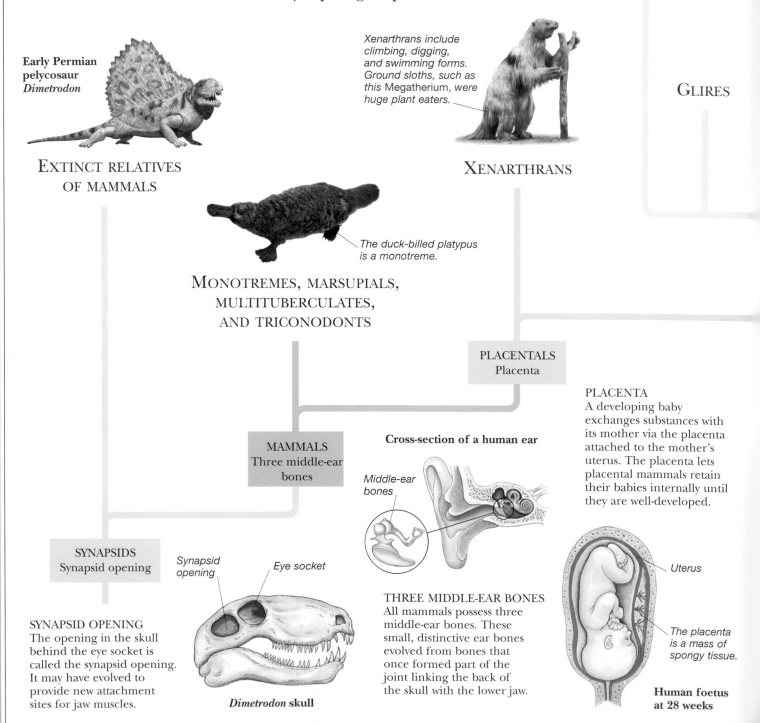

Early Permian pelycosaur *Dimetrodon*

EXTINCT RELATIVES OF MAMMALS

Xenarthrans include climbing, digging, and swimming forms. Ground sloths, such as this *Megatherium, were* huge plant eaters.

XENARTHRANS

CARNIVORES

GLIRES

The duck-billed platypus is a monotreme.

MONOTREMES, MARSUPIALS, MULTITUBERCULATES, AND TRICONODONTS

PLACENTALS
Placenta

PLACENTA
A developing baby exchanges substances with its mother via the placenta attached to the mother's uterus. The placenta lets placental mammals retain their babies internally until they are well-developed.

MAMMALS
Three middle-ear bones

Cross-section of a human ear

Middle-ear bones

SYNAPSIDS
Synapsid opening

Synapsid opening

Eye socket

Uterus

SYNAPSID OPENING
The opening in the skull behind the eye socket is called the synapsid opening. It may have evolved to provide new attachment sites for jaw muscles.

Dimetrodon **skull**

THREE MIDDLE-EAR BONES
All mammals possess three middle-ear bones. These small, distinctive ear bones evolved from bones that once formed part of the joint linking the back of the skull with the lower jaw.

The placenta is a mass of spongy tissue.

Human foetus at 28 weeks

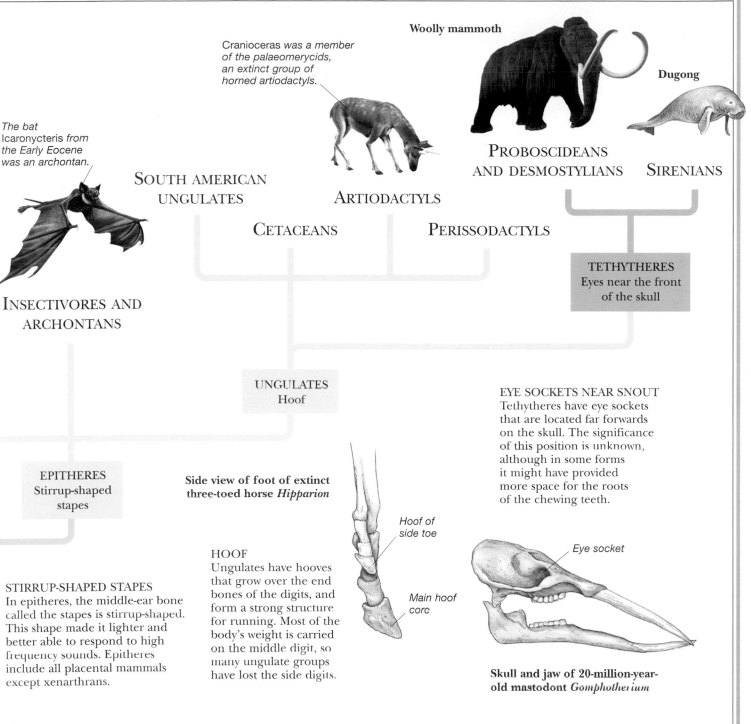

Woolly mammoth

Dugong

Cranioceras was a member of the palaeomerycids, an extinct group of horned artiodactyls.

The bat Icaronycteris *from the Early Eocene was an archontan.*

SOUTH AMERICAN UNGULATES

ARTIODACTYLS

PROBOSCIDEANS AND DESMOSTYLIANS

SIRENIANS

CETACEANS

PERISSODACTYLS

INSECTIVORES AND ARCHONTANS

TETHYTHERES
Eyes near the front of the skull

UNGULATES
Hoof

EYE SOCKETS NEAR SNOUT
Tethytheres have eye sockets that are located far forwards on the skull. The significance of this position is unknown, although in some forms it might have provided more space for the roots of the chewing teeth.

EPITHERES
Stirrup-shaped stapes

Side view of foot of extinct three-toed horse *Hipparion*

Hoof of side toe

Eye socket

HOOF
Ungulates have hooves that grow over the end bones of the digits, and form a strong structure for running. Most of the body's weight is carried on the middle digit, so many ungulate groups have lost the side digits.

Main hoof core

STIRRUP-SHAPED STAPES
In epitheres, the middle-ear bone called the stapes is stirrup-shaped. This shape made it lighter and better able to respond to high frequency sounds. Epitheres include all placental mammals except xenarthrans.

Skull and jaw of 20-million-year-old mastodont *Gomphotherium*

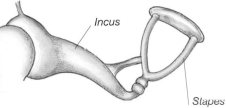

Incus

Stapes

Middle ear bones

SYNAPSID EVOLUTION

Early synapsids appeared during the Carboniferous and the Permian. Their descendants, the small cynodonts of the Triassic, were the direct ancestors of the first mammals. A diversity of primitive mammal groups evolved during the Mesozoic, but only one of these groups – the monotremes – survives today. The largest and most diverse group of mammals – the placentals – evolved in the Cretaceous, and share an ancestor with the marsupials. The placentals underwent a massive burst of evolution at the start of the Cenozoic.

EARLY SYNAPSIDS

SYNAPSIDS ("WITH ARCH") INCLUDE the mammal-like "reptiles" and their descendants, the mammals. They are named for the large hole low in the skull behind each eye. Muscles that worked the jaws passed through this hole, and gave synapsids a wide gape and powerful bite. Synapsids formed a separate group from true reptiles, who gave rise to lizards, dinosaurs, and their relatives. Like living reptiles, however, early kinds were scaly and cold-blooded. Synapsids appeared during the Carboniferous period. Early synapsids are known as pelycosaurs, and were quadrupeds with sprawling limbs. Most pelycosaurs lived in what is now North America and Europe. By early Permian times, pelycosaurs counted for seven out of ten backboned land animals. The early synapsids died out toward the end of the Permian period.

Sunshine could have warmed Dimetrodon's body by heating the blood that flowed through its sail.

SAIL-BACKED KILLER

Dimetrodon was one of the first big land animals to be capable of attacking and killing creatures its own size. This pelycosaur had a large, long, narrow head, with powerful jaws and daggerlike teeth. *Dimetrodon* could grow up to 11 ft 6 in (3.5 m) in length. It survived by attacking and eating large, plant-eating pelycosaurs. *Dimetrodon* lived during the Early Permian in what is now North America and Europe. Its remains have been found in Texas and Oklahoma, and in Europe.

Dimetrodon skull

Canine teeth with serrated blades

TYPES OF TEETH
Most reptiles have teeth of similar shapes. *Dimetrodon*'s teeth had different shapes, like a mammal's. The name *Dimetrodon* means "two types of teeth." The differently shaped teeth had various functions. The pointed upper canine teeth were designed for piercing flesh. The sharp front teeth served for biting and gripping. The small back teeth aided in chewing up chunks of flesh.

Dimetrodon

| Cambrian 540–500 | Ordovician 500–435 | Silurian 435–410 | Devonian 410–355 | Carboniferous 355–295 | Permia... |

PALEOZOIC 540–250 MYA

Tall, rod-shaped bones with short crosspieces held up Edaphosaurus's skin fin, or sail.

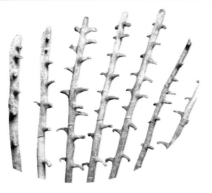

Spines from *Edaphosaurus*'s fin

SKIN SAIL

The skin sail rising from *Dimetrodon*'s back was a special feature whose likely purpose was to help control body temperature. *Edaphosaurus* also had a tall skin sail on its back. Skin sails may have helped pelycosaurs keep cool in hot weather or be active in the morning while their prey was still cold and sluggish. The sail may also have aided recognition among members of a species.

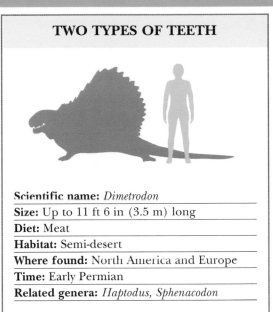

TWO TYPES OF TEETH

Scientific name: *Dimetrodon*
Size: Up to 11 ft 6 in (3.5 m) long
Diet: Meat
Habitat: Semi-desert
Where found: North America and Europe
Time: Early Permian
Related genera: *Haptodus, Sphenacodon*

EARTH LIZARD

Edaphosaurus ("earth lizard") was a large, early plant-eating pelycosaur. Its broad, short head was small for its hefty, 10-ft (3-m) long body. Its barrel-shaped body had room for the large gut needed for digesting bulky plant food, although some scientists believe its peg-shaped teeth were best suited for crushing shellfish. *Edaphosaurus* lived in North America and Europe from the Late Carboniferous to the Early Permian. Its worst enemy was another pelycosaur – the meat-eating *Dimetrodon*.

***Edaphosaurus* skeleton**

Edaphosaurus's skeleton shows it had a relatively deeper tail and shorter limbs than Dimetrodon.

95–250	Triassic 250–203	Jurassic 203–135	Cretaceous 135–65	Tertiary 65–1.75	Quaternary 1.75–present
	MESOZOIC 250–65 MYA			CENOZOIC 65 MYA–present	

TERRIBLE HEADS

DINOCEPHALIAN ("terrible head") therapsids were synapsids from the Permian whose fossils are known from Russia, South Africa, North America, and Brazil. Their heads were massive compared to their bodies, and this quality gave the group its name. Dinocephalians were diverse and abundant, but they did not survive beyond the Permian, and left no descendants. Carnivorous dinocephalians, such as the brithopodid *Titanophoneus*, were long-tailed predators capable of attacking the largest herbivores. Their large, elongate skulls held interlocking incisors – a key dinocephalian feature – and prominent canine teeth. Herbivorous dinocephalians lacked the canine teeth of their predatory, brithopodid-like ancestors. Their enlarged tooth crowns provided a crushing surface for plant material, but were less suited for tearing flesh. Advanced herbivorous dinocephalians, such as *Moschops*, had short tails and grew to the size of rhinos.

Horns of some *Estemmenosuchus* species were complex, with several branches.

The forehead bump may have been present only in males, but more specimens are needed to confirm this theory.

Top view of *Struthiocephalus* skull

HORNED HERBIVORES
Several kinds of herbivorous dinocephalian evolved horns or other unusual structures on their skulls. These may have been used in displays or fights during the breeding season. *Struthiocephalus* was a long-skulled tapinocephalid from Russia that was related to *Moschops*. A large bump that projected from its forehead may have once formed part of a large spike.

Wide mouth, with large incisors and canines that interlocked when the mouth was closed.

ESTEMMENOSUCHIDS
Primitive Russian dinocephalians called estemmenosuchids were famous for the massive bony protuberances that grew from their cheeks and their upper skulls. These protuberances might have been covered in horn, and could have been used in fights or visual displays. Some specimens of *Estemmenosuchus* have larger protuberances than others, and may be males. The canines and pointed incisors of estemmenosuchids suggest carnivorous habits. Fossil skin impressions of *Estemmenosuchus* show that these animals probably lacked scales, and may have had skin glands, like living mammals.

| Cambrian 540–500 | Ordovician 500–435 | Silurian 435–410 | Devonian 410–355 | Carboniferous 355–295 | Permia |

PALEOZOIC 540–250 MYA

TITANOPHONEUS

The large, Russian brithopodid *Titanophoneus* is known from a well-preserved skeleton with a remarkably complete skull. Like other predatory dinocephalians, *Titanophoneus* had a large, elongate skull whose interlocking teeth were used to grab, kill, and dismember large animal prey. Brithopodids had short, powerful limbs and long tails. They bore a superficial resemblance to earlier predatory synapsids, such as the sphenacodontids, whose members included *Dimetrodon*.

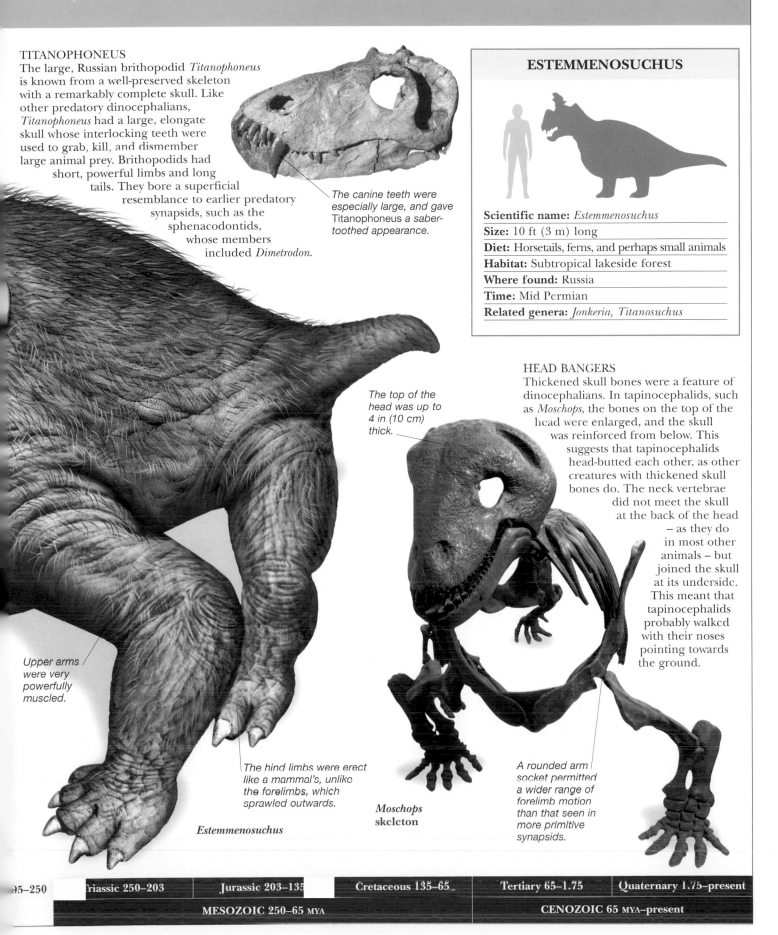

The canine teeth were especially large, and gave Titanophoneus a saber-toothed appearance.

ESTEMMENOSUCHUS

Scientific name: *Estemmenosuchus*

Size: 10 ft (3 m) long

Diet: Horsetails, ferns, and perhaps small animals

Habitat: Subtropical lakeside forest

Where found: Russia

Time: Mid Permian

Related genera: *Jonkeria, Titanosuchus*

The top of the head was up to 4 in (10 cm) thick.

HEAD BANGERS

Thickened skull bones were a feature of dinocephalians. In tapinocephalids, such as *Moschops*, the bones on the top of the head were enlarged, and the skull was reinforced from below. This suggests that tapinocephalids head-butted each other, as other creatures with thickened skull bones do. The neck vertebrae did not meet the skull at the back of the head – as they do in most other animals – but joined the skull at its underside. This meant that tapinocephalids probably walked with their noses pointing towards the ground.

Upper arms were very powerfully muscled.

The hind limbs were erect like a mammal's, unlike the forelimbs, which sprawled outwards.

Estemmenosuchus

Moschops skeleton

A rounded arm socket permitted a wider range of forelimb motion than that seen in more primitive synapsids.

05–250	Triassic 250–203	Jurassic 203–135	Cretaceous 135–65	Tertiary 65–1.75	Quaternary 1.75–present
	MESOZOIC 250–65 MYA			CENOZOIC 65 MYA–present	

TWO DOG TEETH

DICYNODONTS ("TWO DOG TEETH") were short-tailed synapsids with beaked jaws who lived from the Early Permian to the Late Triassic. The unusual dicynodont jaw, combined with their stout, barrel-shaped bodies, suggests that they were herbivorous, and ate fibrous plants, such as horsetails and ferns. However, some dicynodonts may have been omnivorous or carnivorous. Dicynodont limbs were robust, which made these creatures slow-moving, but powerful. Dicynodont forelimbs sprawled sideways, but their hind limbs were erect, like those of mammals. While most Permian dicynodonts were less than 3 ft 3 in (1 m) long, the last Triassic forms reached 10 ft (3 m) in length and perhaps 0.9 ton (1 tonne) in weight. A superficial resemblance to hippopotamuses led dicynodonts to be regarded as amphibious. Perhaps some of them did live this way, but they mostly seem to have been residents of semi-arid, terrestrial environments.

Its skull openings housed large jaw muscles that controlled lower jaw movement.

LYSTROSAURUS

The small, Early Triassic dicynodont *Lystrosaurus* had a distinctive short skull with a deep snout, high nostrils, and stout, broad limb bones. Like most dicynodonts, its jaws appear to have held a beak in life. Its powerful forelimbs and prominent tusks could have been used for digging. *Lystrosaurus*'s short yet flexible neck might have improved its ability to reach plant material. Its ear bones suggest that it relied on sound vibrations conducted to the bones from the ground, rather than through the air.

SINOKANNEMEYERIA

Sinokannemeyeria was a large, long-snouted, Chinese dicynodont with downward-pointing tusks that grew from bulbous projections on its upper jaw. The muscle attachment sites on the back of the skull were quite small, which suggests that *Sinokannemeyeria* did not have the powerful skull muscles needed for shearing plants, unlike other dicynodonts. Most dicynodonts chopped up food by sliding their lower jaws backward and forward. *Sinokannemeyeria* fed by tearing plant material with the front of the snout. The kannemeyeriines descended from ancestors similar to *Lystrosaurus*, and were the only Triassic dicynodonts.

A broad, blunt snout allowed it to grab large mouthfuls of plant material.

Projections that once held tusks

Powerful forelimbs were perhaps used for digging.

Sinokannemeyeria

Cambrian 540–500	Ordovician 500–435	Silurian 435–410	Devonian 410–355	Carboniferous 355–295	Permia

PALEOZOIC 540–250 MYA

SINOKANNEMEYERIA

Scientific name: *Sinokannemeyeria*

Size: 10 ft (3 m) long

Diet: Fibrous plants

Habitat: Woodland near lakes and rivers

Where found: China

Time: Early Triassic

Related genera: *Parakannemeyeria, Rhadiodromus*

BURROW DWELLERS

Some small dicynodonts have features that suggest that they dug burrows. *Cistecephalus* from the Late Permian of South Africa had a robust skeleton with extra muscle attachments similar to those seen in modern animals that dig. The back of *Cistecephalus*'s skull was modified for muscles that power the head forward during digging. A few specimens of the South African dicynodont *Diictodon* were found inside spiral-shaped burrows. Scrape marks on the burrows' walls suggest that *Diictodon* used its beak or blunt claws to dig with.

Cistecephalus **skull**

Solid, wedge-shaped skull with very broad skull roof.

Lystrosaurus **skull**

This prominent tusk bears scratch marks that show it was used for digging.

TEETH AND TOOTHLESSNESS

Late Permian dicynodonts had small teeth that lined their jaws. Later dicynodonts, such as *Lystrosaurus*, lost these small teeth, and retained only the large canines in the upper jaw. In still later dicynodonts, such as *Sinokannemeyeria*, these canines became large tusks that differed in size between the sexes. Tusks may have been used for fighting and display, or could have been used to dig with. Dicynodonts such as *Oudenodon* and *Stahleckeria* were completely toothless.

The large, heavy skull was about 24 in (60 cm) long.

Stout and broad limb bones suggest that Sinokannemeyeria could not run fast.

THE LAST DICYNODONTS

By the Late Triassic, dicynodonts had become rare. The few species known from that time were large beasts – more than 10 ft (3 m) long – and all were found in the Americas. *Placerias* was one of the last dicynodonts, and is known from several individuals that perished at a lake site. Sexual dimorphism (two forms of the same species) is evident in *Placerias* – in some individuals, the pointed projections that house the tusks are larger than in others. The actual tusks were tiny in both sexes.

Placerias

The feet were short and broad with blunt claws.

5–250	Triassic 250–203	urassic 203–135	Cretaceous 135–65	ertiary 65–1.75	Quaternary 1.75–present

MESOZOIC 250–65 MYA   CENOZOIC 65 MYA–present

DOG TEETH

CYNODONTS ("DOG TEETH") WERE SMALL to medium-sized carnivorous synapsids, and were the likely ancestors of mammals. They belonged to the theriodonts ("beast teeth"), the most advanced subgroup of those synapsids called therapsids. Cynodonts had a bony palate that separated the nasal passages from the mouth and let them breathe while they ate – a necessary feature of warm-blooded creatures. Other similarities with mammals include fewer lower-jaw bones and better developed brains than reptiles, broad back teeth with ridged crowns for chewing, and a distinct chest and lower back. Cynodonts appeared in the Permian period, but their heyday was the Triassic, when they lived worldwide. They persisted for 80 million years, before dying out in the Mid Jurassic. No other group of therapsids lasted as long.

Strong, upright lower hindlimbs helped Thrinaxodon to run fast.

Cynognathus **skull**

DOG JAW
Cynognathus ("dog jaw") was one of most dangerous of Early Triassic carnivores. At 3 ft 3 in (1 m) in length, *Cynognathus* was one of the largest cynodonts. *Cynognathus* possessed formidable jaws – long, deep, and capable of inflicting a savagely powerful bite. Its jaws held three kinds of teeth: small nipping incisors, great stabbing canines, and saw-edged, shearing cheek teeth.

TRIDENT TOOTH

Scientific name: *Thrinaxodon*

Size: 19 in (50 cm)

Diet: Small animals

Habitat: Open woodland

Where found: South Africa, Antarctica

Time: Early Triassic

Related genera: *Cromptodon, Tribolodon*

TRIDENT TOOTH

A low-slung, sharp-toothed carnivore, *Thrinaxodon* ("trident tooth") lived in Early Triassic South Africa and Antarctica. *Thrinaxodon* lived in burrows, and ate small creatures. Clues in its remains show that this creature was more mammal-like than its synapsid ancestors. It had a fairly large brain, and tiny pits in its snout that might have held whiskers hint that its body was hairy. An enlarged dentary bone strengthened either side of the lower jaw and contained sockets for its teeth. Its chest and lower back regions were probably separated by a diaphragm – a muscular sheet that contracted to fill the lungs, and would have enabled *Thrinaxodon* to breathe more efficiently than its ancestors.

Cambrian 540–500	Ordovician 500–435	Silurian 435–410	Devonian 410–355	Carboniferous 355–295	Permia

PALEOZOIC 540–250 MYA

EVOLUTION OF THE JAW

Cynodont jaws illustrate key changes in the evolution from early synapsid to mammal. In time, jaw bones vanished or shrank so that the entire lower jaw consisted of the large dentary bone. Two hinge bones gradually moved inside the skull to form two of the mammalian middle-ear bones. Other changes produced the mammals' unique chewing bite.

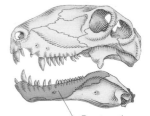

Dentary bone

Skull of the early synapsid *Dimetrodon*

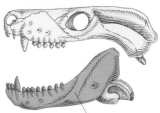

Dentary bone

Skull of the cynodont *Thrinaxodon*

Unlike reptiles, Thrinaxodon's ribs protected only its chest, which gave it a two-part body division into chest and lower back.

Like modern mammals, Thrinaxodon had seven neck vertebrae.

Thrinaxodon

THREE KNOB TEETH

Not all cynodonts were carnivores. Tritylodonts ("three knob teeth") had jaws and teeth designed for eating plants. *Bienotherium* had four incisor teeth, a gap instead of canines, and ridged back teeth much like molars. The great similarity between tritylodont and mammal skeletons suggests that mammals originated from this group of cynodonts.

Bienotherium **skull**

Bienotherium gnawed tough woody plants with its incisors, and crushed them between its back teeth.

.95–250	Triassic 250–203	Jurassic 203–135	Cretaceous 135–65	Tertiary 65–1.75	Quaternary 1.75–present
	MESOZOIC 250–65 MYA			CENOZOIC 65 MYA–present	

THE FIRST MAMMALS

MAMMALS ARE WARM-BLOODED, backboned animals whose females have glands that produce milk to feed their young. All mammals evolved from mammal-like creatures called therapsids. The first mammals were probably Triassic shrewlike animals that shared the same types of jawbones and middle ear bones as living mammals. Yet these creatures did not belong to any of the main living mammal groups – egg-laying monotremes, pouched marsupials, and placental mammals. Some scientists consider the first true mammal to be these groups' common ancestor, which probably appeared in the Early or Mid Jurassic.

MORGAN'S TOOTH

A tiny mammal from early in the Age of Dinosaurs, *Morganucodon* ("Morgan's tooth") is usually grouped with the triconodonts, extinct early mammals named for their three-cusped teeth. The bones of *Morganucodon*'s neck, chest, back, and hips were much like those of living mammals, and it stood more upright and had a relatively bigger brain than today's four-legged reptiles. To avoid dinosaurs, *Morganucodon* probably hid in holes by day and came out to hunt at night.

Early mammals were covered with hair, which suggests that this mammalian feature is primitive.

Lower jawbone of *Taeniolabis*

THE STRANGE MULTIS
Taeniolabis is a post-Mesozoic example of the multituberculates, a major line of rodent-like, plant-eating mammals with many-cusped teeth. They produced more than 200 known species, and varied from creatures no bigger than mice to species the size of beavers. Multituberculates persisted for 100 million years, from the Late Jurassic to the Early Tertiary, when they died out.

Sharp claws helped Morganucodon subdue prey or dig holes in which to hide from its enemies.

Morganucodon

Cambrian 540–500	Ordovician 500–435	Silurian 435–410	Devonian 410–355	Carboniferous 355–295	Permia

PALEOZOIC 540–250 MYA

AN ANCIENT LINE

The duck-billed platypus is one of the egg-laying monotremes – the group of living mammals with the oldest fossil record. The earliest-known monotreme fossils date from 100 million years ago, and were found in Australia. *Steropodon*, an early monotreme, was the size of a cat, and was quite large for a Mesozoic mammal.

The platypus displays the reptilelike posture of early mammals.

Modern duck-billed platypus (*Ornithorhynchus*)

Jeholodens

JEHOLODENS

The first complete skeleton of a triconodont to be discovered was that of *Jeholodens*, which was found in China in 1994. The mouse-sized, insect-eating *Jeholodens* had a body with a strange mixture of features. Its forelimbs were held erect like a modern mammal's, but its hind limbs sprawled in the fashion of reptiles. This unusual combination of features hints that the various parts of mammals' bodies evolved at different rates.

Sensitive whiskers allowed Morganucodon to feel its way in the dark.

MORGAN'S TOOTH

Scientific name:	*Morganucodon*
Size:	4 in (10 cm) long
Diet:	Insects and worms
Habitat:	Forest
Where found:	Western Europe and East Asia
Time:	Early Jurassic
Related genus:	*Megazostrodon*

95–250	Triassic 250–203	Jurassic 203–135	Cretaceous 135–65	Tertiary 65–1.75	Quaternary 1.75–present
		MESOZOIC 250–65 MYA		CENOZOIC 65 MYA–present	

AUSTRALIAN POUCHED MAMMALS

MANY OF THE EARLIEST MAMMALS had a pouch in their skin in which they carried their developing babies. Most mammals later evolved a womb inside their body for the babies and slowly lost their pouch. Marsupials, however, kept this pouch, and are famous for their many Australian representatives. Bandicoots, dasyuromorphs, and diprotodontians all appear as fossils in Oligocene rocks (33.7–23.5 million years ago). The bandicoots are small burrowing omnivores. Dasyuromorphs include marsupial mice, Tasmanian devils, thylacines, and the ant-eating numbats. Diprotodontians include kangaroos, koalas, and possums.

Diprotodon's huge nose probably helped it breathe dry, dusty air. However, some experts suggest that the nose supported a small trunk.

STHENURINES

Modern grassland kangaroos, such as the large sthenurines, evolved in the Pleistocene. Sthenurines may have used their mobile arms to pull down branches. The biggest sthenurines, like *Sthenurus*, were about 10 ft (3 m) tall.

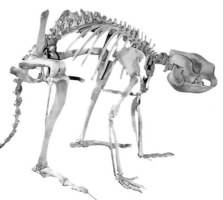

Skeleton of Sthenurus tindalei

Because of its hopping mode of locomotion, Sthenurus has only one main toe.

DIPROTODON

From the Oligocene to the Pleistocene, Australia was populated by heavy-bodied herbivores called diprotodontids. Most diprotodontids were rather like giant wombats. The most famous is *Diprotodon*, a rhinoceros-sized herbivore from the Pleistocene. Diprotodontids gradually died out during the Pleistocene as the tropical forests of Australia were replaced by grasslands. Kangaroos, which grazed on dry grasses, then became dominant.

POUCHED WOLVES

The thylacinids (marsupial wolves) were doglike predators belonging to the dasyuromorph group. *Thylacinus*, the most recent thylacinid, survived on the Australian mainland until about 3,000 years ago and on Tasmania until the 1930s. The last-known specimen died in an Australian zoo in 1936. *Thylacinus* had a long, stiff tail and a very powerful bite.

Thylacinus

Thylacines had sharp teeth and powerful jaws that could be opened very wide. They were predators of other marsupials. During the Pleistocene, a wolf-sized species, Thylacinus potens, hunted the large kangaroos and diprotodontids of the time.

| Cambrian 540–500 | Ordovician 500–435 | Silurian 435–410 | Devonian 410–355 | Carboniferous 355–295 | Permi |

PALEOZOIC 540–250 MYA

Diprotodon's *hippopotamuslike body suggests to some experts that it was amphibious. However, it has been found preserved in dry environments.* Diprotodon was the biggest ever marsupial.

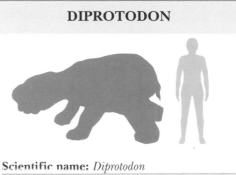

DIPROTODON

Scientific name: *Diprotodon*

Size: 10 ft (3 m) long

Diet: Shrubs and bushes

Habitat: Scrubland, open woodland

Where found: Australia

Time: Pleistocene (1.75–0.01 MYA)

Related genera: *Euowenia, Stenomerus, Nototherium*

Diprotodon *had robust limbs and walked on the soles of its feet.*

Marsupials possess a pouch – a bag made of skin in which the baby is kept. Once born, the baby climbs into the pouch, and for this reason baby marsupials have powerful grasping forelimbs. Within the pouch the baby suckles milk.

A peculiar feature of its hind feet was that the fifth toe was the longest. The sharp claws could have been used in digging.

Studies on tooth wear show that thylacoleonids were predators.

Thylacoleo skull

MARSUPIAL LIONS

One of the most remarkable marsupial groups are the thylacoleonids, also called "marsupial lions." Because of its catlike skull and teeth, *Thylacoleo* (the first thylacoleonid to be discovered) was first interpreted as a carnivorous predator. Later on, some experts argued that it was more likely a fruit-eater. However, the most recent studies show without doubt that it was a predator. Its limbs suggest that it was an able climber and perhaps stalked prey through the trees, jumping onto them from above.

)5–250	Triassic 250–203	Jurassic 203–135	Cretaceous 135–65	Tertiary 65–1.75	Quaternary 1.75 present
		MESOZOIC 250–65 MYA		CENOZOIC 65 MYA–present	

AMERICAN POUCHED MAMMALS

AMERICAN MARSUPIALS (POUCHED MAMMALS), a group called the Ameridelphia, evolved in North America during the Late Cretaceous but underwent most of their evolution in South America. Here they diversified into a major group of predatory species called the borhyaenoids. These included dog- and bearlike forms, and a species that resembled saber-toothed cats. Opossums are one of the most successful American marsupial groups and also moved into Europe, Africa, and Asia. These, and a poorly known separate group called the shrew opossums, are the only American marsupials to survive today. American marsupials never evolved the diversity of the Australian marsupials.

The shape of its body suggests that Thylacosmilus jumped out at its prey from the cover of bushes or tall grass. Perhaps it was colored like a living lion, or maybe it had stripes.

Alphadon

AMERICAN OPOSSUMS
Alphadon, from the Late Cretaceous of North America, is one of the earliest known opossums. About 66 species of opossum are known today from across South America, Mexico, and the US. They are mostly long-tailed climbing marsupials that vaguely resemble rats or weasels.

THYLACOSMILUS
One of the most remarkable marsupials was *Thylacosmilus*, a saber-toothed borhyaenoid that superficially resembled saber-toothed cats. *Thylacosmilus* was roughly the same shape and size as a big cat, but in the details of its skeleton it is clearly very different and more like a giant opossum. Unlike cats and other carnivores, the saber-teeth of *Thylacosmilus* never stopped growing and always had to be worn down at their tips. The roots of the teeth arced upward over the front of the skull, growing above the eyes.

***Lycopsis* skeleton**

THE BORHYAENOIDS
Borhyaenoids were predatory American marsupials known through the whole Tertiary period. The earliest forms, such as *Mayulestes*, were rather like opossums. Some, like *Cladosictis*, were about 3 ft (1 m) long and resembled modern martens. Others, like *Borhyaena*, were giant predators as big as lions or large bears. *Lycopsis* was a borhyaenoid of the Miocene related to *Borhyaena* and *Thylacosmilus*.

Cambrian 540–500	Ordovician 500–435	Silurian 435–410	Devonian 410–355	Carboniferous 355–295	Permi

PALEOZOIC 540–250 MYA

Massive muscles at the back of the skull would have given Thylacosmilus a powerful bite.

Like saber-toothed cats, Thylacosmilus had a flexible, powerful neck.

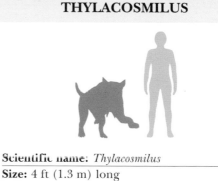

THYLACOSMILUS

Scientific name: *Thylacosmilus*

Size: 4 ft (1.3 m) long

Diet: Probably hoofed mammals and marsupials

Habitat: Grasslands, open woodlands

Where found: Argentina

Time: Miocene (23.5–5.3 MYA) and Pliocene (5.3–1.75 MYA)

Related genera: *Paraborhyaena, Anachlysictis*

POUCHED HOPPERS

The argyrolagids were mouse-sized American marsupials that lived from the Eocene to the Pliocene (53–1.75 million years ago). They had very long hind limbs and small forelimbs and thus appear to have moved by hopping, just like kangaroos or jerboas. *Argyrolagus* from Patagonia is the best-known argyrolagid. At times it has been argued that argyrolagids are not marsupials, but it now seems that they are part of the American marsupial group that also includes the shrew opossums.

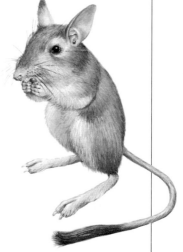

Argyrolagus

Large protective flanges grew downward from the chin. Thylacosmilus might have used these to help guide its saber-teeth into the body of its prey. The flanges would also have protected the teeth from damage when the jaws were closed.

Unlike true cats, Thylacosmilus lacked retractile claws. Even so, its limbs were powerful and capable of grasping. It probably pulled its prey to the ground.

5–250	Triassic 250–203	Jurassic 203–135	Cretaceous 135–65	Tertiary 65–1.75	Quaternary 1.75–present
	MESOZOIC 250–65 MYA			CENOZOIC 65 MYA–present	

STRANGE-JOINTED MAMMALS

A BIZARRE GROUP OF AMERICAN MAMMALS called the xenarthrans are probably the most primitive members of the placental group (mammals that carry their young with the aid of an organ called a placenta). The name xenarthran means "strange joints" and refers to the peculiar extra joints these mammals have between their vertebrae. Sloths, anteaters, and armadillos are the living representatives of xenarthrans. Some xenarthrans, such as anteaters, have no teeth, and in the past the group was called Edentata, meaning "the toothless ones." However, most xenarthrans do have teeth – large ones in sloths and the tanklike glyptodonts. Xenarthrans were important herbivores and insectivores in South America. Some types migrated into North America in the Late Pliocene.

Ground sloth fur is known for some Pleistocene species. It was shaggy and brown.

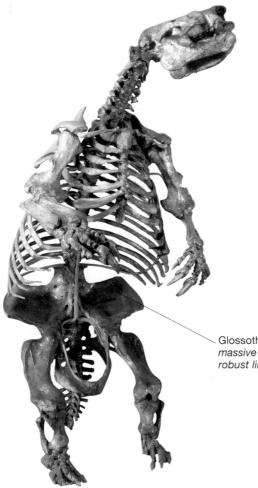

Glossotherium had massive hips and very robust limbs.

MEGATHERIUM
Until relatively recently, there were sloths that lived on the ground and grew to be as big as a modern elephant. These were the ground sloths and, rather than climbing on branches to eat leaves, they reached up with powerful arms and claws to pull branches down toward their mouths. The very biggest ground sloths, such as *Eremotherium* and *Megatherium*, were huge, reaching 20 ft (6 m) in length and weighing about 3 tons. Living sloths are all tree-climbing animals that hang upside down and are no bigger than a medium-sized dog.

Ground sloths had a stout, powerful tail that they probably used as a prop when they reared up on their back legs.

GLOSSOTHERIUM
A medium-sized sloth called *Glossotherium* lived during the Miocene, Pliocene, and Pleistocene in South and North America. Like most sloths, it lived in wooded grasslands and forests. Some sloths inhabited different environments. *Thalassocnus* lived on the beaches of Peru and may have swum in shallow water to eat seaweed. Dwarf ground sloths less than 3 ft (1 m) long lived on the Caribbean islands.

Cambrian 540–500	Ordovician 500–435	Silurian 435–410	Devonian 410–355	Carboniferous 355–295	Permi

PALEOZOIC 540–250 MYA

Megatherium had five fingers, but some other ground sloths lacked the thumb, while others lacked the first two fingers.

MEGATHERIUM

Scientific name: *Megatherium*

Size: 20 ft (6 m) long

Diet: Leaves and twigs

Habitat: Wooded grassland

Where found: South America

Time: Pliocene and Pleistocene (5.3–0.01 MYA)

Related genera: *Pyramiodontherium, Ocnopus, Eremotherium*

All ground sloths, like living tree sloths, had large, curving claws on their fingers. These were probably used as hooks to pull down branches but could also have been used in self-defense.

GLYPTODONT ARMOR
The bodies of glyptodonts were covered by a rigid shell of interlocking hexagonal scales (scutes). Rings of scutes also covered the tail and sometimes over the top of the skull. Some glyptodont specimens have fractured shells, suggesting that they battled one another with their tails.

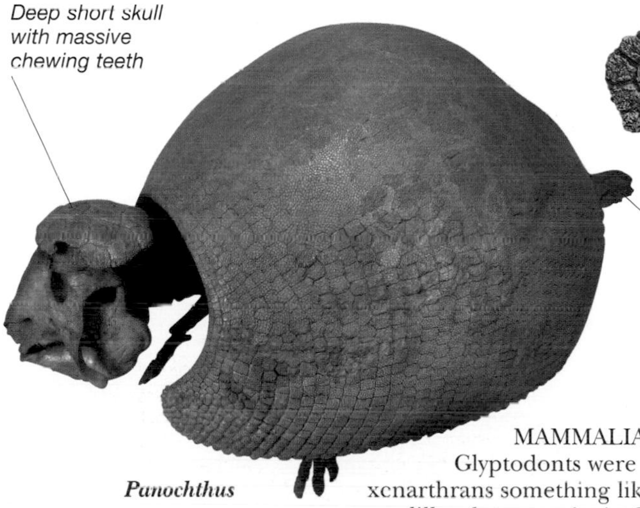

Deep short skull with massive chewing teeth

Some glyptodonts had a tail that could be used as a weapon.

The feet have large claws which curve inward. Fossil tracks show that ground sloths sometimes walked on two legs.

Panochthus

MAMMALIAN TANKS
Glyptodonts were armored xenarthrans something like giant armadillos, known principally from South America. The smallest glyptodonts were about the same size as living armadillos, but the largest kinds, like *Doedicurus, Hoplophorus,* and *Panochthus,* were more than a ton in weight and about 10 ft (3 m) long.

	Triassic 250–203	Jurassic 203–135	Cretaceous 135–65	Tertiary 65–1.75 Quaternary 1.75 present
		MESOZOIC 250–65 MYA		CENOZOIC 65 MYA–present

PLACENTAL PIONEERS

PLACENTALS, THE GROUP OF MAMMALS whose young develop inside their bodies, arose in the Late Cretaceous. The earliest were small, nocturnal omnivores (meat- and planteaters) that resembled living shrews. Nearly all living mammals are classed as placentals, except for the monotremes, which lay eggs, and the marsupials, whose young develop for a short time inside their bodies and are then carried in a pouch. Many primitive placental mammals have marsupial-like pouch bones, but this does not necessarily mean that they all had pouches. The placentals evolved rapidly at the end of the Cretaceous, when the dinosaurs were becoming extinct. Pantodonts and tillodonts, which lived in the Paleocene (65–53 million years ago), were the first placentals to grow larger than the size of a living badger.

ZALAMBDALESTES

One of the best-known early placentals was *Zalambdalestes* from Late Cretaceous Mongolia. It was a long-snouted, four-legged mammal whose slim forelimbs were longer than its hind limbs. It probably looked much like the living elephant-shrews, a group of small, long-legged, omnivorous mammals with mobile snouts. They run fast and leap to escape predators. Some experts believe that *Zalambdalestes* is closely related to elephant-shrews. Other experts argue that *Zalambdalestes* is the earliest lagomorph, which is a group that includes rabbits and their relatives.

The brain of Zalambdalestes was about three-quarters the size of the brain of a living shrew.

Below its long snout, Zalambdalestes had long incisor teeth. There was a gap between the incisors and the teeth at the back of the jaws.

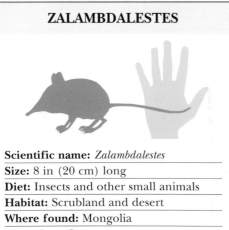

ZALAMBDALESTES

Scientific name: *Zalambdalestes*

Size: 8 in (20 cm) long

Diet: Insects and other small animals

Habitat: Scrubland and desert

Where found: Mongolia

Time: Late Cretaceous

Related species: *Alymlestes, Barunlestes*

Cambrian 540–500	Ordovician 500–435	Silurian 435–410	Devonian 410–355	Carboniferous 355–295	Permia

PALEOZOIC 540–250 MYA

Coryphodon

PANTODONTS

The pantodonts were bulky placental mammals that thrived in the Paleocene and Eocene (65–33.7 million years ago), although they left no descendants. Their feet were tipped with nails or claws, and males had large canine teeth perhaps used for fighting. Their cheek teeth show that they were herbivores (planteaters). *Coryphodon* was a widespread northern hemisphere pantodont the size of a hippopotamus, but its brain was the smallest of any mammal.

TILLODONTS

The tillodonts were a group of Paleocene and Eocene placentals that lived in Asia, North America, and Europe. They had clawed feet and large gnawing teeth, and probably fed on roots and tubers. *Trogosus* was one of the biggest tillodonts and grew to the size of a bear. The tillodonts may be related to pantodonts, and both groups may be distant relatives of the carnivore group, though this is controversial.

Trogosus **skull**

Like many other early placentals, Zalambdalestes had bones near its hips that may have supported a pouch or may have helped to support the side wall of the abdomen. Most of the later placentals lost these bones, whereas the marsupials kept theirs.

UKHAATHERIUM AND RELATIVES

The asioryctitheres were Mongolian Cretaceous placentals that superficially resembled living shrews and other members of the insectivore group. Features of their skull and hip bones show that, despite this resemblance, asioryctitheres were not related to insectivores and they lack advanced features seen in the later groups of placental mammals. The asioryctithere *Ukhaatherium* is known from beautifully preserved, complete skeletons. It was a tiny animal – the complete skeleton is only about 4 in (10 cm) long.

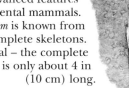

Ukhaatherium **fossil**

Ukhaatherium's *small and pointed teeth were suited to eating insects.*

5–250	Triassic 250–203	Jurassic 203–135	Cretaceous 135–65	Tertiary 65–1.75	Quaternary 1.75–present
		MESOZOIC 250–65 MYA		CENOZOIC 65 MYA–present	

EARLY CARNIVORES

CARNIVORES (CATS, HYENAS, dogs, bears, and all of their relatives) are one of the most successful groups of mammals. Their key feature is their specialized shearing teeth, called carnassials. While many other mammals have carnivorous (meat-eating) habits and some even have carnassials, in true carnivores these teeth are uniquely formed from the fourth upper premolar and the first lower molar. A unique character of primitive carnivores is their retractile claws, which can be pulled back into protective sheaths. Carnivores may have developed in the Late Cretaceous and have a fossil record from the early Paleocene. Miacoids – the earliest carnivores – appeared in North America.

Miacoids had smaller brains for their body size than modern carnivores. Also, their binocular vision was not as good as that of modern carnivores.

MIACIS

One of the best-known miacoids was *Miacis*, an early member of the dog-branch group of carnivores. Like many other early carnivores, *Miacis* was well suited for a climbing lifestyle and had limbs and joints that resemble those of modern climbing carnivores. *Miacis* was probably an agile predator that hunted small animals and might also have eaten eggs and fruit.

Its wrist, elbow, and shoulder joints show that Vulpavus *had flexible, powerful limbs and would have been an agile climber.*

The retractile claws of primitive carnivores were used in climbing and holding prey. They would have been permanently needle-sharp.

LIFE IN THE TREES

The limb skeletons of some miacoids, such as *Vulpavus* from Eocene North America, show that these animals had highly mobile limbs like those of modern carnivores that regularly climb in trees. *Vulpavus* also has sharply curved claws, which supports this idea. However, a climbing lifestyle was probably not true of all miacoids. *Didymictis*, from Paleocene-Eocene North America and Europe, probably lived at ground level and may have been a fast runner or a digger.

Vulpavus skeleton

| Cambrian 540–500 | Ordovician 500–435 | Silurian 435–410 | Devonian 410–355 | Carboniferous 355–295 | Permi |

PALEOZOIC 540–250 MYA

Miacoids may have used their tails as balancing aids and as rudders that helped direct them when leaping from tree to tree. Modern climbing carnivores use their long tails in this way.

***Hyaenodon* skull**

CREODONTS

Hyaenodon was a wolflike animal with carnivorous habits. It is part of a group called the creodonts, which are not regarded as a true carnivores. Living from Paleocene to Miocene times (65–5.3 million years ago), creodonts would have resembled modern civets, cats, or dogs. Slicing teeth at the back of the jaws show that all were committed to a predatory lifestyle.

Early carnivores such as Miacis have five toes on both their hands and feet. Later carnivores have four toes on the foot.

MIACIS

Scientific name:	*Miacis*
Size:	1 ft (30 cm) long
Diet:	Small mammals, reptiles, birds
Habitat:	Tropical forests
Where found:	Europe and North America
Time:	Early Tertiary
Related genera:	*Chailicyon, Vulpavus, Oodectes*

5–250	Triassic 250–203	urassic 203–135	Cretaceous 135–65	Tertiary 65–1.75	Quaternary 1.75–present

MESOZOIC 250–65 MYA	CENOZOIC 65 MYA–present

CATS AND OTHER FELIFORMS

FELIFORMS, including cats, emerged during the Eocene (53–33.7 million years ago). While some feliforms became large predators in open environments, others retained the forest-dwelling lifestyle and long-bodied shape of the ancestral miacoids. Civets and genets, properly called viverrids, are primitive feliforms that have remained largely unchanged. Viverrids may include the ancestors of hyenas and mongooses, which both first appeared in the Oligocene (33.7–23.5 million years ago). Cats are short-skulled feliforms that are more specialized for eating meat than virtually any other mammal. The earliest cats appeared in the Oligocene of Europe, and saber-toothed cats evolved early in the Miocene (23.5–5.3 million years ago).

HYENAS

Though modern hyenas may appear to resemble dogs more than cats, hyenas belong to the cat group of carnivores. Skeletal features show that early hyenas were similar to civets and genets. These bone-crushing hyenas evolved in the Miocene and spread throughout Africa, Asia, and Europe. Early hyenas, such as *Ictitherium*, were much smaller than living hyenas.

Ictitherium **skull**

Smilodon **skull**

ENLARGED CANINES

As cats evolved, they enlarged their canines for biting and their carnassials for slicing but reduced or lost their premolar and molar teeth. The saber-toothed cats enlarged their canines to an extreme. With these specialized teeth, cats administer either a suffocating bite to the neck or sever the spinal cord of a prey animal that they have caught.

The giant canines of saber-toothed cats are oval-shaped in cross-section and can have serrated margins.

TERRIBLE CAT

Some fossil cats, such as *Dinofelis* ("terrible cat") from the Pliocene and Pleistocene, had enlarged canine teeth halfway in between the conical stabbing canines of modern cats and the flattened blades of saber-tooths. As a result *Dinofelis* has been called a "false saber-tooth". However, other skeletal features of *Dinofelis* and its relatives, a group called the metailurines, show that they should probably be classified as true members of the saber-toothed group. *Dinofelis* had body proportions like those of modern forest-dwelling cats such as leopards and jaguars, and it was about the same size as these species.

Cambrian 540–500	Ordovician 500–435	Silurian 435–410	Devonian 410–355	Carboniferous 355–295	Permi

PALEOZOIC 540–250 MYA

Prehistoric *Smilodon* compared with modern tiger

If *Dinofelis* was an inhabitant of forests and woods, it probably had a spotted coat like living forest-dwelling cats.

All cats have shortened, rounded skulls. Their eyes face forward and provide them with an overlapping field of vision which allows them to accurately judge distances.

As well as having remarkable canines, saber-toothed cats also had unusual protruding incisors.

Dinofelis had limb proportions better suited for strength than speed, as was true of nearly all saber-tooths. It may have been a powerful and able climber, like modern leopards and jaguars.

MODERN CAT COMPARISONS

Most saber-toothed cats were large, and the biggest forms, including *Smilodon* and *Homotherium* from the Pliocene and Pleistocene, were larger than the biggest living lions and tigers. Because of their dependence on large prey animals, these cats were vulnerable to extinction when their prey became rare. Unlike saber-toothed cats, the modern cat group, the Felinae, includes both large and small species.

TERRIBLE CAT

Scientific name: *Dinofelis*

Size: 7 ft (2.2 m) long

Diet: Deer, antelopes, apes, other mammals

Habitat: Woodlands

Where found: Europe, Asia, Africa, North America

Time: Pliocene and Pleistocene (5.3–0.01 MYA)

Related genera: *Metailurus*, *Adelphailurus*

295–250	Triassic 250 203	Jurassic 203–135	Cretaceous 135–65	Tertiary 65–1.75	Quaternary 1.75–present
		MESOZOIC 250–65 MYA		CENOZOIC 65 MYA–present	

SABER-TOOTHED CATS

THE MACHAIRODONTINES, otherwise known as saber-toothed cats, were prehistoric members of the cat family and famous for their massive canine teeth. They probably descended from the primitive cat *Pseudaelurus* of the Miocene (23.5–5.3 million years ago). During the Pliocene and Pleistocene (from 5.3 million years ago), they diversified into American, African, European, and Asian species ranging in size from that of a modern puma to that of a lion. The very last saber-toothed cats died out as recently as 10,000 years ago. The most famous is *Smilodon*, a genus known from both North and South America.

Smilodon had immensely powerful arms and shoulders, and an especially powerful and flexible neck. These characteristics suggest that Smilodon frequently grappled large struggling prey to the ground before delivering a killing bite to the neck.

Cambrian 540–500	Ordovician 500–435	Silurian 435–410	Devonian 410–355	Carboniferous 355–295	Permian

PALEOZOIC 540–250 MYA

HUNTING AND SCAVENGING TOGETHER

More carnivore species lived alongside one another in the Pleistocene than they do today, so fighting and competition were probably more severe. Many *Smilodon* specimens show injuries and deformities from hunting and fighting. Some specimens survived major injuries, such as broken hips and jaws. While these injuries were healing, these cats would have been unable to hunt. Perhaps, therefore, *Smilodon* lived in social groups. Injured individuals would have been able to scavenge from kills made by other group members.

In the largest examples of Smilodon, the upper canines were more than 10 in (25 cm) long. These teeth were actually quite fragile and were likely to break if twisted or if they made contact with bone.

SMILODON

Scientific name: *Smilodon*

Size: 5-8 ft (1.7-2.5 m) long

Diet: Large mammals including horses, ground sloths, bison, and camels

Habitat: Grasslands

Where found: North and South America

Time: Pleistocene (1.75–0.01 MYA)

Related genera: *Megantereon, Paramachairodus*

95–250	Triassic 250–203	Jurassic 203–135	Cretaceous 135–65	Tertiary 65–1.75	Quaternary 1.75–present
	MESOZOIC 250–65 MYA			CENOZOIC 65 MYA–present	

DOGS AND OTHER CANIFORMS

CANIFORMS, A GROUP THAT INCLUDES dogs, bears, and seals, evolved in the Eocene (53–33.7 million years ago). Dogs were the earliest caniforms to appear and, until the end of the Miocene (5.3 million years ago), were uniquely North American. The earliest dogs, such as *Hesperocyon*, have both tree-climbing and ground-dwelling characteristics, while some later dogs became catlike predators with shortened skulls and grasping forelimbs. New types of caniform including weasels, raccoons, and bears evolved late in the Eocene. Many became small climbing omnivores (meat- and plant-eaters), others became herbivores (plant-eaters) or miniature underground predators. Others took to life in the water. Bear-dogs lived from the Eocene to the Miocene.

As in most carnivores, dogs have collarbones that are small slivers of bone supported by ligaments. This allows a wider swing of the forelimbs, an advantage in running predators.

DIRE WOLF

Canis dirus ("the dire wolf") was a large wolf from North America in the Pleistocene and one of the most famous fossil dogs. Its fossils are best known from the Rancho La Brea tar pits in California where more than 1,600 dire wolves are preserved. It is thought that these wolves went to feed on animals trapped in the tar and then became trapped themselves. Compared with modern wolves, dire wolves had proportionally larger skulls and teeth, but shorter legs.

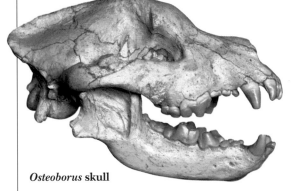

Osteoborus **skull**

Canis dirus *had a proportionally wider head, stronger jaws, and larger teeth than living wolves. These meant that it was better than modern dogs at breaking and eating bones.*

HYENALIKE DOGS
Borophagines were an important group of North American dogs that lived from the Oligocene (33.7 million years ago) to the Pleistocene (10,000 years ago). They are best known for *Osteoborus*, a wolf-sized form with a shortened skull and enlarged crushing molars. Some borophagines were as big as modern lions. *Osteoborus* probably led a hyenalike lifestyle but this was not true of all borophagines – some resembled raccoons or coyotes and might have been omnivorous.

Cambrian 540–500	Ordovician 500–435	Silurian 435–410	Devonian 410–355	Carboniferous 355–295	Permia

PALEOZOIC 540–250 MYA

SEALS AND SEALIONS

Seals, sealions, and walruses evolved from bearlike ancestors in the Oligocene (33.7–23.5 million years ago). Early types resembled otters but possessed flipperlike hands and feet, and enlarged eyes that helped them to see better in the water. By the late Miocene, seals had spread across the world, while walruses and sealions such as *Thalassoleon* had evolved in the northern hemisphere.

Thalassoleon mexicanus skull

Skeleton of Ursus spelaeus

BEARS

The eight living bears belong to a group of bears called the ursines. Most ursines are flat-footed omnivores. Some, like the giant pandas and *Ursus spelaeus*, of the Pleistocene, became cave bears. Extinct bears include the running, doglike hemicyonines, the raccoon-like amphicynodontines, and the swimming bear *Kolponomos*.

The tail is an important social signal in living dogs and probably was in all prehistoric dogs as well.

As with other modern types of dogs, the Dire wolf's hands and feet were specialized for running. It walked only on its fingers and toes, and its blunt claws could not be retracted.

DIRE WOLF

Scientific name: *Canis dirus*

Size: 6 ft 6 in (2 m) long

Diet: Large mammals and other animals, carrion, possibly fruit and nuts

Habitat: Grasslands and woodlands

Where found: North America and northern South America

Time: Pleistocene (1.75–0.01 MYA)

Related species: *Canis lupus, Canis etruscus*

95–250	Triassic 250–203	Jurassic 203–135	Cretaceous 135–65	Tertiary 65–1.75	Quaternary 1.75–present
	MESOZOIC 250–65 MYA			CENOZOIC 65 MYA–present	

ICARONYCTERIS

Fossil bats such as *Icaronycteris* probably hunted at night, using their high-pitched calls and sensitive hearing to detect flying insects. They were likely to have hunted in places where insects gather at night, such as lakesides and the tops of trees. The shape of its wings suggests that *Icaronycteris* flew in cluttered environments such as forests, rather than over open grasslands. Some experts suggest that bats took to hunting at night to avoid the predatory birds that were evolving.

Cambrian 540–500	Ordovician 500–435	Silurian 435–410	Devonian 410–355	Carboniferous 355–295	Permia

PALEOZOIC 540–250 MYA

5–250	Triassic 250–203	Jurassic 203–135	Cretaceous 135–65	Tertiary 65–1.75	Quaternary 1.75–present
		MESOZOIC 250–65 MYA		CENOZOIC 65 MYA–present	

223

INSECTIVORES AND BATS

MOLES, HEDGEHOGS, SHREWS, and other insectivores (also called lipotyphlans) first appeared in the Eocene and share distinctive snout muscles and skull bones. Primitive relatives of shrews, *Batodon* and *Otlestes*, are known from the Late Cretaceous. Bats, the second most species-rich group of living mammals after rodents, share features with primates, colugos, and tree shrews, and are united with them in a group called the Archonta. Like pterosaurs and birds, bats evolved true flapping flight and have modified forelimbs in which the fingers support skin membranes that reach the ankles. Even the very earliest Eocene bats had fully developed wings and were accomplished flying predators that used sonar to detect insects.

Icaronycteris had sharp-clawed feet that could be turned backward, allowing it to hang upside down.

ICARONYCTERIS
The early bat *Icaronycteris* is known from Eocene North America. Other Eocene bats are known from Africa, Australia, and Europe. Their ear bones show that they were able to hear high-frequency sounds. Like modern bats, *Icaronycteris* probably used sonar – after making a high-pitched noise, the bat listens to the echoes and can use these to detect the presence and whereabouts of nearby objects.

Modern desmans have a flexible, sensitive snout. As with most insectivores, their sharp, pointed tooth cusps allow them to catch and chew worms, insects, snails, fish, and frogs.

Lower jaw bone of *Desmana moschata*

A LIFE UNDERGROUND OR IN THE WATER
Prehistoric moles resembled shrews and were less good at burrowing than modern moles, which evolved to be more specialized for life underground than any other mammal. Moles rely on smell and touch and are able to detect the electrical signals made by the muscles of their prey. Desmans are swimming moles that evolved in the Oligocene (33.7–23.5 million years ago) and survive today.

Unlike modern microbats, early forms such as Icaronycteris had claws on their second fingers as well as on their thumbs.

The wing membranes of all bats are made up of layers of skin. Small muscles help control these membranes. Though the membranes are thin, they repair quickly if torn.

Cambrian 540–500	Ordovician 500–435	Silurian 435–410	Devonian 410–355	Carboniferous 355–295	Permia

PALEOZOIC 540–250 MYA

Bats have large ears and acute hearing.

Icaronycteris *had more teeth than modern insect-eating bats.*

FRUIT EATERS, VAMPIRES, AND FISHERMEN

Before the Eocene, bats split into their two main groups, the mostly insect-eating microbats and the mostly fruit-eating megabats. Fish-eating bats evolved in the Miocene (23.5–5.3 million years ago) and survive today. The American fruit- and pollen-eating microbats include horseshoe bats and the vampire bats that feed on the blood of mammals and birds.

Living horseshoe bat

Long, thin fingers support wing membranes.

Macrocranion **fossil**

SPINY AND HAIRY HEDGEHOGS

Modern hedgehogs are split into two groups. True hedgehogs are spiny and short-tailed, while moonrats are furry and long-tailed. However, hedgehogs have a rich fossil record and numerous types are known. Some types were tiny and shrewlike, while Miocene moonrat *Deinogalerix* was nearly 3 ft (1 m) long. *Macrocranion* was a primitive Eocene hedgehog known from Europe and North America. It had a long tail and probably lacked spines. A close relative, *Pholidocercus*, had an unusual fleshy gland on its forehead.

ICARONYCTERIS

Scientific name: *Icaronycteris*

Size: 15 in (40 cm) wingspan, 6 in (15 cm) body length

Diet: Flying insects

Habitat: Forests, caves, riverbanks

Where found: North America

Time: Eocene (53–33.7 MYA)

Related genera: *Archaeonycteris, Palaeochiropteryx*

295–250	Triassic 250–203	Jurassic 203–135	Cretaceous 135–65	Tertiary 65–1.75	Quaternary 1.75 present
		MESOZOIC 250–65 MYA		CENOZOIC 65 MYA–present	

PRIMITIVE PRIMATES

PRIMATES ARE CHARACTERIZED by their grasping hands and feet, large brains, and eyes with an overlapping field of vision. The group includes primitive forms, such as lemurs, and advanced forms such as apes and humans. Primatelike mammals, such as *Purgatorius* from North America, appeared early in the Paleocene, but whether these animals are true primates or not is controversial. Some true primates of the Paleocene and Eocene resembled lemurs while others were like tree shrews. Lemurs, dwarf lemurs, and lorises are the only survivors of the more primitive primate groups. Another important early primate group was the lemurlike adapids, a group known from the Eocene, Oligocene, and Miocene of Africa, Europe, Asia, and North America.

The long plesiadapid skull was unlike that of later primates.

Megaladapis had a dog-like head and might have been responsible for ancient legends of "dog-faced men."

PLESIADAPIS

The plesiadapids were an early primate group, best known for *Plesiadapis* from the Paleocene and Eocene of North America and Europe. *Plesiadapis* had grasping fingers and toes, and a long tail. It probably looked something like a cross between a lemur and a squirrel. Like a number of other early primates, the plesiadapids had prominent incisor teeth that resemble those of rodents. Perhaps they chewed at wood to extract grubs, or to get at sap.

LEMURS LARGE AND SMALL
Lemurs probably evolved from adapids some time in the Miocene or earlier. Prehistoric lemurs were more diverse than they are today. They included gigantic climbing forms, ground-dwelling monkeylike forms, and long-armed forms that probably climbed upside-down like tree sloths. *Megaladapis* was a massive koalalike lemur with a long skull and huge molar teeth. As large as the living orangutan, it died out only 600 years ago.

Megaladapis edwardis skeleton

Like other primitive primates, but unlike monkeys and apes, plesiadapids had claws on their fingers and toes, not nails.

Long finger

Living aye-aye

LONG FINGER EVOLUTION

Aye-ayes (daubentoniids) are a Madagascan group of primates that may be more primitive than lemurs. The living aye-aye (*Daubentonia madagascariensis*) has a remarkable long third finger, which it uses to extract grubs out of holes in trees. Some other mammals, such as the apatemyids from the Paleocene, Eocene, and Oligocene, evolved similar fingers. These fine-fingered mammals seem to have played the role that woodpeckers did elsewhere.

Like squirrels, Plesiadapis could have used its tail for balance when climbing and jumping. The tail may also have been boldly patterned.

NOTHARCTUS

One of North America's last native primates was an Eocene adapid called *Notharctus*. Named in 1870, it was also the first North American fossil primate to be recognized. Thanks in part to the chance discovery of new specimens during the 1980s, *Notharctus* is now one of the best-known early primates. Like other adapids, *Notharctus* had long fingers, thumbs, and toes, and could grip objects powerfully. With its long limbs, flexible back, long tail, and short skull, *Notharctus* would have resembled the agile leaping lemurs of today.

PLESIADAPIS

Scientific name: *Plesiadapis*

Size: 30 in (80 cm) long

Diet: Insects, fruit

Habitat: Subtropical forests

Where found: Western North America, Europe

Time: Late Paleocene (65–53 MYA) and Eocene (53–33.7 MYA)

Related genera: *Platychoerops, Nannodectes*

295–250	Triassic 250–203	Jurassic 203–135	Cretaceous 135–65	Tertiary 65–1.75	Quaternary 1.75–present
		MESOZOIC 250–65 MYA		CENOZOIC 65 MYA–present	

MONKEYS

MONKEYS ARE PART OF A GROUP OF PRIMATES called the anthropoidea, which descended in the Eocene (53–33.7 million years ago) from ancestors related to the living tarsiers of eastern Asia. The teeth of anthropoids are distinguished by enlarged canines, flattened molars, and molar-like premolars. These features and others allowed anthropoids to become better at foraging for food at ground level than other primates. There are two main types of monkeys. The Old World monkeys came to dominate the "Old World" of Africa and Asia. These monkeys share an ancestor with apes and are called the catarrhines (so-named for their downward-pointing nostrils). The New World monkeys, which are also called the platyrrhines (from their flat noses), evolved in the "New World" of South America.

THEROPITHECUS OSWALDI

Old World monkeys invaded grassland environments to exploit grasses and other sources of food. Various species of *Theropithecus*, a seed-eating grassland monkey, evolved in the Pliocene and lived across Europe, Africa, and Asia. *Theropithecus oswaldi* was the largest species and considerably bigger than its living relative, the gelada of Ethiopia.

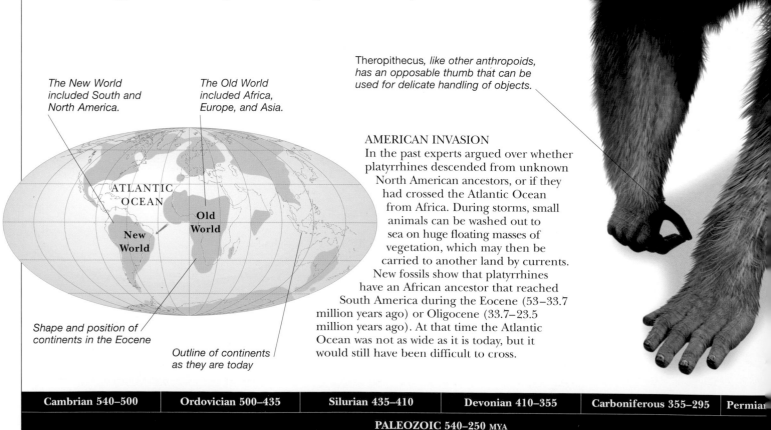

The New World included South and North America.

The Old World included Africa, Europe, and Asia.

Theropithecus, like other anthropoids, has an opposable thumb that can be used for delicate handling of objects.

ATLANTIC OCEAN

Old World

New World

Shape and position of continents in the Eocene

Outline of continents as they are today

AMERICAN INVASION

In the past experts argued over whether platyrrhines descended from unknown North American ancestors, or if they had crossed the Atlantic Ocean from Africa. During storms, small animals can be washed out to sea on huge floating masses of vegetation, which may then be carried to another land by currents. New fossils show that platyrrhines have an African ancestor that reached South America during the Eocene (53–33.7 million years ago) or Oligocene (33.7–23.5 million years ago). At that time the Atlantic Ocean was not as wide as it is today, but it would still have been difficult to cross.

| Cambrian 540–500 | Ordovician 500–435 | Silurian 435–410 | Devonian 410–355 | Carboniferous 355–295 | Permian |

PALEOZOIC 540–250 MYA

Old World monkeys like Theropithecus *use their tails for display and for balance when climbing, but they cannot use the tail to grasp things with. New World monkeys are characterized by prehensile (grasping) tails that are used to hold on to branches when climbing.*

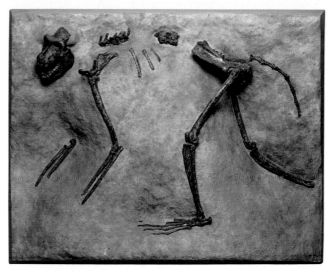

Paracolobus skeleton

OLD WORLD MONKEY EMPIRE

Old World monkeys, many of them agile tree-climbers, replaced monkey-like apes during the Miocene (23.5–5.3 million years ago). One group, the colobids, migrated out of Africa in the Miocene and evolved in Asia into the leaf-eating langurs and proboscis monkeys. *Mesopithecus* and *Paracolobus* were early colobids that probably resembled the living langurs. The colobids have massive, complex stomachs and guts for digesting tough plant foods. Some forms are well adapted for life in the trees. The best-known Old World monkey lineages, such as baboons, mangabeys, and guenons, evolved in the Pliocene (5.3–1.75 million years ago) in Africa.

Unlike earlier primates, anthropoids have nails on all their fingers and toes rather than claws. Nails allow the presence of sensitive pads on the tips of the digits, something not possible if claws cover the ends of the digits.

Upper skull of *Tremacebus*

FOREST-DWELLING NEW WORLD MONKEYS

Unlike Old World monkeys, the New World monkeys never seem to have taken to grassland life and have remained animals of the forests. The earliest known South American monkey is *Branisella* from the Early Oligocene (33.7 million years ago) of Bolivia. *Tremacebus*, from the Late Oligocene (23.5 million years ago) of Patagonia, resembled the living owl monkey. Two giant relatives of spider monkeys, *Protopithecus* and *Caipora*, lived in Pleistocene Brazil (1,750,000–10,000 years ago).

THEROPITHECUS

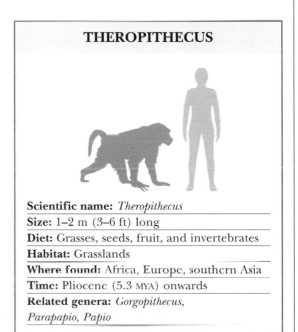

Scientific name: *Theropithecus*

Size: 1–2 m (3–6 ft) long

Diet: Grasses, seeds, fruit, and invertebrates

Habitat: Grasslands

Where found: Africa, Europe, southern Asia

Time: Pliocene (5.3 MYA) onwards

Related genera: *Gorgopithecus, Parapapio, Papio*

95–250	Triassic 250–203	Jurassic 203–135	Cretaceous 135–65	Tertiary 65–1.75	Quaternary 1.75–present
		MESOZOIC 250–65 MYA		CENOZOIC 65 MYA–present	

AUSTRALOPITHECINES

THE GROUP OF AFRICAN APES that includes the ancestors of modern humans were first recognised in 1925. The group is called the australopithecines and contains about ten species of apes. Controversy continues over exactly which species the group should include, their lifestyles, and appearances. It was once thought that the various australopithecine species became more human-like over time, but this idea now seems too simplistic. Studies have shown that some of the earlier species were proportioned in a similar way to modern humans, while some of the later species were more chimp-like. Some had human-like skulls but chimp-like bodies. It also seems that some walked on their knuckles in the same way as living chimps and gorillas, while others walked upright like humans.

Compared to modern humans, australopithecines had enlarged chewing teeth.

Most australopithecines had a brain size of 400–500 cc (25–30 cu in). This is intermediate between that of chimps and early Homo species.

AUSTRALOPITHECUS AFARENSIS

A skeleton from Hadar, Ethiopia, represents the best-known australopithecine species, *Australopithecus afarensis*. This famous specimen, which is about 40% complete, was originally thought to be female and was popularly called "Lucy". However, many experts now believe that "Lucy" was in fact male and so call the skeleton "Lucifer". *Australopithecus afarensis* was small – only 1 m (3 ft 3 in) tall. Its limbs were proportioned much like the limbs of modern humans. Anatomical details of the hips and limbs of "Lucy" suggest that *Australopithecus afarensis* could walk on two legs.

THE TAUNG CHILD
The first australopithecine specimen to be discovered was the skull of a child from Taung, South Africa. This was the species later named *Australopithecus africanus* ("man ape from Africa"). Curiously, the so-called Taung child was found among the fossilized partial remains of numerous medium-sized mammals. On these bones were distinctive nicks like those made by the beak of an eagle. Fragments of an egg shell from a large bird were also found. It therefore seems that a large eagle had fed on, and perhaps killed, the Taung child.

Preserved australopithecine footprints show that, as in modern humans, the big toe was parallel with others.

Cambrian 540–500	Ordovician 500–435	Silurian 435–410	Devonian 410–355	Carboniferous 355–295	Permia

PALEOZOIC 540–250 MYA

The jaw muscles were large and ape-like. They ate a lot of tough plant food.

The molar teeth have thickened layers of enamel.

AUSTRALOPITHECUS AFARENSIS

Scientific name: *Australopithecus afarensis*

Size: 1 m (3 ft 3 in) tall

Diet: Leaves, fruit, tubers, carrion, animals

Habitat: Open woodland, wooded grassland

Where found: Eastern Africa

Time: Pleistocene (1.75–0.01 MYA)

Related species: *Australopithecus anamensis, Australopithecus africanus, Australopithecus garhi*

Lower jaw of *Australopithecus boisei*

ROBUST AUSTRALOPITHECINES
Several australopithecine species, including *Australopithecus robustus, Australopithecus aethiopicus,* and *Australopithecus boisei*, are characterized by deep, massive jaws, robust skulls, and enlarged molar teeth with thickened layers of enamel. Some experts believe that these species should be united in the genus *Paranthropus* – the so-called "robust australopithecines". Others argue that these species do not share the same ancestor.

Though its hips and legs suggest that it could walk bipedally, *Australopithecus afarensis* was probably also an able climber.

The finger bones are curved, unlike the straight bones of modern humans.

AUSTRALOPITHECUS HABILIS
This species was originally named *Homo habilis* and was thought to be the most primitive *Homo* species. The name *Homo habilis* means "handy man" – abundant stone tools found with fossils suggest that it was adept at making and using cutting and scraping tools. Recent discoveries show, surprisingly, that the species had ape-like proportions with long arms and short legs. It may therefore have been less human-like than the old model shown here. Experts now think that *Homo habilis* is actually a type of *Australopithecus* and so it has been renamed *Australopithecus habilis*.

95–250	Triassic 250–203	Jurassic 203–135	Cretaceous 135–65	Tertiary 65–1.75	Quaternary 1.75–present
		MESOZOIC 250–65 MYA		CENOZOIC 65 MYA–present	

EARLY HOMO SPECIES

HUMANS BELONG TO A GENUS OF HOMINID CALLED HOMO, which probably evolved from an advanced species of *Australopithecus* apes. One of the most primitive members of the *Homo* genus is the famous *Homo erectus* ("upright person") from southern Asia and elsewhere. *Homo erectus* was a very successful hominid and lived alongside our own species for thousands of years. Fossils of *Homo erectus* ranging from nearly two million to perhaps 27,000 years old have been found in Africa, Europe, and Asia. Some African fossils that were long confused with those of *Homo erectus* have now been identified as a more primitive species. Discovered by Lake Turkana, Kenya, these have recently been named *Homo ergaster* ("work person"). *Homo ergaster* may have been the earliest *Homo* species.

Homo ergaster *used stone tools to butcher animal carcasses and probably both hunted prey and scavenged from carcasses.*

Homo ergaster *had larger teeth and more powerful jaw and neck muscles than modern humans.*

TURKANA BOY

The best-known *Homo ergaster* specimen, and one of the most complete of all fossil hominids, is the skeleton of the "Turkana boy." The slim and tall proportions suggest that *Homo ergaster* was adapted for moving quickly across the tropical grasslands of the time. Anatomical features suggest that *Homo ergaster* was unlikely to be capable of controlling its breathing precisely enough for complex speech in the way that modern humans can.

WORK PERSON

Homo ergaster is a controversial African hominid recognized in 1975. Its large brain, relatively flat face, and small cheek teeth all suggest that *Homo ergaster* was more closely related to *Homo* species than to the australopithecines. Like other *Homo* species, *Homo ergaster* was taller and larger than most australopithecines. It also took longer to reach adulthood and lived for longer than earlier hominids. In some details, however, *Homo ergaster* resembled australopithecines more than modern humans. Its thorax tapers upward (ours is more cylindrical) and its shoulder girdles were closer together than those of modern people.

Cambrian 540–500	Ordovician 500–435	Silurian 435–410	Devonian 410–355	Carboniferous 355–295	Permia

PALEOZOIC 540–250 MYA

Stone handaxe

SOPHISTICATED TOOLS

The earliest *Homo* species made crude digging and scraping tools, and could use fire. *Homo erectus* refined the use and construction of tools – spears, blades, and chopping tools made from antlers, bones, and stones have been found. *Homo erectus* probably lived in caves but may also have built simple shelters, such as from saplings kept in place by stones. Large hearths are known from some caves used by *Homo erectus* in China. Some have ash layers 7 ft (2 m) deep. The pioneering culture of *Homo erectus* is called Acheulian.

The thorax of Homo ergaster tapers upward.

The skull bones of Homo erectus were thicker than those of modern humans.

Prominent brow ridges

BROW RIDGES AND BIG BRAINS

Homo erectus approached modern humans in the size of its brain. It had a brain capacity of around 67 cu in (1,100 cc) whereas modern humans have a brain capacity of about 90 cu in (1,500 cc). Unlike the brow ridges of neanderthals, which were lightened internally by hollow sinuses, the ridges of *Homo erectus* were mostly solid bone.

Fossilized jaws and teeth suggest that Homo ergaster ate softer food than earlier hominids. It had probably developed cooking skills.

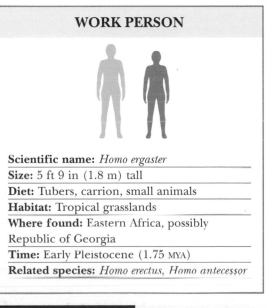

WORK PERSON

Scientific name:	*Homo ergaster*
Size:	5 ft 9 in (1.8 m) tall
Diet:	Tubers, carrion, small animals
Habitat:	Tropical grasslands
Where found:	Eastern Africa, possibly Republic of Georgia
Time:	Early Pleistocene (1.75 MYA)
Related species:	*Homo erectus, Homo antecessor*

05–250	Triassic 250–203	Jurassic 203–135	Cretaceous 135–65	Tertiary 65–1.75	Quaternary 1.75–present
	MESOZOIC 250–65 MYA			CENOZOIC 65 MYA–present	

NEANDERTHALS

THE NEANDERTHALS (HOMO NEANDERTHALENSIS) are the most famous of fossil hominids and are often characterized as Ice Age "cave people." They used tools and fire, probably had a form of language, and may have lived in family groups. Unlike our own species, however, they did not create art, decorate their bodies with paint or jewelry, or demonstrate clear planning to their activities. An older neanderthal-like species, called *Homo heidelbergensis*, was an advanced hominid that might have been ancestral to the neanderthals and perhaps to our own species. It was long regarded as intermediate between *Homo erectus* and *Homo sapiens* and came to be known simply as "archaic *Homo sapiens*." Today most paleontologists recognize it as a distinct species.

NEANDERTHAL

In contrast to fossils of *Homo sapiens*, which have slim proportions suggestive of a tropical climate, neanderthals were stocky with massive, thick-walled, heavily muscled bones. The stocky proportions of neanderthal skeletons show that this species was built for life in cold environments. Neanderthal people have often been depicted as dark and hairy. In reality, we have no idea as to how much body hair they may have possessed. They may have used clothing. Also, because they lived in cold environments, their skin may have been light-colored, as they did not need dark skin to protect from the sun.

HEIDELBERG MAN AROUND THE WORLD
Some researchers believe that various hominid fossils found at locations as far apart as Zambia, Ethiopia, France, and China should be included in the species *Homo heidelbergensis*. European specimens come from Greece, Germany, France, Spain, and England. The famous Broken Hill skull from Zambia, originally named *Homo rhodesiensis*, is thought by some to be an African *Homo heidelbergensis*.

Jaw of *Homo Heidelbergensis* found in Heidelberg, Germany

The chin was less well developed than that of Homo sapiens.

The lower legs and arms were proportionally shorter than those of modern people. Animals from colder climates generally have shorter extremities than those from warmer places.

Cambrian 540–500	Ordovician 500–435	Silurian 435–410	Devonian 410–355	Carboniferous 355–295	Permia

PALEOZOIC 540–250 MYA

Neanderthals had thick-arched brow ridges over the eyes. The function of these brow ridges remains unclear.

BROAD NOSES AND PROMINENT JAWS

Neanderthals had very broad noses that may have helped warm cold air. Their front teeth were large and often heavily worn, suggesting that they were frequently used to hold objects. The cheekbones were also large with an inflated look, while most of the skull and jaws were stretched forward relative to those of modern people. A bulging area on the very back of the skull, called the occipital chignon, is a distinctive feature of neanderthal skulls.

This body is lying on its back with its arms over the chest.

Neanderthals had large brains measuring 80 to 106 cu in (1,300 to 1,740 cc). An average measurement for Homo sapiens is 90 cu in (1,500 cc).

Telltale scratch marks indicate that neanderthals held food between their teeth while cutting off part of it with stone tools.

Their hand bones show that they could carefully manipulate objects but had a more powerful grip than modern people.

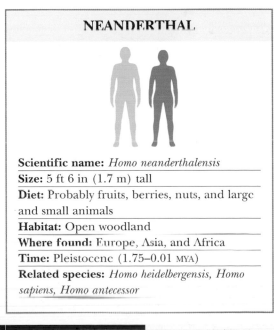

BURYING THE DEAD

A number of neanderthal skeletons, mostly from southwest France, are preserved in a curled up posture and appear to have been buried by other members of their species. Some experts have therefore argued that neanderthals buried their dead. This is hard to prove, as the specimens may simply have died while sleeping and later been covered naturally by sediment. One such skeleton has abundant pollen associated with it, leading to suggestions that bunches of flowers had been placed on the body before burial. This is debatable however.

NEANDERTHAL

Scientific name: *Homo neanderthalensis*

Size: 5 ft 6 in (1.7 m) tall

Diet: Probably fruits, berries, nuts, and large and small animals

Habitat: Open woodland

Where found: Europe, Asia, and Africa

Time: Pleistocene (1.75–0.01 MYA)

Related species: *Homo heidelbergensis, Homo sapiens, Homo antecessor*

)5–250	Triassic 250–203	Jurassic 203–135	Cretaceous 135–65	Tertiary 65–1.75	Quaternary 1.75–present
		MESOZOIC 250–65 MYA		CENOZOIC 65 MYA–present	

HOMO SAPIENS

MODERN HUMANS – HOMO SAPIENS – are perhaps the most successful species of large-bodied mammal ever, inhabiting virtually every habitat on every continent and with more individuals (over six billion) than any other large animal. Fossils, genetics, and studies of living people show that *Homo sapiens* is an African species that evolved from *Homo heidelbergensis* or a similar species around 200,000 years ago. *Homo sapiens* reached Europe at least 40,000 years ago. Evidence such as prehistoric art and ceremonial burial distinguish the advanced culture of our species from other hominids. Around 10,000 years ago *Homo sapiens* began to domesticate plants and animals and develop farming. Having continual supplies of food allowed humans even more time to develop culturally.

Cro-Magnon antler tool

ADVANCED TOOLS
Homo sapiens have developed more types of tools for more different uses than any other animal. The early tools made by our species from stone, bone, antler, or wood are often more complex, and manufactured for more delicate use, than those of other hominids. Important Cro-Magnon tools include spear-throwers and double-pointed blades, barbed harpoons and the burin, a chisel-like tool used to shape other tools as well as produce art and jewelry.

Modern humans and neanderthals have different proportions. Possible hybrids have intermediate proportions.

CRO-MAGNON PEOPLE
Named after a site in the Dordogne, France, Cro-Magnons were a European group of *Homo sapiens* with an African physique. While they were muscular and well built, they lacked the thick bones and notably stocky proportions of neanderthals. Art and symbolism were important in their lives, and they left abundant representations of animals on cave walls and as sculpture. They used natural materials as paints and made ornaments to decorate their bodies.

Though other Homo species may also have used furs and skins as clothing, Homo sapiens created complex garments.

NEANDERTHAL DEBATE
Most anthropologists regard the neanderthals as a separate species from *Homo sapiens*. However, some think that the two may have hybridized (interbred) and that modern people therefore incorporate neanderthal DNA. A 25,000-year-old skeleton from Abrigo do Lagar Velho, Portugal, appears to combine features of both neanderthals and modern humans. Perhaps, rather than killing off the last neanderthals, the modern human population absorbed them by interbreeding.

Cambrian 540–500	Ordovician 500–435	Silurian 435–410	Devonian 410–355	Carboniferous 355–295	Permia

PALEOZOIC 540–250 MYA

Cave paintings at the Lascaux site in France show aurochs (a type of cattle that is now extinct), horses, and other animals.

CAVE ART
Homo sapiens are unique among the hominids in producing art. Paintings and sculpture allowed early artists to express abstract concepts and to impress other tribe members. Perhaps the images also had great spiritual significance. Many prehistoric paintings depict prehistoric animals with remarkable accuracy.

Homo sapiens *has a distinctive skull shape, with a taller forehead and larger and more rounded cranium than other Homo species.*

MODERN HUMAN

Scientific name: *Homo sapiens*

Size: 5 ft 9 in (1.8 m) tall (for Cro-Magnons)

Diet: Seeds, tubers, nuts, fruit, shellfish, fishes, large and small animals

Habitat: Originally woodlands, grasslands, and coastlines; later nearly all land habitats

Where found: Worldwide except most of the polar regions and some remote islands

Time: Quaternary

Related species: *Homo neanderthalensis, Homo antecessor, Homo heidelbergensis*

SPREAD AROUND THE WORLD
From its origins in Africa about 200,000 years ago, *Homo sapiens* spread to Europe and then to Asia. By building boats and using land bridges when the seas were low, *Homo sapiens* then spread from Asia to Australasia and the Pacific islands. Our species is thought to have reached the Americas by 33,000 years ago.

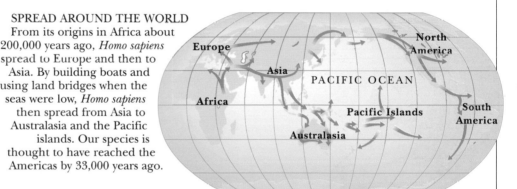

The limb bones of Cro-Magnon people are long and slim, like those of their African ancestors.

95–250	Triassic 250–203	urassic 203–135	Cretaceous 135–65	ertiary 65–1.75	Quaternary 1.75–present

MESOZOIC 250–65 MYA

CENOZOIC 65 MYA–present

PREHISTORIC RABBITS AND RODENTS

RABBITS AND RODENTS probably both appeared in the Paleocene (65–53 million years ago). These superficially similar mammals have gnawing teeth and are mainly plant-eaters. Both might be descended from ancestors such as *Zalambdalestes* from the Late Cretaceous. Rabbits, which are types of lagomorph, have remained fairly similar throughout their history. Rabbitlike pikas (another lagomorph group), were more widespread than rabbits during Miocene times (23.5–5.3 million years ago), but have since declined. Rodents are the largest group of mammals – there are more species (over 1,700) and more individuals than of any other group. Gliding, burrowing, and climbing rodents have fossil records dating from the Eocene (53–33.7 million years ago).

The eyes were small, suggesting that Epigaulus *did not rely on eyesight that much.*

SOUTH AMERICAN RODENTS
South America is home to a distinct group of rodents called caviomorphs. These appear to have arrived from Africa during the Eocene. The giant caviomorphs *Neochoerus* and *Protohydrocoerus* were as large as modern tapirs – they could have weighed 450 lb (200 kg). Biggest of all was *Telicomys*. This was the size of a small rhino and weighed up to a ton.

The horns might have been used in fights, or maybe they helped with digging.

Neochoerus **skull**

The large gnawing incisors could also have been used in digging. Living mole rats and other burrowing rodents use their teeth in this way.

EPIGAULUS

Mylagaulids were a peculiar North American group of powerfully built burrowing rodents. *Epigaulus* is one of the best-known mylagaulids and had spade-like paws and horns above the snout. Though advanced mylagau-lids such as *Epigaulus* were horned, this was not true of the most primitive forms. An old idea is that horned and hornless mylagaulids were males and females of the same species. However, new studies show that both sexes had horns, and that there were different species with and without horns. Mylagaulids were members of the squirrel-beaver group.

Cambrian 540–500	Ordovician 500–435	Silurian 435–410	Devonian 410–355	Carboniferous 355–295	Permia

PALEOZOIC 540–250 MYA

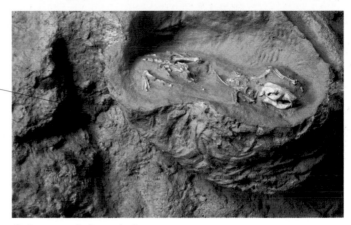

Paleocastor **skeleton in burrow**

Section of
spiral-shaped
burrow

BURROWERS AND BUILDERS

Beavers are large rodents that belong to the same group as squirrels. Some fossil beavers were much like the living beaver. *Paleocastor* was a small burrowing beaver that lived on the plains of North America in the Oligocene and Miocene (33.7–5.3 million years ago). It probably looked like a living prairie dog and is famous for having made vertical spiral-shaped burrows up to 5 ft (2.5 m) deep. These were long known as "Devil's corkscrews." Tooth and claw marks made by *Paleocastor* are preserved on the side walls of the burrows, and some *Paleocastor* skeletons have been found preserved within their burrows.

Broad, spadelike
paws and long
straight claws were
used for digging.

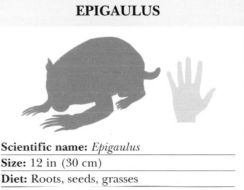

EPIGAULUS

Scientific name:	*Epigaulus*
Size:	12 in (30 cm)
Diet:	Roots, seeds, grasses
Habitat:	Plains
Where found:	North America
Time:	Late Tertiary
Related genera:	*Ceratogaulus*, *Mylagaulus*

RABBITS, HARES, AND PIKAS

The earliest lagomorphs date from the Eocene and include rabbits, hares, and pikas. The pikas, which look like small short-eared rabbits, were abundant in the Miocene but have since declined. Today they live in mountains in North America and Asia. Fossil rabbits such as *Hypolagus* look similar to living types.

Hypolagus **skull**

95–250	Triassic 250–203	Jurassic 203–135	Cretaceous 135–65	Tertiary 65–1.75	Quaternary 1.75–present
		MESOZOIC 250–65 MYA		CENOZOIC 65 MYA–present	

ISLAND GIANTS AND DWARFS

DURING THE PLEISTOCENE, from 1.75 million years ago and until as recently as 8,000 years ago, unusual mammals inhabited the Mediterranean islands. These had been cut off from their ancestors and each other by rising sea levels. The Balearic Islands were home to *Myotragus*, a goatlike creature with unique rodentlike gnawing teeth. *Candiacervus*, a small deer with club-shaped antlers, was an inhabitant of Crete. *Prolagus*, the last European pika (a rabbitlike mammal) lived on Corsica and Sardinia. Hippopotamuses, elephants, and deer on these islands were remarkable for being dwarfs, generally less than half the size of their ancestors. The elephants, for example, grew to little more than half the height of a human. By contrast, other Mediterranean mammals, including lizards, owls, and dormice, became giants. These creatures probably became extinct through a mixture of being hunted by humans, competing with farmed animals, and changes in climate.

Dwarf elephants lived off plant food that grew close to the ground. They might have pushed over small trees and shrubs to reach leaves and fruit.

GIANT DORMICE
Leithia, a giant dormouse from Malta and Sicily, was closely related to living forest dormice. However, it was a giant in comparison with living dormice, reaching about 16 in (40 cm) in total length – about as large as a squirrel. Living dormice are agile climbers, and *Leithia* probably was too. However, whereas living dormice are also mostly nocturnal, *Leithia* might have been more active during the daytime. This is because there were few predators on the islands, so it would not have needed to hide under the cover of darkness.

Like its living relatives, Leithia probably had dark markings around the eyes and a bushy tail.

Cambrian 540–500	Ordovician 500–435	Silurian 435–410	Devonian 410–355	Carboniferous 355–295	Permia

PALEOZOIC 540–250 MYA

DWARF ELEPHANTS

Paleoloxodon falconeri was a miniature island-dwelling elephant with a shoulder height of 3 ft (90 cm). On the Mediterranean islands the territories were smaller than on the main-land, and reduced quantities of food meant that smaller individuals were more likely to survive than large ones. As a consequence, the body size of Mediterranean elephants became progressively smaller as time went by.

Like other elephants, dwarf forms had tusks that they probably used in fights and as tools. They would have used the trunk to bring water and food to the mouth.

DWARF ELEPHANT

Scientific name: *Paleoloxodon falconeri*
Size: 5 ft (1.5 m) long, 3 ft (90 cm) tall
Diet: Leaves, grasses, fruit
Habitat: Forests
Where found: Malta
Time: Quaternary
Related species: *Paleoloxodon melitensis, Paleoloxodon mnaidrensis*

295–250	Triassic 250–203	Jurassic 203–135	Cretaceous 135–65	Tertiary 65–1.75	Quaternary 1.75 present
		MESOZOIC 250–65 MYA		CENOZOIC 65 MYA–present	

TERRIBLE HORNS

DINOCERATANS, THE "TERRIBLE HORNED" MAMMALS, were plant-eating, rhinoceroslike hoofed creatures famous for their paired horns and tusklike canine teeth. The earliest dinoceratan, *Prodinoceras*, first appeared in Asia during the Paleocene (65–53 million years ago), but nearly all later types are from North America. How dinoceratans are related to other mammals is in dispute. They are probably part of the hoofed mammal (ungulate) group and have similarities with some of the South American hoofed mammals. Another idea is that dinoceratans are closely related to pantodonts and tillodonts. A more controversial view is that dinoceratans descend from the anagalids, a small group of rabbitlike mammals.

UINTAH BEAST

The largest and best-known dinoceratan, *Uintatherium*, was as big as a living white rhino. It was named in 1872 after the Uintah Indians, a tribe that, like *Uintatherium*, lived in Utah. When first described, there was controversy over whether *Uintatherium* was an elephant or not. Today it is clear that elephants and dinoceratans are not at all closely related.

Uintatherium
*had a barrel-
shaped body.*

Cast of the skull of *Uintatherium*

HORNS, BUMPS, AND TUSKS
The various shapes on the long skulls of dinoceratans such as *Uintatherium* and *Eobasileus* were probably display structures used to signal sexual maturity. Males appear to have had bigger horns and a more pronounced flange (projection) on the lower jaw. It is likely that they fought using these structures, perhaps pushing against one another with the horns and crests and biting one another with the tusks.

The advanced dinoceratans
had columnlike legs.

Cambrian 540–500	Ordovician 500–435	Silurian 435–410	Devonian 410–355	Carboniferous 355–295	Permian
		PALEOZOIC 540–250 MYA			

In horned dinoceratans, the pair of horns at the back of the skull are always the biggest. The horns were blunt and may have been covered in skin rather than a horny sheath.

UINTAH BEAST

Scientific name: *Uintatherium*

Size: 11 ft (3.5 m) long

Diet: Leaves, fruit, waterplants

Habitat: Forests

Where found: North America

Time: Eocene (53–33.7 MYA)

Related genera: *Eobasileus, Tetheopsis*

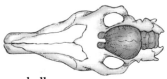

Equus skull

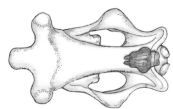

Megacerops skull

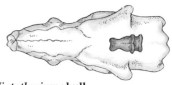

Uintatherium skull

BIG SKULL BUT SMALL BRAIN
Compared to later hoofed mammals, dinoceratans had small brains. While the skull of *Uintatherium* or *Eobasileus* might be nearly 3 ft (1 m) long, the space in the skull for the brain was only about 4 in (10 cm) long. *Megacerops*, a brontothere, was another Eocene giant with a small brain. Smaller brains appear true of most mammals of the time. *Equus*, the modern horse, clearly shows the much bigger brain typical of later mammals.

The enlarged flanges on the lower jaw may have helped protect the tusklike canines. Both the tusks and jaw flanges were better developed in males.

Like elephants, advanced dinoceratans had very short finger, toe, hand, and foot bones and walked only on their toes. Such hands and feet are suited for weight bearing, not for running.

PRIMITIVE HOOFED MAMMALS

FOR MANY YEARS, experts grouped a large number of primitive hoofed mammals together as the Condylarthra. This was always controversial, as the Condylarthra "group" included the ancestors of most later hoofed mammals. Condylarths have recently been redefined, and now consist of a specific group of related hoofed mammals from the early Tertiary. Most condylarths were four-footed plant eaters, ranging from the size of a rat to the size of a sheep. Some condylarths had claws, though others had developed blunt hooves. Their teeth show that they were mainly plant eaters, and some had enlarged, squarish molars and enlarged premolars suited to pulping plant material. Most lived in woods or forests, where they browsed on the undergrowth.

Phenacodus may have been dappled or striped for camouflage in the undergrowth.

PHENACODUS

The most famous condylarth is *Phenacodus*, mostly because experts used to think it was an ancient ancestor of the horse. Like horses, *Phenacodus* had a skeleton suited to a lifestyle of running in the open woodland where it lived. It was about the size of a sheep, and had proportionally longer limbs than many other condylarths. The toes on the outside of its feet were small, meaning that most of its weight was carried on its three middle toes. This suggests that *Phenacodus* was a good runner.

Phenacodus

Phenacodus's *long limbs were quite flexible, so it was not as specialized for running as later ungulates, such as horses. These have stiffened limbs.*

Didolodus

MYSTERIOUS SOUTH AMERICANS

Didolodontids were South American hoofed mammals that were probably closely related to phenacodontids. However, their anatomy is also similar to that of the litopterns – the horse and camellike South American ungulates. Some experts therefore regard didolodontids as primitive members of the South American ungulate group, and as possible ancestors of the litopterns.

Cambrian 540–500	Ordovician 500–435	Silurian 435–410	Devonian 410–355	Carboniferous 355–295	Permian

PALEOZOIC 540–250 MYA

AARDVARK PROTOTYPE?

Ectoconus was a sheep-sized condylarth from North America and perhaps Asia. Its body shape has been compared with that of the aardvark, and for this reason some experts have argued that aardvarks are living members of the condylarth group. Unlike aardvarks, *Ectoconus* would have been no good at digging, as it lacked large, curved claws.

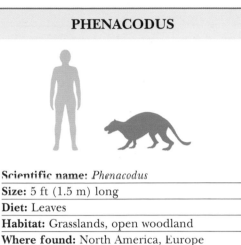

PHENACODUS

Scientific name: *Phenacodus*

Size: 5 ft (1.5 m) long

Diet: Leaves

Habitat: Grasslands, open woodland

Where found: North America, Europe

Time: Paleocene and Eocene (65–33.7 MYA)

Related genera: *Tetraclaenodon, Copecion*

RATLIKE HOOFED MAMMALS

Some condylarths were tiny. *Hyopsodus,* the best-known of the hyopsodontid group, was a rat-sized animal about 1 ft (30 cm) long. It had short legs, a flexible body, and fairly long, clawed digits. It probably foraged in the undergrowth, though it may also have been able to climb trees.

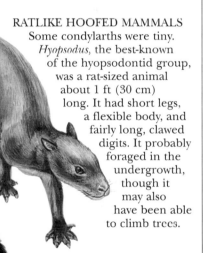

Phenacodus *had five toes on its feet. Each toe ended in a small, blunt hoof.*

Like most condylarths, Phenacodus *had a long, flexible tail.*

95–250	Triassic 250–203	Jurassic 203–135	Cretaceous 135–65	Tertiary 65–1.75	Quaternary 1.75–present
	MESOZOIC 250–65 MYA			CENOZOIC 65 MYA–present	

SOUTH AMERICAN HOOFED MAMMALS

IN THE TERTIARY AND EARLY QUATERNARY, South America was home to a range of unusual hoofed mammals, known as the meridiungulates. Some of these animals resembled hoofed mammals from elsewhere, such as horses and camels. These similarities probably came about because animals with similar lifestyles may evolve in a similar way, even if they live in different places. Exactly how meridiungulates relate to other hoofed mammals is still unclear. Links with condylarths, dinoceratans, and other groups have all been suggested. But despite their diversity, there is evidence that all meridiungulates share a single ancestor.

The bony nostril openings were located between the eyes.

BIG LLAMA

The litopterns were a group of meridiungulates that resembled camels and horses. One of the biggest and best known of the litopterns was *Macrauchenia* ("big llama"). It was about the same size as a large modern camel and had stocky limbs and three-toed feet. *Macrauchenia* is most famous for its nostrils, which were located high up on the top of its head. Some experts think this shows that it had a short trunk, but others dispute this.

Short trunk, like that of a modern tapir

Macrauchenia's long neck resembled that of a camel. It may have grazed from the ground or browsed from trees.

Its vertebrae suggest that Macrauchenia had a small shoulder hump.

Macrauchenia's jaws were lined with 44 large chewing teeth.

It could probably kick powerfully with its hind limbs.

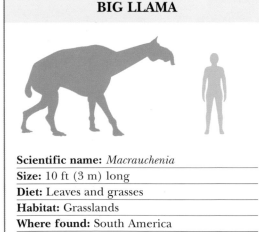

BIG LLAMA

Scientific name: *Macrauchenia*
Size: 10 ft (3 m) long
Diet: Leaves and grasses
Habitat: Grasslands
Where found: South America
Time: Pleistocene (1.75–0.01 MYA)
Related genera: *Windhausenia, Promacrauchenia*

SKELETON OF MACRAUCHENIA
Macrauchenia was discovered by Charles Darwin and named and described by Sir Richard Owen, two of the most important scientists of Victorian times. Darwin in fact wrote of his impression that the skeleton appeared to be from a large llama. From the outside *Macrauchenia* resembled a camel, but, inside, its skeleton was very different from a camel's. The neck bones were more simple and it had more teeth than a camel, for example.

Cambrian 540–500	Ordovician 500–435	Silurian 435–410	Devonian 410–355	Carboniferous 355–295	Permia

PALEOZOIC 540–250 MYA

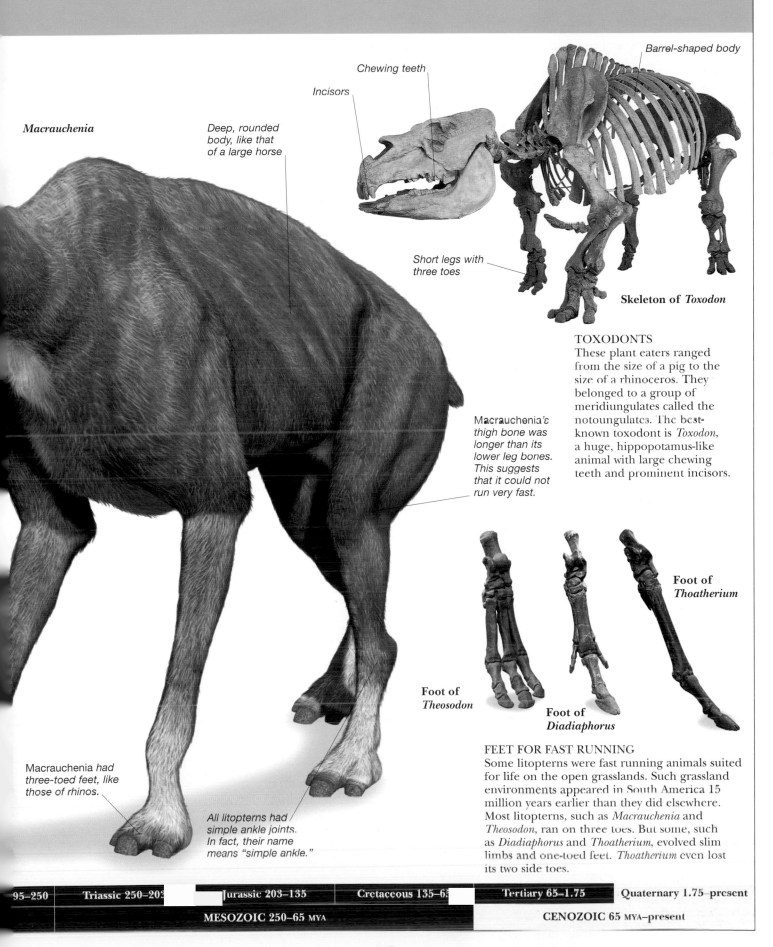

Macrauchenia

Deep, rounded body, like that of a large horse

Chewing teeth

Incisors

Barrel-shaped body

Short legs with three toes

Skeleton of *Toxodon*

Macrauchenia's thigh bone was longer than its lower leg bones. This suggests that it could not run very fast.

Macrauchenia *had three-toed feet, like those of rhinos.*

All litopterns had simple ankle joints. In fact, their name means "simple ankle."

TOXODONTS
These plant eaters ranged from the size of a pig to the size of a rhinoceros. They belonged to a group of meridiungulates called the notoungulates. The best-known toxodont is *Toxodon*, a huge, hippopotamus-like animal with large chewing teeth and prominent incisors.

Foot of
Thoatherium

Foot of
Theosodon

Foot of
Diadiaphorus

FEET FOR FAST RUNNING
Some litopterns were fast running animals suited for life on the open grasslands. Such grassland environments appeared in South America 15 million years earlier than they did elsewhere. Most litopterns, such as *Macrauchenia* and *Theosodon*, ran on three toes. But some, such as *Diadiaphorus* and *Thoatherium*, evolved slim limbs and one-toed feet. *Thoatherium* even lost its two side toes.

95–250	Triassic 250–203	Jurassic 203–135	Cretaceous 135–65	Tertiary 65–1.75	Quaternary 1.75–present
		MESOZOIC 250–65 MYA		CENOZOIC 65 MYA–present	

AT HOME ON THE GRASSLANDS

Macrauchenia lived on grasslands and open woodlands in South America. These habitats must have looked very similar to the pampas grasslands that cover southern South America today. *Macrauchenia*'s teeth suggest that it ate tough vegetation, so it may have fed on grasses as well as from trees. If *Macrauchenia* did have a trunk, it could have used it to grab leaves and branches that would otherwise have been out of its reach. Its long neck and large size would have helped *Macrauchenia* to keep a lookout for predators, such as wolves, lions, and giant running bears.

Cambrian 540–500	Ordovician 500–435	Silurian 435–410	Devonian 410–355	Carboniferous 355–295	Permia

PALEOZOIC 540–250 MYA

URANOTHERES

ONE OF THE MOST PECULIAR groups of mammals is the Uranotheria, a collection of plant-eating, hoofed mammals that includes elephants, seacows, and hyraxes. It might seem strange that these very different creatures are thought to be related, but they share features not seen in other mammals. The earliest members of these groups seem to have been similar in appearance. The first elephants, for example, were not giant creatures with trunks, but dog-sized animals probably similar to modern-day hyraxes. In fact, hyraxes may show how the earliest uranotheres lived – as small, grazing plant eaters. A later group of uranotheres, called the tethytheres, evolved an amphibious lifestyle. Some of these became committed to life in water and eventually evolved into the first seacows.

Arsinoitherium

Two smaller horns grew from the back of the skull.

Arsinoitherium *had a comparatively small and simple brain.*

Males had larger and more pointed horns than females.

Arsinoitherium's *teeth had tall crowns and could have been used to chew very tough plant material.*

ARSINOITHERIUM

Scientific name: *Arsinoitherium*

Size: 12 ft (3.5 m) long

Diet: Tough leaves and stems

Habitat: Woodland, wooded grassland

Where found: Egypt, Oman, southwest Asia

Time: Eocene (53–33.7 MYA)

Related genera: *Crivadiatherium, Paleoamasia*

ARSINOITHERES

These rhinoceros-like uranotheres lived in Asia, Europe, and Africa from the Paleocene until the Oligocene (65–23.5 million years ago). The best-known arsinoithere is *Arsinoitherium* – a large, heavy animal with two massive horns on its skull. The largest individuals of *Arsinoitherium* (probably old males) were about the size of small elephants. Unlike rhinoceros horns, arsinoithere horns were hollow. They have grooves on their surface, showing that there were blood vessels on the outside, and that the horns were probably covered in skin.

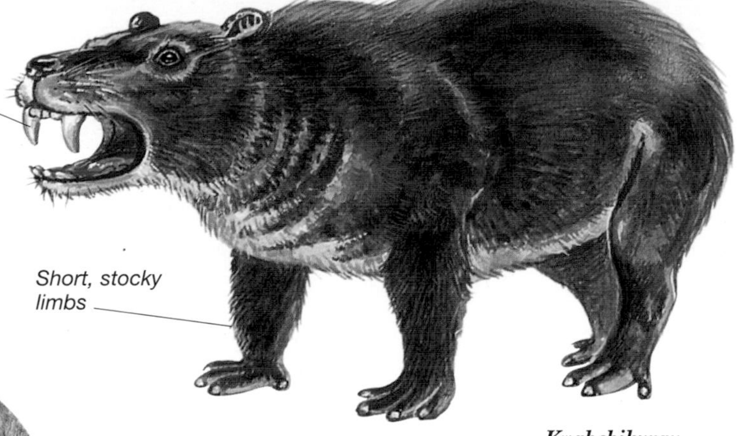

Tusklike
front teeth

Its shoulders
were massive
and powerfully
muscled.

Arsinoitheres probably
digested their food
in an enormous hind
gut region.

Short, stocky
limbs

Kvabebihyrax

HYRAXES

Modern hyraxes are small African mammals that
look like guinea pigs. Fossil hyraxes, however,
were quite different and came in a huge range
of shapes and sizes. *Kvabebihyrax*, shown here,
was the shape of a hippopotamus and may have
been amphibious. *Titanohyrax* was the size of a
small rhinoceros. *Antilohyrax* was a long-legged
runner resembling an antelope. Other fossil
hyraxes had long heads and would have looked
similar to modern-day pigs.

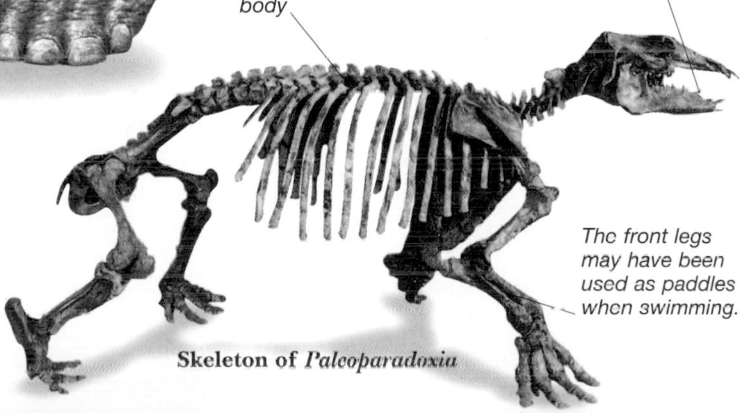

Arsinoitherium's *limbs*
were stout and heavy.

Each foot had five blunt
toes, each tipped with
a small hoof.

It had tusklike front
teeth and cylindrical
chewing teeth.

Broad, heavy
body

The front legs
may have been
used as paddles
when swimming.

DESMOSTYLIANS

Desmostylians, such as *Paleoparadoxia*,
were sea-dwelling uranotheres. They lived
on the edges of the Pacific Ocean during
Oligocene and Miocene times (33.7–5.3
million years ago) and probably fed on
seaweeds. Desmostylians perhaps looked like
a cross between a hippopotamus and a walrus.
Although they lived mainly in the sea, they
could probably walk clumsily on land.

Skeleton of *Paleoparadoxia*

95–250	Triassic 250–203	Jurassic 203–135	Cretaceous 135–65	Tertiary 65–1.75	Quaternary 1.75–present
	MESOZOIC 250–65 MYA			CENOZOIC 65 MYA–present	

HORSES

NONE OF THE PERISSODACTYLS were more suited to life on the grasslands than the horses. Horses appeared in the Eocene (53–33.7 million years ago) and about eight species of them survive today. Successive groups of horse species evolved different features and body sizes to suit their environments. *Hipparion*, shown here, was one of several species of three-toed horse that lived on the Northern Hemisphere grasslands during the Miocene (23.5–5.3 million years ago).

In Hipparion a large bony pocket called the preorbital fossa grew on the side of the snout. This was larger in males than females, though its function remains unknown.

Life in open, grassland environments favored the evolution of large body size and long limbs in horses.

TEETH FOR GRASS-EATING

Advanced horses, such as *Hipparion*, had large, high-crowned molar teeth with complicated chewing surfaces made up of loops of enamel. Their premolars became large and squarish and came to look like the molars. These powerful, resistant teeth allowed advanced horses to eat rough grasses, although they may initially have evolved in response to the accidental chewing of sand and grit.

THREE-TOED FEET

Like modern horses, *Hipparion* was a grassland animal. Earlier horses were probably inhabitants of forests. Unlike modern horses, which only have one toe on each foot, *Hipparion* had three-toed feet. However, most of its weight was borne on the enlarged central toe. *Hipparion* and its relatives were distant cousins of horses such as *Merychippus*, which were the probable ancestors of modern horses.

Cambrian period 540–500	Ordovician 500–435	Silurian 435–410	Devonian 410–355	Carboniferous 355–295	Permia

PALEOZOIC 540–250 MYA

HIPPARION

Scientific name: *Hipparion*

Size: 5 ft (1.5 m) long

Diet: Leaves and grasses

Habitat: Grasslands, open woodlands

Where found: North America, Europe, Asia, and Africa

Time: Miocene and Pliocene (23.5–1.75 MYA)

Related genera: *Cormohipparion, Nannippus, Neohipparion*

Modern horses have special locking mechanisms, called stay apparatus, on their limb bones that allow them to remain standing with a minimum of effort. Hipparion *did not* have stay apparatus.

95–250	Triassic 250–203	Jurassic 203–135	Cretaceous 135–65	Tertiary 65–1.75	Quaternary 1.75 present
		MESOZOIC 250–65 MYA		CENOZOIC 65 MYA–present	

BRONTOTHERES AND CHALICOTHERES

THESE TWO GROUPS OF CREATURES were odd-toed hoofed mammals, or perissodactyls. Brontotheres were large, rhino-like animals known only from North America and Asia in the Eocene (53–33.7 million years ago). Early brontotheres were about the size of sheep, but later ones were giants, up to 8 ft (2.5 m) tall at the shoulder. Some sported horns on the end of their snouts that grew in V or Y shapes. Chalicotheres were horselike perissodactyls with long forelimbs and curved claws on their fingers and toes. First appearing in the Eocene in Asia and Europe, they later spread to Africa and North America and survived into the early Quaternary.

Weak teeth suggest that brontotheres mostly ate soft leaves.

SKULL OF BRONTOPS
Later brontotheres, such as *Brontops*, had very shortenend faces and eyes positioned close to the nose. *Brontops* had two short horns that stuck upward and outward.

BRONTOTHERE HORNS

As brontotheres evolved, their horns became larger. In later brontotheres, males had larger horns than females. This suggests that brontothere males used their horns for displaying and fighting, like the two male *Brontops* shown here. Early brontotheres had tusk-like front teeth, but *Brontops* and other later brontotheres lacked these and instead had a mobile upper lip.

Injuries found on skulls and ribs suggest that brontotheres fought each other with their horns, perhaps for dominance, territory, or mating rights.

Powerful muscles were attached to the massive spines on the shoulder vertebrae and formed a prominent hump.

The surface texture of the horns shows that they were covered in skin.

In some brontotheres one of the wrist bones, a bone called the trapezium, was absent. No one knows why.

Cambrian 540–500	Ordovician 500–435	Silurian 435–410	Devonian 410–355	Carboniferous 355–295	Permia

PALEOZOIC 540–250 MYA

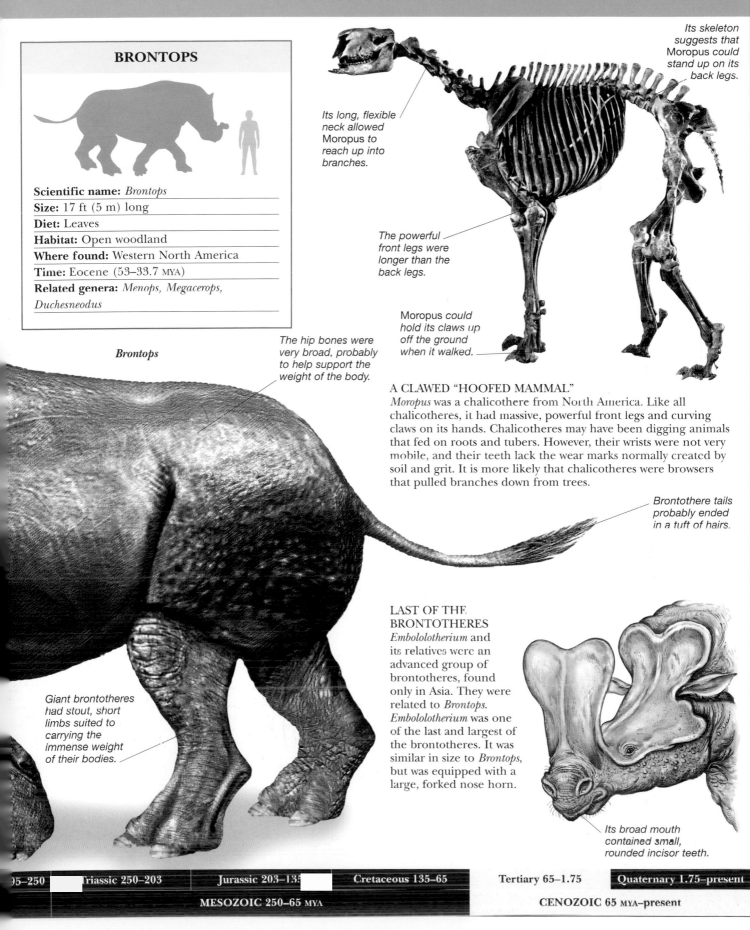

BRONTOPS

Scientific name: *Brontops*

Size: 17 ft (5 m) long

Diet: Leaves

Habitat: Open woodland

Where found: Western North America

Time: Eocene (53–33.7 MYA)

Related genera: *Menops, Megacerops, Duchesneodus*

Brontops

Its long, flexible neck allowed *Moropus* to reach up into branches.

The powerful front legs were longer than the back legs.

Its skeleton suggests that *Moropus* could stand up on its back legs.

Moropus could hold its claws up off the ground when it walked.

The hip bones were very broad, probably to help support the weight of the body.

A CLAWED "HOOFED MAMMAL"

Moropus was a chalicothere from North America. Like all chalicotheres, it had massive, powerful front legs and curving claws on its hands. Chalicotheres may have been digging animals that fed on roots and tubers. However, their wrists were not very mobile, and their teeth lack the wear marks normally created by soil and grit. It is more likely that chalicotheres were browsers that pulled branches down from trees.

Brontothere tails probably ended in a tuft of hairs.

Giant brontotheres had stout, short limbs suited to carrying the immense weight of their bodies.

LAST OF THE BRONTOTHERES

Embolotherium and its relatives were an advanced group of brontotheres, found only in Asia. They were related to *Brontops*. *Embolotherium* was one of the last and largest of the brontotheres. It was similar in size to *Brontops*, but was equipped with a large, forked nose horn.

Its broad mouth contained small, rounded incisor teeth.

05–250	Triassic 250–203	Jurassic 203–135	Cretaceous 135–65	Tertiary 65–1.75	Quaternary 1.75–present
		MESOZOIC 250–65 MYA		CENOZOIC 65 MYA–present	

RHINOCEROSES

TODAY THERE ARE FIVE SURVIVING SPECIES of rhinoceros. They are plant-eaters with horns made from keratin – the same structure that skin, nails, and claws are made from. Fossil rhinoceroses were diverse and evolved many different lifestyles and body shapes. Perhaps the most primitive rhinoceroses were the hyracodontids, or running rhinoceroses. These were hornless, long-legged creatures with simple teeth suited for browsing. Another family, the amynodontids, included amphibious rhinoceroses with short mobile trunks, like the trunks of modern-day tapirs. Amynodontids appear to have been very primitive rhinoceroses, and it has even been suggested that they are not rhinoceroses at all, but part of the tapir group of perissodactyls instead.

ELASMOTHERIUM
The surviving species of rhinoceros are members of the rhinocerotid group. The biggest rhinocerotid was *Elasmotherium*, which reached 16 ft (5 m) in length and had an immense conical horn 6 ft 6 in (2 m) tall on its forehead. *Elasmotherium* lived in the Pleistocene, (1.75–0.01 million years ago).

THE BIGGEST LAND MAMMAL

Paraceratherium was a gigantic hyracodontid rhinoceros. In contrast to the small early hyracodontids, *Paraceratherium* was 18 ft (6 m) tall at the shoulder and weighed around 16 tonnes (15.75 tons), making it the biggest land mammal of all time. Its skull alone was about 4 ft (1.3 m) long. *Paraceratherium* was probably a browser that ate leaves from the tops of trees.

PARACERATHERIUM

Scientific name: *Paraceratherium*

Size: 30 ft (9 m) long

Diet: Leaves and twigs

Habitat: Open woodland

Where found: Eastern Europe, Asia

Time: Oligocene and Miocene (33.7–5.3 MYA)

Related genus: *Forstercooperia*

Despite its great size, Paraceratherium had long, slim legs and could probably run.

Cambrian 540–500	.Ordovician 500–435	Silurian 435–410	Devonian 410–355	Carboniferous 355–295	Permi

PALEOZOIC 540–250 MYA

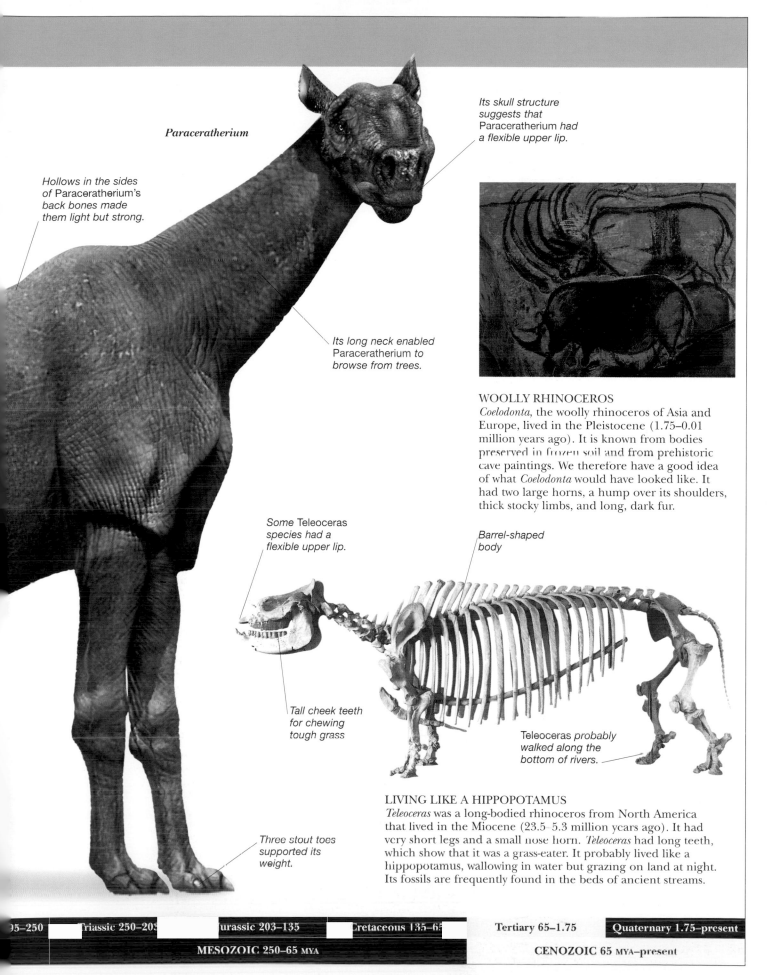

Paraceratherium

Hollows in the sides of Paraceratherium's back bones made them light but strong.

Its skull structure suggests that Paraceratherium *had* a flexible upper lip.

Its long neck enabled Paraceratherium *to* browse from trees.

Some Teleoceras species had a flexible upper lip.

Tall cheek teeth for chewing tough grass

Three stout toes supported its weight.

Barrel-shaped body

Teleoceras *probably* walked along the bottom of rivers.

WOOLLY RHINOCEROS

Coelodonta, the woolly rhinoceros of Asia and Europe, lived in the Pleistocene (1.75–0.01 million years ago). It is known from bodies preserved in frozen soil and from prehistoric cave paintings. We therefore have a good idea of what *Coelodonta* would have looked like. It had two large horns, a hump over its shoulders, thick stocky limbs, and long, dark fur.

LIVING LIKE A HIPPOPOTAMUS

Teleoceras was a long-bodied rhinoceros from North America that lived in the Miocene (23.5–5.3 million years ago). It had very short legs and a small nose horn. *Teleoceras* had long teeth, which show that it was a grass-eater. It probably lived like a hippopotamus, wallowing in water but grazing on land at night. Its fossils are frequently found in the beds of ancient streams.

05–250	Triassic 250–203	Jurassic 203–135	Cretaceous 135–65	Tertiary 65–1.75	Quaternary 1.75–present
	MESOZOIC 250–65 MYA			CENOZOIC 65 MYA–present	

ELEPHANTS

THE TWO MODERN-DAY species of elephant are the living representatives of a much larger group of hoofed mammals, called the proboscideans. The earliest known elephant was *Phosphatherium* from the Paleocene (65–53 million years ago). It weighed only about 33 lbs (15 kg) and was just 2 ft (60 cm) tall at the shoulder. Later elephants increased in size and evolved straight, columnlike legs. They also grew massive tusks in their upper jaws, which they used for fighting and gathering food. The structure of their skulls shows that nearly all fossil elephants had a trunk.

Phiomia probably had a short trunk.

MOERITHERIUM

One of the most primitive known elephants is *Moeritherium*. It lived in Africa in the Eocene (53–33.7 million years ago). *Moeritherium*'s skull indicates that it had an enlarged upper lip, but experts do not know whether this was a true trunk. Its bulky body was similar in shape to a hippopotamus, and its legs were short. These features suggest that *Moeritherium* wallowed in lakes and rivers, perhaps feeding on water plants. Enlarged incisor teeth in both the upper and lower jaws formed small tusks that probably protruded from its mouth.

PHIOMIA
This primitive elephant lived in northern Africa during the Oligocene (33.7–23.5 million years ago). *Phiomia* was larger than *Moeritherium* but still only about as big as a large modern horse. It had columnlike legs, a shorter neck, and a much bigger skull than more primitive elephants. Like later elephants, *Phiomia* had air-filled spaces, called diploe, in its skull. This meant that its skull was light, despite its size.

Primitive elephants like Moeritherium had not yet developed the columnlike legs of later elephants.

Cambrian 540–500	Ordovician 500–435	Silurian 435–410	Devonian 410–355	Carboniferous 355–295	Permi

PALEOZOIC 540–250 MYA

SHOVEL-TUSKERS
Like nearly all primitive elephants, *Phiomia* had tusks in both its upper and lower jaws. Its lower jaw was long and had flattened, square-tipped tusks. This formed a shovel-shaped jaw that could have been used to scoop up water plants, or cut branches or bark from trees. Later, more advanced kinds of elephants, such as *Gomphotherium*, had similar lower jaws.

Skull of Phiomia

Gomphotherium
was about as big
as an Asian elephant.

GOMPHOTHERIUM
A successful group of elephants called gomphotheres spread around the world in the Miocene and Pliocene (23.5–1.75 million years ago). Gomphotheres, such as *Gomphotherium,* inhabited marshes, grasslands, and forests. *Gomphotherium*'s upper jaw tusks were probably used for fighting and display and, as in living elephants, were larger in males than in females. Elephants similar to *Gomphotherium* were the ancestors of mammoths and of modern-day elephants.

DEINOTHERES
These strange elephants had no tusks in their skulls and two down-curved tusks in their lower jaws. These may have been used to dig up roots, strip bark, or wrench branches down from trees. Deinotheres seem to have had shorter trunks than living elephants.

Deinotherium *was 13 ft (4 m) tall at the shoulder.*

The enlarged upper lip and nose may have formed a very short trunk.

Moeritherium's neck was longer than that of more advanced elephants.

MOERITHERIUM

Scientific name: *Moeritherium*
Size: 10 ft (3 m) long
Diet: Water plants
Habitat: Lakes, rivers, riverside forest
Where found: Northern Africa
Time: Eocene and Oligocene (53–23.5 MYA)
Related genus: *Phosphatherium*

5–250	Triassic 250–203	Jurassic 203–135	Cretaceous 135–65	Tertiary 65–1.75	Quaternary 1.75–present
	MESOZOIC 250–65 MYA			CENOZOIC 65 MYA–present	

PLATYBELODON

Platybelodon was a widespread "shovel-tusker" gomphothere. It had a long, scooplike tip to its lower jaw, formed by the tusk and mandible. In some specimens the lower jaw curved downward along its length, while in others it was straighter and curved upward at the tip. *Platybelodon* was once thought to have lived in marshes, where it used its lower jaw to scoop up water plants. Wear patterns on its tusks suggest instead that *Platybelodon* mostly lived in grasslands and forests and cropped tough vegetation from trees.

A FLEXIBLE TRUNK

Old reconstructions of *Platybelodon* show it with a short, wide trunk that would not have been very flexible. This is because the reconstructions were based on evidence from the more primitive *Phiomia*. The nasal openings in *Phiomia's* skull show that its trunk was short and poorly developed. However, *Platybelodon* had the same kind of nasal openings as modern elephants. Like modern elephants therefore, *Platybelodon* probably had a long, flexible trunk.

| Cambrian 540–500 | Ordovician 500–435 | Silurian 435–410 | Devonian 410–355 | Carboniferous 355–295 | Perm |

PALEOZOIC 540–250 MYA

PLATYBELODON

Scientific name: *Platybelodon*

Size: 10 ft (3 m) tall at shoulder

Diet: Leaves, grasses, bark

Habitat: Grasslands, forests

Where found: North America, Africa, Asia, Europe

Time: Miocene and Pliocene (23.5–1.75 MYA)

Related genera: *Ambelodon, Torynobelodon*

LOWER JAW

The wear marks on *Platybelodon*'s lower jaw tusks show that vegetation was often pulled across the tips of the tusks. *Platybelodon* probably used the tusks as blades. It would have grabbed a branch with its long trunk and pulled it repeatedly across the tusks until they sliced through the wood. It seems that most of this branch-cutting happened where the two tusks touched one another, as this is usually the most heavily worn area.

LEGS AND FEET

Like all advanced elephants, *Platybelodon* had straight legs. Its knees were positioned directly above its ankles, so each leg formed a column beneath its body. *Platybelodon*'s ankles were very close to the ground because the bones that formed its feet were very short. Fatty pads under its feet supported the foot bones and helped to spread the animal's great weight as it walked.

05–250	Triassic 250–203	Jurassic 203–135	Cretaceous 135–65	Tertiary 65–1.75	Quaternary 1.75–present
	MESOZOIC 250–65 MYA			CENOZOIC 65 MYA–present	

MAMMOTHS

THE EIGHT SPECIES OF MAMMOTH were all true elephants, closely related to the two living species. Mammoth genetic material, or DNA, was discovered in 1994 and found to be almost identical to that of living elephants. The woolly mammoth (*Mammuthus primigenius*) is perhaps the most famous fossil animal from the Pleistocene (1.75–0.01 million years ago). An inhabitant of the cold Ice Age grasslands, it had a shaggy coat, huge, curving tusks, and a tall, domed skull, but was small compared to some other extinct elephants. As in living elephants, male mammoths probably wandered on their own and fought for dominance with their tusks. Some males even died locked in combat and have been preserved this way as fossils. The last mammoths, a population of dwarf woolly mammoths, lived on Wrangel Island north of Siberia and died out only 4,000 years ago.

Mammoth hair, found on the frozen specimens, can be up to 3 ft (90 cm) long.

Shoulder hump

WOOLLY MAMMOTH

These mammoths lived in herds and fed on grasses and other small plants, which they plucked with the two "fingers" on the tips of their trunks. Several woolly mammoths have been found preserved in the frozen ground of Siberia. Their fur, skin, muscles, and even their stomach contents are still intact. These frozen specimens show that, unlike living elephants, mammoths had very short tails. This is probably because a long tail would be vulnerable to frostbite.

Mammuthus primigenius

Both male and female woolly mammoths had long, curving tusks. They used their tusks in combat and display, and as tools for gathering food.

DIMA THE MAMMOTH

Dima was the name given to a frozen male baby woolly mammoth, recovered in 1977 on the bank of the Berelekh River, Russia, and preserved in a remarkably complete condition. How Dima died has been the subject of debate. It has been suggested that he drowned, fell into a crack in the frozen ground, or became caught in wet mud. X-rays show that Dima had not yet grown the domed skull and tall shoulder hump seen in adult mammoths.

Cambrian 540–500	Ordovician 500–435	Silurian 435–410	Devonian 410–355	Carboniferous 355–295	Permi

PALEOZOIC 540–250 MYA

CAVE PAINTINGS

About 400 prehistoric cave paintings and sculptures of woolly mammoths are known. Most have been found in French or Spanish caves and are about 30,000 years old. The paintings show mammoths with the same features as the mammoths preserved in frozen ground, such as a shoulder hump and small, rounded ears. Some paintings depict mammoths moving in groups while others show mammoths fighting.

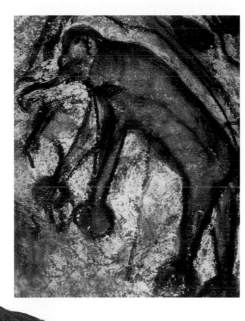

WOOLLY MAMMOTH

Scientific name:	*Mammuthus primigenius*
Size: 11 ft (3.3 m) tall	
Diet: Grasses and other plant material	
Habitat: Woodlands and grasslands	
Where found: North America, Europe, Asia	
Time: From the Pleistocene (1.75–0.01 MYA) to about 4,000 years ago	
Related genus: *Elephas* (includes living elephants)	

The tusks were so long and curved that they crossed over.

Huge columnlike limbs supported its weight.

IMPERIAL MAMMOTH

Mammuthus imperator (Imperial mammoth) was a giant North American Pleistocene mammoth and one of the biggest elephants that ever lived. It was 12 ft (3.7 m) tall at the shoulder and its huge, curving tusks could be 14 ft (4.3 m) long. Many fossils have been found in California, where this mammoth inhabited warm grassland and woodland environments. Warm-weather mammoths probably lacked the furry coats of their cold-climate cousins.

5–250	Triassic 250–209	Jurassic 209–195	Cretaceous 195–65	Tertiary 65–1.75	Quaternary 1.75–present
	MESOZOIC 250–65 MYA			**CENOZOIC 65 MYA–present**	

PIGS, HIPPOS, AND PECCARIES

THE LARGEST AND MOST SUCCESSFUL group of hoofed mammals are the artiodactyls, or even-toed hoofed mammals. All artiodactyls have distinctive ankle and foot bones that allow many of them to run fast. Their feet are symmetrical, and most forms have two or four toes, hence the group's name. Artiodactyls include three major groups that all first appeared in the Eocene. The first group is the suiforms, including pigs, hippopotamuses (hippos for short), peccaries, and various extinct relations. Unspecialized teeth and flexible snouts have allowed them to become omnivores that can eat most kinds of plant material and fungi, as well as carrion and small animals. Many suiforms had, or have, large fang- or tusklike teeth used for fighting and display. These tusks have become massively enlarged in the hippos. The second artiodactyl group, the tylopods, includes the camels. The third group, the pecorans, includes giraffes, deer, and cattle.

DAEODON

Scientific name: *Daeodon*
Size: 10 ft (3 m) long
Diet: Vegetation, carrion, smaller animals
Habitat: Grasslands, open woodland
Where found: North America
Time: Oligocene – Early Miocene
Related genera: *Archaeotherium, Choerodon*

HIPPOPOTAMUSES

The first hippos appeared in the Late Miocene. Two kinds survive today – the large, amphibious *Hippopotamus* and the small, land-living *Hexaprotodon*. The recently extinct *Hippopotamus lemerlei* was a pygmy river-dwelling hippo from Madagascar. Hippos have huge, curving tusks at the front of the mouth. These are larger in males than females and are used in fighting and displaying. Genetic studies suggest that hippos may be related to whales, but this is controversial.

Eyes located on top of the head

Amphibious hippos have elongated snouts and lower jaws.

Skull of *Hippopotamus lemerlei*

Incisors protrude forward, and can be used for digging.

Entelodonts had small brains, but parts of the brain devoted to smell were well developed.

Bony cheek flanges were especially large, with swollen ends.

Skeleton of *Archaeotherium*

ANCIENT BEAST
Entelodonts were pig- to bison-sized suiforms known from Eocene and Miocene Europe, Asia, and North America. They had long legs and deep bodies. Their huge skulls have bony bumps on the cheeks and lower jaws, crushing teeth, and huge, curving canine teeth. *Archaeotherium* was a successful pig-sized entelodont that lived across North America and Asia.

Unlike many other suiforms, entelodonts had only two toes on each foot.

| Cambrian 540–500 | Ordovician 500–435 | Silurian 435–410 | Devonian 410–355 | Carboniferous 355–295 | Permia |

PALEOZOIC 540–250 MYA

Macrogenis **skull**

Powerful neck tendons attached to the shoulder spines helped to support head.

Elongated bony spines grew from shoulder vertebrae.

Daeodon

PECCARIES

Another group of suiforms, which appeared in the Late Eocene (around 40 million years ago), and lived mostly in North America, are the peccaries. They survive to the present as three species. Peccaries look much like pigs and live in similar ways. They have large, vertical canine teeth. Some extinct peccaries, like the Late Miocene *Macrogenis*, had massive triangular protrusions of bone growing out from their cheeks.

Skull bumps became larger with age.

Curving canine teeth with serrated edges

Big crushing molars suggest Daeodon ate bones

KILLER BUFFALO PIG

Daeodon, formerly called *Dinohyus*, is one of the biggest, best known, and last of the entelodonts. Like others of its group, it had tall shoulders, a deep body, and long legs. The bumps on its skull and jaws were probably used for fighting – some fossil specimens have wounds that appear to have resulted from such battles. The bony bumps in *Daeodon* were actually smaller than those of most other entelodonts, though they were still prominent. The teeth and muscle scars of *Daeodon* suggest that it was an omnivore, easily able to break bones and eat animal carcasses. Entelodonts may have been scavengers, finding their food in a similar way to modern hyenas.

Entelodonts had long, slim limbs, suggesting that they were fast runners.

Unlike in smaller entelodonts, the lower leg bones of Daeodon were fused together for strength.

05–250	Triassic 250–203	Jurassic 203–135	Cretaceous 135–65	Tertiary 65–1.75	Quaternary 1.75–present
		MESOZOIC 250–65 MYA		CENOZOIC 65 MYA–present	

CAMELS

CAMELS AND THEIR RELATIVES EVOLVED in the Eocene (55–34 million years ago), and include nearly 100 fossil species. Although modern camels inhabit deserts, they were once abundant grassland and woodland herbivores. Two groups of artiodactyls – the bovoids and the camels and relatives – evolved a special way of digesting plant material called rumination. Once swallowed, food passes to the first of three or four stomach chambers, and is later regurgitated to be chewed a second time ("chewing the cud"). In each stomach chamber, microorganisms break down the plant material further. Ruminant mammals recycle urea, one of the body's waste products, and use it to feed these microorganisms. As a result, less urine is produced, and less water wasted, which is why ruminants have adapted to dry environments like deserts more successfully than other hoofed mammals.

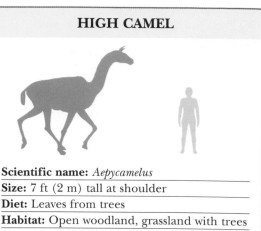

HIGH CAMEL

Scientific name: *Aepycamelus*

Size: 7 ft (2 m) tall at shoulder

Diet: Leaves from trees

Habitat: Open woodland, grassland with trees

Where found: North America

Time: Miocene (23.5–5.3 MYA)

Related genera: *Oxydactylus, Hesperocamelus*

Stenomylus probably lived in large herds.

Skull very short compared to other camels

Long, slender legs would have made Aepycamelus a fast runner.

When standing Stenomylus *was less than 3 ft 3 in (1 m) tall at the shoulder.*

Aepycamelus *walked on the whole length of its toes, unlike earlier* Stenomylus.

NARROW TOOTH
The six living camel species are native to Africa, Asia, and South America. However, most of camel history occurred in North America, and camels still lived here as recently as 11,000 years ago. The first camels were small, and perhaps lived like modern gazelles. *Stenomylus* from the Oligocene (around 30 million years ago) was a small early camel with enormous chewing teeth. Unlike advanced camels, *Stenomylus* had pointed hooves and walked on the tips of its toes.

Cambrian 540–500	Ordovician 500–435	Silurian 435–410	Devonian 410–355	Carboniferous 355–295	Permia

PALEOZOIC 540–250 MYA

FEEDING STRATEGIES
Living camels are grazers that mostly eat grasses. The skulls and teeth of fossil camels, however, show that many of them were browsers, feeding on shrubs and trees. *Oxydactylus* from Miocene North America had long legs and a long neck. Perhaps *Oxydactylus* fed on trees by standing tall on its back legs like the modern Gerenuk antelope.

Feeding Gerenuk

Features of teeth and skull suggest a closer relation to living llamas than to modern camels.

Pointed front teeth were small.

GIANT GIRAFFE CAMEL
Aepycamelus ("high camel") was a large camel with tremendously long leg and neck bones. It was probably a browsing herbivore that, like modern giraffes, fed from trees. Eight *Aepycamelus* species are known, each with a slightly different skull and jaws. They inhabited grasslands with scattered trees, and may have become extinct as the tree cover gradually disappeared. *Aepycamelus* probably shared a number of features with living camels, including a divided upper lip, a long, curved neck, unusual two-toed feet, and legs that are not joined by a sheet of skin to the side of the body. Camels also have special fanglike teeth that the males use in fighting.

Neck bones longer than those of any other camel

Fossil *Oxydactylus* foot

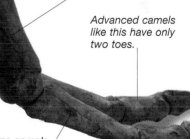

Two "metapodial" bones are fused together in advanced camels.

Advanced camels like this have only two toes.

Primitive Eocene camels still had four toes.

Front and back legs of camels are more equal in size than they are in other hoofed mammals.

Like living kinds of camel, fossil species perhaps had dense, woolly fur.

As in modern camels, two main hand bones were fused together.

CAMEL FEET AND WALKING STYLE
Advanced camels have unique feet. Unlike other artiodactyls, they do not walk on the tips of their toes, but on the whole length of their toes. Soft toe pads help them walk on rocks or sand with ease. Camels walk using a technique called pacing. Both legs on one side of the body move in the same direction at once.

05 250	Triassic 250–203	Jurassic 203–135	Cretaceous 135–65	Tertiary 65–1.75	Quaternary 1.75–present
	MESOZOIC 250–65 MYA			CENOZOIC 65 MYA–present	

DEER AND KIN

SEVERAL NEW GROUPS OF SMALL, forest-dwelling herbivores first appeared during the Miocene (24–5 million years ago). The spread of grasslands allowed some of them to move out of the forest, becoming larger and more successful. Like bovoids, many evolved horns or equivalent structures for fighting and displaying. The most successful of these mammals were the deer – antelope-like animals distinguished by their antlers. Early antlers were simple in shape – any fighting was probably done with fanglike teeth, and some living deer still fight in this way. Giraffids (the giraffes and their relatives) were one of the first groups to move to the grasslands and evolve large body size. Some fossil giraffes were deerlike, and all possessed bony horns called ossicones. Several other groups of deerlike mammals, including the paleomerycids and protoceratids, evolved their own impressive bony horns.

In the largest males, the antlers spanned 12 ft (3.7 m).

GIANT ANTLERS
The largest antlers of all time belong to *Megaloceros*, a giant Pleistocene deer that was still alive 9,000 years ago. Despite the huge size of these antlers, microscopic stress marks show that they were used for fighting and not just display. Antlers are shed each year and, except in reindeer, are grown only by males. Antlers may have first developed from scar tissue resulting from injuries.

Syndyoceras

Protoceras

Synthetoceras

EARLY HORNS
The deerlike protoceratids ("early horns") lived in North America from the Eocene to the Pliocene (55 million to just 2 million years ago). Male protoceratids displayed some of the most spectacular and complex horns ever evolved. In earlier protoceratids, such as *Protoceras*, the horns looked most impressive in side view. Later kinds, including *Syndyoceras* and *Synthetoceras* grew horns more suited for display from the front. Protoceratids had stout limbs and bodies, and their teeth suggest that they ate soft vegetation and they probably had a flexible upper lip like a camel's.

A dappled coat may have helped Cranioceras to hide in dense foliage.

All weight was carried by the middle two toes.

THREE-HORNED DEER RELATIVE

Cranioceras was a paleomerycid – one of a group of deerlike hoofed mammals that lived from the Oligocene to the Pliocene (34–2 million years ago). Many, but not all, paleomerycids had bony horns that grew backward, forward, or upward from above their eyes. In the group that includes *Cranioceras*, a third horn grew upward and back from the rear of the skull. Healed injuries seen on paleomerycid horns show that they were used for fighting – probably to establish mating rights and social dominance. As in most horned mammals, only males possessed horns. While some paleomerycids had long limbs and probably lived in the open, *Cranioceras* and its relatives were short-legged denizens of dense woodlands, about 10 million years ago. Later paleomerycids grew larger, but then smaller just before their final extinction.

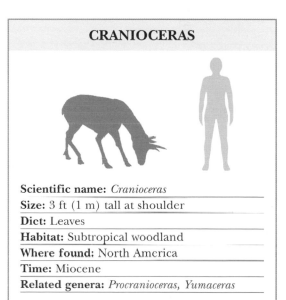

Second pair of ossicones on nose

Long rear ossicones

Giraffokeryx restoration

Paleomerycid horns may have been more like ossicones, suggesting a close link to giraffids.

GIRAFFIDS

Giraffokeryx was a primitive giraffid that lived in Miocene and Pliocene Asia, Europe, and Africa, around 5 million years ago. It had two pairs of pointed, furry, hornlike structures called ossicones. The giraffids are cud-chewing hoofed mammals that probably share an ancestor with bovoids. Only two survive today – the African giraffe (*Giraffa camelopardalis*) and the Okapi (*Okapia johnstoni*). As well as distinctive ossicones, both use a flexible tongue to bring foliage to the mouth. However, many other giraffids thrived between the Miocene era (around 20 million years ago) and the recent past. One major group of extinct giraffids, the sivatheres, had enormous branching ossicones, and would have looked more like deer than giraffes.

Limbs were not as long or slim as those of grassland-dwelling relatives.

Third horn could have been used for display as well as fighting.

CRANIOCERAS

Scientific name:	*Cranioceras*
Size:	3 ft (1 m) tall at shoulder
Diet:	Leaves
Habitat:	Subtropical woodland
Where found:	North America
Time:	Miocene
Related genera:	*Procranioceras, Yumaceras*

95–250	Triassic 250–203	Jurassic 203–135	Cretaceous 135–65	Tertiary 65–1.75	Quaternary 1.75–present
	MESOZOIC 250–65 MYA			CENOZOIC 65 MYA–present	

269

CATTLE, SHEEP, AND GOATS

CATTLE AND THEIR RELATIVES are the most plentiful large, hoofed, grazing animals alive today. Wild and domestic cattle, sheep, goats, antelopes, and musk oxen (but not the antelopelike pronghorns) are grouped together as bovoids, named from the Latin word for ox. All these animals probably evolved more than 20 million years ago from small, hornless, deerlike ancestors. Early forms resembling gazelles gave rise to huge variety, with more than 100 genera by the beginning of the Quaternary, but all bovoids share some common features. These include strong, defensive horns which never shed on the heads of both sexes, and teeth and stomachs adapted for eating and digesting grass. Legs and two-toed feet are also designed for fast running or agile leaping to escape enemies. The cattle family spread first through Europe, Africa, and Asia. By one million years ago, some crossed the Bering Land Bridge into North America where bison, bighorn sheep, and Rocky Mountain goats persist today.

Sharp, strong horns that are never shed

Jaws have high-crowned teeth, which evolved for chewing.

PREHISTORIC ANIMALS IN CAVE PAINTINGS
An artist depicted this great ox on a cave wall at Lascaux in southwest France some 15,000 years ago. At the time, Old Stone Age hunter-gatherers hunted wild herds of cattle for their meat. Perhaps another 7,000 years went by before people learned to tame and farm the least fierce individuals for meat, milk, and hides. The old wild cattle strain is now extinct, but millions of its descendants graze peacefully in pastures worldwide.

ANCESTRAL OX

Bos primigenius, also known as the aurochs, was the ancestor of most domesticated cattle. It was larger than modern cattle, wild and fierce, and roamed the forests of Europe, Asia, and Africa, dying out in recent times. The last wild aurochs was killed in Poland in 1627. Bovoids such as *Bos* and *Bison priscus* left large fossil horn cores of bone. In life, horny sheaths covered these cores, making the horns even longer. Fossils of the prehistoric ox *Pelorovis*, related to the modern African buffalo, have 6 ft 6 in (2 m) horn cores. With the addition of their sheaths, its horns could have spanned as much as 13 ft (4 m). These awesome horns were used by rival males for display and fighting, as well as for self-defense. Although these prehistoric creatures are no more, wild cattle of several genera survive. The best known kinds are bison, buffaloes, and yak.

Cambrian 540–500	Ordovician 500–435	Silurian 435–410	Devonian 410–355	Carboniferous 355–295	Permia
		PALEOZOIC 540–250 MYA			

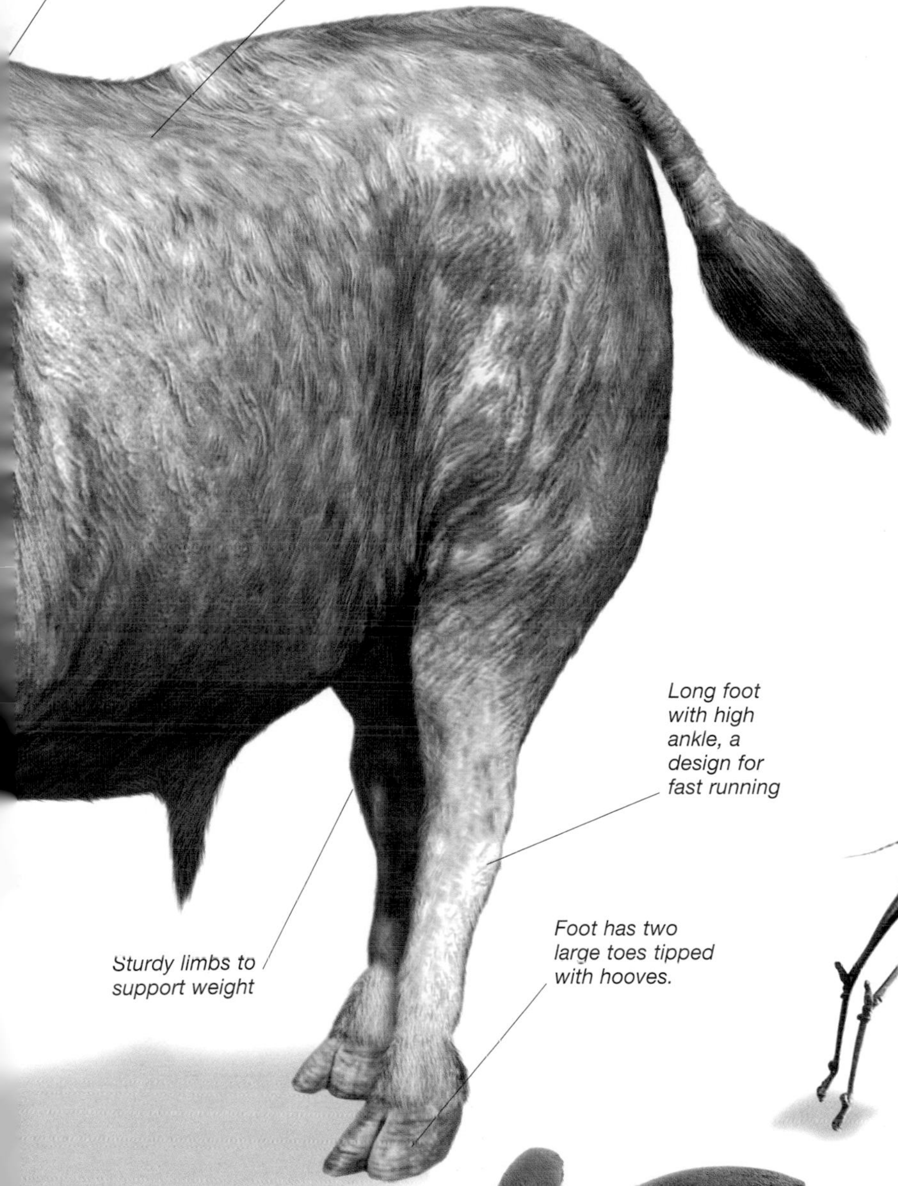

Muscular neck and shoulders

Bos stood up to 6 ft 6 in (2 m) tall at the shoulder.

ANCESTRAL OX

Scientific name: *Bos primigenus*

Size: 10 ft (3 m) long

Diet: Plants

Habitat: Forest glades

Where found: Europe, Africa, Asia

Time: Quaternary

Related species: *Bison, Pelorovis*

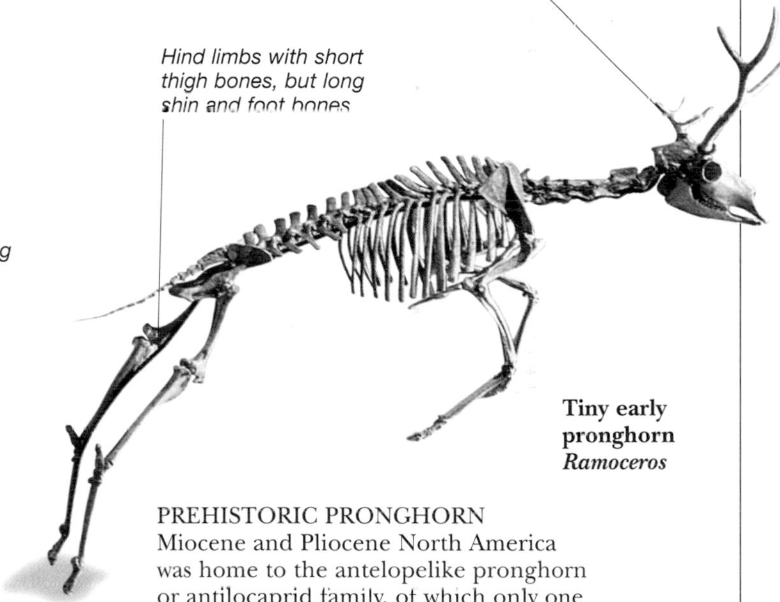

Branched horns with sheaths shed annually

Hind limbs with short thigh bones, but long shin and foot bones

Long foot with high ankle, a design for fast running

Sturdy limbs to support weight

Foot has two large toes tipped with hooves.

Tiny early pronghorn
Ramoceros

PREHISTORIC PRONGHORN
Miocene and Pliocene North America was home to the antelopelike pronghorn or antilocaprid family, of which only one member now survives – the second fastest mammal in the world. *Ramoceros* was a small, prehistoric relative of the living pronghorn. Its long, forked horns may have been used by rival males in pushing contests. Like other antilocaprids, *Ramoceros* shed the sheaths of its horns every year, and new horns formed from hair sprouting on the bony cores. This difference between pronghorns and cattle persuades many scientists that these agile mammals may be more closely related to deer.

EARLY SHEEP AND GOATS
Goats and sheep, including mountain sheep like *Ovis canadensis* shared a common ancestor with other bovoids. This animal probably existed in the Oligocene, more than 20 million years ago. Its descendants gave rise first to antelopes, then to sheep and goats, and finally to cattle.

Ovis canadensis **skull**

295–250	Triassic 250–203	Jurassic 203–135	Cretaceous 195–65	Tertiary 65–1.75	Quaternary 1.75–present
		MESOZOIC 250–65 MYA		CENOZOIC 65 MYA–present	

HOOFED PREDATORS

When someone mentions "hoofed mammals," we tend to think of unaggressive plant-eating creatures: cattle, antelope, and sheep. Early in their evolution, however, the ancestors of these even-toed hoofed mammals included very different creatures – the Acreodi or mesonychians. Like sheep or cows, these had toes tipped with hooves, not claws. But instead of molars shaped for munching leaves, the creatures had massive teeth designed for slicing meat or crushing bones. Acreodi looked a little like, and played the same role as, wolves, hyenas, and bears. They lived across Europe, Asia, and North America for around 30 million years, from the middle Palaeocene (60 MYA) to the early Oligocene (30 MYA).

Long, narrow jaw with teeth rather like a bear's

Head broad at the back with powerful jaw muscles.

Toes tipped with short hooves instead of long sharp claws

Andrewsarchus skull

Massive molars with blunt cusps for crushing

Long, curved, pointed canine tooth for piercing flesh

POWERFUL JAWS

The skull of *Andrewsarchus* shows its powerful jaws and formidable collection of teeth. The canines at the front were long, curved, and piercing for delivering the killer bite to its prey. The back teeth were also pointed – the lower molars bladelike for cutting, and the upper molars broad, designed for crushing. Notches in the top and bottom teeth were much like those in living carnivores, for gripping meat to tear it from the bone. The back teeth, however, were generally not as well-designed for slicing flesh as those of modern carnivores.

GIGANTIC OMNIVORE

The enormous *Andrewsarchus* ("Andrews' flesh-eater") lived in Eocene Mongolia more than 40 million years ago, and was the biggest known carnivorous land mammal of all time. Its skull alone was 33 in (83 cm) long and 22 in (56 cm) wide. The rest of the skeleton has not been discovered, but its body probably grew up to 19 ft (6 m) long or even more. *Andrewsarchus*'s jaws were equipped with long, sharp, curved canine teeth, and massive, crushing back teeth, powerful enough to have killed and crunched the bones of young hoofed mammals, but this enormous beast was probably as unfussy about its diet as a grizzly bear. It would have munched juicy leaves and berries, insect grubs, and small rodents, as well as scavenging from large corpses that it came across.

Cambrian 540–500	Ordovician 500–435	Silurian 435–410	Devonian 410–355	Carboniferous 355–295	Permian

PALEOZOIC 540–250 MYA

Long, heavy body
(exact shape is unknown)

Skull shape shows
Mesonyx had
a strong bite.

Long, lean body
shaped something
like a wolf's

Like Mesonyx,
Andrewsarchus
may have had
a long tail.

Strong limbs must
have supported
its great weight.

Andrewsarchus may
have been flat-footed,
like a bear.

MIDDLE NAIL

Mesonyx ("middle nail") was a member of the mesonychids, the best-known family of the Acreodi. It was a wolflike predator from the Middle Eocene of Wyoming and East Asia (around 45 million years ago). Agile limbs made it a fast runner, and it probably hunted hoofed plant eaters, moving lightly on its toes, not flat-footed like the less advanced Acreodi. However, instead of claws, *Mesonyx*'s toes ended in small hooves. Its long skull had a crest above the braincase to anchor large jaw muscles and give it a powerful bite.

Archaeocetes **skull**

Long, low, narrow
jaws like those
of mesonychids

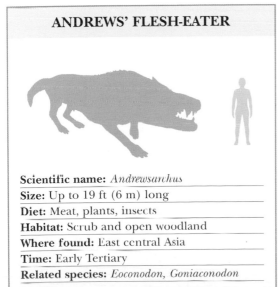

ANDREWS' FLESH-EATER

Scientific name:	*Andrewsarchus*
Size:	Up to 19 ft (6 m) long
Diet:	Meat, plants, insects
Habitat:	Scrub and open woodland
Where found:	East central Asia
Time:	Early Tertiary
Related species:	*Eoconodon, Goniaconodon*

WHALE ANCESTORS

The Acreodi probably became extinct when outcompeted by new kinds of more efficient predators, including the ancestors of carnivores alive today. Meanwhile, though, some of their own ancestors seemingly gave rise to a much longer-lived and more successful group of mammals – the whales. The skulls and teeth of early whales such as *Archaeocetes* strongly resemble those of certain acreodi. Molecular evidence hints that the ancestor of Acreodi and whales gave rise to the hippopotamuses as well.

95–250	Triassic 250–203	Jurassic 203–135	Cretaceous 135–65	Tertiary 65–1.75	Quaternary 1.75–present
		MESOZOIC 250–65 MYA		CENOZOIC 65 MYA–present	

EARLY WHALES

LIVING WHALES ARE FISH-SHAPED, with flipperlike forelimbs, no hind legs, and powerful fluked tails for propulsion. But the earliest Eocene whales were very different from this – some had large hindlimbs and could probably still move on land. Their skeletons show that they had started to swim with an up and down motion of the tail. By the end of the Eocene, fully aquatic whales like *Basilosaurus* had evolved. Eocene whales were predators that mostly inhabited shallow tropical seas. They may have descended from land-dwelling mesonychids that took to foraging for food in shallow water. While mesonychid skulls and skeletons are strikingly similar to those of the first whales, recent DNA studies suggest that whales may actually be artiodactyls most closely related to hippopotamuses. This area is still the subject of much argument.

Square tail vertebrae show that the tail had flukes (fins along its sides)

Long tail flukes provided the main swimming thrust.

Long tail

Long skull, with nostrils close to the tip of snout

Large hindlimbs made Ambulocetus a strong swimmer

Tiny, three-toed hindlimbs would have projected from sides.

Ambulocetus probably spent most of its life on land, taking to the seas to hunt.

Artist's restoration of *Ambulocetus*

FIRST WHALES

The first known whale, *Pakicetus*, comes from the Middle Eocene of Pakistan, a site rich in early whale fossils. Presently known only from skull material, *Pakicetus* was small – probably less than 6 ft 6 in (2 m) long – and not specialized for life in water. However, its ear bones possessed features unique to whales, and its delicate front teeth suggest that it caught fish, perhaps while paddling in shallow water. Other early whales were formidable predators – *Ambulocetus* looked something like a cross between a wolf and a seal and had a long crocodile-like head. Its skull was strong enough to resist the struggles of large mammalian prey.

ECHOLOCATION AT WORK

Throughout their evolution, whales developed a method called echolocation to gain a mental picture of their surroundings. They project noises through a structure on the forehead called the melon. Echoes of the noises are then transmitted to the whale's ears via a fatty pad in its lower jaw. Eocene whales do not appear to have had melons though they do show evidence of sensitive hearing.

The melon sits in a large bony depression on the top of the skull.

Any nearby object, such as another animal, creates an echo.

Cambrian 540–500	Ordovician 500–435	Silurian 435–410	Devonian 410–355	Carboniferous 355–295	Permia

PALEOZOIC 540–250 MYA

Dorudon skull

Nostrils were not located on the forehead in Eocene whales.

Dorudon *and other Eocene whales have two different kinds of teeth.*

It is unknown whether fossil whales had dorsal fins or not.

SKULL EVOLUTION

In early whales like *Pakicetus*, the nostrils were located close to the tip of the snout, as they are in most land mammals. More advanced whales like *Basilosaurus* and *Dorudon* have their nostrils located midway along their snouts. In advanced whales like the Miocene *Prosqualodon*, the nostrils are on the top of the head where they form the blowhole. Whales' nostrils have therefore gradually moved backward, making room for the developing melon in the forehead.

Prosqualodon skull

Teeth of advanced whales are all similar in shape.

EOCENE GIANT

Basilosaurus is one of the biggest fossil whales known, growing to more than 60 ft (20 m). The vertebrae that make up *Basilosaurus*' back and tail are unusual, elongated bones, unlike the shortened vertebrae seen in most whales. These could have made *Basilosaurus* more flexible than living whales. Its huge skull, which can be more than 3 ft 3 in (1 m) long, had curved front teeth and triangular, serrated cheek teeth. Using these, *Basilosaurus* could have grabbed and sliced up fishes as well as other marine mammals.

Unique long body. Other Eocene whales were much shorter.

Ribs were made of very thick, heavy bone.

Unlike modern whales, basilosaurs had a flexible elbow.

Wear on teeth shows that Basilosaurus *preyed on large animals.*

BASILOSAURUS

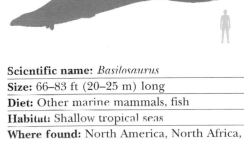

Scientific name: *Basilosaurus*

Size: 66–83 ft (20–25 m) long

Diet: Other marine mammals, fish

Habitat: Shallow tropical seas

Where found: North America, North Africa, South Asia

Time: Late Eocene

Related genera: *Basiloterus Dorudon*

295–250	Triassic 250–203	Jurassic 203–135	Cretaceous 135–65	Tertiary 65–1.75	Quaternary 1.75–present
		MESOZOIC 250–65 MYA		CENOZOIC 65 MYA–present	

Reference Section

In this section, you can scan a pictorial summary of life through time, with pauses for dramatic mass extinctions. Retrace the journeys of prehistoric creatures, from their deaths millions of years ago to their stunning resurrection in museum halls. Along the way, step into the shoes of a paleontologist – spend time on an exotic dig, then learn what goes on when fossils reach the laboratory. Watch scientists reassemble fossil bones and see sculptors recreate lifelike replicas of ancient animals. Get tips on conducting your own fossil hunt. Read about personalities who helped solve puzzles of the past. Then discover where to see exciting fossils on display.

GEOLOGICAL TIME CHART

ROCKS ARE DEPOSITED IN LAYERS, and the layers at the bottom of a sequence are the oldest. The actual ages in years of different rock layers are worked out by techniques that involve measuring the decay of radioactive elements within the rock. Groups of rock layers are classified together to form periods, such as the Triassic and Jurassic. Periods are grouped together to form eras, such as the Mesozoic and Cenozoic. Eras are one of the biggest subdivisions of geological time and are separated from one another by major extinction events in which important fossil groups disappear from the geological record.

MILLION YEARS AGO

4,600-540	PRECAMBRIAN	Origin of life. Evolution of Vendian organisms.

PALEOZOIC ERA

540-500	CAMBRIAN PERIOD	First single-celled and multicellular life.
500-435	ORDOVICIAN PERIOD	First nautiloids and jawed vertebrates.
435-410	SILURIAN PERIOD	First plants and arachnids on land.
410-355	DEVONIAN PERIOD	First vertebrates with four limbs and distinct digits.
355-295	CARBONIFEROUS PERIOD	First reptiles and flying insects on land.
295-250	PERMIAN PERIOD	First sail-back synapsids on land.

MESOZOIC ERA

250-203	TRIASSIC PERIOD	First dinosaurs, mammals, turtles, and frogs.
203-135	JURASSIC PERIOD	First birds appear, dinosaurs rule the land.
135-65	CRETACEOUS PERIOD	First modern mammals. Non-avian dinosaurs die out.

CENOZOIC ERA

65-53		PALEOCENE EPOCH	First owls, shrews, and hedgehogs.
53-33.7	TETIARY	EOCENE EPOCH	First horses, elephants, dogs, and cats.
33.7-23.5		OLIGOCENE EPOCH	First monkeys, deer, and rhinoceroses.
23.5-5.3		MIOCENE EPOCH	First apes, mice, and many new mammals.
5.3-1.75		PLIOCENE EPOCH	First cattle and sheep. Whales diversify.
1.75-0.01	QUATERNARY	PLEISTOCENE EPOCH	First modern humans appear.
0.01-Present		HOLOCENE EPOCH	Extinctions caused by human activity.

Mawsonites · Collenia · Olenellus · Orthoceras · Cyrtoceras · Baragwanathia · Pseudocrinites · Pteraspis · Sandalodus · Edaphosaurus · Diplocaulus · Lystrosaurus · Pterodactylus · Proceratosaurus · Triceratops · Taeniolabis · Phenacodus · Palaeochiropteryx · Hyracotherium · Phiomia · Samotherium · Bison · Balaena · Gigantopithecus · Homo sapiens

Formation of the Earth

PRECAMBRIAN TIME

4,600 MYA

PRECAMBRIAN TIME 4,600-540 MYA

AQUATIC ANIMALS

THE RISE OF LIFE

The first living things were prokaryotes – microscopic, single-celled bacteria-like organisms. They evolved in the Precambrian, probably in the hot water around deep-sea volcanic vents. Their fossils first appear around 3,500 million years ago. Multicellular organisms, or eukaryotes, arose late in the Precambrian, perhaps when single-celled forms took to living in colonies. By the end of the Precambrian, soft-bodied animals were present. Some of these may be ancestors of animals, such as jellyfish and worms, but others might be bizarre dead ends unrelated to later animals.

COLLENIA

Stromatolites are layered structures that resemble stony pillars or platforms. They were widespread in Precambrian times and still exist today in Australia and elsewhere. These bizarre structures were built by colonial microorganisms, such as *Collenia*, which grew in mats using sunlight for energy. When studied under the microscope, stromatolites can be seen to be made up of fossil prokaryotes and other microorganisms.

Round, flattened body, with projection at the center

EDIACARA

This simple, disk-shaped Precambrian organism probably lived a static life on the seafloor, absorbing oxygen directly from the surrounding water. It formed part of the Vendian fauna – a group of soft-bodied organisms first discovered in rocks in southern Australia, and recently found worldwide. Such fossils are highly controversial because they are difficult to interpret. Scientists are not even sure if they were animals or plants.

Body made of three connected segments

DICKINSONIA

This 5-in (13-cm) long segmented animal appears to have lived on or in sandy parts of the seafloor. *Dickinsonia* is known from the Vendian faunas of Australia and Russia. Its identity is controversial. Some experts argue that it was a kind of flat-bodied worm. Others suggest that it was a soft-bodied coral. One expert has even argued that *Dickinsonia* and similar fossils were actually lichens.

This timeline shows each era as a proportion of all geological time. The Precambrian era is more than eight times longer than all the later eras put together.

EARTH FACTS

NORTHERN GONDWANA

SOUTHERN GONDWANA

The Precambrian represents more than 85 percent of geological time during which the Earth changed from a molten ball to a planet with continents, oceans, and an atmosphere. In the latter part of the Precambrian, the first tectonic plates developed, life evolved, and oxygen built up in the atmosphere.

	CENOZOIC
PALEOZOIC	MESOZOIC

540 MYA   250 MYA   65 MYA   TODAY

CAMBRIAN PERIOD

AQUATIC ANIMALS

EXPLOSION OF LIFE

Most of the major groups of animals that exist today evolved in the Cambrian Period. This huge growth in diversity occurred only in the seas – the land was still bare of life other than micro-organisms – and is called the "Cambrian explosion." Soft-bodied animals and stromatolites (bacterial colonies) of the Precambrian were largely replaced by species with hard parts, especially trilobites. Their fossils have been found in abundance in the Burgess Shale, a famous fossil-rich area in the Canadian Rocky Mountains that dates back around 500 million years.

METALDETES

The appearance of shells and other hard parts was a key event in animal evolution that occurred at the very end of the Precambrian. Microscopic fossils of early shelled animals are found worldwide in Cambrian rocks. They include mollusks with coiled shells and worms that lived in straight tubes. Archaeocyathans, such as *Metaldetes*, were early shelled fossils shaped like inverted cones. They probably lived fixed to the seafloor.

Metaldetes *probably resembled a modern sponge.*

Metaldetes taylori

Large eyes

XYSTRIDURA

Trilobites were a tremendously successful and varied group of arthropods, and they make up one third of all fossils known from the Cambrian period. Types such as *Xystridura* had many legs, complex eyes made of numerous individual lenses, and long antennae. Some burrowing trilobites from the Cambrian, however, lacked eyes. Other species were good swimmers, while others could roll into balls for protection.

Each body segment supported a walking leg and a gill-bearing leg.

PIKAIA

Chordates, the group that includes vertebrates, evolved in the Middle Cambrian. One of the first was *Pikaia*, a swimming eel-like animal, 2 in (5 cm) in length. *Pikaia* had a flexible rod called a notochord stiffening its body. In later animals, this developed into the backbone. *Pikaia* swam by contracting blocks of muscle around the notochord to produce a wavelike motion.

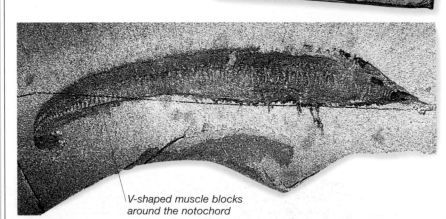

V-shaped muscle blocks around the notochord

540–500 MYA

WIWAXIA

Perhaps distantly related to the mollusks, *Wiwaxia* was 1 in (3 cm) long, dome shaped, and covered in scales. It was equipped with long spines, probably for self-defense. *Wiwaxia* is from the Burgess Shale, but new discoveries show that such animals were widespread in the Cambrian.

Ridged scale

Wiwaxia probably ate algae.

MARRELLA

The most common arthropod in the Burgess Shale is *Marella* – more than 13,000 specimens have been collected to date. Up to 1 in (2 cm) long, this animal had a large head shield, and two pairs of long antennae, although it seems to have lacked eyes. Its body was made up of 24–26 segments, each of which carried a two-branched appendage. The lower branch was a walking leg, while the upper branch carried long gills. The animal was able to both walk and swim.

Indentations may have been sites of muscle attachment.

The head shield supported large backward-pointing horns.

Concave inner surface indicates an older individual.

MOBERGELLA

Among the early shelled fossils of the Cambrian are tiny limpetlike forms, such as *Mobergella* from Scandinavia. These might not have been separate, individual animals but scalelike structures that covered the bodies of larger species. Members of another Cambrian group with hard parts, the halkieriids, were elongate with scaly bodies. It is possible that *Mobergella* may have actually been halkieriid body scales.

EARTH FACTS

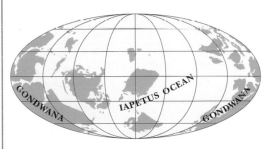

GONDWANA   IAPETUS OCEAN   GONDWANA

During the Cambrian, most of the world's landmasses were united as the supercontinent Gondwana. This was surrounded by the vast Iapetus Ocean. Smaller landmasses that today form Europe, North America, and Siberia lay in tropical and temperate zones. There were no ice caps in the seas, and water levels were high.

ORDOVICIAN PERIOD

AQUATIC ANIMALS

FILTER FEEDERS

Another burst of evolution in the Ordovician gave rise to thousands of new animals. Many were filter feeders that fed on increasing numbers of plankton – microscopic free-floating organisms – in the water. These included mosslike bryozoans, bivalves, and corals, which formed reefs that were home to swimming molluscs and other animals. Trilobites diversified greatly into swimming forms equipped with huge eyes and bottom-feeders with shovel-like snouts for plowing through mud. The earliest jawed vertebrates – a group that includes sharks and bony fish – probably also appeared in the Ordovician.

Estonioceras perforatum

Uncoiled final whorl of shell

ESTONIOCERAS

This swimming mollusc was a nautiloid – a group which survives today as the animal *Nautilus*. It had a loosely coiled shell and was adapted for hunting in fairly deep European waters, grabbing prey with its tentacles. *Estonioceras* was small, just 4 in (10 cm) across, but some of its nautiloid relatives had shells up to 16 ft (5 m) in diameter. At the time, these intelligent Ordovician predators were the largest animals ever to have lived.

Shell could be locked shut by internal pegs and sockets

STROPHOMENA

Among the most abundant of Ordovician animals were brachiopods – filter-feeders whose two shells were joined at a hinge. *Strophomena* was a small brachiopod that probably lived on sand or mud, although many of its relatives cemented themselves to submerged rocks.

AQUATIC PLANTS

ALGAE AND LIFE ON LAND

Colonial blue-green algae – the stromatolites – which had evolved in the Precambrian, were still widespread during the Ordovician. True algae, including globular forms that resembled sponges, lived alongside other reef builders, such as corals, while green algae, the ancestors of land plants, colonized freshwater habitats. Most significantly, plants similar to liverworts and mosses evolved late in the Ordovician and began to colonize the land, which until this time had been barren of life. These plants were still strongly tied to water, needing it for reproduction.

Honeycomb pattern on surface of cluster

MASTOPORA

This reef-forming green alga grew in rounded clusters with a characteristic honeycombed surface pattern. Fossils of the clusters, each about 3 in (8 cm) across, are found worldwide. Limestone secreted by the algae covered the surface, protecting *Mastopora* from hungry herbivores. Superficially resembling a sponge, *Mastopora* was originally thought to be an animal.

Mastopora favus

500–435 MYA

Colony about 3 in
(8 cm) long

CONODONT
Long known only from their small
serrated teeth, conodonts were eel-like
relatives of vertebrates. With large eyes,
they probably hunted and ate small
animals. At 16 in (40 cm) in length,
Promissum, an Ordovician conodont
from South Africa, was the largest known
conodont. The group has a fossil record
that extends from the Late Cambrian
to the Triassic.

Serrations on
the interlocking
teeth were used
to bite and cut
up prey.

ORTHOGRAPTUS
Graptolite fossils first appeared in the Cambrian,
but most groups arose in the Ordovician.
Graptolites formed colonies of interlinked cuplike
structures called thecae, each inhabited by a soft-
bodied filter-feeding animal called a zooid. Some
kinds of graptolites were attached to the seafloor
while others floated in the surface waters.
Orthograptus was a common graptolite whose
colonies consisted of two parallel strips of thecae.

Surface protected
and strengthened by
calcium carbonate

EARTH FACTS

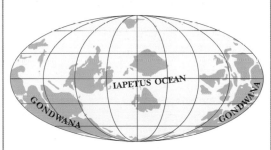

The Gondwanan supercontinent
remained separate from the
landmasses that would become
North America and Europe, though
the Iapetus Ocean had started to
close. The Ordovician was a time of
global cooling. Late in the Period a
huge ice sheet covered much of the
southern hemisphere.

ACANTHOCHONIA
The surface of *Acanthochonia* was made up of numerous
diamond-shaped cells arranged in a spiral pattern. All of these
cells originated from a single central stem, which anchored the
alga to rocks or corals. The rounded alga was only about 2 in
(5 cm) in diameter and lived in coral reefs.

SILURIAN PERIOD

AQUATIC ANIMALS

NEW LIFE

A large-scale extinction event at the end of the Ordovician greatly reduced the richness of animal life early in the Silurian. However, surviving groups – including brachiopods, mollusks, trilobites, and graptolites – soon recovered and increased in diversity in the warm, shallow continental seas of the period. Entirely new aquatic invertebrates, such as primitive sea urchins, also appeared for the first time. Jawless fish still thrived while jawed fish – including armored placoderms and acanthodians or "spiny sharks" – diversified, becoming increasingly important. The very first land-living animals – arthropods including spiders, millipedes, centipedes, and scorpions – evolved from aquatic ancestors during the Silurian.

Small body, about 3 in (6 cm) in length

Birkenia elegans

BIRKENIA

Primitive jawless fish evolved in the Cambrian, but were still thriving well into the Silurian. The small, spindle-shaped *Birkenia* lived in European lakes and rivers. Like other jawless fish, it lacked paired fins, making it unstable when swimming. This poor swimmer was unable to catch fast prey and probably foraged in mud taking in tiny food particles through its vertical slitlike mouth. Its body was covered by deep, overlapping scales arranged in rows. A row of taller defensive scales grew along the top of its back.

LAND PLANTS

THE PIONEERS

The Silurian marks the appearance of the first true land plants, making it a critical time in the evolution of plants. The first land-living plants were mosses and liverworts that grew along the edges of ponds and streams. Among later Silurian forms were the first vascular plants. These contained internal hollow tubes with a woody lining, which helped support the plant and also carried water around its body. Because of the vessels, vascular plants were able to grow to larger sizes and farther from water than mosses and liverworts.

COOKSONIA

Best known from Silurian rocks of southern Ireland, *Cooksonia* was the first upright vascular plant. Lacking leaves and roots, it was composed of cylindrical stems that branched into two at several points along their length. At the ends of the stems were cap-shaped spore-bearing structures. Compared to later vascular plants *Cooksonia* was very small, growing to just 4 in (10 cm) in height, and very simple in shape. It grew along pond and lake margins.

Cooksonia hemisphaerica

Branching stems formed Y-shapes.

PARKA

Green algae are simple plants that grow close to or in water. *Parka* was a green alga from Silurian and Devonian North America and Europe. It had a flattened, loosely branching shape and was only 2 in (4 cm) or so in diameter. A thick protective covering on its outer surface may have helped prevent *Parka* from drying out, suggesting that it may have grown on land rather than in water.

435–410 MYA

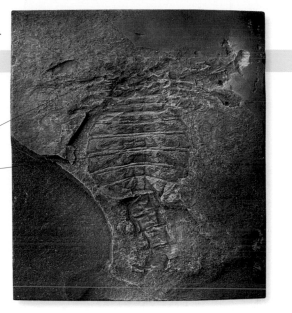

Each arm was free and could be moved by strands of muscle.

The paired legs could have been used for walking or for handling prey.

Abdomen

SAGENOCRINITES

Crinoids, or sea lilies, were important animals of the Silurian seas. Many species survive today in deeper waters. Attached to the seafloor by long, cylindrical stalks, their tentacled heads collect plankton and suspended food from the sea. *Sagenocrinites* was a small crinoid from Silurian Europe and North America. Its head and tentacles were very compact in shape, suggesting that it lived in shallower waters that were constantly churned by waves.

Base of the stem attached to the seafloor

PARACARCINOSOMA

Sea scorpions were Silurian arthropods – relatives of the spiders. They had long tails and many were equipped with large pincers, which they used to grab and dismember their prey. *Paracarcinosoma* was a small sea scorpion, only about 2 in (5 cm) long. It may have lived in brackish and fresh water as well as in the sea. The squarish head, body, and its six pairs of limbs were encased in a hard external skeleton. The last pair of limbs were paddle-shaped and would have been used for swimming.

Stem covered with short fine leaves

BARAGWANATHIA

Closely resembling a club moss, *Baragwanathia* was a relatively complex Silurian plant. It had branching stems about 10 in (25 cm) high, which grew upward from creeping branches that spread across the ground. The stems were clothed in short leaves, giving the plant a "furry" look. *Baragwanathia* lived in the southern hemisphere and is known from Devonian as well as Silurian rocks.

Distinct rounded spore capsules grew on its surface.

Parka decipiens

Baragwanathia longifolia

EARTH FACTS

During the Silurian, the southern continent Gondwana was fringed by other landmasses. Smaller plate fragments moved northward and collided, producing new mountain ranges in North America and Europe. Sea levels rose as Ordovician ice melted and the climate became warmer and less changeable.

DEVONIAN PERIOD

LAND ANIMALS

LIMBS ON LAND

The Devonian was one of the most important periods of vertebrate evolution. The first vertebrates with four limbs and distinct digits evolved from lobe-finned fish during this time, and by the Late Devonian, they had spread widely around the world. Land-dwelling arthropods increased in number throughout the period. Primitive, wingless insects and even winged forms arose while spiders and their relatives became more diverse.

Sharp teeth suggest a diet of fish and other animals.

ACANTHOSTEGA

Among the earliest of four-limbed vertebrates was *Acanthostega* from Greenland. Like its lobe-finned fish relatives, it was a pond-dwelling predator that still had gills and a paddlelike tail. Its limbs suggest that it would not have been good at walking on land. However, fossilized tracks show that some four-footed vertebrates had ventured onto land by this time.

AQUATIC ANIMALS

DEVONIAN DIVERSITY

Heavily armored jawless fish flourished in the Devonian seas and jawed fish were by now also abundant. Among the bony fish, lobe-finned fish were numerous and diverse while ray-finned fish began to become more important. Several groups of trilobites were still widespread and ammonoids and modern-type horseshoe crabs appeared. Their descendants survive to this day.

Pointed fins with a prominent central row of bones.

DIPTERUS

Lungfish such as *Dipterus* were one of the most abundant groups of the Devonian. Five species of these lobe-finned fish survive in modern times. *Dipterus* swam in European waters and, like all lungfish, had large crushing teeth. Fossilized stomach contents show that it was preyed on by placoderms.

LAND PLANTS

LEAVES AND ROOTS

The Devonian Period saw the most important steps so far in the development of land plants. Leaves and roots evolved independently in a number of different groups. For the first time, plants displayed secondary growth – their stems could not only grow in length, but also in diameter. These developments allowed plants to grow far larger than before. The early reedlike pioneers on land gave way to gigantic trees and species with complex leaves. Horsetails, seed ferns, and conifer ancestors appeared late in the Devonian, and it was these forms that would evolve into species that later made up the lush forests of the Carboniferous.

ARCHAEOPTERIS

This widespread and highly successful Late Devonian plant was the first to resemble modern trees. It had an extensive root system and its trunk had branches with reinforced joints at its crown. *Archaeopteris* was also one of the first plants to reach great size, reaching about 65 ft (20 m). Scientists once thought that its woody trunk belonged to a different species and named it *Callixylon*.

Branching, fernlike leaves

Archaeopteris

410–355 MYA

*Seven toes
on each foot*

Ichthyostega

*Limbs served
as props for
walking on land.*

ICHTHYOSTEGA FOSSIL

Ichthyostega was an early four-footed vertebrate. It probably hunted fish and other prey in shallow pools. Features of its limbs suggest that it was relatively advanced and was related to the ancestor of all later four-footed vertebrates. *Ichthyostega* had a short, broad skull and very broad ribs, which helped support its body when it crawled on land.

*Large eye for
excellent vision*

EASTMANOSTEUS

Placoderms were jawed fish that were abundant in Devonian seas. They included predators, armored bottom-dwellers, and flattened ray-like forms. Some Late Devonian placoderms reached 10 m (33 ft) in length, making them the largest vertebrates yet to evolve. *Eastmanosteus*, known from Australia, North America, and Europe, was less than 6 ft 6 in (2 m) long but would still have been a formidable hunter.

PHACOPS

This small trilobite lived in warm, shallow seas. Like many arthropods, each of its body segments supported two sets of limbs. For protection against predators it could roll up its body and tuck its tail beneath its head. Seven of the eight groups of trilobites, including the one to which *Phacops* belonged, died out at the end of the Devonian.

Phacops

ZOSTEROPHYLLUM

Lacking roots and leaves, *Zosterophyllum* was a primitive land plant. Its erect, branching stems grew not from roots, but from a complex underground rhizome (stem). The sides of the stems carried small kidney-shaped capsules in which spores were produced. Reaching a height of around 10 in (25 cm), the plant probably grew along the swampy edges of lakes.

*Clusters of
spore-bearing
stems*

*Zosterophyllum
llanoveranum*

EARTH FACTS

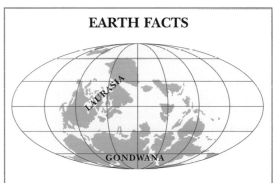

The Devonian world was warm and mild. The huge continent Gondwana lay over the South Pole while modern Europe and North America were positioned close to the equator. Sea levels were high, and much of the land lay under shallow waters, where tropical reefs flourished. Deep ocean covered the rest of the planet.

CARBONIFEROUS PERIOD

LAND ANIMALS

ORIGIN OF THE AMNIOTES
Amniotes, vertebrates whose embryos are enclosed by a watertight membrane, evolved in the Carboniferous. Both major amniote groups – reptiles and the mammal-like synapsids – appeared at the time, while other more primitive land-living vertebrates diversified. At 10 ft (3 m) in length, the synapsid *Ophiacodon* was one of the biggest known land animals of the time. Flying insects evolved and together with arachnids – spiders, scorpions, and mites – increased in size and diversity.

WESTLOTHIANA
Primitive four-footed vertebrates are well known from fossils in North America and Europe. *Westlothiana* was discovered in Scotland, in rocks formed in a lake fed by hot, volcanic springs. Its fossils were found alongside those of four-legged and snake-like tetrapods as well as millipedes, scorpions, and spiders. *Westlothiana* was about 12 in (30 cm) long. Its long body was carried on short legs.

Sharp teeth suggest a diet of insects.

Westlothiana lizziae

AQUATIC ANIMALS

DIVERSE DEPTHS
Sharks and bony fish dominated Carboniferous seas, but ray-finned fish, the actinopterygians, also diversified greatly during this period. Trilobites were still present, but survived as only a handful of groups. Crinoids, brachiopods, echinoderms, and swimming molluscs inhabited the tropical coral reefs of the time.

SYMMORIUM
Many of the Carboniferous sharks were bizarre compared to modern forms. Some were decorated with peculiar spiky crests and spines. *Stethacanthus* had a spine on its back covered with toothlike material, while *Symmorium* looked similar but lacked the spine. Some scientists think that it was the female of *Stethacanthus*.

Internal rodlike structures called ceratotrichia supported the fins.

Pointed teeth show that Symmorium was a predator.

LAND PLANTS

FORESTS AND FLOODPLAINS
Lush tropical forests forming vast swamps and forested deltas were widespread in the Carboniferous. Clubmosses and horsetails were important components of these forests, and some grew to immense sizes. *Lepidodendron* was a clubmoss 130 ft (40 m) tall, while *Calamites* was a 50-ft (15-m) horsetail. Gymnosperms – the group of plants with naked seeds that includes conifers and cycads – began to diversify during the Carboniferous. Toward the end of the period, the huge European and North American floodplains began to shrink as the climate became less wet. The clubmosses were then replaced by ferns and seed ferns from drier habitats.

EQUISETITES
Equisetites is an extinct horsetail, which came from a group that survives today in the form of *Equisetum*. It grew to a height of around 20 in (50 cm) from underground stems (tubers), and its straight stem carried leaves arranged in regular rings or whorls. *Equisetites* dominated the river banks and lake edges of the Carboniferous, and these habitats are still favored today by modern forms of *Equisetum*.

Fossilized tubers and roots of Equisetites

355–295 MYA

Two eyes on a
projecting bump

GRAEOPHONUS

Arachnids, the arthropod group that includes spiders,
scorpions, and their relatives, are well represented in
the Carboniferous fossil record and many new kinds
made their first appearance at this time. *Graeophonus* was
an early member of a group that survives to this day – the
whip scorpions. These have six walking legs and a front
pair of serrated pincers that they use to grab prey. They
lack poisonous fangs, but have sharp jaws.

Growth lines,
or sutures,
on shell

Skeleton made
of cartilage

Forked tail
suggests fast
swimming
speeds.

GONIATITES

This animal is a type
of swimming mollusc
with a coiled shell. It was a
member of a group of ammonoids
(ammonitelike animals) that was
dominant throughout the Paleozoic.
Like all ammonoids, goniatites had gas-
filled shell chambers that allowed it to
float. It probably had complex eyes and
beaklike mouthparts. *Goniatites* lived in
large swarms over reefs in shallow seas.

Straplike leaves

CORDAITES

This coniferlike
land plant grew
in Carboniferous
mangrove swamps,
but died out in
the Permian. It had
characteristic long, leathery
leaves and its straight main trunk grew to a height
of up to 100 ft (30 m), although other species of
Cordaites were shrublike. It produced seeds in loose
cones. The leaves, stems, and seeds of *Cordaites* had
been given different names because they were
originally thought to belong to different species.

*Cordaites
angulostriatus*

EARTH FACTS

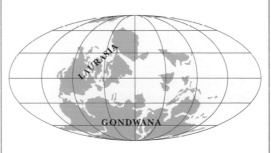

The Carboniferous is known as the
"Age of Coal" because decaying
vegetation from the vast forests was
transformed into coal. The main
landmasses present were the two
huge continents of Gondwana and
Laurasia. Oxygen levels were high,
and this may have allowed giant
terrestrial arthropods to evolve.

PERMIAN PERIOD

LAND ANIMALS

SYNAPSIDS

The most important and diverse land-dwelling vertebrates of the Permian were the primitive synapsids – early members of the group that includes mammals. Most were small or medium-sized animals equipped with powerful skulls and sharp teeth to deal with a diet of flesh or insects. They thrived, along with reptiles and arthropods, including spiders and insects.

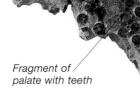

Fragment of palate with teeth

EDAPHOSAURUS

This Permian synapsid had a broad, rounded body with a tall fin on the back. This fin was richly supplied with blood vessels and so could absorb or radiate heat. It may have been used to control the animal's body temperature. *Edaphosaurus* had two types of teeth. Peglike teeth lined its jaws and crushing teeth were located on its palate. These features suggest that it was a herbivore that fed on ferns and other tough Permian plants.

AQUATIC ANIMALS

SEAS OF LIFE

Immense reefs, mostly built by bryozoans (tiny, colonial animals) and sponges, teemed with marine life in Permian times. Shelled animals called brachiopods burgeoned, important new fish groups evolved, and some reptiles – the mesosaurs – returned to live in water. The Permian ended with the biggest mass extinction of all time. Many animals died out, although some, such as fish, were not badly affected.

DERBYIA

Brachiopods were shelled, filter-feeding animals that evolved in the Cambrian and still survive today as lamp shells. Their larvae could swim, but adults lived a static life on the sea floor. *Derbyia* was a large, heavy brachiopod that grew to 3 in (8 cm) in diameter in the Carboniferous and Permian seas. Brachiopods were plentiful in the Devonian, but there were few left by the end of the Permian.

LAND PLANTS

NAKED SEEDS

Plant communities in the Permian were basically similar to those that exist today. During the period, the clubmosses and horsetails that had formed the vast Carboniferous forests largely disappeared and were replaced by gymnosperms, plants that produce their seed "naked," not enclosed in a fruit. Conifers (gymnosperms with needlelike leaves) flourished and two other gymnosperm groups – cycads and gingkos – also evolved. Late in the Permian, many of the conifers developed thick fleshy leaves protected by hairs. These features helped the plants to tolerate the hot and dry climate that typified Late Permian times.

Sword-shaped leaves

Glossopteris

GLOSSOPTERIS

One of the most important Permian gymnosperms was *Glossopteris*. This tree, which grew to 26 ft (8 m), and its close relatives dominated the southern part of the supercontinent Pangea. Fossils of *Glossopteris* have an important place in scientific history. They were found across all the southern continents, thereby providing one of the first pieces of evidence to support the theory of continental drift.

295–250 MYA

Eye socket

DIMETRODON
A stout skull and large, pointed teeth made *Dimetrodon* an awesome predator. This fin-backed synapsid grew to around 10 ft (3 m) in length. It had lightly built limbs so could run fast to catch its prey. Animals like *Dimetrodon* were important because they gave rise to an entirely new group of synapsids, the therapsids, which became dominant in the late Permian.

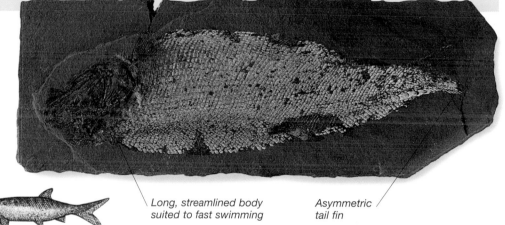

Dimetrodon loomisi skull

PALEONISCUS
Ray-finned fish, which evolved in the Devonian, continued to diversify during the Permian, and a major new group – the neopterygians – appeared. *Paleoniscus* was a primitive ray-finned fish distantly related to the neopterygians. It grew to around 8 in (20 cm) in length. Covered by a coat of overlapping scales, this spindle-shaped predator was a strong swimmer.

Long, streamlined body suited to fast swimming

Asymmetric tail fin

Paleoniscus magnus

MARIOPTERIS
Found in late Carboniferous and early Permian swamps, *Mariopteris* grew to a height of around 16 ft (5 m). Its stem consisted partly of old leaf bases. Some species were treelike, while others were climbing plants.

Small, pointed leaflets

Mariopteris maricata

EARTH FACTS

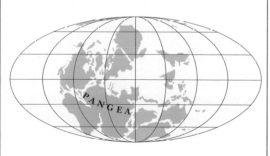

The two major landmasses of the early Permian – Laurasia in the north and Gondwana in the south – collided late in the period to form the supercontinent Pangea. The Pangean climate became hotter and drier. While the south seems to have been relatively cool, tropical conditions prevailed in the north.

PERMIAN EXTINCTION

THE END OF THE PERMIAN PERIOD, 250 million years ago, saw the greatest mass extinction of all time, a period of crisis that has been called "the time of great dying." Perhaps as few as five percent of all species survived. In the seas, reef-dwelling animals were severely affected and trilobites, sea scorpions, and key coral groups disappeared. On land, synapsids and many reptile groups vanished. Some experts think that the Permian extinction happened quickly, but it seems unlikely that a single catastrophe was responsible. It is more probable that a series of several events gradually resulted in the mass extinction. The formation of the supercontinent Pangea, for example, would have destroyed important shallow coastal seas and coastline habitats. Climate changes and volcanic eruptions may also have contributed to the extinction.

FIERY END
A possible cause of the end-Permian extinction is volcanic activity. Huge eruptions of volcanic material are known to have happened in Siberia at this time. Around one million cubic miles of lava poured out, covering enormous areas of the land surface. Eruptions in China also coated the land with ash. The eruptions pumped vast quantities of gas and volcanic dust into the atmosphere. These volcanic clouds might have lowered global temperature by blocking the Sun's rays.

CLIMATIC CRISIS
Climate change characterized the end of the Permian. Rocks from the period indicate that cooling occurred in some areas and ice sheets built up at the poles, causing the global sea level to drop. The white ice sheets reflected sunlight back into space, lowering global temperatures even further. Falling sea levels may have exposed huge areas of coal on the seafloor. This would have released large amounts of carbon dioxide into the atmosphere, so reducing oxygen content. Less oxygen in the atmosphere may have contributed to the extinction of animals with active lifestyles, such as the mammal-like synapsids.

Branching colonies of bryozoans, or moss animals

Rugose corals completely disappeared in the Permian extinction.

Brachiopods like Edriostege, grew on the tops of the reefs.

DESERT DEVASTATION
When the Permian landmasses collided, they produced the vast continent of Pangea. Rains and mists that arose at sea could no longer reach the interior of the land, with the result that some parts of the Permian world became drier and hotter. Deserts grew ever larger, and animals not adapted for life in the arid conditions became extinct.

Cambrian 540–500	Ordovician 500–435	Silurian 435–410	Devonian 410–355	Carboniferous 355–295	Permia

PALEOZOIC 540–250 MYA

DEATH OF A REEF

A Permian coral reef is shown healthy on the left-hand side of the image – and dying as it would have appeared during the Permian extinction – on the right-hand side. Permian reefs – complex environments built by corals and sponges – were inhabited by thousands of different animals and plants. Lowered sea levels and reduced areas of shallow seafloor that resulted from the formation of Pangea destroyed the areas in which reefs could grow. The reefs were gradually killed off, causing an enormous drop in the diversity of marine life. Reduced quantities of oxygen in the Permian atmosphere would also have meant that sea water contained less oxygen than before. Entire oceans would have slowly become stagnant, suffocating the life they contained.

The huge tubular sponge Heliospongia was one of the largest reef organisms of the Permian.

Reef animals would have died off as oxygen levels in the sea dropped.

Gastropods grazed on algae that grew on the reefs.

295–250	Triassic 250–203	Jurassic 203–135	Cretaceous 135–65	Tertiary 65–1.75	Quaternary 1.75–present
	MESOZOIC 250–65 MYA			CENOZOIC 65 MYA–present	

TRIASSIC PERIOD

LAND ANIMALS

THE AGE OF REPTILES

The Triassic was the start of the "Age of Reptiles" and a time when animals from very different lineages lived alongside one another. Synapsids, relatives of the mammals, were still important but were gradually being driven to extinction. Archosaurs, the "ruling reptiles," became important and the first crocodiles, pterosaurs, and dinosaurs all arose late in the Triassic. The first turtles, frogs, and mammal-like animals also appeared.

CYNOGNATHUS

This aggressive Early Triassic predator was a member of the cynodonts – a group of advanced synapsids. Growing to 6 ft 6 in (2 m) in length, it possessed prominent canine teeth, shearing cheek teeth, and large jaw muscles that allowed it to hunt other large synapsids. It may have been warm-blooded and fur-covered like a mammal, and its close relatives were themselves the ancestors of mammals.

AQUATIC ANIMALS

SEA CHANGE

Modern-type corals formed the Triassic reefs and new groups of ammonoid molluscs appeared. Advanced ray-finned fish and the first modern sharks and rays replaced slower, older kinds of marine life. Primitive ichthyosaurs evolved and soon became dolphin-shaped predators. Some were as big as modern whales.

Diamond-shaped scales covered the streamlined body.

DICELLOPYGE

Primitive ray-finned fish like *Dicellopyge* were important predators in the Triassic. This small freshwater fish from southern Africa had a deeply notched tail suggesting that it was a fast swimmer. Its deep skull and jaws were armed with conical teeth that allowed it to catch and eat smaller fish and swimming invertebrates.

LAND PLANTS

DOMINANT CONIFERS

Most plants of the earlier Paleozoic Era reproduced by spores and so relied on moist habitats to reproduce. These groups – including the famous glossopterids of the southern continents – suffered in the drier conditions of the Triassic, when the landscape was increasingly dominated by evergreen trees (conifers and other gymnosperms). Among the more modern kinds of plants, cycads became well established. Ginkgos – relatives of the conifers – became more successful and at least seven genera, including the modern genus *Ginkgo*, lived during Triassic times.

Ginkgo biloba leaf

Leaf fossilized in mudstone

GINKGO

This tree, which evolved in the Triassic, survives essentially unchanged to this day. A native of China, it has been transported around the world for planting in urban parks and gardens, partly because it grows well in heavily polluted air. *Ginkgo* grows to around 115 ft (35 m) in height. It is deciduous, and there are abundant fossils of its leaves. Members of the *Ginkgo* genus typically grew in damp habitats in temperate climates.

250–203 MYA

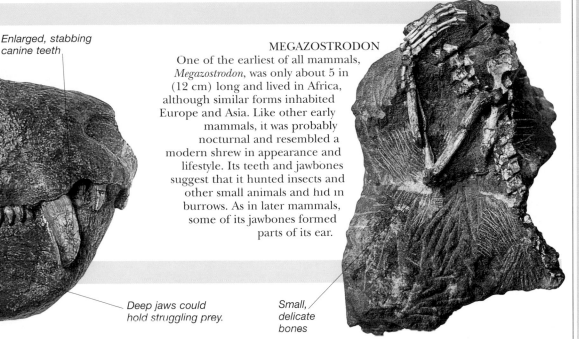

Enlarged, stabbing canine teeth

Deep jaws could hold struggling prey.

MEGAZOSTRODON
One of the earliest of all mammals, *Megazostrodon*, was only about 5 in (12 cm) long and lived in Africa, although similar forms inhabited Europe and Asia. Like other early mammals, it was probably nocturnal and resembled a modern shrew in appearance and lifestyle. Its teeth and jawbones suggest that it hunted insects and other small animals and hid in burrows. As in later mammals, some of its jawbones formed parts of its ear.

Small, delicate bones

Limbs were used as paddles when in the water.

NEUSTICOSAURUS
The sauropterygians were a group of marine reptiles that evolved during the Triassic. The most famous members of the group were the plesiosaurs. *Neusticosaurus* was a small, amphibious, predatory sauropterygian that lived in the shallow seas of Triassic Europe,. where it hunted invertebrates and fish. Fossils of babies preserved without eggshells suggest that these reptiles may have given birth to live young.

Thick, heavy ribs helped keep Neusticosaurus *submerged.*

PACHYPTERIS
Seed ferns (pteridosperms), such as *Pachypteris*, were not ferns at all, but primitive seed plants that lived in swampy areas. They had woody stems studded with dried-out leaf bases. Their tops had fernlike fronds that carried the seeds. The group was very successful late in the Paleozoic, but gradually declined in importance during the Mesozoic, finally becoming extinct in the Cretaceous. *Pachypteris*, which grew worldwide in tropical forests, was one of the last seed ferns to die out in the Cretaceous.

Typical height 6 ft 6 in (2 m)

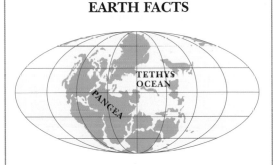

EARTH FACTS

TETHYS OCEAN

PANGEA

The vast supercontinent of Pangea straddled the equator during the Triassic. Hints that it would later split up came from the narrow seaway that separated North America from Europe and another tongue of sea, the Tethys, which encroached on Europe. The climate was generally warm and dry.

JURASSIC PERIOD

LAND ANIMALS

RULE OF THE DINOSAURS

Life on land took on a very different appearance in the Jurassic. Most crocodile-group archosaurs and synapsids were wiped out at the end of the Triassic (but some small synapsids, including early mammals, survived). Giant dinosaurs took over as the dominant animals. On land, plated stegosaurs and long-necked sauropods were preyed upon by large theropods. In the air, new kinds of pterosaurs were seen and the first birds evolved from small predatory dinosaurs.

PTERODACTYLUS

Pterosaurs were reptiles that developed wings and powered flight. They evolved in the Triassic and diversified during the Jurassic, when shorter-tailed, longer-winged forms appeared. *Pterodactylus* was a small Jurassic pterosaur that lived along shorelines, feeding on fish and crustaceans. Just 12 in (30 cm) long, it had a lightly built skeleton and thin, hollow bones. Its wing membrane was supported by the long fourth finger.

This specimen preserves its wing membranes, throat pouch, and foot webbing.

Slender clawed toes

AQUATIC ANIMALS

JURASSIC DIVERSITY

Important marine animals that appeared in the Jurassic include ammonites, belemnites, and modern-type sharks and rays. Teleosts, or bony fish, diversified greatly into long-bodied predatory forms as well as gigantic filter-feeders, which may have been the biggest fish of all time. Crinoids, relatives of today's sea lilies, were important during the period. Giant forms, some with stalks as long as 50 ft (15 m), grew from floating driftwood.

ICHTHYOSAURUS

Advanced ichthyosaurs ("fish lizards"), swimming crocodiles, and new kinds of plesiosaurs all added to the diversity of marine reptiles in the Jurassic. *Ichthyosaurus* was a European fish lizard. It had large, sensitive eyes and a slim snout containing many cone-shaped teeth, both of which helped it catch fish and swimming mollusks. There were several species of *Ichthyosaurus* ranging in size from 3–10 ft (1–3 m) long.

Nostril was located close to the eye socket.

Ring of bony plates

LAND PLANTS

THE AGE OF CYCADS

Cycads, conifers, and ginkgoes were important Jurassic plant groups. So many cycads grew in the forests of the time that the Jurassic is often called "the Age of Cycads." One group of cycadlike plants – the bennettitaleans – were significant because they may have been the ancestors of flowering plants. Jurassic conifers included close relatives of living pines, yews, redwoods, and cypresses. Ferns formed much of the ground cover, and all three major fern groups had probably evolved by the Jurassic. Club mosses, horsetails, and seed ferns continued to survive but were not as important as in earlier times.

CYCAS

Cycads are gymnosperms that reached their greatest diversity and abundance during the Jurassic. *Cycas*, of which about forty species survive today, first appeared in the Jurassic. Some species grew into giant tree-like forms, while others were smaller and more fernlike. Jurassic cycads lived worldwide, but today's species are restricted to the tropical and subtropical zones.

Cycas fronds made of many parallel leaflets

Many cycad leaves were poisonous.

203–135 MYA

Serrated teeth in
lightly built skull

COMPSOGNATHUS
The chicken-sized
Compsognathus was an
advanced predatory dinosaur
from Late Jurassic Europe.
It walked on its two long, slim
hind limbs and probably stalked
its prey of small lizards
and insects. It was similar
in size, habit, and
distribution to the bird
Archaeopteryx, and the
two may have lived side-
by-side in the woodlands
of southern Germany.

Long hind limbs
with four toes

ARCHAEOPTERYX
The first true bird,
Archaeopteryx, evolved in the
Jurassic from small theropod
ancestors. It retains many
features of its reptile past –
three working fingers, true
teeth, and a breastbone
without a keel. This famous
fossil – known as the Berlin
specimen – was discovered
in the Solnhofen limestones
of Germany in 1877.
Remarkably, it preserves
complete impressions of the
wing and tail feathers.

Triangular skull
with forward-
facing eyes

ASPIDORHYNCHUS
Among the new Jurassic teleosts were long-
bodied predators, such as *Aspidorhynchus*.
Growing to around 20 in (50 cm) in length, it
had a pointed skull, large eyes, and sharp
teeth. Its upper jaw was extended beyond the
lower jaw, forming a prominent toothless
"beak." Its tail was symmetrical, and thick
rectangular scales protected its body.
Aspidorhynchus was widely distributed in
shallow, subtropical seas.

WILLIAMSONIA
This plant, which lived
throughout the
Mesozoic, was a member
of the Bennettitales – a
group that may include
the ancestors of flowering
plants. It had a robust stem
that was covered in diamond-
shaped scales and grew large
flowerlike structures. The
Bennettitales had leaves that
resembled those of cycads,
and were probably related
to this group.

Flowers probably
pollinated by insects

Williamsonia

EARTH FACTS

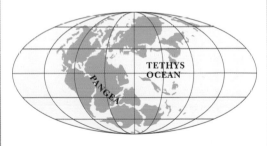

TETHYS
OCEAN

PANGEA

The Pangean supercontinent split as
the Atlantic opened up between the
areas that today form Africa and
North America. The land that would
later become Antarctica, India, and
Australia started to move away from
the rest of Pangea. The climate was
warm, and, with no polar ice caps, sea
levels were high worldwide.

CRETACEOUS PERIOD

LAND ANIMALS

NEW DINOSAURS

Dinosaurs remained the dominant land animals during the Cretaceous. New groups, including tyrannosaurs, duck-billed hadrosaurs, and horned dinosaurs, spread across the northern continents, while birds evolved from toothed *Archaeopteryx*-like species into forms that resembled modern kinds. Snakes developed from lizard ancestors and new groups of insects, including butterflies, ants, and bees appeared feeding on and pollinating the newly evolved flowering plants.

Zalambdalestes probably fed on insects

Stiff tail helped balance the heavy body.

ZALAMBDALESTES

Early Cretaceous mammals were small and insignificant, just as they had been throughout the Triassic and Jurassic, but an important new group emerged later in the Period. Characterized by three-cusped teeth, this group included *Zalambdalestes*, which probably resembled a modern elephant shrew.

AQUATIC ANIMALS

MESOZOIC MARINE REVOLUTION

Marine invertebrates took on a distinctly modern look during the Cretaceous. Crabs and other modern crustaceans appeared, as did predatory gastropod molluscs and burrowing sea urchins. Among fish, the advanced teleosts (bony fish) underwent a massive increase in diversity and relatives of modern herrings, eels, carps, and perches all appeared. Swimming lizards called mosasaurs and the first marine turtles and aquatic birds also evolved.

Mobile skull joint allowed jaws to open wide

MACROPOMA

Coelacanths – fleshy-finned fish that first appeared in the Devonian – grew to sizes of up to 10 ft (3 m) in Cretaceous seas, though the group was in decline later in the Period. *Macropoma* was a European coelacanth, less than 24 in (60 cm) long. It had a short, deep body and large fins that would have aided maneuverability. Its tail had three lobes – a feature common to all coelacanths.

LAND PLANTS

FLOWER POWER

Cretaceous forests were largely dominated by several groups of gymnosperms, particularly conifers, including cypresses, bald cypresses, and monkey-puzzle trees. Other gymnosperm groups, such as cycads and ginkgos, declined in importance. Flowering plants – the angiosperms – arose, first as small, weedlike forms in areas of land disturbed and trampled by herds of dinosaurs. Later in the period, flowering plants, including birches, willows, and magnolias, formed forests in which the dinosaurs lived, but ferns remained important wherever rainfall was high.

BETULITES

Betulites is an extinct member of the birch family, and a close relative of *Betula*, the familiar modern birch tree. Like living birches, it grew in temperate climates, favoring lakesides and other damp habitats. *Betulites* had round or oval leaves that had teeth along their margins – typical of plants that grow in cool or dry environments. Because fossilized *Betulites* leaves are frequently detached from twigs, this tree was probably deciduous.

Leaf fossil in ironstone nodule

Betulites

135–65 MYA

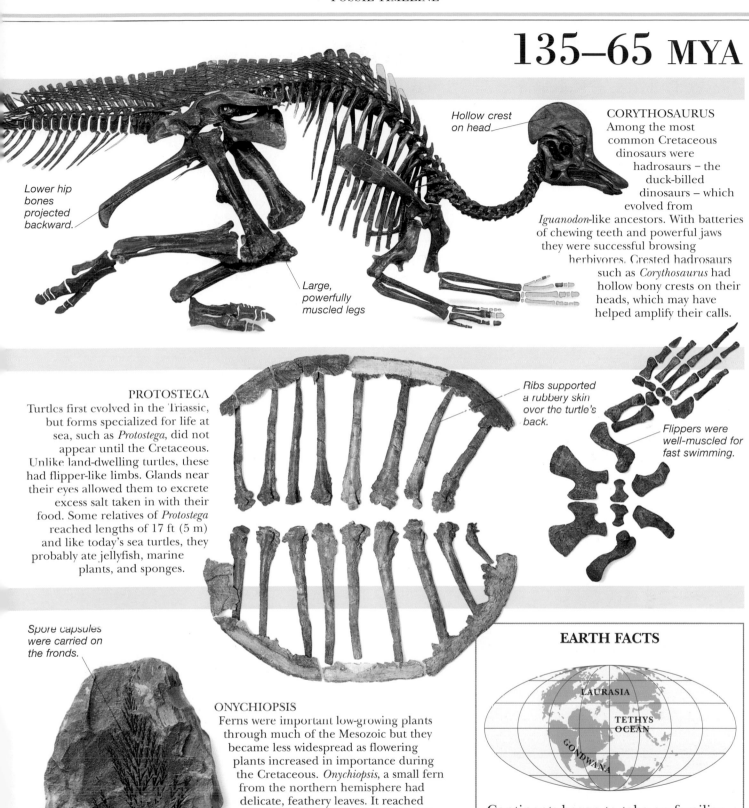

Lower hip bones projected backward.

Large, powerfully muscled legs

Hollow crest on head

CORYTHOSAURUS
Among the most common Cretaceous dinosaurs were hadrosaurs – the duck-billed dinosaurs – which evolved from *Iguanodon*-like ancestors. With batteries of chewing teeth and powerful jaws they were successful browsing herbivores. Crested hadrosaurs such as *Corythosaurus* had hollow bony crests on their heads, which may have helped amplify their calls.

Ribs supported a rubbery skin over the turtle's back.

Flippers were well-muscled for fast swimming.

PROTOSTEGA
Turtles first evolved in the Triassic, but forms specialized for life at sea, such as *Protostega*, did not appear until the Cretaceous. Unlike land-dwelling turtles, these had flipper-like limbs. Glands near their eyes allowed them to excrete excess salt taken in with their food. Some relatives of *Protostega* reached lengths of 17 ft (5 m) and like today's sea turtles, they probably ate jellyfish, marine plants, and sponges.

Spore capsules were carried on the fronds.

ONYCHIOPSIS
Ferns were important low-growing plants through much of the Mesozoic but they became less widespread as flowering plants increased in importance during the Cretaceous. *Onychiopsis*, a small fern from the northern hemisphere had delicate, feathery leaves. It reached about 20 in (50 cm) in height and like all ferns required damp conditions to reproduce. It probably grew around lakes and in sheltered forest environments amongst larger ferns and cycads.

Onychiopsis psilotoides

EARTH FACTS

LAURASIA

TETHYS OCEAN

GONDWANA

Continents began to take on familiar positions during the Cretaceous. By now Pangea had split into Laurasia and Gondwana. These continents were themselves breaking apart into the continents that exist today. Madagascar and India separated from Gondwana and moved north. Large inland seas covered parts of Laurasia.

END OF THE DINOSAURS

THE END OF THE CRETACEOUS PERIOD, 65 million years ago, saw the most famous mass extinction event of all time – although it was certainly not the biggest in terms of species lost. All large land animals disappeared, as did numerous marine invertebrate groups. The theropods – flesh-eating dinosaurs – survived as birds, but all other dinosaurs became extinct. In the seas, plesiosaurs and mosasaurs died out, as did many kinds of bivalves, swimming mollusks, and plankton. Some evidence indicates that a large asteroid struck the Earth at this time. Experts speculate that such an impact would have thrown up enough dust to block out light from the Sun for years or even decades. Perhaps this prolonged cold, dark phase caused Cretaceous plants and animals to die off. However, changes in Cretaceous climate and sea level may already have sent some groups into decline.

LAST SURVIVORS

Scientists are unsure how many dinosaurs were alive at the end of the Cretaceous. It is possible that many species had already become extinct by this time. If so, the whole group was very vulnerable to being wiped out by an extraordinary event, such as meteor impact. *Triceratops* and *Tyrannosaurus* were among the last of the dinosaurs, but many animal groups survived, including insects, some mammals, crocodiles, lizards, and lissamphibians on land, and many fish and invertebrate groups in the sea.

The last dinosaurs may have inhabited a burnt, polluted world with little remaining plant growth.

Cambrian 540–500	Ordovician 500–435	Silurian 435–410	Devonian 410–355	Carboniferous 355–295	Permia
		PALEOZOIC 540–250 MYA			

METEOR EVIDENCE

In 1980, scientists found high levels of the mineral iridium in layers of end-Cretaceous rock. Rare on Earth, iridium is common in asteroids, so the scientists suggested that its presence could be accounted for by an asteroid impact. In 1990, evidence of such an impact – a crater 120 miles (200 km) wide – was found off the coast of Mexico. Named the Chicxulub Crater, it was made by an asteroid around 6 miles (10 km) wide. The similar crater shown here is from much younger rocks in Arizona.

AFTER THE ASTEROID

Many kinds of environmental damage would have followed the impact of the Chicxulub asteroid. This damage could have contributed to the extinction of the dinosaurs and other animals. The impact would have thrown up tidal waves that would have washed ashore on the North American continent, destroying coastal habitats. Hot debris thrown into the atmosphere by the impact may later have rained down to Earth and started huge wildfires.

Triceratops was one of the very last nonavian dinosaurs.

295–250	Triassic 250–203	Jurassic 203–135	Cretaceous 135–65	Tertiary 65 1.75	Quaternary 1.75–present
	MESOZOIC 250–65 MYA			CENOZOIC 65 MYA–present	

PALEOCENE AND EOCENE EPOCHS

LAND ANIMALS

LARGE LANDLUBBERS

At the start of the Paleocene, there were no large animals on the land. Soon the world began to be repopulated by large mammals – which developed from small survivors of the Cretaceous extinction – and by huge flightless birds. Bats, rodents, and true primates made their first appearance, together with many bird groups, including owls, swifts, herons, and eagles. Crocodiles, lizards, turtles, and frogs thrived in the tropical Eocene world, and snakes increased in diversity, feeding on the new rodent types.

PALAEOCHIROPTERYX

Bats probably evolved from tree-climbing ancestors that leapt to catch their insect prey. Early true bats, such as *Palaeochiropteryx* from Eocene Europe, had wings formed from enlarged hands. Though their wings were less advanced than those of modern species, their earbones show that they were already using high frequency calls to locate prey. Like modern bats, they were probably nocturnal, highly agile fliers that fed on flying insects.

AQUATIC ANIMALS

SEA MAMMALS

Modern forms of marine life became firmly established in the Paleocene and Eocene. Fish took on now-familiar forms and new groups of barnacles, crustaceans, and mollusks evolved. The first penguins appeared, and giant forms up to 5 ft (1.5 m) tall inhabited the southern seas. Mammals also took to aquatic life as the first whales and the plant-eating seacows evolved.

WETHERELLUS

This Eocene mackerel was around 10 in (25 cm) in length. Mackerels are fast-swimming marine fish that belong to a group called the scombroids, which are more streamlined than any other group. Swimming in schools, they feed on smaller fish and crustaceans. Some scombroids have heat-generating organs in their eyes and brains that allow these parts of their bodies to function well at low temperatures.

Wide jaws lined with rows of pointed teeth

LAND PLANTS

TROPICAL TIMES

The Paleocene and Eocene world was dominated by tropical forests. Even Europe was home to tropical swamps where ferns, horsetails, and palms formed the forest understory and vines and citrus trees grew overhead. Paleocene trees included forms as diverse as hazel, chestnut, sycamore, alder, magnolia, poplar, and walnut. Trees including beech and sequoias were also present at the time. These forms would later become more important in the temperate forests of the Miocene and beyond. Toward the end of the Eocene, the world cooled. As a result, deciduous and coniferous trees became dominant at higher latitudes, and tropical forests retreated to the equatorial regions.

Nipa burtinii

NIPA

This palm, which survives today only in the mangrove swamps of southeast Asia, grew over large areas of the Northern Hemisphere in the Eocene. Palms are flowering plants that belong to the same group as grasses, orchids, and lilies. They have leaves with parallel veins and their germinating seeds grow one initial leaf (rather than two). Unlike more typical palms, *Nipa* does not have a true stem. Its coconut-like seeds grow at its base.

Rounded Nipa fruit with protective woody shell

65–33.7 MYA

GASTORNIS

Previously known as *Diatryma*, *Gastornis* was a giant, flightless, land bird of Paleocene and Eocene North America and Europe. It stood 7 ft (2.1 m) high and had short, largely useless wings, but its long, stout legs would have made it a fast runner and powerful kicker. Its massive, deep beak was very powerful, suggesting that it could break open bones. Some features indicate that *Gastornis* was most closely related to ducks, geese, and their relatives.

Beak well suited for crushing

Large brain, though smaller than that of living whales

Masses of blood vessels helped control brain temperature.

BASILOSAURUS

One of the best known fossil whales is *Basilosaurus*, a gigantic long-bodied predator from the shallow Eocene seas of the northern hemisphere. It grew to more than 66 ft (20 m) in length and had a huge skull with massive grabbing and slicing teeth. Like most other primitive whales, it had small hind legs with a working knee joint and small, three-toed feet. Relatives of *Basilosaurus* were ancestors of the modern whales.

Figs were an important food for fruit-eating animals.

FICUS

Ficus, the figs, are widespread flowering plants and are part of the same group as oaks. Their fossils first appear in Eocene rocks. Some types of fig grow as shrubs or trees that can reach 100 ft (30 m) in height while others are climbers. Strangler figs are parasites that use trees for support as they grow, eventually killing them. Fig seeds are rounded and grow surrounded by fleshy fruit.

Ficus fruit with woody covering

Ficus

EARTH FACTS

NORTH AMERICA · EUROPE · ASIA · AFRICA · SOUTH AMERICA · INDIA · AUSTRALIA · ANTARCTICA

Tropical forests thrived during Paleocene and Eocene times, even at the poles, but the climate cooled late in the Eocene. North America and Europe were still linked, but a seaway separated Europe from Asia. India and Africa were isolated island continents, while Australia broke away from Antarctica late in the Eocene.

OLIGOCENE AND MIOCENE EPOCHS

LAND ANIMALS

THE MODERN AGE

Many essentially modern animals evolved during the Oligocene and Miocene. Monkeys and apes replaced primitive primates, and some African monkeys crossed the Atlantic to colonize South America. As grasses spread, mammals emerged that resembled today's grazers, such as horses, elephants, and camels. Modern forms of carnivores, birds, lizards, snakes, and frogs also arose.

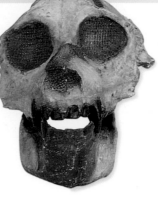

AEGYPTOPITHECUS
This primate lived in Egypt and was among the first members of the Old World monkey group. About the size of a domestic cat, it resembled a modern monkey and probably climbed in trees feeding on fruit and leaves. Compared to its earlier ancestors, *Aegyptopithecus* had fewer teeth, a larger brain, and more forward-looking eyes.

HIPPARION
Horses had existed since the Eocene, but only with the spread of grasslands in the Miocene did they emerge as important large-bodied herbivores. Unlike their forest-dwelling ancestors, new horses like *Hipparion* had longer limbs and high-crowned teeth that allowed them to feed on the tough new grasses.

AQUATIC ANIMALS

FAMILIAR WATERS

By the Miocene, well-known types of fish such as mackerels, flatfish, and advanced sharks, including the Great White, swam the seas, while carp, catfish, and other groups evolved in freshwater. Modern whales developed in the Oligocene, and the first seals evolved from bear-like ancestors. The latter competed with giant diving birds, hastening their extinction.

Leuciscus pachecoi

LEUCISCUS
The fish *Leuciscus* appeared in the Oligocene and survives to this day in North America, Asia, Europe, and Africa. It inhabits freshwater streams and pools, where it uses its specialized toothless jaws to feed on aquatic plants. Like other members of the catfish–carp group, *Leuciscus* has special ribs that transmit vibrations from its swim bladder to its inner ears, providing it with sensitive hearing.

These Leuciscus *probably died as their home lake dried up.*

Body around 4 in (10 cm) long

LAND PLANTS

TEMPERATE LANDS

During the Oligocene and Miocene, the tropical forests of the Eocene gradually gave way to drier grasslands. First, the lower temperatures of the Oligocene restricted tropical forests and allowed temperate woodlands consisting of broad-leaved deciduous trees to spread across the continents. Then the warmer and drier conditions of the Miocene coincided with the evolution of grasses – ground-hugging plants that could grow with little water. The grasses spread across the landscape, forming vast savannah and prairie environments in the south. Temperate forests of conifers, oaks, birches, elms, and willows remained in the north.

ACER
The maples (*Acer*) and their relatives first evolved in the Oligocene, and many species survive today in temperate forests around the world. All are deciduous trees, some of which grow to 82 ft (25 m) in height. Maple leaves are three-lobed with long stalks. Flowers are produced in drooping clusters and are followed by distinctive winged fruits. The wings allow the fruit to be caught by the wind and carried long distances from the parent tree.

Acer

Wing of Acer fruit preserved in limestone

33.7–5.3 MYA

PALAEOCASTOR

Rodents were abundant from the start of the Oligocene and diversified throughout the period. Early squirrels, mice, and porcupines emerged, as did beavers like *Palaeocastor*. This burrow-dwelling animal lived on the plains of North America and dug distinctive corkscrew-shaped burrows. It probably resembled a modern marmot.

Hipparion had a long, slim skull and high-crowned teeth.

Limbs well-suited for digging

Large chewing teeth

PACHYDYPTES

Penguins, flightless marine birds that evolved from close relatives of albatrosses, appeared in the Eocene and continued to be successful throughout the Oligocene and Miocene. All forms lived in the Southern Hemisphere. *Pachydyptes*, a giant penguin from New Zealand, was similar in appearance to living penguins and, like the modern forms, fed on fish caught underwater.

Stout upper arm bone

Color caused by mineral impurities

Species of *Quercus* can reach 130 ft (40 m) in height.

QUERCUS

The oak, *Quercus*, is one of the most distinctive of large trees and is an important component of many temperate forest environments. *Quercus* is a widespread and diverse genus, which first appeared in the Eocene. Some forms have lobed leaves. Some are deciduous, others evergreen. As shown in this Miocene tree trunk, their wood bears distinctive growth rings.

Quercus

EARTH FACTS

During the Oligocene, South America separated from Antarctica, allowing ocean currents to move around Antarctica for the first time. The Antarctic ice cap now began to form, cooling the climate. By Miocene times, India had collided with mainland Asia, causing the Himalayas to rise. Africa also connected with Eurasia.

PLIOCENE EPOCH   5.3–1.75 MYA

LAND ANIMALS

GRASSLAND GRAZERS
Pliocene animals were largely similar to today's forms. Hoofed mammals, such as one-toed horses, camels, elephants, and antelopes became more diverse as they exploited the newly developing grassland habitats. Large saber-toothed cats hunted the plains and forests of the Americas, Africa, Asia, and Europe and the first humans evolved from chimplike ancestors.

Teeth suggest a diet of leaves not grasses.

TETRALOPHODON
Elephants appeared in the Paleocene, but during the Miocene and Pliocene advanced forms, closely related to today's species, spread to most parts of the world. *Tetralophodon* was an elephant that lived in Africa, Asia, and Europe. It had a long skull but, unlike living elephants, sometimes possessed lower jaw tusks. *Tetralophodon* may have been one of the first members of the Elephantidae, the group to which mammoths and living elephants belong.

Tetralophodon longirostrus

AQUATIC ANIMALS

WHALE DIVERSITY
By the Pliocene, modern whales had largely replaced more primitive forms. Sperm whales, humpbacks, killer whales, and many modern kinds of dolphins were all present. As North and South America were brought together, the land bridge blocked movement of marine animals from the Atlantic to the Pacific. As a result, numerous fish and other animals unique to the Caribbean Sea evolved.

BALAENA
The right whale, *Balaena*, which grows to 65 ft (20 m) in length, has been hunted to near extinction by humans. Its enormous mouth has long, fine baleen plates that are used to filter food from seawater. Like all advanced whales, it has a shell-shaped ear bone connected to the skull by ligaments. After death, the ear bone often drops away from the carcass.

Balaena

Fossilized ear bone

LAND PLANTS

RETREATING TROPICS
Conditions became drier and cooler during the Pliocene and grasslands continued to spread. Arid steppe and pampas environments replaced the warmer, more wooded savannahs of the Miocene, with the result that grazing animals flourished at the expense of browsers. Tropical plants started to disappear from high latitudes and bands of cooler-adapted forests, made up of conifers, birches, and other trees, began to spread across northern North America, Europe, and Asia. Willow trees and fruiting trees frequented the river valleys of the northern hemisphere. Such forests would become even more widespread during the Pleistocene ice ages.

GRASSES
Grasses are among the most important groups of plants alive today. They provide shelter and food for countless animal species. The spread and diversification of grasses started in the Miocene and continued through the Pliocene as conditions became drier. Winds that swept the Pliocene plains spread grass seeds, helping these plants dominate the dry interiors of continents as well as waterside habitats. Because grasses grow from the bottom of their leaves (rather than the tops, as in other plants), they recover very quickly from damage caused by fire and grazing.

Grasses produce huge quantities of pollen and seed.

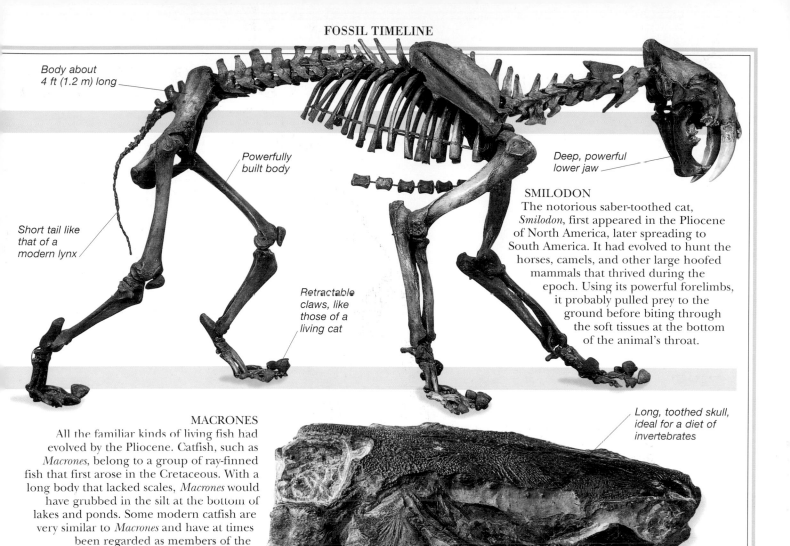

Body about
4 ft (1.2 m) long

Powerfully
built body

Short tail like
that of a
modern lynx

Retractable
claws, like
those of a
living cat

Deep, powerful
lower jaw

SMILODON

The notorious saber-toothed cat,
Smilodon, first appeared in the Pliocene
of North America, later spreading to
South America. It had evolved to hunt the
horses, camels, and other large hoofed
mammals that thrived during the
epoch. Using its powerful forelimbs,
it probably pulled prey to the
ground before biting through
the soft tissues at the bottom
of the animal's throat.

MACRONES

All the familiar kinds of living fish had
evolved by the Pliocene. Catfish, such as
Macrones, belong to a group of ray-finned
fish that first arose in the Cretaceous. With a
long body that lacked scales, *Macrones* would
have grubbed in the silt at the bottom of
lakes and ponds. Some modern catfish are
very similar to *Macrones* and have at times
been regarded as members of the
same genus.

Sensitive barbels
grew from the
upper jaw.

Long, toothed skull,
ideal for a diet of
invertebrates

Macrones *were
about 20 in
(50 cm) long*

LIQUIDAMBAR

These trees, sometimes called
sweetgum, grew to around
82 ft (25 m) in height. Distributed
worldwide, they formed an
important part of Pliocene
temperate woodlands. The
twigs of *Liquidambar* had
corky "wings" and their
fruits were collections of
woody burrlike capsules,
carried on long stems.
Today, sweetgum trees are
economically important.
Their wood is used to
make furniture and pulp
for paper.

Distinctive
star-shaped
five-lobed leaf

Leaves were
shed in the
autumn.

*Liquidambar
europeanum*

EARTH FACTS

In the Pliocene, a land bridge formed
between North and South America.
Animals could move from one
continent to the other, but ocean
currents were blocked, diverting
warm water northwards. India
continued to push the Himalayas
ever higher. The climate grew cooler
and Antarctica froze over.

PLEISTOCENE EPOCH 1.75–0.01 MYA

LAND ANIMALS

MAMMALS AND HUMANS

During the Pleistocene, temperatures dropped in the northern hemisphere. Animals adapted to warmer climates, for example lizards, snakes, and lissamphibians, were pushed southward. In their place there developed numerous large, fur-covered mammals that were better suited to the cold. Among these were new mammoths, giant rhinos, cave lions, and giant deer. New human species emerged in Africa, Europe, and Asia and began to have an effect on the diversity of large animals.

HOMO SAPIENS

Our own species – *Homo sapiens* – first emerged in Pleistocene Africa. It soon spread throughout Europe and Asia and even crossed vast oceans to colonize the American continents and Australasia. *Homo sapiens* was the most adaptable and successful of the several species of *Homo* alive in the Pleistocene. It probably had a more complex language and culture, and a better understanding of tools than the other species, which it gradually replaced.

AQUATIC ANIMALS

COLD WATERS

Marine invertebrate life in the Pleistocene was largely unchanged from the Miocene and Pliocene. However, corals and other reef animals were affected as sea levels fell. The colder climate worldwide meant that cold-water seabirds and marine mammals – which today are found only in polar waters – were far more widely distributed. Auks and walruses, for example, lived as far south as Japan and southern Europe.

Pinguinus impennis

PINGUINUS

The Great Auk, *Pinguinus impennis*, was a flightless seabird that inhabited the cool seas of the northern hemisphere during the Pleistocene. It occurred as far south as north Africa and Florida. Like the living penguins, it would have "flown" underwater chasing after its prey of fish and crustaceans. *Pinguinus* survived into the Holocene but was mercilessly hunted by humans for its feathers and oil. The very last Great Auks died before 1860.

LAND PLANTS

GRASSLANDS AND TAIGA

During the Pleistocene, grasslands developed in the chilly northern latitudes. These supported not only grasses, but cold-adapted plants such as ground-hugging lichens, mosses, dwarf sedges, and miniature willow and birch trees. Taiga – a new kind of coniferous forest – colonized the area between the cold northern grasslands (steppes) and the temperate deciduous forests farther south. During warm spells, grapevines, hazels, and oaks returned to the north. Tropical forests retreated, and the South American and African rainforests may have been split into small "islands" by bands of grassland. Climate changes at the end of the Pleistocene resulted in the decline of the steppes.

PICEA

Spruces (*Picea*) are pine trees that formed much of the taiga – the vast forests that spread through the northern hemisphere in the Pleistocene. Today more than thirty species of spruce live in subtropical, temperate, or mountainous regions of the world. *Picea* trees are typically tall and narrow with drooping branches, giving them a "layered" appearance. They have rectangular needles and thin, scaly bark. Their cones are long and are attached by a long stalk.

Cones release winged seeds.

Woody cone covered with bracts in diamond pattern

Small brain

Some Diprotodon skeletons have marks indicating that they were hunted by prehistoric people.

DIPROTODON

Herds of this giant marsupial are thought to have roamed the Australian grasslands of the Pleistocene. This rhinoceros-sized herbivore was equipped with large chewing teeth set into thick, heavy jaws. *Diprotodon* and its relatives were most abundant during the Miocene, but declined as Australia became drier. Their role was taken over by the large grazing kangaroos that still survive to this day.

Strong, heavy, columnlike limbs

HYDRODAMALIS

Steller's sea cow (*Hydrodamalis gigas*) was a kelp-eating marine mammal related to the modern dugong of the tropical Indian Ocean. It lived in the cold Arctic seas, protected from the icy water by layers of fat beneath its barklike skin. Like *Pinguinus*, it survived into the Holocene and was hunted to extinction by 1767.

Short feet well suited for bearing the animal's weight

Flippers blunt and stumplike

Whalelike tail flukes

Buttercups can have yellow, white, red, or blue flowers.

RANUNCULUS

Buttercups (*Ranunculus*) are flowering plants that grow in grassland, wetland, and woodland environments. They are among the oldest groups of flowering plants and were successful and widespread in the temperate environments of the Pleistocene. Today, about 2,000 members of the buttercup family are found as herbs, shrubs, and vines. Buttercup flowers are poisonous. Their shiny coating irritates the digestive tracts of animals that eat them.

Ranunculus spread across North America, Europe, and Asia in the Pleistocene.

EARTH FACTS

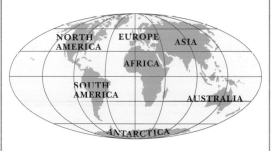

Huge ice sheets covered northern North America, Europe, and Asia. Southern South America, Australia, New Zealand, and Antarctica were also icier than today. Pleistocene sea levels were around 330 ft (100 m) lower than the present day, and dry land linked North America to eastern Asia and Australia to New Guinea.

HOLOCENE EPOCH

LAND ANIMALS

DIVERSITY IN DECLINE

The Holocene has been dominated by humans. The result of their success has been a large drop in the diversity of life on Earth. The human species has multiplied like no other before, and has spread to the most isolated places on the planet. Humans have destroyed the habitats of other species to feed and house growing populations. They have hunted creatures to extinction, and created pollution that threatens animal and plant life worldwide.

Prominent curved beak and naked facial skin

DODO

The dodo (*Raphus cucullatus*) was a giant flightless pigeon that lived on the island of Mauritius in the Indian Ocean. Dodos were not shy of the people that visited Mauritius in the 1500s and 1600s. This made them very easy to catch, and by about 1680 the species was extinct. Thousands of other island-dwelling species suffered the same fate.

AQUATIC ANIMALS

WATER LOSSES

As on land, the most significant aspect of life in the Holocene seas has been destruction caused by humans. Some seals and sea cows have been hunted to extinction, and whaling carried out between about 1850 and 1950 almost wiped out some of the great whale species. Industrial-scale fishing has changed the balance of life in the seas, while rivers and oceans are increasingly used as dumps for chemicals, sewage, and solid waste.

SALMON

Found in rivers, lakes, and seas throughout the northern hemisphere, salmon have been an important food source for people for thousands of years. Today wild salmon are hunted for sport, and some species are farmed. Salmon numbers have been hit by water pollution and by the construction of dams, which prevent the fish from migrating upstream to breed.

LAND PLANTS

HUMAN INFLUENCE

At the start of the Holocene, elm, birch, and conifer woodland colonized those parts of the northern hemisphere that had previously been covered by ice. Vast tracts of these woodlands, as well as wetlands and tropical forests, were later destroyed as humans cleared and drained land for agriculture. Humans cultivated a few selected species of grasses – the cereal crops – which today dominate huge areas at the expense of natural plant communities. Other apparently natural habitats, such as moorlands, heaths, and grasslands, are actually created and maintained by human activity, such as deliberate burning and grazing of livestock.

Salmon require water with a high oxygen content.

OAK MOSS

Although it is called "oak moss," *Evernia prunastri* is in fact a lichen – an alga and a fungus growing together symbiotically. This greenish-gray, bushy lichen grows throughout much of the northern hemisphere. Some scientists believe that lichens may have been the first multicellular organisms on Earth. Today, many lichens are dying off as a result of pollution. Some types, however, have successfully colonized buildings and now flourish in towns and cities.

Branching, leafy thallus (body)

0.01 MYA–PRESENT

GIANT PANDA

Giant pandas are Asian bears specialized for eating bamboo. Three species evolved in the Pleistocene but only one, *Ailuropoda melanoleuca*, survived into the Holocene. Many of the large bamboo forests that pandas need have been cut down and the few surviving panda populations are now widely separated. Pandas are also slow to breed and are hunted by poachers.

DOLLY THE SHEEP

People have always "engineered" domestic animals by breeding from carefully selected individuals. Advances in genetics now let biologists manipulate the genetic material of living things. This means that embryos can be cloned, a process that resulted in Dolly the sheep, born in 1997. In the future, genetic engineering will increasingly be used to modify the features of living things and even create new species.

BLUE WHALE

The invention of the explosive harpoon in the late 1800s enabled humans to hunt the giant Blue Whale (*Balaenoptera musculus*) to near extinction. It is still an endangered species, though its numbers have recovered to about 10,000 worldwide. Blue whales are among the largest animals ever to have lived. They can reach 100 ft (30 m) in length and weigh more than 100 tons (100 tonnes).

DUCK

Ducks are omnivorous water birds that evolved at the end of the Cretaceous. The Mallard (*Anas platyrhynchos*) is a freshwater species native to Europe, Asia, and North America. It has been domesticated and introduced worldwide. As with other domesticated birds, people have bred types of Mallard that have fancy plumage or grow especially fat.

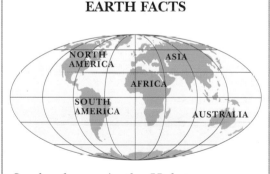

WHEAT

Early in the Holocene people began to domesticate wild grasses. They deliberately cross-bred the types which produced the most seeds, or grew the fastest. Emmer is a primitive kind of wheat (*Triticum*) first domesticated in the Middle East. People soon found that by cross-breeding emmer with other kinds of grasses they could produce hardier, even more productive wheats.

Wheat is milled to produce flour.

EARTH FACTS

NORTH AMERICA · ASIA · AFRICA · SOUTH AMERICA · AUSTRALIA

Sea levels rose in the Holocene as the Pleistocene ice retreated. Global warming caused by pollution continues this trend today. By the start of the Holocene the land bridge that linked Asia with North America was under water and New Guinea was separated from Australia. Africa and Australia continue to move northward.

FINDING FOSSILS

NEW FOSSILS ARE DISCOVERED all the time, but only become known as collectors, enthusiasts, and researchers share their knowledge and announce their discoveries. Many finds are made in areas that have been searched for years or decades and yet continue to produce material as new rocks are exposed and new fossils unearthed. Many of the world's most prolific fossil-bearing sites, such as the Gobi Desert and the Cretaceous rocks of southern England, are famous and are regularly visited by organized expeditions and local collectors. Other areas, including the African deserts, remote parts of South America, and the polar regions, have only recently been discovered as rich sources of fossils.

Lyme Regis, England

Shale cliffs formed in the Jurassic

Sea constantly erodes cliffs, causing rock falls.

Fallen rock containing cluster of ammonite fossils

Chalk (limestone)

Rock sandstone

Rock clay

SEDIMENTARY ROCK TYPES
Sedimentary rocks are made from ground-up fragments of other rocks, as well as material from living organisms. Clays and mudstones are made up of minuscule mud particles, while limestones contain the remains of billions of tiny organisms, cemented together by the mineral calcium carbonate. Sedimentary rocks mostly form on the seafloor, where fresh sediments are continuously deposited after being washed off the land. Many sedimentary rocks contain rounded lumps called concretions. These are produced by chemical changes, often caused by the presence of a fossil.

WHICH ROCKS?
Most fossils are found in sedimentary rocks that form in layers from deposits of sand and mud – those with tiny particles can preserve fossils in incredible detail. Metamorphic rocks have been modified by heat and pressure below the Earth's surface, so any fossils they once contained have usually been destroyed. Igneous (volcanic) rocks rarely contain fossils, since they burn organic material away when molten, but fossil footprints may still be preserved on the surface of lava. Permanently frozen ground, such as the permafrosts of Siberia, can also preserve organisms.

Different colors indicate materials that reflect radio waves differently.

Stripes indicate outcrops of Cretaceous sedimentary rock.

Radar-bright cliff face

MAPS, PHOTOS, AND SATELLITE IMAGES
Geological maps show the different types or units of rock that are exposed on the Earth's surface. They are widely used when searching for potential fossil-bearing sites. Investigations by geologists have determined the ages of the rocks and the environments in which they were deposited. Aerial photographs and satellite images can be used in conjunction with geological maps so that the locations of exposed rocks can be pinpointed. These tools are vital when investigating remote or poorly known areas.

Satellite radar image of Egyptian desert

FINDING FOSSIL REMAINS

Individual collectors investigate cliffs, seashores, and other places and find hundreds of fossils, often of new species. Many digs are the result of an initial small discovery made by a local collector. They are carried out by amateurs or teams of scientists, close to where these people live or work. Larger-scale expeditions often aim to investigate specific fossil environments – they expect to bring back many specimens, and may hope to discover several new species. Such expeditions often travel to remote areas – they are expensive, involve months of planning, and may involve teams from several different countries. It may also be necessary to obtain special permission from governments.

Fossil-hunting expedition in West Africa

EXPOSURES

Fossils are mostly discovered where fossil-bearing rocks have been exposed by the actions of water, wind, or people. Eroding cliffs and riverbanks are the best places to find fossils since constant erosion means that new fossils are always being exposed. Fossils eroded from cliffs and from rocks exposed at sea may be washed around in the surf for years, and seashores may be littered with fossils. As a result, seashores are one of the best places to find fossils. Where people have exposed rocks - in quarries, road cuts, and building sites – fossils may also be exposed. Places where rock surfaces are not covered by soil and plants, such as rocky deserts, are also important places for the discovery of fossils. To find specific kinds of fossils, fossil hunters examine particular kinds of rocks deposited at specific times and in specific environments. This means that knowledge of the geological history of an area is important for successful fossil hunting.

Rock outcrops in the Gobi Desert date to the Late Cretaceous.

Fossil hunters may have to walk for miles across the desert in search of promising exposed fossils.

Site walking in the Gobi Desert

Exposed shells in limestone

ONSITE ACTIVITIES

Palaeontologists looking for fossils may spend hours walking a site, peering at the ground or at the surfaces of exposed rocks. Rather than digging holes and hoping to find fossils by chance, palaeontologists generally look for places where they have already been exposed by erosion. Palaeontologists learn to spot fossils by looking for shapes or textures – bones are often noticed because of their smooth, shiny outer surface or their honeycombed internal fabric. Shells, teeth, and other fossils often have distinctive shapes and surface textures.

TECHNIQUES OF EXCAVATION

REMOVING AND TRANSPORTING A FOSSIL can take one amateur fossil hunter a matter of minutes, or involve a whole team of paleontologists working painstakingly over weeks or even months. Every year, major museums send digging parties to rich fossil sites around the world. In the field, they can face a variety of challenges, from delicate and crumbling rocks to huge lumps of bone that require heavy lifting equipment to transport, and may even have to be cut into pieces on site. Major excavations may use cranes, helicopters, digging machines, and even explosives.

Small excavation tools

TOOLS OF EXCAVATION
Excavation tools range from toothbrushes and scalpels to shovels and hammers. Once the position of the fossil itself is known, heavy tools can be used to remove most of the overburden (overlying rock). Gloves, protective goggles, and hard hats are needed to prevent injury from flying shards of rock. As the rock layer around the fossil is reduced, smaller and more delicate tools are used. Sieves are also used to sift through the overburden for small fossils, which may prove very useful for establishing a larger fossil's context.

EXCAVATION IN PROGRESS
Normally, the surrounding rock is not completely removed from a fossil until it is safely back in the laboratory. In the field, most specimens are excavated as part of a block that contains the whole fossil and helps protect it during transport. Freeing a specimen from the rock, and removing the rock that lies on top of it – known as the overburden – can be difficult. Some rocks are so hard that explosives and heavy-duty machinery like bulldozers and power drills may be needed. However, not all rocks are so difficult to remove – some soft sandstones and mudstones can be simply washed or brushed away from the fossils they contain.

Protective gear

MAPPING THE SITE

Recording the precise positions and relationships of fossils on a site can reveal important clues about how an organism died and how it came to be preserved. Before anything is removed from the site, it is divided up using a grid, photographed, and accurately mapped. The different fossils are also clearly labeled so there is no confusion when they are freed from the rock and taken back to the laboratory. The end result is a detailed site map that can be almost as important as the fossils themselves.

Site mapping in progress

MOVING FOSSILS

Many fossils are fragile and prone to cracking and breaking, so glue and resin are painted or sprayed on to help keep them together. Small fossils collected in the field can be kept safe wrapped in paper or stored in sample bags. Large fossils may need to be wrapped in plaster or have their most fragile parts protected by polyurethane foam. Some blocks containing fossils may be so large that they have to be split apart for ease of transport.

REMOVAL

Final removal of the fossil is a delicate moment. Often rock from below the fossil block is dug out first, leaving just a stump that has to be chiseled through or broken off. Once freed, the block can be turned over, and its underside stabilized. It may then have to be transported for hundreds of miles from remote areas by jeep, plane, boat, or even horse-drawn cart.

Plaster and bandages

Paintbrushes

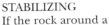

STABILIZING

If the rock around a fossil is crumbly or the fossil itself has been exposed to the elements, it often needs stabilizing before it can be moved. Stabilizing helps to keep a fossil block together and protect it from damage during transport. Stabilization methods range from simply painting the exposed parts with glue or resin, to wrapping the whole block with bandages of burlap cloth soaked in plaster of Paris – just like putting a broken leg in a cast.

Stabilizing a fossil prior to removal

FAMOUS FOSSIL SITES

Rich fossil beds are scattered all around the world, preserving the remains of life from a variety of different ages. However, only a few very specific geological environments are able to preserve fossils well. The most widespread are fine-grained sedimentary rocks, but other preserved remains have been found trapped in Siberian ice, or drowned in Californian tar pits. Paleontologists know that our view of the prehistoric world can never be comprehensive, because we see it through such narrow windows into the past.

SIBERIA
The wildernesses of northern Siberia are covered with thick layers of permafrost, which have trapped and preserved the remains of Ice Age animals such as mammoths. This unique method of preservation retains soft body parts as well as bones and immense tusks.

LYME REGIS
The slate cliffs of Lyme Regis in southwest England were among the earliest fossil sites, well known by the early 1800s. They preserve animals from the Jurassic seas, including ichthyosaurs and plesiosaurs.

Ichthyosaurus

SOLNHOFEN
Germany's Solnhofen quarry was once a shallow tropical sea with scattered islands. The fine Solnhofen limestones have preserved the delicate remains of fish, as well as island-dwellers like *Compsognathus* and the early bird *Archaeopteryx* (discovered in 1861).

MESSEL
The Messel quarry in Germany preserves the remains of an entire ecosystem from Early Tertiary times – the period when mammals were diversifying and asserting themselves. Fossil mammals found at Messel since its discovery in the late 19th century include opossums, bats, rodents, early primates, and primitive horses. Other finds from the site are insects, frogs, predatory fish, reptiles and crocodiles, birds, snakes, and plants.

Fossil bat from Messel deposits

OLDUVAI GORGE
The Olduvai Gorge in Tanzania is an important site because it preserves some of the earliest-known human remains, alongside prehistoric mammals such as antelope, zebra, pigs, hippopotamuses, and elephants. Discovered in the early 1960s by husband and wife paleontologists Louis and Mary Leakey, early hominids from Olduvai Gorge include *Australopithecus habilis*, *Australopithecus boisei*, and *Homo ergaster*.

THE KAROO
South Africa's Karoo Basin is a storehouse of fossils from the Permian to the Jurassic, charting the rise and diversification of synapsids and reptiles. Animals from the Karoo include *Lystrosaurus*, *Euparkeria*, *Dicynodon*, and *Thrinaxodon*.

THE FLAMING CLIFFS

The Flaming Cliffs of Mongolia's Gobi Desert have yielded some of the world's best-known dinosaurs since their discovery in the 1920s by Roy Chapman Andrews. The cliffs preserve fossils from the Late Cretaceous, including *Protoceratops*, *Oviraptor*, and *Velociraptor*.

RANCHO LA BREA

These tar pits, near Los Angeles, are a unique site where Ice Age animals were trapped in the pools of liquid asphalt that form on the suface. The first bones were discovered in the 1870s, but proper excavation did not get underway until the early 1900s. The pits have so far revealed more than 565 species, ranging from mammals such as mammoths, saber-toothed cats, and dire wolves, to insects, fish, and frogs.

COMO BLUFF

This vast Jurassic deposit of mainly sauropod skeletons in Wyoming was discovered in the 1870s, during the building of the Union Pacific Railroad. It included remains of giants such as *Apatosaurus*, *Diplodocus*, and *Camarasaurus*. Nearby Bone Cabin Quarry, excavated by American Museum of Natural History scientists from the 1890s onward, yielded hundreds more specimens.

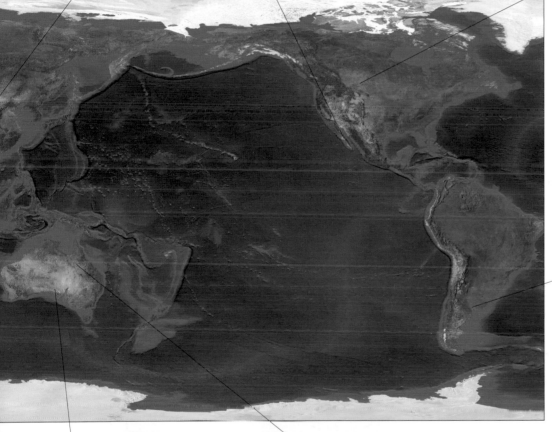

VALLEY OF THE MOON

This barren valley in Western Argentina is the source of some of the earliest dinosaur fossils. In among the rhynchosaurs and other ruling reptiles from the Late Triassic period are two early theropod dinosaurs – *Eoraptor* and *Herrerasaurus*. This remote site was discovered in the 1950s, but its true richness was only revealed in the late 1980s.

The Ediacara fossil *Spriggina*

EDIACARA

Ediacara, in Australia's Flinders mountain range, was a sea in Precambrian times, and preserves some of the earliest known remains of complex organisms. The creatures found here resemble sea jellies, sponges, sea pens, annelid worms, and even arthropods.

RIVERSLEIGH

The Riversleigh quarry in Queensland, Australia, holds the record for density of fossil finds. Discovered in 1900, it was not seriously excavated until 1983. The diggers found a huge range of fossils from late Tertiary period, including marsupial mammals such as kangaroos, diprotodontids, and marsupial lions, as well as crocodiles, snakes, and giant flightless birds.

FOSSILS IN THE LAB

FINDING AND EXCAVATING A FOSSIL is only the first step in understanding it. Paleontologists actually spend far more time in the laboratory than in the field. This is where the fossil is removed from its protective field jacket and the often painstaking task of separating the fossil from the rock around it takes place. Removing rock and cleaning and piecing fossils together may involve mechanical tools such as hammers and brushes, as well as chemicals. X-ray technology can be used to reveal how much of a fossil is preserved while it is still encased in the rock. Once it is prepared, a fossil's anatomy can be studied to reveal its secrets. The results of these studies are published in scientific journals.

CATALOGING FINDS

Expeditions usually return with hundreds of small fossils in addition to their major finds. These can help give context to other material found around them, and so are carefully cataloged. Over the years, paleontologists have built up lists of index fossils – rapidly changing, widespread, and common animals that can be identified from tiny fragments. Because the age of these fossils is precisely known, remains found alongside, above, or below them can also be dated.

FREEING FOSSILS FROM ROCK

Once a fossil is in the laboratory, the protective jacket put on it in the field can be removed. As rock that surrounds the fossil in its block is removed, exposed elements may need strengthening with glues and protective resins. Removing rock from all the fine details of a fossil can be a delicate and time-consuming process, and jackhammers, drills, knives, files, and brushes are used according to how much rock needs removing. Sometimes CAT-scan images of the fossil in the rock are used to guide the preparation process. In the final stages, particularly for small fossils, removal of rock particles may be performed with fine tools under the microscope.

Saw is used to clean away small areas of rock.

Hammer and chisel can only be used for removing large chunks of rock.

Drill is used for the most delicate final cleaning.

Hammer and chisel

Dental drill

Cleaning a fossil in an acid bath

ACID PREPARATION

By using acids, paleontologists can remove the rock from around a fossil, without damaging the fossil itself. Dilute acetic or formic acids are used to remove limestones, while other acids are used to break down silica- or iron-rich rocks. The results of acid preparation can be spectacular, but the process must be carefully monitored as acid can sometimes dissolve fossils from the inside. Some acids are dangerous and can burn human skin, so people using them must wear safety masks, gloves, and clothing.

SCIENTIFIC DESCRIPTION

Once a fossil is fully prepared, a paleontologist can begin to describe the anatomy of a fossil and compare it with material from related or similar species. Unique features may show that a fossil is a new genus or species, in which case it has to be given a new name. By comparing the features of a new fossil with others, it can be incorporated into a phylogeny (evolutionary sequence of events) and provide new information on the evolution of a group. Using what is known of living animals, paleontologists can reconstruct muscles and degrees of motion possible at joints. This can provide information on how fossil animals may have looked and behaved when alive.

Scientific illustration of the Cambrian arthropod Opabinia

ILLUSTRATION

Paleontological illustration and restoration is an art in itself, and the key to describing what an ancient animal really looked like. Illustrations can vary from precise drawings of the fossil still in its rock, to complete and labelled reconstructions of the articulated skeleton, like the one shown here. For precision, scientists often use a camera lucida – a simple device that projects an image of the fossil onto paper, allowing its outline and details to be traced. Although drawings are less accurate than photographs, they are useful because they can combine features that could never be seen at the same time in the fossil itself.

REVIEW AND PUBLICATION

Once a fossil has been studied, its description is published as a scientific paper for the rest of the scientific community to read and refer to in later work. The paper is a technical article published in a specialist journal. It may be a description of a new species, a re-evaluation of long-known species, or a study of the evolution, structure, or biology of a group. Diagrams and photos are used to illustrate the features or concepts discussed in the paper. Although mistakes happen, most scientific papers that make it to publication are reliable, since they have already been peer-reviewed. Before publication, the paper is sent out to other experts in the field, who can comment on it and recommend changes. Often, when a new and spectacular animal is discovered, the media become interested, the story appears in newspapers, and the discoverer can become famous.

American Museum of Natural History paleontologists excavating fossils in Mongolia

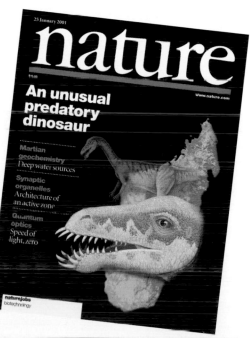

A new dinosaur appears on the cover of *Nature*.

STUDYING FOSSILS

PALEONTOLOGISTS STUDY THE ANATOMY of fossils to reveal evidence about lifestyle, diet, growth, and movement. Anatomical details also provide a great deal of information on the evolutionary relationships between species. A lot of paleontological work therefore concentrates on the accurate description of a fossil's anatomy. Tomography – the use of X-rays to view internal structures three-dimensionally – and microscopy, the use of microscopes, have become increasingly sophisticated and allow improved investigation of anatomy. Paleontologists can now see inside fossils without breaking them open and can view delicate internal structures never examined before.

Large forward-facing eyes indicate stereoscopic (3-D) vision.

Large nostrils show a keen sense of smell.

Saber-toothed cat skull

ANATOMY

The anatomy of a fossil animal provides a wealth of information, not just on the possible lifestyle and structure of the creature it preserves, but on the evolution of the group to which it belongs. By comparing an animal's bones with those of similar forms, paleontologists formulate ideas about the evolutionary relationships between species. Soft tissues like muscles and organs are rarely preserved in fossils, but their probable structures can be inferred by comparing the anatomy of fossil animals with living ones.

SKULL AND TEETH

By looking at the evidence for eyeballs, nasal tissue, and ears, paleontologists can learn about a fossil animal's senses. Teeth provide an indication of lifestyle – carnivorous animals typically have sharp-edged or conical, pointed teeth, while herbivores typically have leaf-shaped or flattened chewing teeth. The arrangement of teeth in the mouth can also provide information about the animal's feeding strategy – for instance whether a carnivore was a predator or scavenger.

Saber teeth show the animal was a fearsome hunter.

Birdlike beak indicates Gallimimus may have had birdlike feeding habits.

Internal anatomy based on a modern bird's

Hip acted as a pivot point – Gallimimus's tail balanced the rest of its body.

Tail muscles reconstructed from ridges on tail vertebrae.

Skin covering based on modern reptile – dinosaur skin is rarely preserved.

Long neck for snapping up insects and other small prey

Long arms could have been used to collect vegetation or grab prey.

Birdlike muscular gizzard for crushing food, based on findings of gizzard stones associated with dinosaur fossils

Sharp foot claws were probably used as defensive weapons.

Shins longer than thighs are similar to those found in ostriches, so Gallimimus was a fast runner.

Anatomical model of Gallimimus

MUSCLES AND ORGANS

Scars, crests, and ridges on fossil bones can show where muscles were attached in life – something that can be tested by looking at the muscles and bones of living animals. The positions and sizes of muscles in fossil animals, and the amount of movement possible at bony joints are measured. These are used to reconstruct the way the animal might have moved and what it was capable of when alive. Internal organs are more difficult to reconstruct, although some exceptional fossils can preserve traces of these structures, and comparisons with living animals can also be valuable.

PALEOPATHOLOGY

The study of ancient diseases and injuries
is called paleopathology. These can be
recognized by preserved changes or
peculiar growths in bones and may
indicate that fossil animals endured
disease or injury when alive. Features
seen regularly in many members of a
fossil species – such as injured horns
in fossil antelopes or broken teeth in
carnivores – indicate that these structures
were often used in combat or defense.

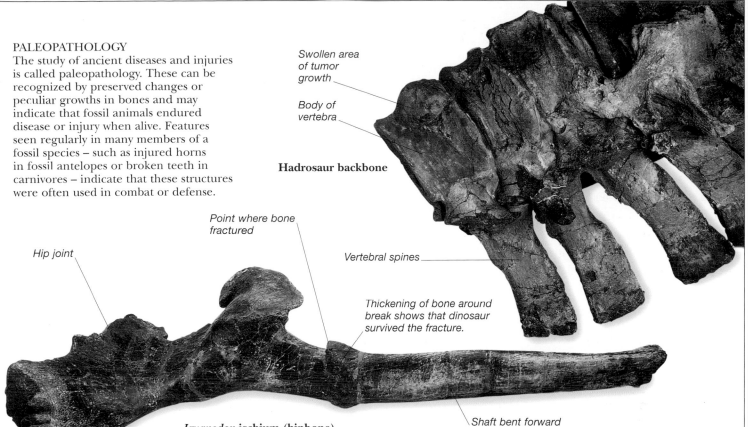

Swollen area
of tumor
growth

Body of
vertebra

Hadrosaur backbone

Point where bone
fractured

Hip joint

Vertebral spines

Thickening of bone around
break shows that dinosaur
survived the fracture.

Iguanodon **ischium (hipbone)**

Shaft bent forward
after repair

LOOKING CLOSER

Microscopy has been used to study fossils
since the earliest days of paleontology, but
recent advances have allowed scientists to
look much more closely at prehistoric
evidence. Scanning electron microscopes
allow far more detail to be seen in fossil
bones. They have also revealed fossilized
microorganisms for the first time, helping
paleontologists to learn more about the
environment the larger animals lived in.
Tomography involves the use of X-rays to look
inside an object. It has been used to look at
structures such as the complex hollow tubes
within the skull of duck-billed dinosaurs.

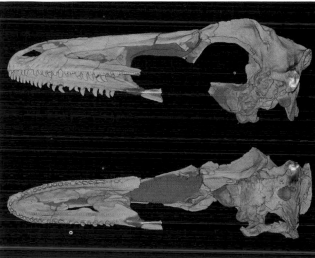

CT scan of a theropod dinosaur skull

MICROSCOPY

By examining fossils with microscopes,
paleontologists can study fossil
microorganisms, like bacteria and
plankton. Paleobotanists routinely
use microscopes to analyse the cells
and spores of fossil plants. Scanning
electron microscopes (SEMs) are
powerful tools that can magnify the
image of an object a million times

SEM image of fossil pollen grain

CT SCANS

CT (computerized tomography) scans enable
paleontologists to look inside fossil skulls and
other structures without destroying them. In
conventional X-rays, objects are compressed into
a single plane, but in CT, the X-rays are used to
produce a three-dimensional computer model
that can be manipulated within digital space.
Detailed structures that can only normally be
examined when a fossil is broken open, such as
the shape of the brain or the location of nerves
and blood vessels, can be viewed in this way.

PALEOBOTANY

THE STUDY OF FOSSIL PLANTS, or paleobotany, is the means by which scientists understand plant evolution. Fossilized plants are used by scientists to reconstruct prehistoric environments, and to understand the relationship among seed plants. Since the fossil record for plants is less complete than for animals, many questions about plant evolution are still unanswered. The oldest fossil plants are Precambrian calcareous algae, which lived in shallow seas and built stacked "mats" known as stromatolites. Plants did not begin to spread onto the land until about 410 million years ago. Early land plants were no more than simple shoots with a creeping root system. Ferns appeared in the Devonian period, while conifers and palmlike cycads appeared in the Mesozoic era. The flowering plants, which dominate the world today, did not appear until the Cretaceous period.

Woody plants, such as this cycad, are easily fossilized.

Cycad

COMMON FOSSIL PLANT PARTS
Most of the plant fossils that are found were deposited near lakes and swamps. Parts such as leaves, roots, fruit, and seeds are frequently preserved in detail. Windborne spores and pollen are tough because they are composed of a resistant organic material. Their microfossils are often found in rocks with no other evidence of life. Fragile petals are rarely fossilized.

IDENTIFYING FOSSIL PLANTS

Large plants often become fragmented during fossilization. Scientists then face the problem of matching the separate plant parts. Frequently, individual names are given to the various parts of the fossilized plant, such as its roots and cones. Many fossilized parts of the Carboniferous club moss *Lepidodendron* have been found. Sometimes the same part appears fossilized in different ways, such as in an impression or a cast. Scientists combine information on each part, drawn from a variety of fossil types, to build a picture of the complete plant.

Fossilized bark of *Lepidodendron*

Lepidostrobus **encased in ironstone**

The fossilized cone of the club moss Lepidodendron is called Lepidostrobus.

A cast of the inside of the stump and roots, created when fine sediment filled the hollow stump.

The fossilized root-bearing branches, or rhizophores, of Lepidodendron are called Stigmaria.

Fossilized tree stump of *Lepidodendron*

RECONSTRUCTING ANCIENT CLIMATES

Plant fossils can be used as indicators of prehistoric climates. Scientists study the density of stomata – pores through which gases pass in and out of plants – on fossilized leaves. The greater the density of the stomata, the lower the level of carbon dioxide in the atmosphere. Pleistocene pollen can be used to identify ice ages. During cold phases, arctic plant species predominated, while warm interglacial phases were reflected in a preponderance of subtropical species.

Glossopteris covered the continents once joined as Gondwana.

Distribution of *Glossopteris* during the Permian period

BIOGEOGRAPHY

The mapping of plant fossils is very useful in proving the movement of continents. For example, if finds of the Permian plant *Glossopteris* are plotted on a modern map, its distribution is meaningless. It is hard to understand how the same plant could be scattered over such vast distances and contrasting climates. However, if the *Glossopteris* finds are plotted on a reconstruction of the Permian world, they form a relatively continuous belt that runs across the cooler latitudes found in the southern continents.

Fossil pollen grain magnified hundreds of times

The fossil remains of plane trees are found in Late Cretaceous rocks of the northern hemisphere.

Eocene daisy pollen grain

Cretaceous plane tree pollen grain

FOSSIL POLLEN

The specialized study of fossilized pollen and spores is known as palynology. Pollen grains have distinctive shapes, so they are useful for identifying plants. Pollen and seeds can even provide information on the reproductive structure of ancient plants. Fossil pollen is also vital in dating rocks from which no other fossil remains have been recovered.

Lepidodendron grew to a height of more than 165 ft (50 m), and had rhizophores that could spread out for 40 ft (12 m).

PALEOECOLOGY

SCIENTISTS USE FOSSILS to reconstruct ancient communities and environments. By closely examining fossil organisms and the rocks in which they were deposited, paleoecologists can understand the environment in which the organisms lived. Paleoecology uses knowledge of modern ecological patterns to reconstruct past lifestyles. As in the modern world, ancient environments consisted of a range of habitats that included valleys, deserts, swamps, forests, reefs, and lakes. Each habitat contained a range of ecological niches, and each niche was inhabited by an animal or plant that had adapted to specific environmental conditions. Examination of a collection of fossils from a certain habitat allows scientists to reconstruct an entire ecosystem and to understand the ways in which extinct organisms may have coexisted and survived.

Scientist with an ice core sample

Glacial ice contains frozen air bubbles that give information on past atmospheres.

PAST ENVIRONMENTS

Frozen air bubbles trapped deep within a glacier reveal the makeup of ancient atmospheres. Similarly, the analysis of oxygen molecules trapped in the shells of marine organisms can indicate the temperature of the oceans and the atmosphere when the animal was alive. The distribution of plants can provide information about ancient climatic conditions. When the global climate was warmer than it is today, forests covered much of the globe and warm-habitat plants were found at higher latitudes. Finds of certain plant fossils can therefore give clues about the Earth's temperature at a particular point in global history.

Analysis of Cambrian trilobites shows that the seas were rich in carbonates and phosphates.

Trilobite *Xystridura*

Canis dirus and Thylacinus evolved lean bodies that enabled them to pursue prey over great distances.

***Thylacinus*, an Australian marsupial**

***Canis dirus*, the dire wolf, a North American placental mammal**

Thylacinus walked on its toes, just like Canis dirus.

Specialized shearing teeth called carnassials are unique to wolves and other carnivores.

ANCIENT SEAS

Fossils of marine organisms can reveal much about Earth's changing coastlines. They also indicate fluctuating sea levels during Earth's history. The shallow seas of the Cretaceous can be traced in deposits of chalk – the compressed bodies of millions of tiny algae called coccolith. Fossils can also provide more specific information. The shells of Foraminifera – Pleistocene marine protozoans – coiled to the left when sea temperatures were below 9°C (48°F), and coiled to the right when sea temperatures were higher.

PROVINCIAL ECOLOGY

Comparison of ancient ecosystems found in similar physical environments but different provinces (locations) can show how organisms adapted to environmental conditions. Life in Australia evolved in geographic isolation for millions of years, yet some marsupial mammals evolved so that they resembled placental mammals that lived in similar ecological niches on other continents.

RECONSTRUCTING ECOSYSTEMS

Paleoecologists piece together a prehistoric landscape by interpreting the fossils found in a particular habitat. Occasionally, scientists unearth a fossil site where extensive remains of plants, vertebrates, and invertebrates enable them to reconstruct an entire ecosystem with great confidence. At a quarry in Messel, Germany, scientists discovered fossils that allowed them to reconstruct an almost complete Early Tertiary community. The Messel site yielded fossils of more than 60 species of plant, as well as fossils for a complete succession of plant-eating insects, insect-eating vertebrates, and carnivorous predators.

Fossils of *Velociraptor* and *Protoceratops* locked in battle

Velociraptor aimed its feet at Protoceratops's neck in an attempt to slash its throat.

FROZEN IN TIME

Fossils can reveal interactions between ancient populations. Sometimes confrontations between species may be preserved – a predator's teeth marks can be visible on an animal's bones. In rare instances, fossil organisms are found joined in mortal combat. The stomach contents of a fossilized animal may yield an example of the species upon which it preyed. The Cretaceous fish *Rhacolepis* is often found preserved in the stomachs of larger fish, such as *Notelaps*.

Plant-eating dinosaurs such as Corythosaurus may have lived in herds to increase their protection against carnivorous predators.

Corythosaurus herd grazing

LIVING TOGETHER

Fossils can preserve evidence of physical and biological activity within a prehistoric population. Fossilized trackways show whether animals lived alone, in small groups, or in herds. Rare finds of preserved dinosaur eggs can indicate whether dinosaurs nested together, and can suggest how long the young remained in the nest. Fossilized animal droppings provide information on an animal's diet.

COMPARATIVE DATING

To FIT A FOSSIL into the wider picture of prehistory, paleontologists must know how old it is. In most cases, they work this out by studying its relationship to surrounding rocks and other fossils. Fossils only form in sedimentary strata – accumulated layers of rock formed by layers of compressed sediment. More recent strata, normally those relatively closer to the surface, will naturally contain younger fossils. Some fossils can also be important dating tools themselves – they can display distinctive changes in shape and structure over comparatively short timescales. Changes in fossils found within rock strata divide the part of the geological timescale covered in ths book into three great eras, subdivided into periods.

STUDYING STRATA

Unconformities (breaks in a layered sequence of rocks) complicate the structure of rock strata, but also give important clues to geological history. An unconformity is an old, buried erosion surface between two rock masses, such as where a period of uplift and erosion once removed some layered rock before the build up of sediment resumed.

Disconformity – an irregular, eroded surface between parallel strata

Parallel unconformity

Eroded outcrop of igneous rock

Unconformity

Sediments above unconformity indicate that it was under water – perhaps in a riverbed.

A missing layer of strata shows a gap in sedimentation, perhaps caused by a fall in water level.

STRATIGRAPHY

The examination of rock strata, called stratigraphy, is a vital tool for interpreting Earth's history. The basic principle of stratigraphy is that younger rocks are deposited on top of older ones – but unfortunately strata do not always lie neatly on top of each other in the order in which they formed. Continental drift and mountain building fold, fault, and contort rock strata, sometimes turning them completely upside down. Changing sea levels can accelerate or halt the build up of sediments, and upwelling molten rocks can also disrupt the sediments. Any interruption to the steady sequence of strata is called an unconformity.

Limestone containing Eocene Alveolina fossils

BIOSTRATIGRAPHY

Geological changes mean that a stratigraphic "column" does not always reflect a neat chronological sequence. Fossils of established age found in the rocks can be vital in establishing the history and current arrangement of the strata. They can also help to establish links between strata from very different localities, a process known as correlation. By matching and comparing rock and fossil samples from diverse locations, geologists have been able to devise a general stratigraphic history.

*Angular unconformity –
rocks below tilt at
different angles from
those above.*

*This unconformity is
the eroded surface
of folded strata,
once mountaintops.*

INDEX FOSSILS

Scientists subdivide the geological
timescale into many units: aeons, eras,
periods, epochs, ages, and zones. A
zone is a small unit of geological time,
defined by the evolutionary history of
certain organisms, known as index
fossils. The most useful index fossils are
organisms that evolved rapidly and spread
widely so they define a limited time zone
over a large geographical area. Common
fossils, such as ammonites, brachiopods,
and trilobites are used as index fossils.
They are widely distributed and are
easily recovered from marine
sediments, and they show enough
variation over time to provide easily
recognizable chronological markers.

*Pleuropugnoides –
Carboniferous only*

Fossil brachiopods

*Derbiya –
Carboniferous
to Permian*

*Dyke of igneous
rock intruding
into older strata*

*Disconformity shows
where a riverbed
once ran.*

Paleocene nummulite microfossils

MICROFOSSILS AS DATING TOOLS

The smallest of fossils can also be
used as index fossils. They are
particularly useful for dating
rocks that have been recovered
from boreholes such as those
used in oil exploration. A very
narrow rock core can yield a large
number of useful fossils. Dating
rocks and correlating finds between
boreholes is a vital tool in finding
and recovering mineral wealth from
great depths.

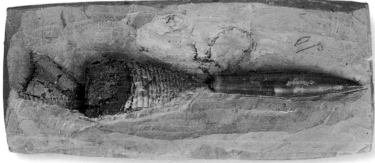

**Cretaceous
belemnite**

COMMON INDEX FOSSILS

Index fossils are used to date rocks on a
worldwide basis. A number of distinctive
organisms are closely associated with
different geological periods. Trilobites are
used for dating in the Cambrian,
graptolites in the Ordovician and Silurian,
ammonites and belemnites in the Jurassic
and Cretaceous. Microfossils become
important in the Mesozoic era, and small
unicellular fossils called foraminiferans are used
in the Tertiary. In some periods, such as the
Triassic, index fossils are rare because of a lack of
marine sediments. The history of these periods is
therefore particularly hard to decipher.

Ordovician graptolite

Early Jurassic ammonites

CHRONOMETRIC DATING

THE DISCOVERY OF NATURAL RADIOACTIVITY has revolutionized dating in geology and paleontology. By measuring the rate at which certain elements in rock formations decay into other forms, the age of the rocks can be calculated. This "chronometric" dating method converts the sequence of rock formations, established by stratigraphy and comparative dating, into an absolute scale measured in millions of years. For example, it has established that the oldest-known rocks on Earth, from northwestern Canada, are about 3,900 million years old. Other chronometric dating methods track changes in the planet's magnetic field, or measure traces left by the decay of radioactive uranium. Chronometric and fossil dates are complementary – fossils are still used to measure fine divisions, while chronometric dates provide a broad framework.

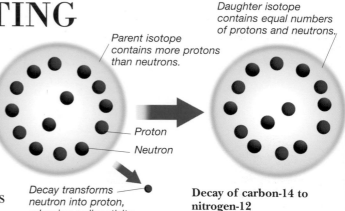

Parent isotope contains more protons than neutrons.

Daughter isotope contains equal numbers of protons and neutrons.

Proton

Neutron

Decay transforms neutron into proton, releasing radioactivity.

Decay of carbon-14 to nitrogen-12

ISOTOPES AND RADIOACTIVITY
The central nucleus of any atom is made up of two types of subatomic particle – protons, which govern its chemical behavior and determine which element it forms, and neutrons, which give it extra mass. But most elements can exist in different isotopes – atoms with the same numbers of protons but different numbers of neutrons and therefore different weights. Radioactivity occurs when an excess of neutrons in a parent isotope makes the atom unstable. It splits or decays into other elements, releasing radioactivity in the process.

RADIOMETRIC DATING
Radiometric dating measures the proportions of isotopes (atoms of different atomic weight) in so-called radioactive elements. When a molten rock cools and hardens, the isotopes in its radioactive elements decay into lighter ones at a steady rate, so their proportions slowly but steadily change. The amount of an isotope left in a sample indicates how much time has passed since this radioactive clock was set to zero. The decay rate of a specific isotope is measured by its half-life – the time taken for half of the parent atoms in a sample to decay. After one half-life, only 50 percent of the parent isotopes will be left. After two half-lives, 25 percent, and so on.

Measuring isotopes with a mass spectrometer

Computer displays results.

Sample injected in liquid form

PREPARATION AND MEASUREMENT
In order to measure the proportions of different isotopes in a sample, scientists use a machine called a mass spectrometer, which measures the relative amounts of isotopes with different masses. The proportion of radioactive isotopes left in the mineral indicates how much time has passed since its radioactive clock was set. Scientists measure a number of different decay processes. The decay of uranium-235 is used for measuring the oldest rocks because it involves a slow series of decays through several forms. Potassium-40's decay into argon is also widely used because potassium is so widespread.

Preparing a sample for radiometric dating

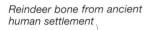
Reindeer bone from ancient human settlement

Sample of material is scraped off, powdered, and dissolved into liquid form for mass spectrometry.

RADIOCARBON DATING

One of the most successful radiometric dating methods is based on the decay of the radioactive isotope carbon-14 (C-14). This isotope is constantly absorbed from the atmosphere by living things, and a fixed proportion of the carbon in any living organism will be radioactive. But when a creature dies, it no longer absorbs carbon, and the C-14 within it starts to decay. Radiocarbon dating is used to provide accurate dates for organic materials, such as shells, bones, and charcoal. However, because C-14 decays relatively quickly (its half-life is 5,730 years), it cannot date material more than around 70,000 years old – there is simply not enough C-14 left in older organisms. The method is very accurate and has revolutionized studies of early humans. It can be used, for example, to date isolated sites – such as abandoned campfires – where no other remains have been found.

FISSION-TRACK DATING

This recent dating method measures the spontaneous fission (breaking apart) of the radioactive isotope uranium-238 within minerals such as zircon. In this unique type of radioactive decay, the nucleus of a single parent uranium atom splits into two fragments of similar mass with such force that a trail of crystal damage, known as a fission track, is made in the mineral. The number of tracks present increases over time, at a rate dependent on the mineral's overall uranium content. A microscope is used to measure the number of fission tracks and the uranium content of a mineral, and the age of the rock is calculated from these measurements.

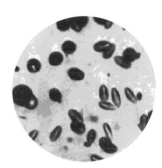

Close-up of fission tracks

Zircon crystal

Satellite map of mid-ocean floor

Mid-ocean ridges show where new basaltic rock forms as the seafloor spreads apart.

Ridges farther from the center were formed further back in time.

Basaltic rock preserves the direction and strength of the Earth's magnetism as it solidifies.

PALEOMAGNETISM

The Earth's magnetic field has reversed at irregular intervals throughout its history – magnetic North periodically becomes magnetic South. Magnetic minerals in rocks become aligned with the Earth's magnetic field and become fixed in that magnetic orientation when the rock is formed. By studying the volcanic rocks steadily produced over millions of years at the spreading centers of Earth's ocean floors, scientists have built up a complete record of Earth's magnetic reversals. Rock samples from elsewhere – for example volcanic flows with fossil footprints in them – can be matched with this overall record of Earth's magnetism to determine where they fit into the sequence.

RECONSTRUCTING FOSSILS

THE DETECTIVE WORK REQUIRED to put a fossil animal back together can be very complex. Usually, only the hard parts of an organism become fossilized, and often only small fragments of these are found. Paleontologists have to identify the fossil from remains such as shells, teeth, or bones. They usually assume that the missing pieces, with few exceptions, will resemble those of the animal's closest relatives, and use these as a guide for making replacement parts. Once a complete skeleton has been assembled, scientists can reconstruct the size, shape, and posture of the living creature. By examining fossil remains of plants and other organisms, they can even reconstruct the entire ecosystem where the animal once lived. Nevertheless, reconstructions are only models, representing our current state of knowledge – our picture of extinct life forms changes with each new find, and many fossil reconstructions undergo substantial revisions.

Latex coating painted onto fossil Barosaurus _pelvis_

MAKING THE MOLD
There are many techniques for copying fossils. Generally, a mold is made by painting the outside with layers of latex or silicone rubber, which sets into a solid but flexible mirror-image of the original. This can then be peeled away to reveal an impression of the original fossil.

MAKING A REPRODUCTION
Most excavated fossils are too delicate or too cumbersome to put back together and display in a museum. Many fossils are also only impressions rather than exact replicas of the original structure that formed them, and so could not be rebuilt anyway. For reconstruction of a skeleton, replica bones are usually cast in materials that are light, strong, and durable. The first step in reproducing a fossil is to make a mold from the original, which can then be used to cast replicas. When parts of a fossil animal are missing, skilled sculptors recreate bones based on the animal's relatives, and the mold is then made from these clay sculptures.

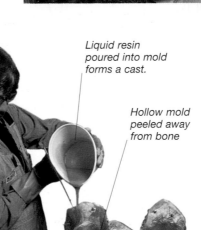

Liquid resin poured into mold forms a cast.

Hollow mold peeled away from bone

CASTING
The mold is now filled with a modeling material, such as fiberglass-reinforced plastic, or plaster of Paris. This hardens as it dries. If the fossil in question is already an impression, the molding substance can be poured directly into it. When the fossil is more fragile than the surrounding rock, acid is used to dissolve the fossil and create a rock mold.

Mold is removed from cast for finishing.

REMOVING THE MOLD
The mold is now gently separated from the cast. Any rough edges on the replica fossil are carefully filed away, and the replica is painted so that it resembles the original fossil. In some cases, casts of sculpted replacement bones are deliberately colored differently in order to highlight them.

MAKING THE FRAMEWORK

Steel supports for bones of a reproduction are designed by a structural engineer. They must be as light and slender as possible, yet carry the finished model's weight when it is mounted into a realistic posture. The framework is prepared by blacksmiths and metalworkers, and each bone cast is cut and drilled so steel tubes can run through the center.

CONNECTING THE PIECES

Once the bones of an animal have been replicated, they are laid out in relation to each other. A mount maker then reconstructs the animal's posture based on available evidence such as fossil footprints and computer models of how the animal may have moved. Sometimes, reconstructions can put forward new and controversial ideas – for example, the huge *Barosaurus* at the American Museum of Natural History (AMNH) in New York is mounted rearing on its hind legs. Paleontologists are still arguing about whether *Barosaurus* could really have done this, but the reconstruction speaks volumes about the way our view of dinosaurs has changed since the 1970s.

AMNH *Barosaurus* display

FINAL ASSEMBLY

Frequently fossil reproductions are made in special laboratories, and have to be shipped, piece by piece, to museums for display. Using photographs and detailed plans as a guide, museum technicians first arrange the pieces in the correct position on the display floor. The model is then assembled from the base upward. As the parts are mounted, the steel framework is welded together to ensure that the reproduction is stable.

Long steel tubes link neck vertebrae.

Barosaurus's center of mass is very far back over its hips – evidence that it may have reared.

Steel joists through leg bones support weight.

Predatory Allosaurus – several dinosaurs 0are often displayed together in a scene.

Baby Barosaurus hides behind its mother.

RESTORING FOSSIL ANIMALS

FLESHING OUT THE BONES of a fossil animal to restore its appearance when alive is a painstaking scientific process. Paleontologists have to combine information from other, comparable finds with a detailed knowledge of the anatomy of modern animals. They comb their excavation sites for extra clues, which can reveal the terrain in which the animal lived, the food it ate, and its interaction with other animals. Despite this careful detective work, some of the choices made when restoring extinct animals are simply a matter of educated guesswork – skin texture and color, for example, can rarely be confirmed by fossil finds. The history of paleontology has been one of continual revision – as more information is gathered about extinct life-forms, restorations are updated and, in some cases, radically reinterpreted.

EARLY ATTEMPTS
The first dinosaur restorations to gain public attention were the life-sized models exhibited at London's Crystal Palace in 1854. Designed by paleontologist Richard Owen, they showed dinosaurs as lumbering, elephantlike creatures walking on four legs. This view was overtaken in the early 20th century by the work of artists and illustrators. They used their skills as draftsmen, and their understanding of wild animals, to create memorable illustrations of extinct animals, placed within the context of fully-imagined prehistoric landscapes. Among the pioneers of this new type of dinosaur restoration were Erwin Christman and Charles Knight, who worked at the American Museum of Natural History.

Megalosaurus **restoration**

Megalosaurus **jaw**

RESTORING A FOSSIL
Most restorations are based on fossilized bones, since soft parts are rarely preserved. Bones can give an expert detailed information about the creature's anatomy, size, and stance, while muscle attachment points can also indicate the design of the musculature. A detailed drawing or model of an accurately reconstructed skeleton is the starting point for any full-scale restoration. Using this as a framework, specialized artists and sculptors can, in consultation with paleontologists, reconstruct the layers of muscle and flesh that overlaid it in life.

RESEARCH
Reconstruction is based on the best available research about the animal and its relatives. Fossil trackways reveal information about stance and movement. Fossilized stomach contents, teeth, and claws can also provide useful information about diet and lifestyle. Skin impressions are rare, but the few finds indicate that dinosaurs were covered with non-overlapping scales. Skin color is a matter of guesswork, based on our understanding of how camouflage and display coloring works in living animals.

Fossilized dinosaur skin

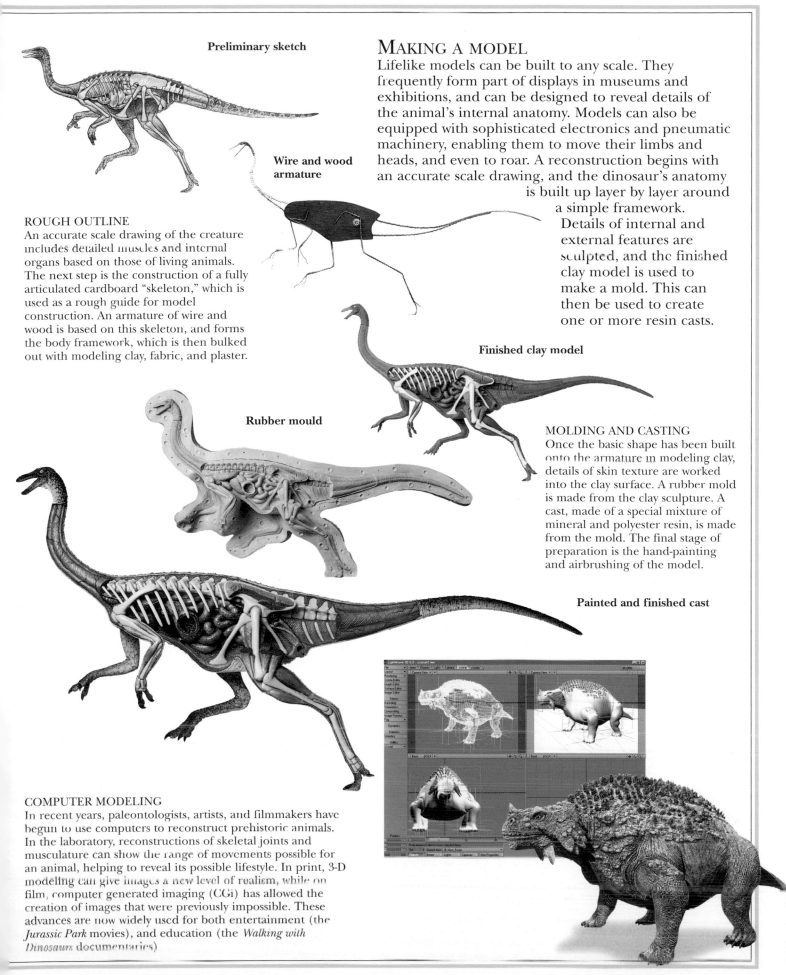

Preliminary sketch

MAKING A MODEL

Lifelike models can be built to any scale. They frequently form part of displays in museums and exhibitions, and can be designed to reveal details of the animal's internal anatomy. Models can also be equipped with sophisticated electronics and pneumatic machinery, enabling them to move their limbs and heads, and even to roar. A reconstruction begins with an accurate scale drawing, and the dinosaur's anatomy is built up layer by layer around a simple framework. Details of internal and external features are sculpted, and the finished clay model is used to make a mold. This can then be used to create one or more resin casts.

Wire and wood armature

ROUGH OUTLINE

An accurate scale drawing of the creature includes detailed muscles and internal organs based on those of living animals. The next step is the construction of a fully articulated cardboard "skeleton," which is used as a rough guide for model construction. An armature of wire and wood is based on this skeleton, and forms the body framework, which is then bulked out with modeling clay, fabric, and plaster.

Finished clay model

Rubber mould

MOLDING AND CASTING

Once the basic shape has been built onto the armature in modeling clay, details of skin texture are worked into the clay surface. A rubber mold is made from the clay sculpture. A cast, made of a special mixture of mineral and polyester resin, is made from the mold. The final stage of preparation is the hand-painting and airbrushing of the model.

Painted and finished cast

COMPUTER MODELING

In recent years, paleontologists, artists, and filmmakers have begun to use computers to reconstruct prehistoric animals. In the laboratory, reconstructions of skeletal joints and musculature can show the range of movements possible for an animal, helping to reveal its possible lifestyle. In print, 3-D modeling can give images a new level of realism, while on film, computer generated imaging (CGi) has allowed the creation of images that were previously impossible. These advances are now widely used for both entertainment (the *Jurassic Park* movies), and education (the *Walking with Dinosaurs* documentaries)

FOSSIL HUNTER

FOSSIL HUNTING can be a rewarding pastime –
where it is allowed. In some countries,
collecting fossils is illegal on public, and
sometimes even on private, land. Elsewhere,
fossil hunters are allowed to collect and keep
the fossils they find. Before hunting for fossils,
you must find out which rules apply in the area
you will be searching. The following 10 pages
provide all the information an amateur
collector needs to get started. The first two
pages explain how to find suitable sites to look
for fossils, what to wear and take on a fossil
hunt, and safe practices to follow in the field.
The next two pages describe how to collect
fossils, and how to prepare finds for storage
and display. The six pages that complete the
fossil hunter section provide a mini fossil
identification key for vertebrates,
invertebrates, and plants.

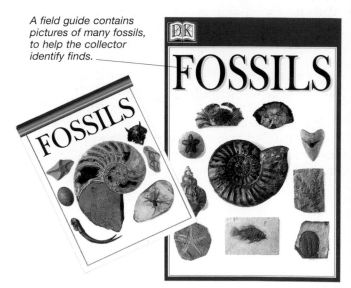

A field guide contains
pictures of many fossils,
to help the collector
identify finds.

RESEARCH AND REFERENCE

Fossils are not found in every rock, so before
a fossil hunt can begin it is vital to research,
not just the fossil-collecting rules of that area,
but the geology of the area. Maps, guides, and
other fossil hunters are all useful sources of
information. Many fossil sites are listed and
described in geological guidebooks, at regional
museums, and at tourist information centers.
Famous fossil sites, or those that are known to
yield scientifically valuable specimens, are usually
protected, and collecting fossils at these places
is strictly prohibited. When out on a field trip,
a field guide is useful to help you identify
and understand the fossils you might see.

Geological map

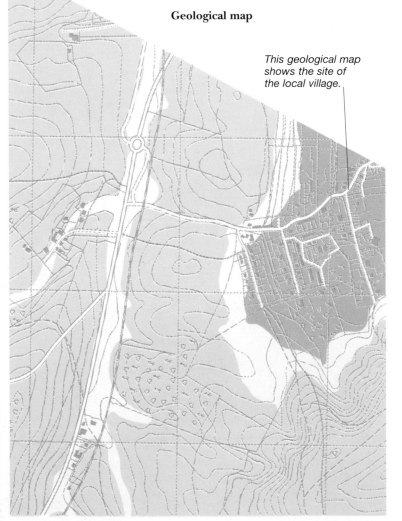

This geological map
shows the site of
the local village.

Key to geological units

Upper chalk

Lower chalk

Clay

A plastic sieve
is used to sift fine
sand and dirt, and
leave larger items.

MAP MATTERS
A geological map shows the
pattern of rock formations
in different areas. Each band
of color on this type of map
represents a different geological
unit – rock of a certain age –
and shows what type of rock
is at the surface. Units may
be named after the site where
they were first described. Fossils
usually occur in sedimentary
rock, such as chalk, limestone,
and sandstone. A regular map
printed on top of the geological
map helps the user establish
a unit's location.

WHAT TO WEAR

Most fossils are found in rough, rocky terrain, so fossil hunters should wear sturdy boots for walking. It is wise to check weather forecasts before setting off, and to wear clothing that is suitable for the climate. In cold or wet weather, collectors should take sufficient warm and waterproof clothing. If it is going to be sunny, a long-sleeved shirt and high-protection sun cream will provide added protection. Field equipment can be carried in a knapsack, along with adequate supplies of food and water. Most importantly, the careful collector should take a small first-aid kit, in case of cuts or grazes.

A woolly hat keeps the head warm.

Long, waterproof jacket for protection during wet weather.

magnifying glass

Compass

Camera for taking pictures of a location or find.

Protective sun cream is applied to the skin in sunny weather.

Thick socks make boots more comfortable.

Tape measure for measuring the size of finds.

Tough pants or jeans are practical.

Sturdy boots

Summer clothes   **Winter clothes**

A notebook and pencil are useful for recording notes and sketches of finds in the field.

EQUIPMENT

Tools can only be used at sites where fossil collecting is permitted. They should be kept to a minimum to reduce weight. When working in soft sediment – such as sand or clay – a trowel can be used to clear the area around the fossil. Sieves are used for separating fossils easily from sand and gravel. Newspaper or plastic bags can be used to protect fossil finds. A notebook, pen, magnifying glass, and camera will help the collector to examine, identify, and record finds.

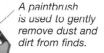
A paintbrush is used to gently remove dust and dirt from finds.

Adult supervising child collector

SAFE PRACTICES

Before starting a fossil hunt, collectors should ensure that they will not trespass and should obtain permission to visit a site, if necessary. Children should always be accompanied by an adult. There is a danger of rock fall at cliff faces, so collectors should stay away from overhangs. When hunting at coastal sites, collectors should be aware of incoming tides, which can be dangerous. It is vital to check safety guidelines at quarries before venturing on-site.

HIDDEN TREASURE

ONCE THE AMATEUR FOSSIL HUNTER has identified a likely fossil site, the process of scanning the landscape for fossils can begin. If the amateur hunter is allowed to take samples away, finds should be carefully wrapped and taken home, where the next part of the fossil-hunting adventure takes place. The first task is to carefully clean fossil finds and to strengthen any fragile specimens. Then, fossils should be identified by comparing finds with illustrations and detailed descriptions, which can be found in many specialist books. Once identified, the specimens should be labeled and cataloged in a card index on which information about individual specimens can be recorded. Fossils can be stored in special collection cabinets or in plastic boxes and cardboard trays.

SIFT AND SORT
A sieve is an effective way to carefully separate fossils from sand and gravel. It is often the best way to find fossils on a riverbank. Sieves with either plastic or wire mesh screens can be used. Two or three shovelfuls of sand should be dug up and tipped into the sieve. Using a gentle circular motion, the sand should be gradually allowed to run through the sieve, leaving large fragments of rock and fossil, which can be easily sorted out.

Sieving can be done with an ordinary fine-mesh garden sieve.

An ammonite fossil can clearly be seen embedded in seashore rocks.

OUT AND ABOUT
Hunting is easiest in places where rocks have become exposed to reveal their fossil wealth, such as beaches, road cuttings, quarries, and the banks of streams that cut into rock. Fossils found loose on the seashore are usually heavier than shells and are of a uniform color – generally dark gray or white. Fossils found inland are often embedded within a lump of rock called a nodule, which can be gently eased out of surrounding rocks. It is important that records are kept of exactly where and in what kind of rock each fossil was found. Finds should be wrapped in paper towels or newspaper for protection.

A CLOSER LOOK

Fossils are often very small, so it may be difficult to see fine detail with the naked eye. A magnifying glass is useful for examining finds up close.

The most useful magnification is x8 or x10. In some places, such as national parks, fossils cannot be picked up. When the handling of fossils is allowed, the magnifying glass should be held 2 in (5 cm) from the eye, with the fossil held the same distance from the glass.

Brightly colored string tied to the magnifying glass makes it easy to find if dropped in the field.

Fossil is protected in cotton balls in a shallow display box.

IDENTIFICATION AND STORAGE

Notes taken in the field are useful when identifying fossil finds. These notes can be checked against information in reference books to confirm a fossil's identity. Fossils should be stored in a cool, dry place. Specially designed wooden display cabinets can be used, but most collectors opt for simpler storage arrangements, such as cardboard boxes, jam jars, and matchboxes. Each find should be carefully labeled. A good method is to give the fossil a number that refers to its record in a catalog or card index. Records should hold as much information about the fossil as possible, including its name, where it was found, and the date of its collection.

A toothbrush or paintbrush should be used carefully to remove dust.

CLEANING AND MENDING

It is best to practice cleaning techniques on unimportant fossils. Brushes can be used to remove any dirt that surrounds a fossil. Vinegar, a weak acid, will remove rock from chalky specimens. Forceps or tweezers can be used when handling tiny specimens. Fragile fossils can be strengthened with a coating of a 10 percent solution of water-soluble glue in water with a drop or two of detergent. If a sample is retrieved in pieces, it can be glued together using an acetone-soluble glue.

Spoon plaster into the fossil, ensuring all cracks are filled.

Fossil

Plaster cast of the fossil

MAKING A MODEL

Sometimes a fossil takes the form of an imprint in the rock. It is then possible to make a plaster of Paris model, using the fossil as a mold, to see what the creature looked like. First, the fossil should be cleaned and the surface brushed with petroleum jelly to prevent the plaster from adhering. Plaster of Paris should be mixed and spooned onto the fossil, ensuring all indentations are filled. The mold should be left to set. Then the cast can be pryed away from the fossil to reveal the replica.

INVERTEBRATES

THE MOST ABUNDANT FOSSILS are of invertebrate animals. Invertebrates lived in high concentrations and frequently in conditions where fossilization was likely to occur, such as shallow seas and reefs. Hard invertebrate shells are able to withstand the rigors of fossilization. Arthropods and molluscs are well-represented in the fossil record, while more delicate, land-dwelling creatures are not very well preserved.

CORAL

Coral are marine animals with a skeleton of calcium carbonate, saclike body (polyp), mouth, and tentacles. Many coral species live in branching colonies and form large, moundlike coral reefs in tropical oceans. Other coral forms remain relatively solitary and are often found fossilized in shale, which indicates that they preferred the muddy ocean bed. Coral are among the most common fossils on Earth. They are abundant in Paleozoic limestone and shale. Fossilized coral can be hornlike, tubelike, or treelike. The size of a colony varies from less than 0.3 in (1 cm) to several feet.

Trachyphyllia

External wall of this solitary coral

BRYOZOANS

Bryozoans live in colonies that are made up of thousands of individual organisms. Most colonies are about 1.2 in (3 cm) across, but they may reach widths of 24 in (60 cm). Branching, twiglike bryozoans are found in limestone and may be preserved in surfaces that have weathered away.

Schizoretepora

These tiny fossils are best seen with a hand lens.

AMMONITES

Female shell is larger than its male counterpart

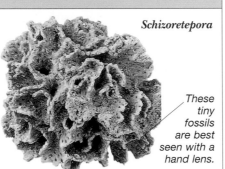

Ammonites are extinct invertebrates whose chambered shells were straight or coiled. Some shells had wavy sutures (joins). Ammonites were abundant and diverse in Mesozoic seas, but they suffered a marked decline in diversity in the Late Cretaceous and became extinct by the end of the Cretaceous. Ammonites were creatures of open tropical seas and their fossils are found in great numbers in limestone from tropical reefs. Their fossils are also found in shale from lagoons and deeper water. The smallest ammonites were only about 0.1 in (3 mm) in width, although coiled ammonites over 10 ft (3 m) in diameter have been found.

Alternate long and short ribs

Mantelliceras

TRILOBITES

Elrathia

The most numerous organisms of the Early Paleozoic, trilobite fossils are common in Cambrian, Ordovician, and Silurian rocks worldwide. Their remains can be found in all types of sedimentary rock. They ranged from several inches to about 35 in (90 cm) in length. Many fossil finds are exoskeletons discarded during molting, not fossils of the animals themselves.

GASTROPODS

The spiral whorls of the shell are encircled by ridges, or keels.

Gastropods are successful molluscs that use a flattened foot for crawling. They have a head with eyes and a mouth, and carry their viscera (abdominal organs) coiled in a spiral shell. Evolutionary changes can be traced in the shape of the shell. The most ancient gastropod shells show no coiling. Eventually, shells began to coil on a single plane. Later forms had complex, three dimensional coils that twist and spiral. Marine gastropods live mainly in shallow waters, though some have been found at depths of over 3 miles (5 km). Gastropod fossils are usually preserved in certain limestone, either intact or as empty molds. They range in size from 0.7 to 4.7 in (2 to 12 cm).

Ecphora **shell**

BIVALVES

Concentric ridges

Crassatella **shell**

Bivalves include oysters, clams, and mussels. The bodies of bivalves are held within two symmetrical, chalky shells (valves) that are joined by an elastic ligament. Shells may grow to over 12 in (30 cm) in diameter. Bivalves are most abundant in shallow marine waters, where they burrow in soft sediment. Fossil molds of shells are frequent finds, as many shells dissolved after being encased in rock. Single shells are also common, since shells often separated after the creature's death.

BRACHIOPODS

Platystrophia **shell**

The brachiopod body is surrounded by two shells (valves) joined by a hinge. Fossils can be found attached to the sea floor, in muddy shale, and in mudstone. Brachiopod shells are often found in joined pairs, since shells tend to stay closed after the animal's death. Fossil shells average 0.7 to 3 in (2 to 7 cm) in length.

CRINOIDS

Crinoids, or sea lilies, consist of a cup, a number of feather arms that catch food, and a long stem that anchors them to the sea floor or driftwood. Crinoids were so abundant in Paleozoic seas that their calcite stems formed vast masses of limestone. The typical diameter of a crinoid cup was 1 in (2.5 cm), and whole specimens average about 6 in (15 cm) in length. The best specimens are found in limestone, such as the Silurian rocks of England and the Mississippian rocks of the US. A complete fossil crinoid is rarely found, as the body separates when the animal dies. Crinoid stems, with their button-shaped discs, are often found under logs.

Cyathocrinites

Branching arms

Cup

ECHINOIDS

Hemiaster

Echinoids, or sea urchins, have rigid calcite skeletons covered by spines for defense. Their geological record stretches back to the Ordovician, but it was not until the Mesozoic that they proliferated. They are abundant in Jurassic and Cretaceous rocks. Isolated spines are common finds.

BELEMNITES

Guard made of calcium carbonate

Belemnitella **guard**

Belemnites had an internal, chambered shell that was enclosed by soft, muscular tissue. Their strong, cylindrical guards preserved well, and are abundant in Mesozoic marine rock. Fossilized guards vary in length from 0.3 in (1 cm) to specimens tens of inches in length. These guards are a fraction of the size of the living animal, whose body and long tentacles extended beyond the guard.

VERTEBRATES

THE EARLIEST FOSSILS of vertebrates are tiny "scale bones" that belonged to jawless fish and are found in Late Cambrian rocks. Despite their long evolutionary history and great abundance, complete fish fossils are rather rare – sea water, currents, and swirling sediment break up and disperse fossil remains. Although higher vertebrates, such as reptiles and mammals, live in a wide range of environments, their fossil remains are also uncommon. The best sites for preservation are in shallow marine rocks, along old river channels, and in caves. The most common vertebrate parts to be fossilized are teeth, which are made of durable enamel.

CARTILAGINOUS FISH

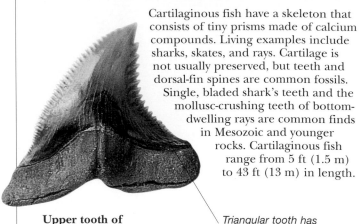

Cartilaginous fish have a skeleton that consists of tiny prisms made of calcium compounds. Living examples include sharks, skates, and rays. Cartilage is not usually preserved, but teeth and dorsal-fin spines are common fossils. Single, bladed shark's teeth and the mollusc-crushing teeth of bottom-dwelling rays are common finds in Mesozoic and younger rocks. Cartilaginous fish range from 5 ft (1.5 m) to 43 ft (13 m) in length.

Upper tooth of the shark *Hemipristis*

Triangular tooth has serrated cutting edge.

ARMORED FISH

Overlapping bony plates

Bothriolepis **body shield**

Armored fish, or placoderms, first appeared in the Devonian and are now extinct. They were distinguished by their primitive jaws, which were armed with slicing plates. They also had heavily armored head shields and trunks. Small scales protected the rest of the body and the tail. Armored fish lived on the seabed in marine and fresh water. Although their average length was no more than 5.5–16 in (14–40 cm), some species grew to a great size – *Dunkleosteus* was more than 10 ft (3 m) long.

JAWLESS FISH

The oldest fossil fish lack jaws – the mouth is simply an opening – and they are covered by thick plates and scales. They had heavy head skeletons, but their cartilaginous internal skeletons were lighter. Early species lived in the sea, but by the Silurian, jawless fish had moved into fresh and brackish (somewhat salty) water. These heavily armored fish make robust fossils. Headshields are well-represented in the fossil record, and are particularly common in red rocks from the Silurian and Devonian.

Head shield of *Pteraspis*

A series of immovable bony plates formed an effective defense.

BONY FISH

Fish that belong to this class are characterized by a bony internal skeleton. The majority of living fish are part of this group, although they do not share common ancestors. The complex classification of bony fish is based on fin structure. Ray-finned fish have fins supported by bony rods, while lobe-finned fish have fleshy fins, supported by a single bone at the base. This group includes the coelacanth, the most famous "living fossil." Ray-finned fish are very diverse and abundant, yet they have left comparatively few remains, as water breaks up and disperses fish skeletons. Fish fossils can be found in shale, especially in marine black shale or in shale deposited in lakes.

Priscacara **skeleton**

AMPHIBIANS

Frog fossil

The Carboniferous is popularly known as the "age of the amphibians," since the group achieved an unequalled dominance in the vertebrate world at that time. Most amphibian fossils are of wholly or partially aquatic amphibians, and are found in rocks formed from Carboniferous coal swamps. Fossils of land-dwelling Paleozoic amphibians are recognized by their distinctive teeth and flattened skulls.

ANAPSID REPTILES

Highly textured surface

Shell of turtle *Trionyx*

Reptiles are grouped into subclasses according to the number of skull openings and the arrangement of skull bones behind the eye sockets. The Anapsida were the earliest reptiles. The first forms, which appeared about 300 million years ago, were small, lizardlike creatures that had evolved from an amphibian ancestor. Although anapsid reptiles adapted to a wide range of environments, fossil finds are comparatively rare. Terrestrial surfaces are not conducive to preservation, and fossils frequently became scattered and fragmented.

DIAPSID REPTILES

The Diapsida evolved during the Carboniferous, and achieved maximum diversity during the Mesozoic era, when diapsid reptiles, such as dinosaurs, marine reptiles, and pterosaurs, dominated life on Earth. Fossils are found worldwide, and include skeleton parts, teeth, and body armor.

Scutes of crocodile *Goniopholis*

BIRDS

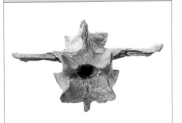

Hesperornis **vertebra**

The diapsid reptiles called birds evolved from one of the carnivorous dinosaur families. The earliest bird remains come from Jurassic rocks. More modern birds quickly diversified at the end of the Cretaceous, when many other reptiles became extinct. Fossilized birds are very rare because the evolution of flight led to generally light and fragile skeletons.

MAMMALS

Mammals are animals that suckle their young. Early mammals were present in the Triassic period. During the Cenozoic era, mammals have become the dominant group, and have colonized most of the Earth's surface. Teeth make up most mammal fossil remains. Their variety reflects the specialized nature of mammal teeth, which have evolved to carry out different activities. Repositories for fossil teeth include the sediment that fills caves and fissures in limestone. Other fossil finds include jaw bones and other skeletal parts, and horns. Hair is rarely fossilized.

Lower jaw of bear

The jaw and tooth of this bear are well-adapted for crushing and chewing.

PLANTS

LAND PLANTS BEGAN TO EVOLVE in the Silurian, initially in bogs, rivers, and lakes. By the end of the Devonian, plants occupied almost every terrestrial habitat. Plant fossils are very common in Carboniferous and Tertiary rocks. Much of the coal (rock formed from fossil plants) that is mined comes from Carboniferous rocks, and plant fossils are usually found in coal beds. Plant fossils are commonly found in rocks that were once part of freshwater lakes or river deltas, and in the fossilized remains of peat. The chance of fossilization is much better in low-lying, swampy areas, and in temperate climates. Plant fossils are usually separated into seeds, leaves, and stems – finds of complete plants are extremely rare. Many plants are preserved as three-dimensional casts or as carbonized impressions.

HORSETAILS

Asterophyllites

Carbonized branches attached to jointed stems.

Horsetails were once widespread and varied, and even included trees that reached up to 66 ft (20 m) in height. Fossils of these jointed plants, with their featherlike appearance, are easy to recognize. Horsetails thrived in the Carboniferous and are frequently found in the soft, dark shale associated with coal seams. They are also found in freshwater sediment from the Jurassic and the Cretaceous.

ALGAE

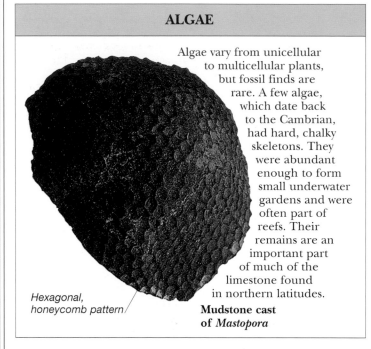

Algae vary from unicellular to multicellular plants, but fossil finds are rare. A few algae, which date back to the Cambrian, had hard, chalky skeletons. They were abundant enough to form small underwater gardens and were often part of reefs. Their remains are an important part of much of the limestone found in northern latitudes.

Hexagonal, honeycomb pattern

Mudstone cast of *Mastopora*

CLUB MOSSES

Lepidodendron **bark**

Club mosses date from the Late Silurian. Many Carboniferous trees were club mosses, and their trunks were important in coal formation. Club mosses have long, narrow leaves, and produce spores from their cones. Their extensive root systems were often fossilized.

EARLY LAND PLANTS

Spore capsule

Zosterophyllum

The earliest land plants, found in Silurian and Devonian rocks, were simple shoots that emerged from a ground-hugging root. Spore-bearing capsules appeared along the sides or at the tips of upright, spiked branches. These early plants vary in size from no more than 3 in (7.5 cm) to about 3 ft 3 in (1 m) tall. The best fossil remains of these early land plants occur as dark markings on shale.

FERNS

The fossil record of ferns extends back to the Mid Devonian, and they thrived during the Carboniferous. Ferns were found in a wide range of environments – from tropical forests to temperate zones – but they required a humid environment for reproduction. Ferns are characterized by delicate fronds, or leaves. They reproduced by means of minute spores, which formed in clusters on the underside of the fronds. Although many ferns were small, they occasionally grew to the size of trees, extending to heights of 13–16 ft (4–5 m). Tree ferns broke apart after fossilization, and today are only represented by fragmentary fossils of fronds and trunks.

Leaf bases were preserved in this silicified fossil – silica became incorporated into the decaying wood as it fossilized.

Section of *Osmunda* stem

CONIFERS

The ancestry of the conifers stretches back to the forests of the Carboniferous, and these trees are still very much in evidence today. Conifer trees grew to an average height of 98 ft (30 m), and had long, slender trunks. Some ancient conifers, such as *Sequoia*, reached heights of about 230 ft (70 m), and formed extensive forests in subtropical regions. Today, these conifers are restricted to coastal California. In temperate climates, conifer trunks terminated in needle-shaped leaves, while in tropical climates the leaves were flat and broad. Seeds were contained in fir cones, which often became carbonized (reduced to carbon) or silicified, and preserved as robust fossils. Some species of conifer, such as the *Araucaria*, or monkey puzzle tree, have survived with little change since the Jurassic.

Diamond pattern of woody bracts on cone

Carbonized spruce cone

CYCADS

Cycad leaves

The palmlike cycads grew in the forests of the Mesozoic era. They were distinguished by leafless stems that were crowned by a mass of stiff, large leaves. A cycad plant reproduced by means of a large, seed-bearing cob, which emerged from the crown of the tree. Fossil finds of cycads are likely to come from Triassic, Jurassic, and Cretaceous rocks. Living cycad species can still be found today.

SEED FERNS

Trigonocarpus seeds

This extinct group of plants shared a common ancestor with ferns. They bore true seeds, which hung from the underside of fronds, and could be several inches long. Fossilized seeds are common in Late Paleozoic rocks, but are rarely found attached to plants. Most seed ferns were bushy shrubs, but some were climbers or trees, and could reach heights of 26 ft (8 m).

BENNETTITES

The fossilized trunks of the bennettites – an extinct Mesozoic group of cycad-like plants – are among the most spectacular fossils. Bennettites are distinguished by their palmlike leaves and star-shaped flowers. Some of the trees of these tropical plants reached heights of about 10 ft (3 m).

Star-shaped flower

Carbonized flower of *Williamsonia*

ANGIOSPERMS

Fossils of angiosperms (flowering plants) are common in Tertiary rocks, although some fossils date from the Cretaceous. Fossilization preserved leaves, seeds, wood, and even pollen. Delicate plant remains were best preserved in deposits laid down in lakes and riverbeds, such as shale.

Silicified palm tree stem

AMBER

Amber is the hardened, resinous sap of a tree. This sap was usually produced by conifers, although some angiosperms also exuded amber-producing sap. Most amber is less than 70 million years old, although some types may be more than 100 million years old. In many cultures, amber is valued as a precious stone. Amber is also vitally important because it acts as a fossil trap. Small insects and animals that became embedded in the sap while it was still viscous were preserved in exquisite detail. Amber frequently preserved the remains of delicate insects that are otherwise very poorly represented in the fossil record. This fossil resin is usually associated with coal and shale deposits. The Baltic coast, the Isle of Wight, and New Zealand are well-known amber locations.

Clear amber

BIOGRAPHIES

DOUGLAS AGASSIZ
1807–73

Swiss-American naturalist who made important studies of fossilized fish. In 1826, Agassiz was chosen to classify a large collection of fish that had been captured in the Amazon River region of Brazil. He then undertook a detailed study of the extinct fish of Europe. By 1844, Agassiz had named nearly 1,000 fossil fish, a pioneering work in the study of extinct life. By studying the movements of Swiss glaciers, Agassiz proved that large sheets of ice had covered much of Europe during a recent ice age.

LUIS AND WALTER ALVAREZ

An American father and son team who, in 1980, publicized the discovery of a worldwide layer of clay rich in the rare element iridium, which was present in rocks from the K-T boundary, the border between the Cretaceous and Tertiary periods. Luis (1911–88) and Walter (born 1940) argued that about 66 million years ago the iridium was deposited by the impact of a meteorite. They speculated that the catastrophic meteoritic impact might have been responsible for the extinction of the dinosaurs. Luis was an experimental physicist who was awarded the Nobel Prize for Physics in 1968 for his work on radioactive decay.

ROY CHAPMAN ANDREWS
1884–1960

A naturalist, explorer, and author who led a number of pioneering expeditions to central and eastern Asia. He acquired an outstanding collection of fossils for the American Museum of Natural History (AMNH), and was its director from 1934 to 1941.

After Andrews' graduation in 1906, his first expeditions, undertaken for the AMNH, were to Alaska and Japan, where he studied aquatic mammals. Andrews' most important expeditions, however, took place between 1919 and 1930, when he traveled to the Gobi Desert, Outer Mongolia. During these expeditions, Andrews' teams discovered the first known fossilized dinosaur nests and hatchlings. His teams also discovered prehistoric mammals and many new dinosaurs, including *Protoceratops, Oviraptor,* and *Velociraptor.*

MARY ANNING
1799–1847

A pioneering English fossil collector, Anning was born in Lyme Regis, England, an area famously rich in fossils. Her father was a carpenter and seller of fossil specimens. In 1811, Anning discovered the fossil skeleton of a Jurassic ichthyosaur. This skeleton can be seen in London's Natural History Museum. Anning went on to discover the first plesiosaur in 1821 and the first pterodactyl in 1828. Most of the fossils collected by Anning were sold to institutions and private collections, but often no record was kept of her role in their discovery.

ROBERT BAKKER
BORN 1945

An American paleontologist credited with bringing about the so-called dinosaur renaissance. Bakker has promoted a number of revolutionary ideas, including the theory that dinosaurs are hot-blooded relatives of birds, rather than cold-blooded giant lizards. His reconstructions of dinosaurs show them standing upright, not dragging their tails. Bakker views dinosaurs as intelligent, well-adapted creatures, whose extinction is problematic and intriguing. As part of his mission to popularize dinosaurs, Bakker acted as consultant on the 1993 epic dinosaur film *Jurassic Park.*

ELSO BARGHOORN
BORN 1915

An American paleontologist who, in 1956, discovered the two-billion-year-old Precambrian gunflint fossils. The silica-rich flint rocks of Ontario contain some of the best-preserved Precambrian microfossils in the world. In 1968, Barghoorn showed that fossils of biomolecules, such as amino acids, can be preserved in three-billion-year-old rocks.

ROLAND T. BIRD
1899–1978

A Harley Davidson-riding fossil collector, who played a key role in the excavations at Home Quarry, Wyoming – one of the world's greatest deposits of dinosaur bones. In the 1930s and 1940s, Bird worked for the American Museum of Natural History as a field collector. In 1938, he found sauropod tracks near the Paluxy River, Texas. This find indicated that sauropods walked on land and refuted the belief that these giant animals were aquatic dinosaurs. Bird was also one of the first scientists to find evidence of herding behavior among the dinosaurs.

DEREK BRIGGS
BORN 1950

Briggs is known for his work on the Burgess Shale, a 530-million-year-old mudstone deposit in British Columbia, Canada. He described a number of arthropods found there, including *Perspicaris* and *Sanctacaris*. He also discovered, with others, a number of new Burgess Shale sites, which showed that these animals were common inhabitants of the Cambrian seas. Recently, Briggs has pioneered research into the fossilization of soft-tissue animals.

JOACHIM BARRANDE
1799–1883

The Austrian geologist and paleontologist Barrande worked as a tutor to the French royal family, and followed them into exile in Prague in 1830. Barrande dedicated himself to the study of the Paleozoic trilobite fossils of Bohemia. He published the first volume of his life's work – *The Silurian System of Central Bohemia* – in 1852. The initial publication was followed by 23 volumes of text and plates.

WILLIAM BEEBE
1877–1962

A noted American biologist and explorer, and a writer on natural history who proposed theories about birds' early ancestors. In 1934, he descended, along with Otis Barton, in a bathysphere to a record depth of 3,028 ft (923 m) in the waters off Bermuda.

Beebe in 1932, standing next to his bathysphere.

An enthusiastic fossil collector from an early age, Beebe became curator of ornithology at New York Zoological Gardens in 1899. In 1909, he embarked on a 17-month-long journey to 22 countries to study pheasants, and produced a monumental work on the subject. In 1915, Beebe described a hypothetical ancestor to *Archaeopteryx*, which he called *Tetrapteryx*. He also proposed that ornithomimosaur dinosaurs were insectivores. Beebe became an enthusiastic diver in the late 1920s. He designed the bathysphere – a steel-hulled diving sphere moored to the ocean's surface – to allow the exploration of deep waters.

BARNUM BROWN
1879–1968

The greatest dinosaur hunter of the 20th century, whose most famous discovery was the first specimen of *Tyrannosaurus rex* ever found. From 1910 to 1915, Brown recovered a spectacular variety of complete dinosaur skeletons from the Red Deer River in Alberta, Canada. These discoveries amounted to several large skeletons, representing 36 species of dinosaur and 84 species of other vertebrates. In the 1930s, Brown excavated a wealth of Jurassic fossils at Howe Ranch, Wyoming. Always impeccably dressed, Brown combined a great enthusiasm for dinosaur fossils with a canny business sense. He could generate huge publicity and, with it, funding. As a representative of the American Museum of Natural History, Brown acquired fossils from all over the world.

RINCHEN BARSBOLD
BORN 1935

Mongolian paleontologist and director of the Institute of Geology at the Mongolian Academy of Sciences, Barsbold discovered many new dinosaurs, naming *Adasaurus* and Enigmosauridae in 1983, *Conchoraptor* in 1985, *Anserimimus* in 1988, and *Nomingia* in 2000. *Barsboldia*, a 30-ft (10-m) long, duck-billed dinosaur, which lived in Mongolia in the Late Cretaceous, was named after Barsbold in 1981 by his fellow scientists Teresa Maryanska and Halszka Osmólska.

ALEXANDRE BRONGNIART
1770–1847

French mineralogist and geologist who devised the division of reptiles into four orders – saurians, batrachians, chelonians, and ophidians. Working alongside Georges Cuvier, Brongniart pioneered stratigraphy, the examination of successive rock layers to reveal past environments and life forms. In 1822, Brongniart and Cuvier mapped the Tertiary strata of the Paris basin, and collected local fossils.

WILLIAM BUCKLAND
1784–1856

English clergyman and geologist who dedicated himself to a systematic examination of the geology of Great Britain. In 1819, Buckland discovered the first *Megalosaurus*. His first great work, *Observations on the Organic Remains contained in caves, fissures, and diluvial gravel attesting the Action of a Universal Deluge*, was published in 1823. Buckland's treatise *Geology and Mineralogy* (1836) went through three editions. In 1845, Buckland was appointed Dean of Westminster Abbey.

ERIC BUFFETAUT
BORN 1950

Leading French paleontologist who has worked on developing a complete picture of dinosaur evolution in Thailand. In that country Buffetaut discovered the oldest known sauropod dinosaur, *Isanosaurus attavipachi* from the Upper Triassic, and also numerous dinosaur footprints. In his work on the Late Cretaceous dinosaurs of southern France, he found the first European remains of a gigantic pterosaur, whose wing span was 29.5 ft (9 m). He also discovered the first Late Cretaceous birds from France. Buffetaut has worked in a number of countries, including Spain, Canada, and Pakistan.

GEORGES-LOUIS DE BUFFON
1797–1888

French naturalist and popularizer of natural history. His treatise *Histoire Naturelle (Natural History)* has appeared in several editions, and it has been translated into many languages.

Buffon's skill was to express complex ideas in a clear form. In 1739, he became keeper of the Jardin du Roi and the royal museum in Paris, and began to collect materials for his great work. The volume of his celebrated *Natural History* that appeared in 1749 was the first of 44, their publication extending over 50 years. Beautifully illustrated, the volumes are highly prized by collectors, but the work caused a sensation when it was first published. The most famous volume, *Epoques de la nature (Natural Epochs)*, was the fifth in the series and appeared in 1799. The final eight volumes did not appear until after Buffon's death.

EDWARD DRINKER COPE
1840–97

A prolific American paleontologist who discovered more than 1,000 species of extinct vertebrates in the US.

From 1864 to 1867, Cope was professor of comparative zoology and botany at Haverford College, Pennsylvania. He devoted the next 22 years to exploration and research, concentrating on the area between Texas and Wyoming, where he discovered several extinct species of fish, reptiles, and mammals. While working for the US Geological Survey as a paleontologist, Cope studied the evolutionary history of the horse and of mammal teeth. Cope published more than 1,200 books and papers, and contributed greatly to the understanding of Tertiary vertebrates.

LUIS CHIAPPE
BORN 1962

Argentinian paleontologist who is curator of vertebrate paleontology at the Los Angeles County Museum. Chiappe is one of the world's leading authorities on ancient birds, and on the relationship between birds and dinosaurs. In 1998, while working in the Río Colorado region of Patagonia, Chiappe's team made a major discovery. They unearthed thousands of dinosaur eggshells, along with the first dinosaur embryos to be found in the southern hemisphere, and the first conclusively identified eggs belonging to sauropods.

JENNIFER CLACK
BORN 1947

English paleontologist who revolutionized theories about tetrapods, the first vertebrate animals with legs. Clack's examination of Devonian fossils revealed that legs evolved for navigating in water and later became adapted for walking on land. Clack discovered a complete specimen of *Acanthostega* in the 1980s, and in 1998 she described *Eucritta*.

FRANCIS CRICK
BORN 1916

English biophysicist who, along with James Watson and Maurice Wilkins, won the Nobel Prize for Physiology and Medicine in 1962 for his determination of the molecular structure of deoxyribonucleic acid (DNA). This was one of the most important scientific discoveries of the 20th century. Their double-helix model of DNA helps scientists track the evolution of extinct creatures. DNA can be used to test the relationships between animals long extinct and to compare them with modern relatives. Since 1967, Crick has been distinguished professor of biological studies at the Salk Institute in California.

EDWIN H. COLBERT
BORN 1905

American paleontologist, whose research into vertebrate paleontology took him all over the world. One of the foremost paleontologists of the 20th century, Colbert's *Wandering Lands and Animals* (1973) studied fossils of similar land animals on different continents, and added biological support to the theory of continental drift, proposed by Alfred Wegener. In 1947, he excavated the Ghost Ranch site in New Mexico, where he found more than 500 skeletons of *Coelophysis*, which lived some 220 million years ago.

GEORGES CUVIER
1769–1832

French naturalist and founder of comparative anatomy who led the way in the reconstruction of vertebrate animals, and was an early proponent of stratigraphy. Cuvier dedicated himself to comparative anatomy and to the systematic classification of mollusks, fish, and fossil mammals and reptiles. He produced a number of comprehensive works on the structure of living and fossil animals, and believed that the development of life on Earth was greatly affected by periodic catastrophes. With Alexandre Brongniart, he explored the geology of the Paris Basin using the newly developed principle of stratigraphy.

CHARLES DARWIN
1809–82

English naturalist who influenced scientific thought through his theory of evolution.

In 1831, Darwin traveled to the Galápagos Islands aboard the HMS *Beagle*, as naturalist for a surveying expedition. His observations on the relationship between living animals, newly extinct animals, and fossil finds led him to speculate that species evolved by a process of natural selection. When Darwin's theories were first published in 1859, in *On the Origin of Species by Natural Selection*, a storm of controversy arose. The scientific debate increased when Darwin developed his ideas in *The Descent of Man* (1871). Darwin's theories are now a cornerstone of paleontological research.

PHILIP J. CURRIE
BORN 1949

Canadian paleontologist and curator at the Royal Tyrrell Museum of Paleontology, Drumheller, Canada, Currie is a major research scientist. He was one of the describers of *Caudipteryx*, and has written a number of accessible dinosaur books, including *Dinosaur Renaissance* (1994) and *Newest and Coolest Dinosaurs* (1998). In his research, Currie specializes in Permian fossil reptiles including diapsid reptiles from Africa and Madagascar, and early kinds of synapsids from Europe and the US.

JAMES DWIGHT DANA
1813–95

American geologist, mineralogist, and zoologist who made important studies of mountain-building, volcanic activity, and the origin and structure of continents and oceans. Dana was a geologist on a US expedition to the Pacific Ocean during 1838–42, and later became a professor at Yale University. Dana's reputation was made by a number of definitive texts, including *System of Mineralogy* (1837) and *Manual of Geology* (1862).

RAYMOND DART
1883–1988

South African anthropologist and paleontologist whose discovery of fossil hominids in Africa greatly contributed to an understanding of human evolution. In 1924, Dart recovered the "Taung" skull from a region near the Kalahari Desert. He recognized its humanlike features and named the new species *Australopithecus africanus*. His claim that this species had dental features and an upright posture that approached that of humans was initially met with scepticism. Later finds in South Africa and in Tanzania's Olduvai Gorge confirmed Dart's theory.

LOUIS DOLLO
1857–91

Belgian paleontologist who was responsible for the first reconstruction of *Iguanodon*. In 1878, Dollo worked alongside Louis De Pauw to study the famous *Iguanodon* skeletons found in a coal mine at the village of Bernissart in Belgium. In 1893, Dollo proposed the Law of Irreversibility in Evolution, which argues that complex structures cannot be regained in their original form once that form is lost.

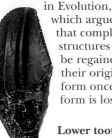

Lower tooth of *Iguanodon*

DONG ZHI-MING
BORN 1937

Chinese paleontologist and prolific dinosaur hunter. As a student in the 1950s, Dong studied under the father of Chinese paleontology, Yang Zhongdian. Dong has become China's most famous paleontologist, and has led fossil-finding expeditions to the Gobi Desert, Mongolia, and China's Yunnan province. Among Dong's many Asian discoveries are *Yangchuanosaurus* (1978), *Chungkingosaurus* (1983), *Alaxasaurus* (1993), and *Archaeoceratops* (1998).

EARL DOUGLASS
1862–1931

American paleontologist who, while working for the Carnegie Museum in Pittsburgh, discovered 350 tons (355 tonnes) of fossilized dinosaur skeletons at the Carnegie Quarry in Utah (now renamed the Douglass Quarry). He spent many years digging up the skeletons and shipping them to Pittsburgh. Among his discoveries were specimens of *Allosaurus*, *Apatosaurus*, *Diplodocus*, and *Stegosaurus*.

EUGENE DUBOIS
1858–1940

Dutch anatomist and geologist who discovered the remains of Java Man, the first-known fossils of the early human *Homo erectus*.

Skull of Homo erectus from Kenya, now called H. ergaster.

Originally an anatomy lecturer, Dubois became increasingly interested in human evolution. In 1887, he traveled to the East Indies to look for hominid remains, and in 1891, at Trinil, Java, he found a hominid jaw fragment, skullcap, and thighbone. The million-year-old specimen had distinctive brow ridges and a flat, receding forehead. Dubois named it *Pithecanthropus* ("apeman") *erectus*, to show that it represents an intermediate stage in human evolution.

NILES ELDREDGE
BORN 1943

American paleontologist whose work focuses on achieving a better "fit" between the fossil record and evolutionary theory.

In 1972, Eldredge and Stephen Jay Gould launched the theory of punctuated equilibria, which proposes that new species are created from a series of rapid bursts interposed with long periods of little change, rather than by steady evolution over time.

DIANNE EDWARDS
BORN 1942

Welsh paleobotanist who discovered the earliest fossils of vascular plants in Silurian rocks in Britain. Edwards studies the Silurian and Devonian plant fossils found in South Wales, the Welsh Borders, and Scotland. She has shown how vascular plants, which use roots to obtain water and nutrients, evolved and colonized the land.

JIM FARLOW
BORN 1951

American paleontologist and zoologist who researched the function of *Stegosaurus*'s plates, and the shape and function of theropod teeth. Farlow is also interested in dinosaur footprints, and has measured the feet of bird, theropod, and ornithopod skeletons in museums all around the world.

PETER GALTON
BORN 1942

English paleontologist who has named a number of dinosaurs, including *Lesothosaurus* (1978) and *Aliwalia* (1985). Galton successfully demonstrated that hadrosaurs did not drag their tails, but used them to counterbalance their heads. In the 1970s, Galton suggested that birds and dinosaurs should be grouped as the Dinosauria.

JACQUES GAUTHIER
BORN 1948

American paleontologist who is professor of geology and geophysics at Yale University, and curator of vertebrates in the Peabody Museum. Gauthier has worked extensively on the evolution of lizards, birds, and crocodilians. Gauthier has examined many characteristics of birds to show that they are part of the dinosaur family tree.

CHARLES WHITNEY GILMORE
1874–1945

American paleontologist who studied North American and Asian dinosaurs, and worked extensively in the Gobi Desert. Gilmore named several dinosaur genera, including *Alamosaurus* and *Bactrosaurus*. The dinosaur *Gilmoreosaurus*, found in China in 1979, was named in his honor.

MARTIN GLAESSNER
1906–89

Australian geologist who produced the first detailed descriptions of the Ediacaran fossils from the Flinders Range mountains of southern Australia. Glaessner was the first to make major inroads toward understanding the Precambrian record of multicellular life. In 1961, he recognized that the Ediacaran fossils were the oldest-known multicelled organisms.

WALTER GRANGER
1872–1941

One of the first paleontologists at the American Museum of Natural History. Granger was chief paleontologist on the museum's Central Asiatic expeditions of the 1920s. In 1898, Granger led the expedition that discovered the *Apatosaurus* skeleton that became the first sauropod ever to be mounted for exhibition.

JAMES HALL
1811–98

American paleontologist who was an outstanding field geologist, and became geologist for New York state. Hall's masterwork is the book *The Paleontology of New York* (1847–94), a comprehensive review of the Paleozoic invertebrate fossils of the state of New York.

STEPHEN JAY GOULD
BORN 1941

American paleontologist, biologist, and science writer, whose popular books trace various controversies in the history of evolutionary biology and paleontology.

Gould's early work at Harvard University focused on the evolution of West Indian land snails. He later developed the theory of punctuated equilibria with Niles Eldredge, which proposes that new species are created from a series of rapid bursts interposed with long periods of little change. Gould has written many popular works, including *Time's Arrow, Time's Cycle* (1990), which examines the measurement of Earth history.

Gould explored the reasons for the extinction of dinosaurs in his book Bully for Brontosaurus *(1991).*

ERNST HAECKEL
1834–1919

German biologist and outstanding field naturalist who was the first prominent German to support Darwin's theories of evolution, which he promoted enthusiastically in Germany. Haeckel was the first to draw up a genealogical tree, laying out the relationship between the various orders of animals. He coined the word "phylum" for the major group to which all related classes of organisms belong. He traced the descent of humans from single-celled organisms through chimpanzees and so-called *Pithecanthropus erectus*, which he saw as the link between apes and human beings.

GERHARD HEILMANN
1859–1946

Danish doctor who wrote *The Origin of Birds* (1916), which examined the similarities between theropod dinosaurs and birds. Heilmann thought that theropods lacked collarbones, and concluded that they could not be birds' ancestors since a feature could not vanish and later reappear during evolution. His theory was unchallenged by scientists until the recent discovery of dinosaurs with collarbones.

JAMES HUTTON
1726–97

Scottish geologist who sought to understand the history of the Earth by studying the origins of minerals and rocks. In his *Theory of the Earth* (1785), Hutton argued that the present rocks of the Earth's surface were formed from the waste of older rocks. He traced the dynamic processes that shape the land and the processes of erosion that flatten it.

WILLI HENNIG
1913–76

A German zoologist and supporter of the theory of cladistics, which groups organisms according to the historical sequence by which they descended from a common ancestor.

Hennig used his early research on the larvae of Diptera, an order that includes flies and mosquitoes, to refine his cladistics theory. In 1949, Hennig became head of the systematic entomology department in Leipzig. In 1950, he proposed his cladistics principles in the book *Phylogenetic Systematics*. The erection of the Berlin Wall in 1961 drove him to West Germany, where he became director of phylogenetic research at the Museum of Natural History in Stuttgart.

FERDINAND HAYDEN
1829–87

American geologist whose bold exploration of the western territories of the US led to the first finds of horned dinosaurs.

Hayden's love of exploration began in the early 1850s. During his geological surveys conducted for the US government, Hayden collected fossils and recorded the geological composition of the western territories. His geological survey of the Upper Missouri in 1855 produced the first finds of *Troodon* and *Palaeoscincus.*

Hayden at camp during a survey, c. 1874

DOROTHY HILL
1907–97

Paleontologist from Queensland, Australia, best known for her work on Paleozoic corals. In her early fieldwork, Hill outlined the structure of Mesozoic sediments in the Brisbane Valley. She became interested in corals while working on a Carboniferous fossil reef at Mundubbera. Hill went on to write three volumes of *The International Treatise on Invertebrates*, which won scientific acclaim worldwide.

EDWARD HITCHCOCK
1793–1864

The first great, modern dinosaur tracker, Hitchcock described thousands of dinosaur tracks, many from his native New England, but he never attributed these tracks to dinosaurs. Instead, Hitchcock theorized that the tracks belonged to large extinct birds. In the late 20th century, it was argued that birds are the direct descendants of a group of carnivorous dinosaurs known as coelurosaurs. Hitchcock had stumbled onto a connection – his tracks were in fact made by the ancient theropod relatives of birds. In his work Hitchcock accumulated an impressive collection of Early Jurassic tracks, many of which are still on display at Amherst College in Massachusetts.

JAMES HOPSON
BORN 1935

Vertebrate paleontologist and professor in the department of organismal biology and anatomy at the University of Chicago, Hopson has researched the evolutionary history of the synapsids, a major branch of the vertebrates. He is interested in tracing the structural changes that occurred during the evolution from Late Paleozoic synapsids to the more modern mammals of the Late Mesozoic. In his work, Hopson has estimated dinosaur brain size and has proposed theories on the function of hadrosaurid crests.

JOHN HORNER
BORN 1946

American paleontologist and Curator of Paleontology at the Museum of the Rockies in Montana. In 1978, Horner discovered the fossilized skeleton of a duck-billed baby *Maiasaura* dinosaur in Montana. He also excavated a cache of dinosaur nests found at Egg Mountain, Montana. Horner has proposed a number of new theories about dinosaurs, most notably the idea that some dinosaur parents nurture their hatchlings. He has also argued that *Tyrannosaurus rex* was not a deadly hunter, but was, in fact, a scavenger that ate carrion.

ZOFIA KIELAN-JAWOROWSKA
BORN 1925

Polish paleontologist who was the first woman to organize and lead fossil-hunting expeditions to the Gobi Desert, conducted from 1963 to 1971. In Mongolia, Kielan-Jaworowska discovered Cretaceous dinosaurs and rare finds of Mesozoic mammals. Her book *Hunting for Dinosaurs* (1969) popularized the paleontology of the Gobi region. She has published more than 200 scientific papers, as well as many books and articles.

THOMAS HUXLEY
1825–95

English biologist who supported the ideas of Charles Darwin, and recognized the anatomical links between birds and reptiles.

The young Huxley voyaged to the Torres Strait where he studied ocean life. Darwin's theories enthused him, and he rebuffed many of Darwin's critics in a series of papers and lectures. Huxley studied fossil reptiles and birds, and in 1867 he linked them in an order that he called Sauropsida to demonstrate their close relationship. He listed several characteristics that are shared between typical dinosaurs and modern birds.

JEAN-BAPTISTE DE LAMARCK
1744–1829

French naturalist who developed ideas on invertebrates and the diversity of animal life.

As botanist to the king of France, Lamarck produced comprehensive botanical works. He was the first to use the presence of a vertebral column to distinguish between vertebrate and invertebrate animals. Lamarck was also a pioneer in evolutionary theory. He promoted the idea that species were not unalterable, and that more complex forms developed from pre-existent, simpler forms. Lamarck also developed a theory on the inheritance of acquired characteristics.

DONALD JOHANSON
BORN 1943

Physical anthropologist who discovered the first known skeleton of *Australopithecus afarensis*. In 1973, Johanson found the knee-joint of an australopithecine in Ethiopia. He was able to demonstrate that these hominids walked in an upright fashion, like humans. The following year, he discovered "Lucy", the oldest fossil hominid ever found.

Johanson holds the skull of "Lucy", a 3.1-million-year-old hominid.

CHARLES KNIGHT
1874–1953

Famous dinosaur illustrator who worked at the American Museum of Natural History's department of vertebrate paleontology during the 1920s and 1930s. Knight's interest in drawing wild animals eventually led to his association with the museum, where he studied and reconstructed the appearance of extinct animals. His most famous murals are *Life in an Ice Age* (1911–21) and *The Age of Mammals in North America*, which was completed in 1930.

LAWRENCE LAMBE
1863–1919

Pioneering Canadian paleontologist and fossil hunter who investigated dinosaur fossils in the Alberta region for the Canadian Geographical Survey. Lambe named *Euoplocephalus* (1910), *Chasmosaurus* (1914), and *Edmontosaurus* (1917). The dinosaur *Lambeosaurus lambei*, which was discovered by Charles H. Sternberg in 1913, was named in Lambe's honour.

JOSEPH LEIDY
1823–91

American scientist who was professor of anatomy at the University of Pennsylvania. A well-respected anatomist and a specialist on intestinal parasites, Leidy became famous as a vertebrate paleontologist. He examined many of the newly discovered fossil finds from the western states and, in a series of important books and papers, laid the foundations of American paleontology. His *Extinct Fauna of Dakota and Nebraska* (1869) contained many species unknown to science and some that were previously unknown on the American continent.

GIUSEPPE LEONARDI
DATES UNAVAILABLE

An Italian dinosaur expert who became a paleontologist while studying to become a priest. Leonardi traveled to Brazil in the 1970s in search of meteorites, and later returned there to live. He has traveled to the most remote terrain in South America in search of dinosaur tracks from different periods. He also discovered what may be one of the world's oldest amphibian tracks, dating from the Late Devonian. He has mapped remote sites in inaccessible locations, and has synthesized information about fossilized footprints on a continental scale.

MARY AND LOUIS LEAKEY

A husband and wife team whose fossil finds proved that human evolution was centered on Africa, and that the human species was older than had been thought.

The Leakeys hold a 600,000-year-old skull found in Tanzania, Central Africa.

Louis Leakey (1903–72) was born in Kenya of English parents. In 1931, he began work in the Olduvai Gorge, Tanzania, aided by his second wife, Mary (1913–98), an English paleoanthropologist. In 1959, Mary discovered a 1.7-million-year-old fossil hominid, now thought to be a form of australopithecine. Between 1960 and 1963, the Leakeys discovered remains of *Homo habilis*, and Louis theorized that their find was a direct ancestor of humans.

CAROLUS LINNAEUS
1707–78

Swedish botanist whose *Systema naturae* (1735) laid the foundations for the classification of organisms.

Linnaeus was the first to formulate the principles for defining genera and species. He based a system of classification on his close examination of flowers. The publication of this system in 1735 was followed by the appearance of *Genera Plantarum* (1736), a work that is considered the starting point of modern botany.

Carolus Linnaeus

WILLARD LIBBY
1908–80

American chemist whose method of radiocarbon dating proved an invaluable tool for paleontologists and archeologists. As part of the Manhattan Project (1941–45), Libby helped to develop a method for separating uranium isotopes. In 1947, he discovered the isotope Carbon-14. Its decay within living organisms is used to date organic materials, such as shell and bone. Libby was awarded the Nobel Prize for Chemistry in 1980.

MARTIN LOCKLEY
BORN 1950

Leading expert on dinosaur trackways, professor of geology at the University of Colorado, and curator of the Denver Fossil Footprints Collection. Lockley's primary research interests include fossil footprints, dinosaur trackways, and paleontological history. His research has taken him from his home bases of Colorado and Utah to Europe, and Central and East Asia.

RICHARD LYDEKKER
1849–1915

English naturalist and geologist who catalogued the fossil mammals, reptiles, and birds in the British Museum. Lydekker's magnificent 10-volume set of *Catalogues* was published in 1891. In 1889, he published the two-volume *A Manual of Palaeontology* together with H.A. Nicholson. Lydekker was also responsible for naming the dinosaur *Titanosaurus* (1877).

CHARLES LYELL
1797–1875

Scottish barrister and geologist who studied the geology of France and Scotland, and in 1827 gave up a career in law for a life spent studying geology. In his work *The Principles of Geology* (1830–33), Lyell devised the names for geological epochs that are now in universal usage, including Eocene and Pliocene. His *Elements of Geology*, which was published in 1838, became a standard work on stratigraphy and paleontology. In Lyell's third great work, *The Antiquity of Man* (1863), he surveyed the arguments for humans' early appearance on Earth, discussed the deposits of the last Ice Age, and lent his support to Darwin's theory of evolution.

WILLIAM DILLER MATTHEW
1871–1930

American paleontologist who worked extensively on the fossil record of mammals. Matthew was curator of the American Museum of Natural History from the mid-1890s to 1927. One of his key theories, that waves of faunal migration repeatedly moved from the northern continents southward, mistakenly relied on the notion that the continents themselves were stable. Matthew also did early work on *Allosaurus* and *Albertosaurus*, and on the early bird *Diatryma*. He named *Dromaeosaurus* in 1922. He was one of the first to study the effect of climate on evolution.

STANLEY MILLER
BORN 1930

American chemist who conducted experiments in the 1950s to demonstrate the possible origins of life on Earth.

While working in Chicago in 1953, the 23-year-old Miller passed electrical discharges – equivalent to a small thunderstorm – through a mixture of hydrogen, methane, ammonia, and water, which he believed represented the constituents of Earth's early atmosphere. After some days, his analysis showed the presence of organic substances, such as amino acids and urea. Miller's experiments revolutionized scientific understanding of the origins of life on Earth.

Stanley Miller with the glass apparatus used to recreate the conditions found on primitive Earth.

CHARLES OTHNIEL MARSH
1831–99

American paleontologist and pioneer of dinosaur studies. Marsh described 25 new genera of dinosaurs and built up one of the most extensive fossil collections in the world. After studying geology and paleontology in Germany, Marsh returned to America and was appointed professor of paleontology at Yale University in 1860. He persuaded his uncle, George Peabody, to establish the Peabody Museum of Natural History at Yale. On scientific expeditions to the western United States, Marsh's teams made a number of discoveries. In 1871, they found the first American pterodactyl fossils. They also found the remains of early horses in the US. Marsh described the remains of Cretaceous toothed birds and flying reptiles, and Cretaceous and Jurassic dinosaurs, including *Apatosaurus* and *Allosaurus*.

HERMANN VON MEYER
1801–69

German paleontologist who named and described *Archaeopteryx* (1861), *Rhamphorhynchus* (1847), and *Plateosaurus* (1837). Meyer was one of the first to view dinosaurs as a separate group, which he called "saurians" in 1832. Meyer started publication of the journal *Paleontographica* in 1846, and used it to publish much of his research on fossil vertebrates.

MARK NORELL
BORN 1957

American paleontologist and curator of vertebrate paleontology at the American Museum of Natural History, who has carried out extensive fieldwork in Mongolia. In 1993, Norell and Michael Novacek discovered a site in the Gobi Desert called Ukhaa Tolgod, a basin rich in fossils. There they found an 80-million-year-old fossil oviraptorid embryo still cloaked in shattered eggshell, as well as a mature oviraptorid that had been buried while sitting on a nest of eggs. In 1995, Norell found a dromaeosaur nest containing eggs, which had been buried by a prehistoric sandflow. He has worked with Chinese colleagues to describe feathered dinosaurs from Liaoning, China.

ALEXANDER OPARIN
1894–1980

Russian biochemist who studied the origins of life from organic matter. Oparin theorized that simple organic and inorganic materials might have combined into complex organic compounds, which, in turn, formed primordial organisms. His most important work is *The Origin of Life on Earth* (1957). In 1935, Oparin helped to found a biochemical institute in honor of his mentor, the botanist A.N. Bakh. He remained director of the institute until his death.

JOHN OSTROM
BORN 1928

American vertebrate paleontologist who is professor emeritus of geology at Yale University. Ostrom is a specialist in the evolution of birds, and has argued that birds evolved from warm-blooded dinosaurs. He made a revolutionary study of the dinosaur *Deinonychus*, which he and others discovered in 1964. Ostrom named the dinosaurs *Microvenator*, *Tenontosaurus*, and *Sauropelta*.

HENRY FAIRFIELD OSBORN
1857–1935

American paleontologist who greatly influenced the art of museum display and made important contributions to the study of dinosaurs.

Osborn was president of the American Museum of Natural History (AMNH) from 1908 to 1935, and was also professor of zoology at Columbia University from 1896 to 1935. During his tenure at the AMNH, he accumulated one of the finest fossil collections in the world and was a celebrated popularizer of palaeontology. In 1905, he described and named *Tyrannosaurus rex*. Osborn proposed the concept of adaptive radiation – that primitive plants or animals might evolve into several species by spreading over a large area and adapting to different ecological niches.

RODERICK MURCHISON
1792–1871

English geologist who pioneered the mapping and study of Paleozoic rocks. He also defined and named the Silurian and Devonian systems.

Originally a soldier, Murchison prepared his first paper for the Royal Geological Society in 1825. With Charles Lyell and Adam Sedgwick as his companions, he explored France, Italy, and the Alps to study their geology. Investigations into the geology of the Welsh borders led, in 1839, to his establishment of the Silurian system – a series of rock formations, each containing distinctive organic remains, which can be found all over the world. Investigations in southwestern England and the Rhineland led to the definition of the Devonian system. Further geological expeditions took him to Russia and the Scottish highlands.

RICHARD OWEN
1804–92

English anatomist and paleontologist who coined the word "dinosaur" in 1842. Owen was responsible for the foundation of the Museum of Natural History in South Kensington, London. Trained as a doctor, he went on to become an expert in comparative anatomy. In 1856, he became superintendent of the natural history department of the British Museum. He supervised the removal of the collections to a new building in South Kensington. A pioneer in vertebrate paleontology, he conducted extensive research on extinct reptiles, mammals, and birds. His most important work in this field is his four-volume *History of British Fossil Reptiles* (1849–84). Owen was responsible for the first full-scale dinosaur reconstructions, which were displayed in Crystal Palace Gardens, London.

KEVIN PADIAN
BORN 1951

Professor of integrative biology who is curator in the Museum of Paleontology at the University of California. Padian is one of the world's leading authorities on the events that took place during the transition from the Triassic period to the Jurassic period, a time that signalled the rise of the dinosaurs. He has written extensively on the relationship of birds to dinosaurs, and studies pterosaurs to see what their anatomy illustrates about the origins of flight. Padian also studies fossil footprints, and is interested in the history of paleontology.

ADAM SEDGWICK
1785–1873

English clergyman and geologist who became the Woodwardian professor of geology at Cambridge University. Sedgwick carried out extensive fieldwork in southwestern England, the Isle of Wight, and Yorkshire. Following fieldwork in Wales in 1831, he applied the name Cambrian to the oldest group of fossiliferous strata. In 1836, while working with Roderick Murchison, Sedgwick demonstrated that the fossils of the Devon limestones were of an intermediate type, between those of the Silurian and Carboniferous systems. They introduced the name Devonian for the slates and limestone of southwestern England, and jointly published *On the Physical Structure of Devonshire,* a memoir.

ALFRED SHERWOOD ROMER
1894–1973

American paleontologist who is known for his theories about vertebrate evolution.

Romer saw anatomical adaptations to environmental change as the key to evolutionary progress. In 1933, he became professor of biology at Harvard University and published *Vertebrate Paleontology,* an important work that shaped academic thinking for decades.

PAUL SERENO
BORN 1957

An American paleontologist known for his fieldwork and research on early dinosaurs.

Attached to the University of Chicago, Sereno has worked extensively in South America, Asia, and Africa. He named the oldest-known dinosaur, *Eoraptor,* and discovered the first complete skull of *Herrerasaurus.* In 1994, Sereno found and named the predatory African dinosaur *Afrovenator.* He has also rearranged dinosaur cladograms – in particular, the ornithischian groupings.

HARRY GOVIER SEELEY
1839–1909

Seeley was the pioneer, in 1887, of a radical new dinosaur classification scheme. He noticed that all dinosaurs possessed a pelvis that followed one of two distinctive designs – birdlike or reptilelike. He divided the dinosaurs into two orders, Ornithischia ("bird-hipped") and Saurischia ("reptile-hipped"). In his book *Dragons of the Air* (1901), Seeley assessed early research and opinion on pterosaurs.

ARMAND DE RICQLÈS
BORN 1938

French professor of comparative anatomy who is known for his research on dinosaur bone structure. Using the link between bone structure and rate of bone growth, Ricqlès examined the structure of fossil bones. His findings led him to suggest that certain groups of dinosaurs might have been warm-blooded, a theory that is a popular topic of debate among paleontologists.

Paul Sereno studies dinosaur skeletons from around the world to learn more about dinosaur evolution.

GEORGE GAYLORD SIMPSON
1902–84

An important paleontologist and the author of hundreds of technical papers and popular books, Simpson was curator of the department of geology and paleontology at the American Museum of Natural History from 1945 to 1959. An expert on the Mesozoic era and the Paleocene epoch, Simpson was one of the first paleontologists to make use of genetics and statistical analysis. He studied the extinct mammals of South America, and contributed much to the understanding of transcontinental migration.

REG SPRIGG
1919–94

Australian geologist who discovered the then oldest-known fossils in 1946. Sprigg stumbled across the 580-million-year-old Precambrian fossils in the Ediacaran Hills of the Flinders Range in South Australia. Since their discovery, "Ediacaran" fossils have been found all over the world. Sprigg continued to pursue his geological career, and led oil exploration in Australia. He mapped the Mount Painter uranium field for the South Australian Geological Survey in 1944.

THE STERNBERG FAMILY

Led by their father, Charles H. (1850–1943), the Sternberg family made many spectacular dinosaur discoveries in North America. In the 1860s, Charles H. discovered thousands of fossils, and developed techniques for "jacketing" fossil bones in a protective cast. Charles M. (1885–1981) was famous for his ability to "read" the ground for dinosaur bones. George (1883–1959) discovered the duck-billed *Edmontosaurus* (1909). Levi (1894–1976) developed a latex casting technique that was used to duplicate fossils.

WILLIAM SMITH
1769–1839

English geologist who is known as the "father of English geology." He was a pioneer of geological mapping and stratigraphic geology.

Smith was a canal engineer who studied rocks while carrying out engineering surveys around England. He realised that particular rock layers (strata) could be identified by the fossils they contained. By taking vertical sections and identifying rock outcrops at the surface, Smith was able to produce three-dimensional geological maps. In 1794, he produced his first geological map, of the region around Bath. In 1815, he published a 15-sheet geological map of England, Wales, and part of Scotland.

MARIE STOPES
1880–1958

English paleobotanist, suffragette, and pioneer of birth control.

In 1905, Stopes became the first female science lecturer at Manchester University. She was an expert on fossil plants and primitive cycads, and demonstrated how plant remains alter to become coal. Stopes's later career was ruled by her interest in women's health issues.

Marie Stopes studied botany in England and Germany.

NIELS STENSEN
1638–86

A Danish scientist and physician to Ferdinand II who recognized the organic processes that fossilize bone, and contributed to the creation of laws on the dating of sedimentary rock strata. In 1666, Stensen examined a shark's skull and observed that organic processes had turned the teeth – which he called "tongue stones" – to stone. From these observations, Stensen developed an understanding of the processes of fossilization. Stensen also drew stratigraphic sections of the rocks in the Tuscany region. He has therefore been seen as the father of both modern paleontology and geology.

LEIGH VAN VALEN
BORN 1935

American paleontologist and professor in the department of ecology and evolution at the University of Chicago, Van Valen has pointed out the similarities between the mesonychid mammals of the Paleocene epoch and the early whales called protocetids. He has also proposed an ecological succession model for the extinction of the dinosaurs.

CHARLES D. WALCOTT
1850–1927

American geologist who discovered the Burgess Shale fossils. Walcott joined the US Geological Survey, and became its director in 1894. He described and interpreted the great Paleozoic region of central Nevada, and examined the Cambrian formations of the Appalachian Mountains. Later, he worked on the Cambrian formations of the Rocky Mountains. In 1909, Walcott made his most famous find when he discovered the deposit of Cambrian fossils known as the Burgess Shale in British Columbia, Canada. Walcott had unearthed the largest find of perfectly preserved fossils from any era. He excavated some 70,000 specimens and passed them on to the Smithsonian Institute, of which he had become head in 1907.

JAMES WATSON
BORN 1928

American molecular biologist and discoverer, with James Crick and Maurice Wilkins, of the molecular structure of deoxyribonucleic acid (DNA). For this discovery Watson was awarded the Nobel Prize for Physiology and Medicine in 1962. He wrote about his research in *The Double Helix* (1968). From 1989 to 1992, Watson was director of the US National Center for Human Genome Research.

ALFRED WEGENER
1880–1930

German meteorologist and geologist who developed the theory of continental drift, which revolutionized the scientific study of the Earth in the 20th century.

Wegener died, aged 50, on his third expedition to the Greenland ice sheet.

From 1924 Wegener held the chair in meteorology and geophysics at the University of Graz, Austria. He began to develop his theory of continental drift from 1910, but it was not fully articulated until the publication of his *Origin of Continents and Oceans* in 1929. In that book he argued that India, Africa, South America, Australia, and Antarctica were once united in a supercontinent, which he named Pangea. This landmass broke up and drifted apart 200 million years ago. Wegener's evidence for this theory was the jigsaw "fit" of separated continents, as well as matching finds of rocks and fossils. His ideas were initially met with hostility, and only gained support with the development of plate tectonics theory.

ABRAHAM GOTTLOB WERNER
1750–1817

The father of German geology, who proposed a "Neptunist" theory of geology – that the minerals present in the ancient ocean that once covered the Earth were gradually deposited as rock. Werner's belief in a primeval ocean as the origin of all of Earth's rocks was highly influential. His followers were called Neptunists, while opponents, who recognized the importance of subterranean heat in the formation of the Earth's crust, were known as Vulcanists. A mineralogist and teacher, Werner examined the rocks of Saxony to demonstrate geological succession – the idea that the rocks of the Earth are laid down in layers that reveal the Earth's history. Although his Neptunist ideas have been disproven, his work on the chronological succession of rocks is still widely respected.

SAMUEL WENDELL WILLISTON
1852–1918

American biologist, paleontologist, and entomologist, who is chiefly remembered for his contributions to vertebrate paleontology, in particular his monumental research on Cretaceous and Permian reptiles and amphibians. Williston found the first *Diplodocus* remains in 1877, and formulated a theory on the evolution of flight. He also conducted extensive research into the Diptera – an order of insects that includes flies, mosquitoes, and midges.

JOHN WOODWARD
1655–1728

English professor who built an extensive collection of fossils and minerals, and devised one of the earliest classifications of fossils. Woodward's collection was left to the University of Cambridge, and is currently on display in the Sedgwick Museum, Cambridge, England.

THE PAST ON DISPLAY

MILLIONS OF FOSSILS are displayed around the world in museums of natural history. In some countries, amateur enthusiasts can also visit sites where fossils are being excavated. Alternatively, travel back in time by exploring websites about prehistoric life.

Fossil bear at the American Museum of Natural History

DISPLAYS IN THE UK

NATURAL HISTORY MUSEUM
Cromwell Road, London SW7
www.nhm.ac.uk
You will immediately be face-to-face with a huge 85-ft (26-m) long skeleton of *Diplodocus* as you enter the Life Galleries at this superb museum. Use the touch-screens, videos, and interactive exhibits to learn about prehistoric life and the theory of evolution. Don't miss the amazing robotic dinosaurs, especially the anima-tronic *T-rex* with its terrifyingly sharp teeth. The museum's website includes virtual reality fossils and a Dino Directory, which you can search by time, country, and body shape.

OXFORD UNIVERSITY MUSEUM OF NATURAL HISTORY
Parks Road, Oxford
www.oum.ox.ac.uk
Dinosaurs and other Mesozoic reptiles found locally, dinosaur eggs from China, and a dodo are among the fantastic sights.

SEDGWICK MUSEUM
Downing Street, Cambridge
www-sedgwick.esc.cam.ac.uk
Huge ammonites, giant marine reptiles, and a prehistoric hippopotamus found in a local gravel pit are among the million fossils that have been collected by this museum.

HUNTERIAN MUSEUM
University Avenue, Glasgow
www.hunterian.gla.ac.uk
Come here to see the first and second dinosaur fossils ever to be found – a tooth each from *Iguanodon* and *Megalosaurus*. Plus view finds from the Gobi Desert in Mongolia, and lots more.

DINOSAUR ISLE EXPERIENCE
Sandown, Isle of Wight
An animatronic *Neovenator* – a meat-eating dinosaur that once roamed the Isle of Wight – is just one of the exciting displays. Also go on fossil walks and watch scientists at work.

DISPLAYS IN THE USA

AMERICAN MUSEUM OF NATURAL HISTORY
Central Park West at 79th Street, New York
www.amnh.org
The displays include saurischian and ornithischian dinosaurs, and extinct mammals. "Ology" on the museum's website is especially for children, with great quizzes, games, and activities.

FIELD MUSEUM OF NATURAL HISTORY
1400 S.Lake Shore Dr, Chicago
www.fmnh.org
Exhibits cover 3.8 billion years of life on Earth from single cells to dinosaurs and humans. Be sure to visit "Sue," the world's largest and best preserved *Tyrannosaurus rex*, found in 1990 in the badlands of South Dakota.

CARNEGIE MUSEUM OF NATURAL HISTORY
4400 Forbes Ave, Pittsburgh
www.clpgh.org/cmnh
Brontosaurus, Stegosaurus, and *Camptosaurus* are among displays of the largest land animals ever to live. Trace the evolution of camels and horses, and help out in the Bonehunters Quarry.

SMITHSONIAN MUSEUM OF NATURAL HISTORY
10th Street and Constitution Avenue, Washington, DC
www.mnh.si.edu
Amazing dioramas recreate scenes from the Jurassic and Cretaceous periods, the last Ice Age, and life in the ancient seas. You are also allowed to touch and examine fossils in the Discovery Room, and arrange to watch scientists at work in the Fossil Laboratory.

LOS ANGELES COUNTY MUSEUM OF NATURAL HISTORY
900 Exposition Blvd, Los Angeles
www.lam.mus.ca.us
A cast of the complete skeleton of the largest-necked dinosaur ever discovered – called *Mamenchisaurus* – is here, and there are also dramatic models of *Allosaurus* and *Carnotaurus*. Activities include fossil rubbings in the Discovery Center.

DINOSAUR NATIONAL MONUMENT QUARRY
Jensen, Utah
www.nps.gov/dino/dinos.htm
The world's largest site from the Jurassic period was discovered in 1909 and is still being excavated. More than half of all the different types of North American dinosaurs have been found here, including the long-necked, plant-eating sauropods. An extraordinary sandstone cliff, in which over 1,600 bones have been exposed, forms one wall of the Visitor Center.

Robotic *Tyrannosaurus rex* at London's Natural History Museum

DISPLAYS AROUND THE WORLD

THE ROYAL TYRRELL MUSEUM OF PALEONTOLOGY
Drumheller, Alberta, Canada
www.tyrrellmuseum.com
See what the undersea world was like in the Cambrian period, with its strange and exotic creatures. Primitive plants are grown in the Paleoconservatory, and there are great displays of Alberta's rich fossil heritage. If you can't visit in person, try the virtual tour on the museum's website, which also has an A-Z encyclopedia of fossils.

CANADIAN MUSEUM OF NATURE
Ottawa, Ontario, Canada
www.nature.ca/nature_e.cfm
Horned, duck-billed, and "ostrich mimic" dinosaurs feature in the exhibits, which were found in the badlands of Southern Alberta and Saskatchewan. On the website are games presented by the Virtual Museum of Canada including "Dig This! the Cretaceous Period" and "Palaeo Pursuit."

QUEENSLAND MUSEUM
Brisbane, Queensland, Australia
www.Qmuseum.quld.gov.au
Learn about the weird prehistoric creatures that used to roam Queensland. Quizzes to test your knowledge about Australian dinosaurs and a poster to color on the website.

MUSÉE PARC DES DINOSAURES
Béziers, France
www.musee-parc-dinosaures. com/anglasi/index.htm
The largest museum-park of fossils in Europe, located within a paleontological site in Southern France. Excavation news is posted on the website, which has an English version.

ROYAL BELGIAN INSTITUTE OF NATURAL SCIENCES
Brussels, Belgium
www.kbinirsnb.be/general/eng/ main_e.htm
Exhibits include the world's largest group of *Iguanodon* – 30 skeletons discovered in a coal mine at Bernissart in 1878.

ZIGONG DINOSAUR MUSEUM
Zigong, Sichuan, China
Excellent museum that is built over the site of some incredible excavations. Twelve dinosaurs in good condition are displayed here, and some bones are still *in situ*. The dinosaurs are sometimes taken out of China and displayed at temporary exhibitions round the world.

ARGENTINE MUSEUM OF NATURAL SCIENCES
Buenos Aires, Argentina
Numerous remarkable dinosaur fossils found in Patagonia are on show at this center of paleontological study.

PREHISTORIC LIFE IN CYBERSPACE

Dino Data
www.dinodata.net
Great site for serious dinosaur enthusiasts, with all the facts at your fingertips.

Dino Master Quest
www.goldenbooks.com/ dino/intro.html
Spin the Wheel of Knowledge with a cartoon professor in this animated time travel for younger children.

Dinorama
www.nationalgeographic.com/ dinorama
Smart, stylish website by the National Geographic – includes models and animation.

Dinosauria On-Line
www.dinosauria.com
Award-winning site for enthusiasts, with a gallery of images and discussion group.

Dinosaurs and Other Prehistoric Creatures
www.discovery.com/guides/ dinos/dinos.html
Saber-tooth tigers, mammoths, and other ancient animals from the Discovery Channel.

Discovering Dinosaurs
www.dinosaurs.eb.com
From *Encyclopedia Britannica* – how our ideas about dinosaurs have changed over the years.

Fossil Zone
www.discovery.com/exp/ fossilzone/fossilzone.html
A visual treat for dinosaur fans from the TV Discovery Channel, including hi-tech animation and sounds.

Imax: T-Rex
www.imax.com/t-rex
Become a virtual paleontologist and use the time machine to travel back to the era of the legendary *Tyrannosaurus rex*.

Prehistoric Illustrated
www.prehistoricillustrated.com
Gallery of prehistoric creatures plus the latest news and research on extinct animals.

Project Exploration
www.projectexploration.org
Join junior paleontologists as they head into the mountains of Montana, in search of fossils.

Walking with Dinosaurs
www.bbc.co.uk/dinosaur
Amazing video clips of dinosaurs brought to life by computer wizardry from the BBC.

Zoom Dinosaurs
www.EnchantedLearning.com/ subjects/dinosaurs
Ask questions and vote for your favorite dinosaur, plus games and the best dinosaur jokes ever!

The Hall of Saurischian Dinosaurs at the American Museum of Natural History, New York

GLOSSARY

A

Acanthodians (ae-KAN-tho-DEE-anz: "spiny sharks") Extinct fish that had fins supported by strong, immovable spines. Their heyday was the Devonian period.

Acetabulum The hip socket.

Actinopterygians (ak-tin-op-ter-IG-ee-nz) The ray-finned fish, a major group of osteichthyans (bony fishes).

Adaptations The ways in which organisms evolve in response to their environment.

Aerofoil The curved suface of a wing that aids flight by creating an upward force.

Agnathans (ag-NAY-thanz: "without jaws") A class of primitive vertebrates, the "jawless fish," that flourished mainly in Early Paleozoic times. They include extinct groups and the living hagfish and lampreys.

Algae Primitive plants and plant-like organisms that grow in wet conditions. Cyanobacteria ("blue-green algae") were among the first organisms to evolve and helped to create the oxygen-rich atmosphere essential for other lifeforms.

Allosaurs (AL-o-SORE-z: "strange lizards") Big, meat-eating dinosaurs – a group of rather primitive tetanuran theropods.

Amber The fossil form of the sticky resin produced by trees. Perfectly preserved insects and other organisms have been found fossilized in amber.

Ammonites An extinct group of cephalopods that teemed in Mesozoic seas. They had a coiled, chambered shell.

Amniotes Tetrapod vertebrates whose young develop within a special protective membrane called the amnion. Amniotes include reptiles, birds, and mammals.

Amphibians Cold-blooded tetrapod vertebrates whose young use gills to breathe during the early stages of life. Living amphibians include frogs, newts, and salamanders, whose ancestors originated in the Carboniferous period.

Amphibious Inhabiting both water and land. Crocodiles and otters are amphibious (but they are not amphibians).

Anapsids A group of primitive reptiles with no skull opening behind the eye. Besides extinct forms, anapsids may include turtles and tortoises.

Ancestor An animal or plant from which others have evolved.

Angiosperms (AN-JEE-o-spermz: "seed vessels") Flowering plants which have seeds enclosed in an ovary. The group includes broad-leaved trees and grasses.

Ankylosaurs (ANG-ki-lo-SORE-z or ang-KIE-lo-SORE-z: "fused lizards") Four-legged, armored, plant-eating, ornithischian dinosaurs with bony plates that covered the neck, shoulders, and back. A horny beak was used for cropping plants.

Annelids Worms with segmented bodies. Because they lack skeletal structures, their fossil evidence is usually restricted to trails and burrows.

Anthracosaurs (an-THRAK-o-SORE-z) Extinct amphibious tetrapods, including kinds that mainly lived on land, may have included the ancestors of the reptiles.

Anthropoids/the Anthropoidea The higher primates: monkeys, apes, and humans.

Anthropology The study of humankind. Anthropologists examine and analyze the structure of human societies and the nature of human interactions and beliefs.

Antorbital fenestra A hole in the skull in front of each eye; a hallmark of the archosaurs.

Appendages Limbs, gills, antennae, or other parts projecting from a creature's body.

Araucaria A genus of large evergreen conifers, characterized by small leaves arranged in spirals. Living members include the monkey puzzle tree and Norfolk Island pine.

Archaebacteria Primitive single-celled organisms, thought to be among the earliest life forms to have evolved, over 3.5 billion years ago. Many thrive in extreme conditions, such as scalding water.

Archaic Primitive, or of an ancient time.

Archean/Archaean The second eon of the geological timescale, about 3.8–2.5 billion years ago.

Archosaurs (AR-ko-SORE-z: "ruling lizards") A major group of reptiles that originated in the Triassic. It includes dinosaurs, pterosaurs, and crocodilians.

Arthropods Invertebrates with segmented bodies and a hard (outer) exoskeleton. They form the largest phylum (major division) in the animal kingdom, with well over a million living species. Extinct arthropods include trilobites and eurypterids; living ones include insects and spiders.

Artiodactyls (AR-tee-o-DAK-tilz) Hoofed mammals (ungulates) with an even number of toes. Pigs, camels, deer, giraffes, and cattle are living examples.

Australopithecines (os-TRAL-o-PITH-e-seen-z: "southern apes") Extinct apelike hominids including the ancestors of humans.

Aves Birds. Some scientists restrict the name Aves to modern birds (*see also Neornithes*), calling the most primitive birds Avialae. Birds probably evolved from theropod dinosaurs in the Late Jurassic.

B

Belemnites An extinct group of squidlike creatures. They were characterized by an internal chambered shell, enclosed entirely by soft, muscular tissue.

Bennettitales An extinct group of plants with palmlike foliage, and similar in appearance to the living sago palms, or cycads. They produced star-shaped flowerlike reproductive structures.

Bilateral Having two sides. The wings of a butterfly are one of many examples of bilateral symmetry in the animal kingdom.

Bipedal Walking on the hindlimbs rather than on all fours.

Biostratigraphy The branch of geology that examines the fossil content of rock layers.

Biozone A division of geological time identified by the presence of particular species fossilized in rock layers.

Bivalves Aquatic molluscs, such as clams, that are enclosed by a hinged shell. The two halves of the shell are usually mirror images of each other.

Blastopore An opening in an embryo. In some organisms, the blastopore will become the mouth or anus, in others, part of the digestive system.

Bovoids (boe-VOYD-z: "oxlike") Artiodactyl hoofed mammals including pigs, hippopotamuses, camels, pronghorns, deer, giraffes, cattle, and their kin.

Brachiopods Marine invertebrates with a two-valved shell. They are classified by whether or not the valves are hinged. They evolved in the Cambrian period but are now a minor group.

Bryozoans Marine invertebrates that grow in branching or fan-like colonies measuring a few inches across. They have flourished since the Ordovician period, in both deep and shallow waters.

Burgess Shale The site in British Columbia, Canada, where an important discovery of Middle Cambrian fossils occurred. Among the 130 species identified are sponges, jellyfish, worms, and arthropods.

C

Caecilians Burrowing, wormlike amphibians, which have poorly developed eyes and no limbs.

Calcareous Any rock containing calcium carbonate.

Calcified To be converted to calcium carbonate, such as when bones or shells have formed chalk, limestone, or marble.

Calcite A widely distributed rock-forming mineral, common in the shells of invertebrates. It is the chief constituent of limestone.

Cambrian The first period of the Paleozoic era, about 540–500 million years ago. This was when most of the main invertebrate groups appeared in the fossil record.

Carbonate A substance containing carbon with calcium or magnesium, for example limestone or dolomite.

Carboniferous The fourth period of the Paleozoic era, about 355–295 million years ago. During this period, extensive forests covered the land, and were colonized by insects and four-legged vertebrates including amphibious tetrapods, and the first reptiles and synapsids.

Carbonized Describing organic matter that has decomposed under water or sediment, leaving a carbon residue. The residue preserves many features of plants, insects, and fish.

Carinates A group of birds with deeply keeled breastbones.

Carnassials The bladelike cheek teeth of carnivores, designed to slice meat into pieces.

Carnivores/The Carnivora A group of sharp-toothed, meat-eating mammals, including cats, dogs, bears, and their relatives and ancestors. People often call other meat-eating animals carnivores, too.

Carnosaurs Large carnivorous dinosaurs with big skulls and teeth. All such theropods were once called carnosaurs. The name is now used only for *Allosaurus* and its relatives.

Cartilaginous Having a skeleton of cartilage (a firm but flexible substance) rather than bone.

Catarrhines Primates with down-pointing nostrils that are close together, for example monkeys, apes, and humans.

Caudal Of, or relating to, a tail.

Cenozoic The era that covers the last 65 million years. It is subdivided into the Tertiary period (65–1.75 million years ago) and Quaternary period (1.75 million years to the present).

Cephalopods Marine molluscs with big eyes and a well-developed head surrounded by a ring of tentacles. Examples include ammonites, belemnites, octopuses, squid, and cuttlefish.

Ceratopsians (ser-a-TOP-see-anz: "horned faces") Bipedal and quadrupedal, plant-eating, ornithischian dinosaurs with a deep beak and bony frill at the back of the skull. They include the horned dinosaurs.

Ceratosaurs (se-RAT-o-SORE-z or SER-a-to-SORE-z: "horned lizards") One of the two major groups of theropods.

Cetaceans (se-TAE-see-anz: "whales") Marine mammals with a streamlined, fishlike body and limbs evolved as flippers. They include dolphins, whales, and porpoises.

Chelonians (ke-LO-nee-nz: "tortoises") Broad-bodied reptiles, protected by a rooflike shell. They comprise turtles, tortoises, and their ancestors.

Chimaeras Cartilaginous fish characterized by long, tapering tail fins.

Chondrichthyans (kon-DRIK-thee-anz: "cartilage fish") Sharks, chimaeras, and kin: fish with a cartilaginous skeleton and jaws.

Chondrosteans (kon-DROS-tee-anz: "cartilage-boned") Primitive ray-finned fish comprising the sturgeons and paddlefish.

Chordates Animals that have a notochord.

Chronological Arranged in order of occurrence.

Civet A catlike mammal with glands that secrete a strong, musky scent. Civets are in the same family as mongooses.

Clade A group of organisms (such as dinosaurs) sharing anatomical features derived from the same ancestor.

Cladistic (kla-DIS-tik) Describing a method of classifying plants and animals by grouping them in clades.

Cladogram (KLAD-o-gram) A branching diagram showing the relationships of different clades.

Class In the Linnaean system of classification, a group of organisms containing one or more related orders (sometimes grouped in subclasses).Classes include Aves (birds), Reptilia (reptiles), and Mammalia (mammals).

Cold-blooded Depending upon the heat from the sun for body warmth.

Continental drift The movement of continents across the surface of the Earth over time.

Cretaceous The last period of the Mesozoic era, about 135–65 million years ago.

Crinoids (sea lilies) Plant-shaped echinoderms that are either free-floating or anchored to the sea-floor by long stalks. They form an important fossil group in Paleozoic rocks.

Crustaceans A large class of arthropods named after the hard carapace, or "crust," that encases their bodies. Living examples include crabs, shrimp, and woodlice.

Ctenophores (TEN-o-FORE-z) Marine animals with jellyfish-like bodies and cilia (short vibrating hairs). Living examples include the sea gooseberries.

Cycads (sie-kadz) Palmlike, seed-bearing plants that are topped by a crown of fernlike leaves. They may be short and shrublike, or grow as high as 65 ft (20 m).

Cynodonts (SIE-no-dontz: "dog teeth") Extinct, doglike synapsids that included the ancestors of mammals.

D

Descendant A living thing that is descended from another.

Devonian period The third period of the Paleozoic era, about 410–355 million years ago. In Devonian times, tetrapods (four-legged vertebrates) were evolving from fish.

Diapsids (die-AP-sidz) A major group of reptiles, typically with two holes in the skull behind each eye. Diapsids include lizards, crocodiles, dinosaurs, and birds. Their ancestors originated in Late Carboniferous times.

Dicynodonts (die-SIE-no-DONT-z: "two dog teeth") Extinct, four-legged therapsids with long, downward-pointing tusks.

Digit A finger, thumb, or toe.

Dinosaurs (DIE-no-sore-z: "terrible lizards") A great group of advanced archosaurs with erect limbs.

Diplodocids (di-PLOH-do-sidz: "double beams") A family of huge saurischian dinosaurs: long-necked, long-tailed, plant-eating sauropods. Diplodocids included *Diplodocus* and *Apatosaurus.* ·

Diprotodonts (die-proe-toe-DON-tz: "two first teeth") The largest of the extinct giant marsupials, diprotodonts were rhinoceros-like creatures, with huge rodent-like incisor teeth and massive skulls. These forest-dwellers browsed on low-growing trees and shrubs.

Disconformity A break between parallel rock layers representing a time when no sediment was deposited. It indicates an environmental change in the affected area.

Diversify To become more varied. In evolution, for example, when a few species evolve into many species, which are adapted to different environments.

DNA Deoxyribonucleic acid, whose molecules carry genetic instructions from one generation to the next. *(See Genes.)* The complex double-helix structure of DNA was discovered in the 1950s.

Domesticated Bred to be tame, as with cows, sheep, and dogs, which now live alongside human beings.

Dominant and recessive Terms describing inherited characteristics that depend on the type of gene inherited from each parent. For example, in humans brown-eye genes are dominant, while blue-eye genes are recessive.

Dromaeosaurids (DROH-mee-o-SORE-idz: "running lizards") Bird-like, bipedal, carnivorous dinosaurs. Most grew no longer than 6 ft (1.8 m). Dromaeosaurids lived in all northern continents.

E

Echinoderms (i-KIE-no-dermz: "sea urchin skins") Marine invertebrates with a hard, chalky skeleton and a five-rayed symmetry. They evolved during the Cambrian period and include starfish, sea lilies, sea cucumbers, and sea urchins.

Echinoids (I-KIE-noydz) Sea urchins – echinoderms with a rigid, globular (rounded) outer skeleton of spiny plates, pierced by narrow tube feet for walking.

Ecosystem A natural system that is made up of a community of living organisms and the environment in which they live.

Ectotherm A cold-blooded animal.

Ediacarans Fossil organisms named after those found in the Ediacaran Hills of South Australia. These complex, soft-bodied animals were found in rocks that were about 580 million years old.

Elasmobranchii (ee-LAZ-mo-BRAN-kee. "metal plate gills") The main group of chondrichthyan fish, including the sharks, skates, and rays.

Elasmosaur (ee-LAZ-mo-SORE: "metal plate lizard") A long-necked type of plesiosaur: a bulky, Mesozoic marine reptile with paddle-like limbs.

Elytra The hard outer wingcases of beetles and some other insects.

Embryo An animal or plant in its early stage of development from a fertilized egg or seed.

Eocene The second epoch of the Tertiary period, about 53–33.7 million years ago. Hoofed mammals, whales, and primates diversified in this epoch.

Eon The longest unit of geological time. From oldest to youngest, the four eons are called Hadean, Archean (Archaean), Proterozoic, and Phanerozoic. The Phanerozoic eon comprises the Paleozoic, Mesozoic, and Cenozoic eras.

Epoch An interval of geological time that is longer than an age and shorter than a period.

Era A unit of geological time that ranks below an eon.

Erosion The wearing away of the surface of the Earth by natural forces, such as wind and moving ice and water.

Eukaryotes (yoo-KARRY-oatz: "having a true nucleus") All organisms made of cells with a nucleus. Eukaryotes evolved from prokaryotes at least 800 million years ago.

Eurypterids (yoo-rip-ter-idz: "wide wings") Sea scorpions, living in salt- and freshwater in the Paleozoic era. Some grew more than 6 ft 6 in (2 m) long.

Evolution The process by which one species gives rise to another. It occurs because individual organisms pass on mutations (chance changes in genes controlling such things as body size, shape, and color). Individuals with beneficial mutations pass these on, so their kind multiplies. In this way new species eventually arise.

Excavation Digging out and removing fossils or other substances from the ground.

Exoskeleton An external skeleton. External skeletons appeared among various marine invertebrates in Cambrian times.

Extinction The dying out of a plant or animal species. This may be caused by increased competition for resources, or unfavorable changes in the environment, such as alterations in climate or sea level or an asteroid striking the Earth.

F

Fenestra A small hole, or opening, in a bone.

Flagellum A long, whiplike appendage found on some microscopic organisms.

Foraminiferans Minute aquatic organisms with a single or multi-chambered shell. Their fossils are important indicators of the ages of some rocks.

Fossil The remains of a prehistoric organism preserved in the Earth's crust.

Fossilization Any fossil-forming process. As organic substances decay, they may be reduced to a carbon residue, a process called carbonization. Bones and shells may be impregnated by mineral-bearing solutions, in a process known as permineralization. Original hard parts may be dissolved away and entirely replaced by a mineral substance, in a process known as petrifaction.

G

Gastropods The largest, most successful class of molluscs. Their internal organs are generally carried in a spiral shell, they have a head with eyes and mouth, and a flattened foot for crawling. Living members of the class include snails, cowries, and limpets.

Genes Microscopic units of cells that control inherited characteristics. They are passed on from parents to their young.

Genets Catlike mammals of the genus *Genetta*, characterized by spotted fur and a long, bushy tail. Native to Africa and southern Europe.

Genus (plural: genera) A group of related organisms ranked between the levels of family and species.

Geological Concerning geology, the scientific study of the composition, structure, and origins of the Earth's rocks.

Gharial A large Indian reptile related to crocodiles. It has a long, very narrow snout.

Giraffids (ji-RAF-idz: "giraffes") A family of hoofed, plant-eating mammals – artiodactyls with long necks and forelegs.

Girdles (hip and shoulder girdles) The hip bones and shoulder bones of tetrapod vertebrates, forming structures that support the limbs.

Glossopteris (glos-OP-ter-is: "tongue fern") A Permian seed-fern found on all southern continents when they were grouped as Gondwana.

Glyptodonts (GLIP-to-dontz: "carved teeth") Large, armadillo-like mammals from South America with hard, thick, bony shells; now extinct.

Gondwana The vast southern supercontinent that included South America, Africa, Antarctica, Australia, and India. Gondwana persisted from Precambrian times until the Jurassic period, when these lands began to move apart.

Graptolites (GRAP-to-lietz: "writing on the rocks") Extinct, tiny, colonial marine animals whose branching tubular exoskeletons left impressions in shale. These fossils help scientists date others from the Ordovician and Silurian periods.

H

Habitat The natural home of an organism.

Hadean The first eon of the geological time scale, about 4.6–3.8 billion years ago.

Hadrosaurs (HAD-ro-SORE-z: "bulky lizards") The duck-billed dinosaurs – large, bipedal/quadrupedal Late Cretaceous ornithopods that used their ducklike beaks for browsing.

Hagfish A living kind of jawless fish (agnathan).

Hallux The innermost digit ("big toe") of the hindfoot of tetrapod vertebrates.

Herbivore Any animal that eats only plants. The teeth, stomach and digestive system of herbivores are adapted to breaking down fibrous plant material.

Hesperornithiformes (HES-per-OR-nith-i-form-eez: "western bird forms") Toothed, flightless, foot-propelled diving birds of Late Cretaceous times.

Holocene The most recent epoch of geological history, lasting from 10,000 years ago to the present.

Hominids The group of primates that includes humans and their living and extinct relatives.

Hybrid The offspring of two species.

I

Iapetus Ocean The precursor of the Atlantic Ocean, between the ancient continents of Laurentia (mainly North America) and Baltica (northern Europe). The ocean closed during the Ordovician period.

Ichthyosaurs (IK-thi-o-SORE-z: "fish lizards") Fishlike Mesozoic marine reptiles that resembled modern dolphins.

Igneous rocks Rocks formed from magma: molten matter originating deep down in the Earth.

Iguanodontians (i-GWAHN-o-dont-i-anz: "Iguana teeth") Large, bipedal/quadrupedal, plant-eating dinosaurs: ornithopods that flourished in the Early Cretaceous.

Ilium One of the three (paired) hip bones.

Inherited Passed down through the generations.

Insectivore Any insect-eating organism, including certain plants, but especially the group of mammals including moles, shrews, and hedgehogs.

Invertebrates Animals without backbones.

Ischium One of the three (paired) hip bones.

J

Jerboa A small desert rodent with long hindlegs.

Jurassic The middle period of the Mesozoic era, about 203–135 million years ago. At this time dinosaurs dominated the land, the first birds evolved, and mammals began to diversify.

Juvenile A young or immature individual.

K

Kin Family – individuals that are genetically related.

L

Lamprey A living type of jawless fish, with a sucker mouth and horny teeth.

Lancelets Small, invertebrate, fish-like chordates that bury themselves in the sand.

Lepospondyls (LEP-o-SPON-dilz) Small, salamander-like and snakelike amphibious and aquatic tetrapods that flourished in Carboniferous and Permian times.

Lissamphibians (LISS-am-FIB-ee-anz) Living amphibians and their closest ancestors. Lissamphibians include caecilians, frogs, and salamanders.

Lophophorates (LOF-o-FOR-aitz) Invertebrate animals that possess a lophophore, a fan of tentacles around the mouth. The lophophorates include the bryozoans and brachiopods.

Lungfish A group of lobe-finned, bony fish that evolved in the Devonian. They have both gills and lungs and can breathe in water and air.

M

Mammals Warm-blooded, hairy vertebrates that secrete milk and suckle their young. Living mammals range from tiny shrews to the blue whale, the largest creature ever, and between them occupy a great variety of habitats. Mammals possibly arose in Triassic times.

Maniraptorans (man-i-RAP-tor-anz: "grasping hands") Predatory dinosaurs including birds. They were advanced tetanuran theropods with long arms and hands.

Maneuverability An ability to perform complex movements with ease and agility.

Marginocephalians (mar-JIN-o-se-FAL-ee-anz: "bordered heads") Ornithischian dinosaurs with a skull ridge or shelf – the pachycephalosaurs and ceratopsians.

Marsupials Mammals that give birth to small, undeveloped young that grow and mature in a skin pouch on the mother's stomach. Living examples include kangaroos and wallabies. Marsupials survive only in Australasia and the Americas.

Mastodons (MAS-to-dons) An extinct group of large mammals with trunks, tusks, and thick hair. They were related to the elephants.

Megalosaurs (MEG-a-lo-SORE-z: "great lizards") A mixed group of large carnivorous dinosaurs. They were primitive tetanuran theropods less advanced than the allosaurs.

Mesoderm The middle layer of cells in an embryo. In vertebrates the mesoderm develops into muscles, bones, the circulatory system, and various internal organs and glands.

Mesosaurs (MEZ-o-SORE-z: "intermediate lizards") Primitive, somewhat lizardlike aquatic reptiles of Permian times. They swam by waggling their flattened tails.

Mesozoic The "middle life" era, about 250–65 million years ago, containing the Triassic, Jurassic, and Cretaceous periods. This was the Age of the Dinosaurs – their extinction is marked by the end of the era.

Metamorphosis Change of shape, as when the young of some creatures take on adult form, for instance a tadpole becomes a froglet, and a caterpillar becomes a pupa and then a winged butterfly.

Metatarsals Foot bones between the ankle and toes.

Metazoans Many-celled animals (this applies to the vast majority of animals).

Microfossils Fossils too small to be seen with the naked eye. They include the shells of some microscopic, single-celled organisms, plant spores, pollen grains, and the bony scales of certain fish.

Miocene The fourth epoch of the Tertiary period, about 23.5–5.3 million years ago.

Mitochondrion A structure within a cell containing enzymes (special proteins) for energy production and respiration.

Molluscs A great group of invertebrates including bivalves, gastropods, and cephalopods, many important as marine fossils.

Monotremes Primitive, egg-laying mammals that evolved by the Mid-Cretaceous. Only the platypus and echidnas (spiny anteaters) survive.

Mosasaurs (MOZE-a-SORE-z) Large, Cretaceous marine reptiles – long-jawed aquatic lizards with slender bodies and flipperlike limbs. They were fierce predators.

Multituberculates Small, rodent-like mammals of Late Jurassic to Early Cenozoic times. Many were mouse-sized, the largest as big as a beaver.

N

Natural selection The natural "weeding out" of weaker individuals that guides evolution. As generations of individuals mutate, those whose mutations are favorable (making them stronger, faster, etc.) survive in greater numbers to reproduce and pass on their mutations to the next generation.

Nautiloids (NOR-til-OY-dz) A type of cephalopod living in a straight or coiled, chambered shell. Nautiloids swim by squirting water out of the body cavity. They reached their peak in the Ordovician and Silurian but only a single genus survives: the pearly nautilus of the Pacific and Indian oceans.

Neanderthal (nee-AN-der-taal) An extinct species of hominid that is closely related to our own species.

Nematodes Parasitic and free-living worms with a slender, unsegmented cylindrical shape; also called roundworms.

Neoceratopsians (NEE-o-sera-TOP-see-anz: "new horned faces") Small to large, mainly four-legged ceratopsians, many with huge, horned heads.

Neornithes (nee-ORN-ith-eez: "new birds") Birds of the modern type, with a toothless beak, and distinctive bones not found in earlier forms.

Neural Relating to the nerves or central nervous system.

Niche A set of environmental conditions that are uniquely well suited to the survival of a particular species.

Nocturnal Relating to the night. Nocturnal creatures are active during the hours of darkness and sleep during daylight.

Notochord A flexible internal rod stiffening the body of chordates. It forms the basis of the backbone in vertebrate animals.

Nummulites Foraminiferans with disc-shaped and lens-shaped shells; plentiful in some Tertiary rocks.

O

Olfactory Relating to the sense of smell.

Oligocene The third epoch of the Tertiary period, about 33.7–23.5 million years ago. Many of the modern animal families flourished, but with species that are now extinct.

Onychophorans (ON-ik-o-FOR-anz) Long, wormlike invertebrates with many stumpy limbs. They are closely related to arthropods. The earliest lived in the Cambrian period.

Ordovician The second period of the Paleozoic era, about 500–435 million years ago. All creatures known from this time lived in water.

Organelle A specialized structure within a cell.

Ornithischians (or-ni-THIS-kee-anz: "bird hips") One of the two major dinosaur groups (see also *Saurischians*). The pelvis of ornithischians is similar to the pelivis of birds.

Ornithodirans (or-ni-thoe-DIRE-anz: "bird necks") The group of archosaurs that includes dinosaurs, pterosaurs, and birds.

Ornithopods (or-ni-thoe-POD-z: "bird feet") A group of large and small ornithischian dinosaurs: plant-eaters that walked on their long hindlimbs or at least hurried along on them.

Ossicle A small bone or bonelike body part, for instance the calcite plates of echinoderms.

Osteichthyans (OS-tee-IK-thi-anz: "bony fish") Fish with a bony not cartilaginous skeleton. They include the ray-finned actinopterygians and lobe-finned sarcopterygians.

Osteostracans (OS-tee-o-STRAK-anz: "bone shields") Early jawless fish whose head and gills were enclosed in a heavy bony shield.

Overburden Sediment or other material that must be removed to reach an underlying deposit of fossils or minerals.

Oviraptorids (OH-vi-RAP-tor-idz: "egg stealers") A family of long-legged, beaked, birdlike maniraptoran theropod dinosaurs.

P

Pachycephalosaurs (pak-i-SEF-a-lo-SORE-z: "thick-headed lizards") Bipedal ornithischian dinosaurs: marginocephalians with immensely thick skulls.

Paleobotany The study of fossil plants. This is useful in understanding ancient ecology, and can also help scientists to match the dates of different rock samples.

Paleocene The first epoch of the Tertiary period, about 65–53 million years ago. Large mammals appeared during this epoch.

Paleoecology The study of the relationships between fossil organisms and their ancient environments. Comparisons are often made with modern ecosystems.

Paleontology The scientific study of fossil plants and animals.

Paleozoic ("ancient life") The geological era from 540–250 million years ago, comprising the Cambrian, Ordovician, Silurian, Devonian, Carboniferous, and Permian periods.

Palpebral A bony eyelid, as seen in some ankylosaurs.

Palynology The study of microscopic pollen and spores and their spread. Palynology is a branch of paleoecology and paleobotany.

Pampas Treeless, grass-covered plains.

Pangea (pan-JEE-a) The supercontinent formed at the end of the Paleozoic era. Pangea consisted of all the major continental blocks and stretched from pole to pole.

Parareptiles (PAR-a-REP-tile-z: "near/beside reptiles") Primitive reptiles, including the mesosaurs. Some people have used the term to include all the reptiles known as anapsids.

Pareiasaurs (par-EE-a-SORE-z) A group of early reptiles characterized by massive bodies and strong limbs. Their skulls had many bony protuberances.

Peccary A piglike type of hoofed mammal native to the Americas.

Pelvis The hip girdle. (*See Girdles.*)

Period The unit of geological time between era and epoch. Periods are an era's main subdivisions.

Perissodactyls (per-IS-o-DAK-tilz) The "odd-toed" hoofed mammals, including horses, rhinoceroses, tapirs, their ancestors, and various extinct forms.

Permafrost Permanently frozen ground. The surface thaws in the higher temperatures of summer, but water cannot drain away through the frozen subsurface.

Permian The last period of the Paleozoic era, about 295–250 million years ago. The end of the Permian saw a worldwide mass extinction of life-forms.

Phalanges (singular: phalanx) Toe and finger bones.

Phanerozoic ("visible life") The current eon of geological time, spanning the last 540 million years, characterized by the evolution of plants and animals. The Phanerozoic comprises the Paleozoic, Mesozoic, and Cenozoic eras.

Phragmocone (FRAG-mo-kone) The cone-shaped internal shell of belemnites. It is divided into chambers.

Phylum A major subdivision of the animal kingdom, comprising a class or classes.

Phytosaurs (FIE-to-SORE-z) Heavily armored, semiaquatic Triassic archosaurs: reptiles resembling modern crocodiles and with similar habits.

Pikas Small, short-eared relatives of hares and rabbits. They live in rocky, mountainous parts of Asia and North America.

Placentals Mammals whose unborn young are nourished by a special organ called a placenta. Placental mammals have replaced marsupials in most parts of the world.

Placoderms (PLAK-o-dermz: "plated skins") A class of jawed fish, protected by armorlike plates. They flourished in Devonian times.

Placodonts (PLAK-o-dontz: "plated teeth") Aquatic reptiles of the Triassic period. Some "rowed" with paddle-shaped limbs, others swam with webbed digits and by waggling their tails.

Planarian A type of flatworm often found in freshwater.

Plastid In a plant cell, a structure containing pigments, food, or other substances.

Platyhelminthes Flat-bodied worms, also called flatworms.

Pleistocene The first epoch of the Quaternary period, 1.75 million to 10,000 years ago. It was marked by a series of ice ages (really one ice age with cold and warm phases).

Plesiosaurs (PLEE-SEE-o-SORE-z) Large Mesozoic marine reptiles that that swam with flipper-shaped limbs. Many were long-necked, reaching lengths of 10–40 ft (3–12 m).

Pliocene The last epoch of the Tertiary period, about 5.3–1.75 million years ago. The first species of the genus *Homo* appeared in this epoch.

Precambrian The great span of time from the Earth's formation to the Cambrian Period. Scientists divide the Precambrian into three eons. (*See Eon.*)

Predator Any animal or plant that preys on animals for food.

Prehensile Designed to grasp something by wrapping around it. For example, South American monkeys have prehensile tails.

Preservation Keeping something, for example a fossil, free from harm or decay.

Primates The group of mammals that includes lemurs, monkeys, apes, humans, and their ancestors.

Primitive At an early stage of evolution or development.

Proboscideans Elephants and their extinct ancestors and relatives – mostly large mammals possessing a long flexible trunk.

Prokaryotes (pro-KARRY-oatz: "before a true nucleus") Tiny, primitive organisms without a cell nucleus. They comprise the bacteria and archaebacteria.

Pronghorns Antelope-like North American mammals that shed their horns' outer covering.

Only one species survives today.

Prosauropods Early plant-eating saurischian dinosaurs including big four-legged forms resembling the sauropods that replaced them. Prosauropods lived from Late Triassic to Early Jurassic times.

Proterozoic The third eon of the geological timescale, from about 2.5 billion to 540 million years ago. The first eukaryotes appeared in this time.

Protozoans A great and varied group of tiny one-celled organisms, for example the foraminiferans.

Psittacosaurs (SIT-a-ko-SORE-z or si-TAK-o-SORE-z: "parrot lizards") Bipedal, plant-eating Cretaceous dinosaurs with a deep beak somewhat like a parrot's. They were ceratopsian ornithischians related to the later neoceratopsians (horned dinosaurs).

Pterodactyloids (TER-o-DAK-tee-loidz) Short-tailed pterosaurs that replaced long-tailed early forms.

Pterosaurs (TER-o-SORE-z: "winged lizards") Skin-winged, Mesozoic flying reptiles – archosaurs related to the dinosaurs.

Pubis One of the three (paired) hip bones.

Pygidium The tail of a trilobite or certain other kinds of invertebrate.

Pygostyle The short tailbone of a bird, formed of fused vertebrae.

Q

Quadrupedal Walking on all fours.
Quaternary The most recent period of geological history, covering the last 1.75 million years. It is divided into the Pleistocene and Holocene epochs.

R

Reconstruction Rebuilding, for instance reassembling scattered fossil bones to reconstruct the skeleton of an extinct animal.

Reptiles Lizards, snakes, turtles, crocodiles, dinosaurs, and their extinct and living relatives. Living reptiles are cold-blooded, scaly vertebrates that reproduce by laying eggs or giving birth on land.

Reptiliomorphs Small, lizardlike tetrapods that gave rise to true reptiles.

Rhinocerotidae ("nose horns") A family of plant-eating hoofed

mammals related to tapirs and horses. Living rhinoceroses are large, thick-skinned quadrupeds with a horn or two horns on their snouts.

Rhomboidal Having the shape of a rhombus (a sloping square).

Ribosome A type of particle making proteins in a cell.

Rodents A group of small mammals including mice, rats, squirrels, porcupines, and their extinct ancestors. Rodents have sharp front teeth used for gnawing grains, nuts, and seeds.

S

Sacrum Fused vertebrae that are joined to the pelvis.

Sarcopterygians (SAR-KOP-ter-ig-ee-anz: "flesh fins") The lobe-finned or fleshy-finned bony fish, comprising lungfish, coelacanths, and so-called rhipidistians including the ancestors of all four-legged vertebrates.

Saurischians (sore-IS-kee-anz: "lizard hips") One of the two major dinosaur groups (*see also Ornithischians*). The pelvis of most saurischians is similar to that of lizards.

Sauropodomorphs (sore-o-POD-o-morfz: "lizard-foot forms") Mostly large to immense, four-legged, long-necked, plant-eating saurischian dinosaurs. They comprised the prosauropods and sauropods.

Sauropods (SORE-o-podz: "lizard feet") Huge, plant-eating, quadrupedal saurischian dinosaurs, including the largest-ever land animals. They lived through most of Mesozoic time.

Sauropterygians (SORE-op-te-RIG-ee-anz) Mesozoic marine reptiles including the nothosaurs, placodonts, and plesiosaurs.

Scutes Bony plates with a horny covering set in the skin of certain reptiles to protect them from the teeth and claws of enemies.

Sediment Material deposited by wind, water, or ice.

Silurian The third period of the Paleozoic era, about 435–410 million years ago. It was named after the Silures, an ancient tribe in Wales.

Sirenians (sigh-REE-nee-anz) Large plant-eating aquatic mammals. Sea cows and dugongs are the only living examples.

Skull The head's bony framework that protects the brain, eyes, ears, and nasal passages.

Species In the classification of living things, the level below a genus. Individuals in a species can breed with each other to

produce fertile young.

Stegosaurs (STEG-o-SORE-z: "plated/roof lizards") Four-legged ornithischian dinosaurs – plant-eaters with two tall rows of bony plates and/or spines running down the neck, back, and tail.

Stereoscopic A type of eyesight or photography where both eyes or two lenses slightly apart focus on an object to give a three-dimensional effect.

Stratigraphy The study of layers of sedimentary rock (strata).

Stromatolite A mound made of blue-green algae interlaid with lime "mats." Stromatolites abounded in intertidal waters in Precambrian times, before algae-eating sea creatures appeared. Fossil stromatolites are early evidence of widespread life.

Supercontinent A prehistoric landmass containing two or more major continental plates. Examples include Gondwana and Pangea.

Symbiosis The living together of individuals of different species that benefit from this arrangement.

Synapsids The group of tetrapod vertebrates that includes the extinct pelycosaurs and therapsids, and the therapsids' descendants – mammals.

T

Tardigrades Tiny invertebrates whose bodies are composed of four segments, each bearing a pair of unjointed limbs. They live in damp moss, on flowering plants, in sand, in freshwater, and in the sea.

Tarsiers Small nocturnal primates with big eyes and ears, long tails, and long hindlegs for leaping from tree to tree. They live in Southeast Asia.

Teleosts A great group of the ray-finned bony fish (actinopterygians). Most living fish are teleosts.

Temnospondyls (TEM-no-SPON-dilz: "cut vertebrae") A group of early tetrapods including weak-limbed aquatic fish-eaters but also sturdier forms living mainly on land.

Tertiary The first period of the Cenozoic era, about 65–1.75 million years ago. It contained five epochs: Paleocene, Eocene, Oligocene, Miocene, and Pliocene.

Tetanurans (TET-a-NYOOR-anz: "stiff tails") One of the two major groups of theropod dinosaurs.

Tetrapods (TETRA-podz: "four

feet") Four-legged vertebrates and those two-legged and limbless vertebrates descended from them.

Thecodonts (THEEK-o-DONT-z: "socket-teeth") A mixed group of archosaurs including various extinct forms, among them the ancestors of dinosaurs, crocodilians, and pterosaurs.

Therapsids (ther-AP-sidz: "mammal arches") Prehistoric synapsids that included cynodonts, the immediate ancestors of mammals. They lived from Early Permian to Mid-Jurassic times.

Theropods (THER-o-podz: "beast feet") The predatory dinosaurs, many armed with sharp teeth and claws. They ranged from hen-sized creatures to the colossal tyrannosaurids.

Thylacines (THIE-la-seenz: "pouched") Also called Tasmanian wolves, these were foxlike marsupials. Until about 10,000 years ago, they were found on the mainland of Australia and New Guinea. The last known thylacine was captured in 1930 in Tasmania.

Thyreophorans (THIHR-ee-OFF-o-ranz: "shield bearers") Four-legged, plant-eating dinosaurs comprising the armored ankylosaurs, plated stegosaurs, and their close relatives.

Titanosaurs (tie-TAN-o-SORE-z: "gigantic lizards") Very large, four-legged, plant-eating dinosaurs. The titanosaurs were sauropods and included perhaps the largest land animals ever.

Topography The surface of the land, including its variations in height.

Trace fossils Traces left by prehistoric creatures. They include fossil burrows, footprints, eggs, droppings, bite marks, and fossil impressions of skin, hair and feathers.

Triassic The first period of the Mesozoic era, about 250–203 million years ago. Dinosaurs emerged in the Triassic period.

Triconodonts (try-KON-o-dontz "three cone teeth") An extinct group of primitive mammals, known across North America, and from Europe to China.

Trilobites (TRY-lo-bite-z: "three lobed") Paleozoic marine arthropods with external skeletons divided lengthwise into three lobes. Variations in trilobite shapes and features are an accurate indicator of the age of the sediments in which they are found.

Tylopods (TIE-lo-podz: "padded feet") Artiodactyl (even-toed),

hoofed mammals including camels, the llama, alpaca, guanaco, and vicuña, and their extinct relatives.

Tyrannosaurids (ti-RAN-o-SORE-idz: "tyrant lizards") A family of huge, bipedal, carnivorous dinosaurs: tetanuran theropods with large heads, short arms, two-fingered hands, and massive hindlimbs. They flourished in Late Cretaceous North America and Asia.

U

Ungulates Hoofed mammals.
Unspecialized Not specialized – not adapted, or set apart, for a specific purpose.

V

Vendian The last Precambrian period of Earth history, about 600–540 million years ago. Many-celled Ediacaran-type creatures appeared in the sea during this period.

Vertebrates Animals with an internal bony or cartilaginous skeleton including a skull and a backbone made up of vertebrae

Vertebrae (singular: vertebra) The linked bones forming the backbones of vertebrate animals. According to what part of a backbone they form, scientists describe them as cervical (neck), dorsal (back), sacral (hip), and caudal (tail) vertebrae.

Viscera Organs inside the body cavity, for example the intestines, heart, and liver.

W

Warm-blooded Keeping body temperature at a constant level, often above or below that of the surroundings.

Z

Zone fossils (index fossils) Types of fossil useful for determining the relative ages of rocks, and matching the ages of rocks from different parts of the world.

ADDITIONAL PRONUNCIATION GUIDE

Acanthostega
(a-kan-tho-STEEG-uh: "spiky roof")
Aepycamelus
(ee-pi-CAMEL-us: "high/lofty camel")
Archaeopteryx
(AHR-kee-OP-ter-iks: "ancient wing, feather")
Australopithecus afarensis
(AWS-tra-lo-pith-ee-cus: "southern ape from Afar")
Caudipteryx (kaw-DIP-ter-iks or kaw-dip-TAYR-iks or KAW-dee-tayr-iks: "tail wing, feather")
Cheirolepis (kyr-o-LEE-pis)
Cladoselache (clade-o-su-LAK-e)
Coelurosauravus
(seel-uro-sawr-AV-us)
Compsognathus
(komp-SOG-na-thus or KOMP-sog-NAY-thus: "elegant jaw")
Confuciusornis
(con-foo-shush-OR-nis: "Confucius bird")
Corythosaurus
(ko-RITH-o-SAWR-us or KOR-i-tho-SAWR-us: "helmet lizard")
Daeodon (DAY-oh-don)
or Dinohyus (dine-oh-high-us)
Deinonychus (dine-on-EE-kus: "terrible claw")
Diadectes (DIE-a-deck-teez)
Dilophosaurus
(die-loph-UH-saw-rus: "double-crested lizard")
Diplocaulus (dip-low-COR-luss)
Dunkleosteus (dunk-lee-OS-tee-us)
Echioceras (eck-ee-o-SAIR-us: "spiky horn")
Edmontonia
(ed-mon-TOHN-ee-a: "from Edmonton")
Epigaulus (ep-ee-GAW-lus)
Eryops (eer-EE-ops. "long face")
Estemmenosuchus
(es-tem-EE-nah-soo-kus)
Euoplocephalus
(YOO-o-plo-SEF-a-lus: "well-armoured head")
Herrerasaurus
(he-RER-a-SAWR-us: "Herrera's lizard")
Hylonomus (hiy-LON-uh-mus: "forest mouse")
Icaronycteris
(ick-ah-row-NICK-ter-is)
Ichthyosaurus
(ick-THEE-uh-SAWR-us: "fish lizard")
Lepidotes (lep-ee-DOTE-eez)
Lesothosaurus
(le-SOH-toh-SAWR-us: "Lesotho lizard")

Macrauchenia (mack-row-CHEE-nee-uh: "big llama" or "big neck")
Mastodonsaurus (MAS-toe-don-saw-rus: "mastodon lizard")
Meganeura (meg-uh–NUR-us)
Megatherium
(meg-uh-THEER-ee-um: "big beast")
Metriorhynchus
(met-ree-oh-RINK-us)
Miacis (my-ASS-is)
Moeritherium
(moh-rih-THEER-ee-um)
Morganucodon
(more-gan-OOH-kud-don)
Oviraptor (OH-vi-RAP-tor: "egg robber")
Pachycephalosaurus
(pak-i-SEF-a-lo-SAWR-us: "thick-headed lizard")
Palaeoloxodon falconeri (pale-ee-o-LOCKS-uh-don ful-con-ear-ee)
Panderichthys (pan-der-ICK-theez)
Paraceratherium
(para-sair-uh-THEER-ee-um)
Phacops (fake-OPS)
Phenacodus (fenn-ah-co-DUSS)
Plateosaurus (PLAT-ee-o-SAWR-us "broad, strong lizard")
Platybelodon
(plat-ee-BELL-uh-don)
Plesiadapis (ples-ee-ah-DAP-is)
Psittacosaurus (SIT-a-ko-SAWR-us or si-TAK-o-SAWR-us: "parrot lizard")
Pteranodon (TAIR-an-oh-don: "wing, no teeth")
Pteraspis (TAIR-as-pis)
Pterygotus (tear-ee-GOTE-us)
Scelidosaurus (SKEL-i-do-SAWR-us: "hindleg lizard")
Sinokannemeyeria
(SIEN-o-kanna-may-urh-ee-a)
Styracosaurus
(STIHR-a-ko-SAWR-us or stie-RAK-o-SAWR-us: "spiked lizard")
Suchomimus (SOOK-o-MIEM-us: "crocodile mimic")
Tanystropheus
(tan-ee-STROFE-ee-us: "stretched joints")
Therizinosaurus
(THER-i-ZIN-o-SAWR-us: "reaping lizard")
Theropithecus
(THAIR-oh-pith-ee-cus)
Thrinaxodon (thrin-AX-uh-don)
Thylacosmilus
(thigh-LACK-uh-smy-lus)
Tuojiangosaurus
(too-JUNG-uh-saw-rus)
Uintatherium
(u-IN-tah-theer-ee-um: "Uintah beast")
Zalambdalestes
(za-LAMB-duh-less-tees)

INDEX

In this index main entries for each subject are shown in **bold** type. Scientific names are given in *italics*.

PICTURE CREDITS

Aero Vironment Inc: Martyn Cowley 99bl;

American Museum Of Natural History; 10clb, 45tl, 76bl, 93c, 126bl, 155tl, 157cr, 161br, 208bl, 212 213b, 216bl, 220cl, 221tl, 221tr, 226bl, 227bl, 238cl, 239tr, 239bc, 246cb, 247br, 251br, 254tr, 263cr, 264bl, 264br, 265tl, 271cr, 271bc, 272bl, 313bl, 317tl, 319bl, 321cr(below); 325tc, 332cr, 332br, 344tl, 344bc, 349br, 351c, 352cl, 355tl; A. E. Anderson 86bl, 257br; AMNH Photo Studio 196bl, 197bc, 199br, 200tr; J. Beckett 134cr (above); J. Beckett/Denis Finnin 90-91; Bierwert & Bailey 91bl; Blackwell/Finnin/Chesek 124bl; C. Chesek 2bl, 48bl, 60bl, 135cr,286-287c; Jim Coxe 28c; Mick Ellison 130bl; D. Finnin/ C. Chesek 197t; D.Finnin 3b, 38b, 40cl, 40br, 44c, 49tr, 95cr, 130tr, 135tr, 229tr 229cb, 288c; Kirschner 78-79t; Menke 317tr; Rota 79bl;

Ancient Art & Architecture Collection: 257tr, 263tc;

Aquila Photographics: J.J. Brooks 141tr;

Ardea London Ltd: Francois Gohier 199tc;

Barleylands Farm Museum: 35tr;

J. Beckett: 142tc;

BBC: 23tc;

Bridgeman Art Library, London / New York: 237tl;

Bristol City Museum and Art Gallery: 168tr;

British Antarctic Survey: Chris Gilbert 324tc;

Carnegie Museum of Natural History: Mark A.Klinger 148t, 170bl, 205cr;

Jean-Loup Charmet: 10t;

Robert Clark: 161tl;

Cleveland Museum of Natural History: 41bc;

CM Studio: 201br;

Bruce Coleman Collection: 248-249, 310-311t; Mark Carwardine 310-311c; Sarah Cook 227tc; Janos Jurka 172-173; Steven Kaufman 292bl; Hans Reinhard 49br; Jens Rydell 225tr;

S. Conway Morris: 279bl, 280bl, 280-281c, 281tc, 281cr;

Corbis: 14cl, 16tr, 16cb, 16br, 18tr, 18c, 18l, 252-253, 260-261, 292cl, 335br, 336b, 345tr, 350bc, 351tr, 352tc, 353bc, 355bc, 357bl; O.Alamany & E.Vicens 316br; Tom Bean 12br, 148br, 218-219; Jonathan Blair 316cla, 316clb; Gianni Dagli Orti 270bl; Juan Echeverria 10bc; Marc Garanger 240-241; Derek Hall/Frank Lane Picture Agency 312tr; Dave G.Houser 317tc; Peter Johnson 122tc; Bob Krist 222c; Diego Lazama Orezzoli 317bc; The Purcell Team 267tl; Charles O'Rear 317br; Martin B.Withers/Frank Lane Picture Agency 316bc;

Peter Cormack: James L. Amos 280tr; Layne Kennedy 281tr;

Esto Photographics: Scott Frances 359br;

Mary Evans Picture Library: 357tc;

Exhibit Museum of Natural History, University of Michigan: 292-293;

Getty Images Stone: Earth Imaging 316cr;

Graves Museum: 137br, 137t;

Dr. Pat Herendeen: 321bc;

John Holmes: 103tl, 333tl, 333tc, 333cl, 333cr;

Hulton Archive: 332tr, 345bc, 346ct, 347cl, 347cb, 349tr, 354tr, 354bc, 356cb;

Hunterian Museum: 2c, 11tr, 34ca, 39bc, 279c, 302tc, 45br; Dr. Neil D.L. Clark 283tl;

Gerado Kurtz: courtesy of University of Madrid 143bl;

Dave Martill: 83tr;

Museo Arentino De Cirendas Naterales, Buenos Aires: 150tr;

Muséum National d'Histoire Naturelle: Paleontologie (Paris), D. Serrette 11bl;

Museum of the Rockies: Bruce Selyem 136br;

N.A.S.A.: 312b;

National Museum of Natural History/Smithsonian Institution: 167tr;

National Museum of Wales:

262bc;

The Natural History Museum, London: 3t, 13tr, 23tcr, 31tr, 32c, 37tr, 45c, 45cr, 45clb, 64bl, 74bl, 80b, 82tr, 87bl, 87tr, 89br, 94cl, 124br, 140c, 155tr, 168bl, 168cr, 194tr, 207br, 216cl, 217tr, 224bl, 225bl, 230l, 231c, 231br, 233tc, 233tr, 234bl, 235tl, 235tr, 236tr, 242tr, 247tr, 261tr, 273tr, 275tl, 279t, 282bl, 282t, 283bl, 284tc, 284bl, 285cl, 285c, 286bc, 287bl, 288bc, 289bl, 290tc, 290br, 291cr, 291bl, 291t, 294tr, 294c, 294br, 295bl, 295cl, 295bcb, 296c, 296t, 297tr, 297cr, 297bl, 298c, 298bc, 298tc, 299c, 299cr, 299bl, 302c, 302br, 303c, 303bl, 303tr, 304tc, 304c, 304br, 305cr, 306tc, 306cr, 307cr, 307bl, 307t, 308c, 308b, 308tc, 309t, 313br, 313tr , 318cr, 318bl, 318br, 340cl, 340cr, 340bc, 340t, 341tr, 341bl, 341br, 342tr, 342cl, 342cr, 342bl, 343cl, 343b, 358bl;

Nature Magazine: 319br;

N.H.P.A.: 96-97; Daniel Heuclin 300-301; Trever McDonald 44-45;

Oxford Scientific Films: Hjalmar R. Bardarson 292tr; Max Gibbs 48tr; Mark Jones 272tc; Maurice Tibbles 92br; Norbert Wu 33tr;

Popperfoto: Reuters 316tc;

Dr. Mark A. Purnell, University of Leicester: 3bc;

Luis Rey: 127cr;

Royal British Columba Museum: 195trc, 262-263;

Royal Museum of Scotland: 34tr, 37cla, 59b, 286c, 288tr;

Science Photo Library: Martin Dorhn/Stephen Winkworth 98-99; James King-Holmes 328bl, 329tl; David Parker 301tl; Geoff Tompkinson 328cr,

Senckenberg Nature Museum: 140l, 154c;

Paul Sereno/University of Chicago: 106bl, 117br;

J & B Sibbick: 14cb, 15cr;

Smithsonian Institute: 156tr;

South African Museum: Clive Booth 198bl, 201tr;

Topham Picturepoint: Press Association 311tr;

Royal Tyrell Museum: 136l, 165tc;

University Museum, Oxford: 19cl, 58c;

University Museum of Zoology, Cambridge: 58bc, 59t, 201c, 286tr, 287tc;

Dr. RT Wells, Flinders University: Photo by F. Coffa 206cl;

Professor Harry Whittington: 319cr;

Yorkshire Museum: 153t, 200-201b, 230r, 231l, 232l;

Jerry Young: 57ca.

All other images © Dorling Kindersley. For further information see: www.dkimages.com

Specially commissioned illustraions:

Bedrock: 4bl, 5tl, 6tl, 7tl, 7tr, 11c, 17tl, 21inset, 26-27, 29cl, 34ca, 36ca, 37tl, 41c, 46-47, 55inset, 62-63, 65c, 68 69, 70tl, 70tr, 71tc, 71tr, 72-73, 74-75, 76-77, 78-79c, 80-81, 82-83, 86-87, 88-89, 101inset, 104tl, 104tr, 112-113, 116-117, 124-125, 126-127, 128-129, 138tc, 143c, 143tr, 145cr, 146 147, 150 151, 156 157, 158-159, 160-161, 165tl, 178-179, 184-185, 193inset, 194tl, 195tl, 195tc, 196-197, 198-199, 202-203, 204-205, 206-207, 208-209, 214-215, 216-217, 217tr, 218-219, 220-221, 222-223, 224-225, 226-227, 228-229, 244-245, 246-247, 248-249, 252-253, 254-257, 256-257, 260-261, 265r, 266-267, 268-269, 270-271, 272-273, 277inset, 332cr, 333br;

Tim Brown: 11cr, 14tr, 14bl, 64c, 67c, 123tc, 140b, 144t, 145tr, 328tr, 329cr;

Peter Bull: 17br, 19cb, 19la, 19fl, 22-23bl to br, 25cr, 25tr, 30bl, 33tcr, 34-35bl to br, 36-37bl to br, 47cb, 56-57bl to br, 70-71bl to br, 90br, 91t, 98bl, 98br, 99tr, 99tl, 104-105bl to br, 138-139bl to br, 164-165bl to br, 194-195bl to br, 255br, 256tr;

Gary Cross: 212-213tc;

Encompass Graphics: 236cr;

Malcolm McGreggor: 58c, 61rc, 66-67t, 77c, 112bl, 127tl, 152b, 208tl, 209l, 209br, 269tr, 274cr;

Luis Rey: 20-21, 52-53c, 54-55, 100-101, 192-193, 276-277;

Peter Visscher: 19tc, 19tl, 22cc, 19ca, 34tc, 37tc, 56cl, 56tl, 56tla, 57tc, 104tc, 138tr, 139tl, 139tc, 139tca, 164tl, 195tl, 213cr, 213tr, 324bl, 336t, 337tl, 337bl;

Robin Carter/Wildlife Art Ltd: 81tl, 81bl, 82bl, 89bl, 94bl, 244bl, 245tl, 245br.

ACKNOWLEDGMENTS

With special thanks to:
the American Museum of Natural History for their patient
help and expert advice. In particular: Maron Waxman,
Editorial Director, Department of Special Publishing;
Mark Norell, Curator of Vertebrate Paleontology;
Jin Meng, Assistant Curator of Vertebrate Paleontology

Special Photography:
Denis Finnin, Roderick Mickens, and Megan Carlough for
photography at the American Museum of Natural History; Trish Gant
of Dorling Kindersley for photography at the Yorkshire Museum

Dorling Kindersley Picture Library:
Sally Hamilton, Rachel Holt,
Diane Le Grande

Jacket Design:
Nicola Powling, Dean Price

Additional Editorial Assistance:
Margaret Hynes, Carey Scott

Additional Design Management:
Julia Harris, Gill Shaw

Additional Picture Research:
Marie Osbourne, Sarah Pownall

Additional DTP Assistance
Siu Yin Ho

Proofreading:
Lee Simmons, Claire Watts

Design assistance:
Polly Appleton, Sheila Collins, Venice Shone

Index:
Lynn Bresler